FIAT
Panda
Owners
Workshop
Manual

Peter G Strasman

Models covered
Fiat Panda 45, 45 Comfort & 45 Super (S) including
limited edition models; 903 cc

Does not cover four-wheel-drive models

(793-9L1)

ABCDE
FGHIJ
KLMNO
PQRS

THE
BOOK

Haynes Publishing Group
Sparkford Nr Yeovil
Somerset BA22 7JJ England

Haynes Publications, Inc
861 Lawrence Drive
Newbury Park
California 91320 USA

Acknowledgements

Thanks must go to the FIAT Motor Company (UK) Ltd for the supply of technical information and the use of certain illustrations. The Champion Sparking Plug Company provided the illustrations showing various spark plug conditions and Sykes-Pickavant supplied some of the workshop tools. Thanks must also go to all those people at Sparkford who assisted in the production of this manual.

A book in the **Haynes Owners Workshop Manual Series**

Printed by J. H. Haynes & Co. Ltd, Sparkford, Nr Yeovil, Somerset BA22 7JJ, England

ISBN 0 85696 793 9

British Library Cataloguing in Publication Data
Strasman, Peter G.
   Fiat Panda owners workshop manual.–
   (Owners Workshop Manuals)
   1. Panda automobile
   I. Title II. Series
   629.28'722   TL215.P/
   ISBN 0-85696-793-9

Contents

Introductory pages

About this manual   5
Introduction to the Fiat Panda   5
General dimensions, weights and capacities   6
Wheel changing, jacking and towing   7
Buying spare parts and vehicle identification numbers   9
General repair procedures   10
Tools and working facilities   11
Conversion factors   13
Safety first!   14
Routine maintenance   15
Recommended lubricants and fluids   19
Fault diagnosis   20

Chapter 1
Engine   24

Chapter 2
Cooling and heating systems   54

Chapter 3
Fuel system   63

Chapter 4
Ignition system   74

Chapter 5
Clutch   82

Chapter 6
Transmission   86

Chapter 7
Driveshafts, hubs, wheels and tyres   106

Chapter 8
Braking system   112

Chapter 9
Electrical system   124

Chapter 10
Steering   147

Chapter 11
Suspension   155

Chapter 12
Bodywork   160

Index   173

Wiring diagrams   177

Fiat Panda 45 Super Hatchback

About this manual

Its aim

The aim of this manual is to help you get the best value from your vehicle. It can do so in several ways. It can help you decide what work must be done (even should you choose to get it done by a garage), provide information on routine maintenance and servicing, and give a logical course of action and diagnosis when random faults occur. However, it is hoped that you will use the manual by tackling the work yourself. On simpler jobs it may even be quicker than booking the car into a garage and going there twice, to leave and collect it. Perhaps most important, a lot of money can be saved by avoiding the costs a garage must charge to cover its labour and overheads.

The manual has drawings and descriptions to show the function of the various components so that their layout can be understood. Then the tasks are described and photographed in a step-by-step sequence so that even a novice can do the work.

Its arrangement

The manual is divided into twelve Chapters, each covering a logical sub-division of the vehicle. The Chapters are each divided into Sections, numbered with single figures, eg 5; and the Sections into paragraphs (or sub-sections), with decimal numbers following on from the Section they are in, eg 5.1, 5.2, 5.3 etc.

It is freely illustrated, especially in those parts where there is a detailed sequence of operations to be carried out. There are two forms of illustration: figures and photographs. The figures are numbered in sequence with decimal numbers, according to their position in the Chapter – eg Fig. 6.4 is the fourth drawing/illustration in Chapter 6. Photographs carry the same number (either individually or in related groups) as the Section or sub-section to which they relate.

There is an alphabetical index at the back of the manual as well as a contents list at the front. Each Chapter is also preceded by its own individual contents list.

References to the 'left' or 'right' of the vehicle are in the sense of a person in the driver's seat facing forwards.

Unless otherwise stated, nuts and bolts are removed by turning anti-clockwise, and tightened by turning clockwise.

Vehicle manufacturers continually make changes to specifications and recommendations, and these, when notified, are incorporated into our manuals at the earliest opportunity.

Whilst every care is taken to ensure that the information in this manual is correct, no liability can be accepted by the authors or publishers for loss, damage or injury caused by any errors in, or omissions from, the information given.

Introduction to the Fiat Panda

The Fiat Panda is inexpensive to buy, run and service and is an ideal vehicle for the home mechanic to work on.

Provided the limitations of its size and performance are appreciated, the car offers reliable, versatile transport with a good standard of equipment and acceptable ride, especially on the Super version.

General dimensions, weights and capacities

Dimensions
Overall length	3380 mm (133.2 in)
Overall width	1460 mm (57.5 in)
Overall height	1445 mm (56.9 in)
Wheelbase	2160 mm (85.1 in)
Front track	1254 mm (49.4 in)
Rear track	1249 mm (49.2 in)
Turning circle	9.2 metres (30.19 feet)

Weights
Kerb weight	680 kg (1499 lbs)
Maximum laden weight	1080 kg (2381 lbs)

Capacities
Engine oil including filter:	
Up to engine number 6263501	3.5 litres (6.2 pts)
From engine number 6263502	3.3 litres (5.8 pts)
Transmission	2.36 litres (4.15 pt)
Steering gear	140 cc (0.25 pt)
Driveshaft CV joint	55 g
Brake hydraulic fluid	0.39 litre (0.69 pt)
Fuel tank	35.0 litres (7.7 gals)
Coolant	5.2 litres (9.2 pts)

Wheel changing, jacking and towing

Wheel changing

To change a roadwheel, apply the handbrake and then release (but do not remove) the wheel bolts.

Remove the spare wheel from the engine compartment (photos).

Using the jack supplied with the car, insert it fully into its sill location and raise the car (photos).

Remove the wheel bolts and the wheel. On Super models, the wheel bolts hold the plastic trim plate in position (photo).

Locate the spare wheel on the hub and screw in the bolts.

Lower the car and remove the jack then fully tighten the wheel bolts.

Jacking

The jack supplied with the car should only be used for roadside wheel changing. *When overhauling or repairing the car, use a trolley or substantial hydraulic or mechanical jack. Always supplement the jack with axle stands.*

To raise the front or rear ends, place the jack under the centre brackets as shown (photos).

Towing

Towing hooks are provided at front and rear. Always unlock the steering gear when being towed.

Jack location

Spare wheel location

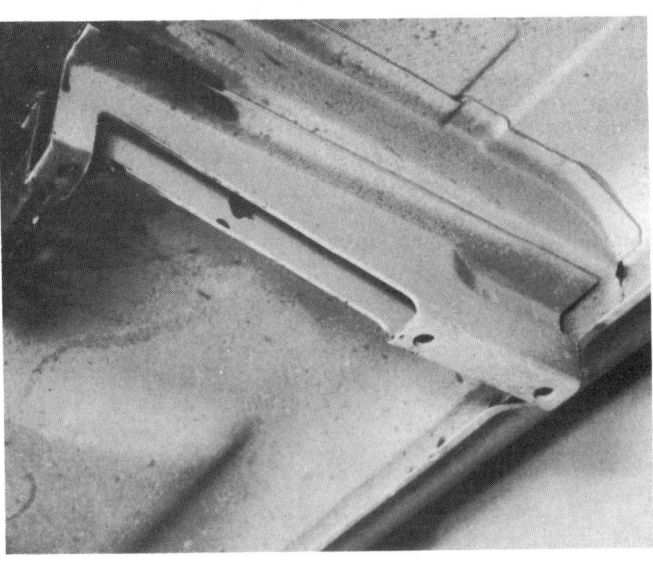

Sill jacking point

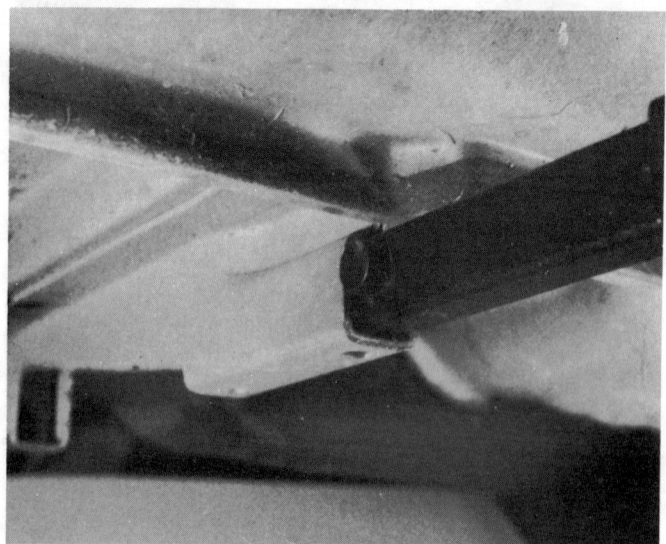

Jack located in sill jacking point

Roadwheel trim plate

Front jacking point

Rear jacking point

Jacking car

A   *Front end*   *B*   *Rear end*

Buying spare parts
and vehicle identification numbers

Buying spare parts

Spare parts are available from many sources, for example: FIAT garages, other garages and accessory shops, and motor factors. Our advice regarding spare parts is as follows:

Officially appointed FIAT garages – this is the best source of parts which are peculiar to your car and otherwise not generally available (eg complete cylinder heads, internal gearbox components, badges, interior trim etc). It is also the only place at which you should buy parts if your vehicle is still under warranty; non-FIAT components may invalidate the warranty. To be sure of obtaining the correct parts it will always be necessary to give the storeman your car's engine and chassis number, and if possible, to take the old part along for positive identification. Remember that many parts are available on a factory exchange scheme – any parts returned should always be clean! It obviously makes good sense to go straight to the specialists on your car for this type of part for they are best equipped to supply you.

Other garages and accessory shops – these are often very good places to buy material and components needed for the maintenance of your car (eg oil filters, spark plugs, bulbs, fan belts, oils and grease, touch-up paint, filler paste etc). They also sell general accessories, usually have convenient opening hours, charge lower prices and can often be found not far from home.

Motor factors – good factors will stock all of the more important components which wear out relatively quickly (eg clutch components, pistons, valves, exhaust systems, brake cylinders/pipes/hoses/seals/shoes and pads etc). Motor factors will often provide new or reconditioned components on a part exchange basis – this can save a considerable amount of money.

Vehicle identification numbers

Modifications are a continuing and unpublicised process in vehicle manufacture quite apart from major model changes. Spare parts manuals and lists are compiled upon a numerical basis, the individual vehicle numbers being essential to correct identification of the component required.

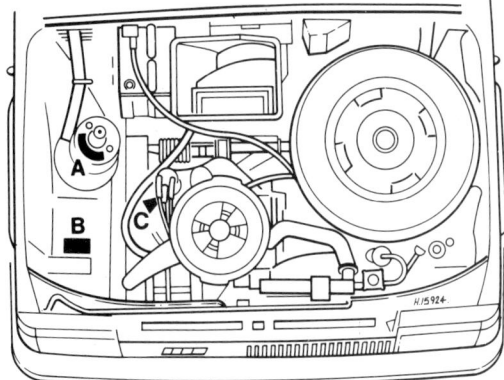

Location of vehicle identification numbers

A   *Chassis type and number*   C   *Engine type and number*
B   *Manufacturers plate*

The Chassis type and number is located within the engine compartment on the right-hand suspension strut turret.

The manufacturer's plate is also located within the engine compartment on the right-hand wing valance (photo). The engine number is stamped on the cylinder block (photo).

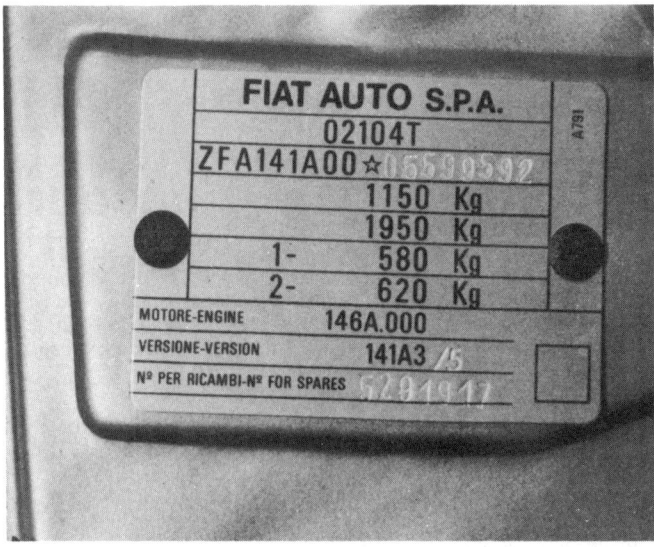

Vehicle identification plate

Engine number

General repair procedures

Whenever servicing, repair or overhaul work is carried out on the car or its components, it is necessary to observe the following procedures and instructions. This will assist in carrying out the operation efficiently and to a professional standard of workmanship.

Joint mating faces and gaskets

Where a gasket is used between the mating faces of two components, ensure that it is renewed on reassembly, and fit it dry unless otherwise stated in the repair procedure. Make sure that the mating faces are clean and dry with all traces of old gasket removed. When cleaning a joint face, use a tool which is not likely to score or damage the face, and remove any burrs or nicks with an oilstone or fine file.

Make sure that tapped holes are cleaned with a pipe cleaner, and keep them free of jointing compound if this is being used unless specifically instructed otherwise.

Ensure that all orifices, channels or pipes are clear and blow through them, preferably using compressed air.

Oil seals

Whenever an oil seal is removed from its working location, either individually or as part of an assembly, it should be renewed.

The very fine sealing lip of the seal is easily damaged and will not seal if the surface it contacts is not completely clean and free from scratches, nicks or grooves. If the original sealing surface of the component cannot be restored, the component should be renewed.

Protect the lips of the seal from any surface which may damage them in the course of fitting. Use tape or a conical sleeve where possible. Lubricate the seal lips with oil before fitting and, on dual lipped seals, fill the space between the lips with grease.

Unless otherwise stated, oil seals must be fitted with their sealing lips toward the lubricant to be sealed.

Use a tubular drift or block of wood of the appropriate size to install the seal and, if the seal housing is shouldered, drive the seal down to the shoulder. If the seal housing is unshouldered, the seal should be fitted with its face flush with the housing top face.

Screw threads and fastenings

Always ensure that a blind tapped hole is completely free from oil, grease, water or other fluid before installing the bolt or stud. Failure to do this could cause the housing to crack due to the hydraulic action of the bolt or stud as it is screwed in.

When tightening a castellated nut to accept a split pin, tighten the nut to the specified torque, where applicable, and then tighten further to the next split pin hole. Never slacken the nut to align a split pin hole unless stated in the repair procedure.

When checking or retightening a nut or bolt to a specified torque setting, slacken the nut or bolt by a quarter of a turn, and then retighten to the specified setting.

Locknuts, locktabs and washers

Any fastening which will rotate against a component or housing in the course of tightening should always have a washer between it and the relevant component or housing.

Spring or split washers should always be renewed when they are used to lock a critical component such as a big-end bearing retaining nut or bolt.

Locktabs which are folded over to retain a nut or bolt should always be renewed.

Self-locking nuts can be reused in non-critical areas, providing resistance can be felt when the locking portion passes over the bolt or stud thread.

Split pins must always be replaced with new ones of the correct size for the hole.

Special tools

Some repair procedures in this manual entail the use of special tools such as a press, two or three-legged pullers, spring compressors etc. Wherever possible, suitable readily available alternatives to the manufacturer's special tools are described, and are shown in use. In some instances, where no alternative is possible, it has been necessary to resort to the use of a manufacturer's tool and this has been done for reasons of safety as well as the efficient completion of the repair operation. Unless you are highly skilled and have a thorough understanding of the procedure described, never attempt to bypass the use of any special tool when the procedure described specifies its use. Not only is there a very great risk of personal injury, but expensive damage could be caused to the components involved.

Tools and working facilities

Introduction

A selection of good tools is a fundamental requirement for anyone contemplating the maintenance and repair of a motor vehicle. For the owner who does not possess any, their purchase will prove a considerable expense, offsetting some of the savings made by doing-it-yourself. However, provided that the tools purchased are of good quality, they will last for many years and prove an extremely worthwhile investment.

To help the average owner to decide which tools are needed to carry out the various tasks detailed in this manual, we have compiled three lists of tools under the following headings: *Maintenance and minor repair, Repair and overhaul*, and *Special*. The newcomer to practical mechanics should start off with the *Maintenance and minor repair* tool kit and confine himself to the simpler jobs around the vehicle. Then, as his confidence and experience grow, he can undertake more difficult tasks, buying extra tools as, and when, they are needed. In this way, a *Maintenance and minor repair* tool kit can be built-up into a *Repair and overhaul* tool kit over a considerable period of time without any major cash outlays. The experienced do-it-yourselfer will have a tool kit good enough for most repair and overhaul procedures and will add tools from the *Special* category when he feels the expense is justified by the amount of use to which these tools will be put.

It is obviously not possible to cover the subject of tools fully here. For those who wish to learn more about tools and their use there is a book entitled *How to Choose and Use Car Tools* available from the publishers of this manual.

Maintenance and minor repair tool kit

The tools given in this list should be considered as a minimum requirement if routine maintenance, servicing and minor repair operations are to be undertaken. We recommend the purchase of combination spanners (ring one end, open-ended the other); although more expensive than open-ended ones, they do give the advantages of both types of spanner.

Combination spanners - 10, 11, 12, 13, 14 & 17 mm
Adjustable spanner - 9 inch
Engine sump/gearbox drain plug key
Spark plug spanner (with rubber insert)
Spark plug gap adjustment tool
Set of feeler gauges
Brake bleed nipple spanner
Screwdriver - 4 in long x $\frac{1}{4}$ in dia (flat blade)
Screwdriver - 4 in long x $\frac{1}{4}$ in dia (cross blade)
Combination pliers - 6 inch
Hacksaw (junior)
Tyre pump
Tyre pressure gauge
Oil can
Fine emery cloth (1 sheet)
Wire brush (small)
Funnel (medium size)

Repair and overhaul tool kit

These tools are virtually essential for anyone undertaking any major repairs to a motor vehicle, and are additional to those given in the *Maintenance and minor repair* list. Included in this list is a comprehensive set of sockets. Although these are expensive they will be found invaluable as they are so versatile - particularly if various drives are included in the set. We recommend the $\frac{1}{2}$ in square-drive type, as this can be used with most proprietary torque wrenches. If you cannot afford a socket set, even bought piecemeal, then inexpensive tubular box spanners are a useful alternative.

The tools in this list will occasionally need to be supplemented by tools from the *Special* list.

Sockets (or box spanners) to cover range in previous list
Reversible ratchet drive (for use with sockets)
Extension piece, 10 inch (for use with sockets)
Universal joint (for use with sockets)
Torque wrench (for use with sockets)
'Mole' wrench - 8 inch
Ball pein hammer
Soft-faced hammer, plastic or rubber
Screwdriver - 6 in long x $\frac{5}{16}$ in dia (flat blade)
Screwdriver - 2 in long x $\frac{5}{16}$ in square (flat blade)
Screwdriver - 1$\frac{1}{2}$ in long x $\frac{1}{4}$ in dia (cross blade)
Screwdriver - 3 in long x $\frac{1}{8}$ in dia (electricians)
Pliers - electricians side cutters
Pliers - needle nosed
Pliers - circlip (internal and external)
Cold chisel - $\frac{1}{2}$ inch
Scriber
Scraper
Centre punch
Pin punch
Hacksaw
Valve grinding tool
Steel rule/straight-edge
Allen keys
Selection of files
Wire brush (large)
Axle-stands
Jack (strong mechanical or hydraulic type)

Special tools

The tools in this list are those which are not used regularly, are expensive to buy, or which need to be used in accordance with their manufacturers' instructions. Unless relatively difficult mechanical jobs are undertaken frequently, it will not be economic to buy many of these tools. Where this is the case, you could consider clubbing together with friends (or joining a motorists' club) to make a joint purchase, or borrowing the tools against a deposit from a local garage or tool hire specialist.

The following list contains only those tools and instruments freely available to the public, and not those special tools produced by the vehicle manufacturer specifically for its dealer network. You will find occasional references to these manufacturers' special tools in the text of this manual. Generally, an alternative method of doing the job without the vehicle manufacturers' special tool is given. However, sometimes, there is no alternative to using them. Where this is the case and the relevant tool cannot be bought or borrowed, you will have to entrust the work to a franchised garage.

Valve spring compressor
Piston ring compressor
Balljoint separator
Universal hub/bearing puller
Impact screwdriver
Micrometer and/or vernier gauge
Dial gauge
Stroboscopic timing light
Dwell angle meter/tachometer
Universal electrical multi-meter
Cylinder compression gauge
Lifting tackle
Trolley jack
Light with extension lead

Buying tools

For practically all tools, a tool factor is the best source since he will have a very comprehensive range compared with the average garage or accessory shop. Having said that, accessory shops often offer excellent quality tools at discount prices, so it pays to shop around.

Remember, you don't have to buy the most expensive items on the shelf, but it is always advisable to steer clear of the very cheap tools. There are plenty of good tools around at reasonable prices, so ask the proprietor or manager of the shop for advice before making a purchase.

Care and maintenance of tools

Having purchased a reasonable tool kit, it is necessary to keep the tools in a clean serviceable condition. After use, always wipe off any dirt, grease and metal particles using a clean, dry cloth, before putting the tools away. Never leave them lying around after they have been used. A simple tool rack on the garage or workshop wall, for items such as screwdrivers and pliers is a good idea. Store all normal wrenches and sockets in a metal box. Any measuring instruments, gauges, meters, etc, must be carefully stored where they cannot be damaged or become rusty.

Take a little care when tools are used. Hammer heads inevitably become marked and screwdrivers lose the keen edge on their blades from time to time. A little timely attention with emery cloth, a file or grindstone will soon restore items like this to a good serviceable finish.

Working facilities

Not to be forgotten when discussing tools, is the workshop itself. If anything more than routine maintenance is to be carried out, some form of suitable working area becomes essential.

It is appreciated that many an owner mechanic is forced by circumstances to remove an engine or similar item, without the benefit of a garage or workshop. Having done this, any repairs should always be done under the cover of a roof.

Wherever possible, any dismantling should be done on a clean, flat workbench or table at a suitable working height.

Any workbench needs a vice: one with a jaw opening of 4 in (100 mm) is suitable for most jobs. As mentioned previously, some clean dry storage space is also required for tools, as well as for lubricants, cleaning fluids, touch-up paints and so on, which become necessary.

Another item which may be required, and which has a much more general usage, is an electric drill with a chuck capacity of at least $\frac{5}{16}$ in (8 mm). This, together with a good range of twist drills, is virtually essential for fitting accessories such as mirrors and reversing lights.

Last, but not least, always keep a supply of old newspapers and clean, lint-free rags available, and try to keep any working area as clean as possible.

Spanner jaw gap comparison table

Jaw gap (in)	Spanner size
0.250	$\frac{1}{4}$ in AF
0.276	7 mm
0.313	$\frac{5}{16}$ in AF
0.315	8 mm
0.344	$\frac{11}{32}$ in AF; $\frac{1}{8}$ in Whitworth
0.354	9 mm
0.375	$\frac{3}{8}$ in AF
0.394	10 mm
0.433	11 mm
0.438	$\frac{7}{16}$ in AF
0.445	$\frac{3}{16}$ in Whitworth; $\frac{1}{4}$ in BSF
0.472	12 mm
0.500	$\frac{1}{2}$ in AF
0.512	13 mm
0.525	$\frac{1}{4}$ in Whitworth; $\frac{5}{16}$ in BSF
0.551	14 mm
0.563	$\frac{9}{16}$ in AF
0.591	15 mm
0.600	$\frac{5}{16}$ in Whitworth; $\frac{3}{8}$ in BSF
0.625	$\frac{5}{8}$ in AF
0.630	16 mm
0.669	17 mm
0.686	$\frac{11}{16}$ in AF
0.709	18 mm
0.710	$\frac{3}{8}$ in Whitworth; $\frac{7}{16}$ in BSF
0.748	19 mm
0.750	$\frac{3}{4}$ in AF
0.813	$\frac{13}{16}$ in AF
0.820	$\frac{7}{16}$ in Whitworth; $\frac{1}{2}$ in BSF
0.866	22 mm
0.875	$\frac{7}{8}$ in AF
0.920	$\frac{1}{2}$ in Whitworth; $\frac{9}{16}$ in BSF
0.938	$\frac{15}{16}$ in AF
0.945	24 mm
1.000	1 in AF
1.010	$\frac{9}{16}$ in Whitworth; $\frac{5}{8}$ in BSF
1.024	26 mm
1.063	$1\frac{1}{16}$ in AF; 27 mm
1.100	$\frac{5}{8}$ in Whitworth; $\frac{11}{16}$ in BSF
1.125	$1\frac{1}{8}$ in AF
1.181	30 mm
1.200	$\frac{11}{16}$ in Whitworth; $\frac{3}{4}$ in BSF
1.250	$1\frac{1}{4}$ in AF
1.260	32 mm
1.300	$\frac{3}{4}$ in Whitworth; $\frac{7}{8}$ in BSF
1.313	$1\frac{5}{16}$ in AF
1.390	$\frac{13}{16}$ in Whitworth; $\frac{15}{16}$ in BSF
1.417	36 mm
1.438	$1\frac{7}{16}$ in AF
1.480	$\frac{7}{8}$ in Whitworth; 1 in BSF
1.500	$1\frac{1}{2}$ in AF
1.575	40 mm; $\frac{15}{16}$ in Whitworth
1.614	41 mm
1.625	$1\frac{5}{8}$ in AF
1.670	1 in Whitworth; $1\frac{1}{8}$ in BSF
1.688	$1\frac{11}{16}$ in AF
1.811	46 mm
1.813	$1\frac{13}{16}$ in AF
1.860	$1\frac{1}{8}$ in Whitworth; $1\frac{1}{4}$ in BSF
1.875	$1\frac{7}{8}$ in AF
1.969	50 mm
2.000	2 in AF
2.050	$1\frac{1}{4}$ in Whitworth; $1\frac{3}{8}$ in BSF
2.165	55 mm
2.362	60 mm

Conversion factors

Length (distance)

Inches (in)	X	25.4	= Millimetres (mm)	X	0.0394	= Inches (in)
Feet (ft)	X	0.305	= Metres (m)	X	3.281	= Feet (ft)
Miles	X	1.609	= Kilometres (km)	X	0.621	= Miles

Length (distance)						
Inches (in)	X 25.4	= Millimetres (mm)	X 0.0394	= Inches (in)
Feet (ft)	X 0.305	= Metres (m)	X 3.281	= Feet (ft)
Miles	X 1.609	= Kilometres (km)	X 0.621	= Miles

Volume (capacity)

Volume (capacity)				
Cubic inches (cu in; in^3)	X 16.387	= Cubic centimetres (cc; cm^3)	X 0.061	= Cubic inches (cu in; in^3)
Imperial pints (Imp pt)	X 0.568	= Litres (l)	X 1.76	= Imperial pints (Imp pt)
Imperial quarts (Imp qt)	X 1.137	= Litres (l)	X 0.88	= Imperial quarts (Imp qt)
Imperial quarts (Imp qt)	X 1.201	= US quarts (US qt)	X 0.833	= Imperial quarts (Imp qt)
US quarts (US qt)	X 0.946	= Litres (l)	X 1.057	= US quarts (US qt)
Imperial gallons (Imp gal)	X 4.546	= Litres (l)	X 0.22	= Imperial gallons (Imp gal)
Imperial gallons (Imp gal)	X 1.201	= US gallons (US gal)	X 0.833	= Imperial gallons (Imp gal)
US gallons (US gal)	X 3.785	= Litres (l)	X 0.264	= US gallons (US gal)

Mass (weight)

Mass (weight)				
Ounces (oz)	X 28.35	= Grams (g)	X 0.035	= Ounces (oz)
Pounds (lb)	X 0.454	= Kilograms (kg)	X 2.205	= Pounds (lb)

Force

Force				
Ounces-force (ozf; oz)	X 0.278	= Newtons (N)	X 3.6	= Ounces-force (ozf; oz)
Pounds-force (lbf; lb)	X 4.448	= Newtons (N)	X 0.225	= Pounds-force (lbf; lb)
Newtons (N)	X 0.1	= Kilograms-force (kgf; kg)	X 9.81	= Newtons (N)

Pressure

Pressure				
Pounds-force per square inch (psi; lbf/in^2; lb/in^2)	X 0.070	= Kilograms-force per square centimetre (kgf/cm^2; kg/cm^2)	X 14.223	= Pounds-force per square inch (psi; lbf/in^2; lb/in^2)
Pounds-force per square inch (psi; lbf/in^2; lb/in^2)	X 0.068	= Atmospheres (atm)	X 14.696	= Pounds-force per square inch (psi; lbf/in^2; lb/in^2)
Pounds-force per square inch (psi; lbf/in^2; lb/in^2)	X 0.069	= Bars	X 14.5	= Pounds-force per square inch (psi; lbf/in^2; lb/in^2)
Pounds-force per square inch (psi; lbf/in^2; lb/in^2)	X 6.895	= Kilopascals (kPa)	X 0.145	= Pounds-force per square inch (psi; lbf/in^2; lb/in^2)
Kilopascals (kPa)	X 0.01	= Kilograms-force per square centimetre (kgf/cm^2; kg/cm^2)	X 98.1	= Kilopascals (kPa)

Torque (moment of force)

Torque (moment of force)				
Pounds-force inches (lbf in; lb in)	X 1.152	= Kilograms-force centimetre (kgf cm; kg cm)	X 0.868	= Pounds-force inches (!bf in; lb in)
Pounds-force inches (lbf in; lb in)	X 0.113	= Newton metres (Nm)	X 8.85	= Pounds-force inches (lbf in; lb in)
Pounds-force inches (lbf in; lb in)	X 0.083	= Pounds-force feet (lbf ft; lb ft)	X 12	= Pounds-force inches (lbf in; lb in)
Pounds-force feet (lbf ft; lb ft)	X 0.138	= Kilograms-force metres (kgf m; kg m)	X 7.233	= Pounds-force feet (lbf ft; lb ft)
Pounds-force feet (lbf ft; lb ft)	X 1.356	= Newton metres (Nm)	X 0.738	= Pounds-force feet (lbf ft; lb ft)
Newton metres (Nm)	X 0.102	= Kilograms-force metres (kgf m; kg m)	X 9.804	= Newton metres (Nm)

Power

Power				
Horsepower (hp)	X 745.7	= Watts (W)	X 0.0013	= Horsepower (hp)

Velocity (speed)

Velocity (speed)				
Miles per hour (miles/hr; mph)	X 1.609	= Kilometres per hour (km/hr; kph)	X 0.621	= Miles per hour (miles/hr; mph)

Fuel consumption*

Fuel consumption*				
Miles per gallon, Imperial (mpg)	X 0.354	= Kilometres per litre (km/l)	X 2.825	= Miles per gallon, Imperial (mpg)
Miles per gallon, US (mpg)	X 0.425	= Kilometres per litre (km/l)	X 2.352	= Miles per gallon, US (mpg)

Temperature

Degrees Fahrenheit = (°C x 1.8) + 32   Degrees Celsius (Degrees Centigrade; °C) = (°F - 32) x 0.56

*It is common practice to convert from miles per gallon (mpg) to litres/100 kilometres (l/100km), where mpg (Imperial) x l/100 km = 282 and mpg (US) x l/100 km = 235

Safety first!

Professional motor mechanics are trained in safe working procedures. However enthusiastic you may be about getting on with the job in hand, do take the time to ensure that your safety is not put at risk. A moment's lack of attention can result in an accident, as can failure to observe certain elementary precautions.

There will always be new ways of having accidents, and the following points do not pretend to be a comprehensive list of all dangers; they are intended rather to make you aware of the risks and to encourage a safety-conscious approach to all work you carry out on your vehicle.

Essential DOs and DON'Ts

DON'T rely on a single jack when working underneath the vehicle. Always use reliable additional means of support, such as axle stands, securely placed under a part of the vehicle that you know will not give way.

DON'T attempt to loosen or tighten high-torque nuts (e.g. wheel hub nuts) while the vehicle is on a jack; it may be pulled off.

DON'T start the engine without first ascertaining that the transmission is in neutral (or 'Park' where applicable) and the parking brake applied.

DON'T suddenly remove the filler cap from a hot cooling system – cover it with a cloth and release the pressure gradually first, or you may get scalded by escaping coolant.

DON'T attempt to drain oil until you are sure it has cooled sufficiently to avoid scalding you.

DON'T grasp any part of the engine, exhaust or catalytic converter without first ascertaining that it is sufficiently cool to avoid burning you.

DON'T syphon toxic liquids such as fuel, brake fluid or antifreeze by mouth, or allow them to remain on your skin.

DON'T inhale brake lining dust – it is injurious to health.

DON'T allow any spilt oil or grease to remain on the floor – wipe it up straight away, before someone slips on it.

DON'T use ill-fitting spanners or other tools which may slip and cause injury.

DON'T attempt to lift a heavy component which may be beyond your capability – get assistance.

DON'T rush to finish a job, or take unverified short cuts.

DON'T allow children or animals in or around an unattended vehicle.

DO wear eye protection when using power tools such as drill, sander, bench grinder etc, and when working under the vehicle.

DO use a barrier cream on your hands prior to undertaking dirty jobs – it will protect your skin from infection as well as making the dirt easier to remove afterwards; but make sure your hands aren't left slippery.

DO keep loose clothing (cuffs, tie etc) and long hair well out of the way of moving mechanical parts.

DO remove rings, wristwatch etc, before working on the vehicle – especially the electrical system.

DO ensure that any lifting tackle used has a safe working load rating adequate for the job.

DO keep your work area tidy – it is only too easy to fall over articles left lying around.

DO get someone to check periodically that all is well, when working alone on the vehicle.

DO carry out work in a logical sequence and check that everything is correctly assembled and tightened afterwards.

DO remember that your vehicle's safety affects that of yourself and others. If in doubt on any point, get specialist advice.

IF, in spite of following these precautions, you are unfortunate enough to injure yourself, seek medical attention as soon as possible.

Fire

Remember at all times that petrol (gasoline) is highly flammable. Never smoke, or have any kind of naked flame around, when working on the vehicle. But the risk does not end there – a spark caused by an electrical short-circuit, by two metal surfaces contacting each other, or even by static electricity built up in your body under certain conditions, can ignite petrol vapour, which in a confined space is highly explosive.

Always disconnect the battery earth (ground) terminal before working on any part of the fuel system, and never risk spilling fuel on to a hot engine or exhaust.

It is recommended that a fire extinguisher of a type suitable for fuel and electrical fires is kept handy in the garage or workplace at all times. Never try to extinguish a fuel or electrical fire with water.

Fumes

Certain fumes are highly toxic and can quickly cause unconsciousness and even death if inhaled to any extent. Petrol (gasoline) vapour comes into this category, as do the vapours from certain solvents such as trichloroethylene. Any draining or pouring of such volatile fluids should be done in a well ventilated area.

When using cleaning fluids and solvents, read the instructions carefully. Never use materials from unmarked containers – they may give off poisonous vapours.

Never run the engine of a motor vehicle in an enclosed space such as a garage. Exhaust fumes contain carbon monoxide which is extremely poisonous; if you need to run the engine, always do so in the open air or at least have the rear of the vehicle outside the workplace.

If you are fortunate enough to have the use of an inspection pit, never drain or pour petrol, and never run the engine, while the vehicle is standing over it; the fumes, being heavier than air, will concentrate in the pit with possibly lethal results.

The battery

Never cause a spark, or allow a naked light, near the vehicle's battery. It will normally be giving off a certain amount of hydrogen gas, which is highly explosive.

Always disconnect the battery earth (ground) terminal before working on the fuel or electrical systems.

If possible, loosen the filler plugs or cover when charging the battery from an external source. Do not charge at an excessive rate or the battery may burst.

Take care when topping up and when carrying the battery. The acid electrolyte, even when diluted, is very corrosive and should not be allowed to contact the eyes or skin.

If you ever need to prepare electrolyte yourself, always add the acid slowly to the water, and never the other way round. Protect against splashes by wearing rubber gloves and goggles.

When jump starting a car using a booster battery, for negative earth (ground) vehicles, connect the jump leads in the following sequence: First connect one jump lead between the positive (+) terminals of the two batteries. Then connect the other jump lead first to the negative (–) terminal of the booster battery, and then to a good earthing (ground) point on the vehicle to be started, at least 18 in (45 cm) from the battery if possible. Ensure that hands and jump leads are clear of any moving parts, and that the two vehicles do not touch. Disconnect the leads in the reverse order.

Mains electricity

When using an electric power tool, inspection light etc, which works from the mains, always ensure that the appliance is correctly connected to its plug and that, where necessary, it is properly earthed (grounded). Do not use such appliances in damp conditions and, again, beware of creating a spark or applying excessive heat in the vicinity of fuel or fuel vapour.

Ignition HT voltage

A severe electric shock can result from touching certain parts of the ignition system, such as the HT leads, when the engine is running or being cranked, particularly if components are damp or the insulation is defective. Where an electronic ignition system is fitted, the HT voltage is much higher and could prove fatal.

Routine maintenance

Maintenance is essential for ensuring safety and desirable for the purpose of getting the best in terms of performance and economy from the car. Over the years the need for periodic lubrication has been greatly reduced if not totally eliminated. This has unfortunately tended to lead some owners to think that because no such action is required the items either no longer exist or will last forever. This is certainly not the case; it is essential to carry out regular visual examinations as comprehensively as possible in order to spot any possible defects at an early stage before they develop into major and expensive repairs.

Engine compartment with spare wheel and air cleaner removed

1	Battery	5	Jack	9	Washer fluid reservoir	13	Alternator
2	Fuse box	6	Ignition coil	10	Carburettor	14	Radiator
3	Suspension strut turret	7	Distributor	11	Thermostat housing	15	Wheel brace
4	Brake master cylinder	8	Coolant expansion tank	12	Oil filler cap		

16

Front end viewed from underneath

1 Sill jacking point
2 Suspension lower arm
3 Driveshaft
4 Brake caliper
5 Radius rod
6 Sump pan drain plug
7 Exhaust downpipe
8 Gearchange control rods
9 Transmission lower mounting
10 Transmission
11 Radiator
12 Tie-rod end
13 Coolant pump

Rear end viewed from underneath

1 Leaf spring
2 Rear axle tube
3 Shock absorber

4 Silencer
5 Fuel tank

6 Handbrake cable equaliser
7 Handbrake cables

Weekly or every 400 km (250 miles)

Check engine oil level (photo)
Check brake reservoir fluid level
Check tyre pressures and tread wear (photos)
Check operation of all lights
Top up washer fluid reservoirs and check operation of washers and wipers (photo)
Check coolant level (photo)
Check battery electrolyte level

At first 1000 miles (1500 km) – new cars

Check torque of cylinder head bolts (Chapter 1, Sec 5)
Adjust valve clearances (Chapter 1, Sec 11)
Check carburettor idle speed and mixture setting (Chapter 3, Sec 10)
Check handbrake adjustment (Chapter 8, Sec 13)
Check front wheel alignment (Chapter 10, Sec 12)
Check dwell angle and ignition timing (Chapter 4, Secs 3 and 4)
Renew engine oil (Chapter 1, Sec 2)
Check transmission oil level (Chapter 6, Sec 2)

Every 6000 miles (10 000 km) or six monthly – whichever occurs first

Renew engine oil and filter (Chapter 1, Sec 2)
Check and re-gap spark plugs (Chapter 4, Sec 9)
Check disc pad and brake shoe lining wear (Chapter 8, Sec 3)

Check steering rack gaiters and driveshaft gaiters for splits or damage (Chapter 7, Sec 3; Chapter 10, Sec 4)
Check and top up transmission oil (Chapter 6, Sec 2)
Check drivebelt tension and condition (Chapter 2, Sec 7)
Check tyres for wear or damage (Chapter 7, Sec 7)
Lubricate all hinges and controls
Check condition of exhaust system (Chapter 3, Sec 15)
Check clutch cable adjustment (Chapter 5, Sec 2)
Check dwell angle and ignition timing (Chapter 4, Secs 3 & 4)

Every 12 000 miles (20 000 km) or annually – whichever occurs first

Renew spark plugs (Chapter 4, Sec 9)
Renew air cleaner element (Chapter 3, Sec 2)
Check brake hoses for condition (Chapter 8, Sec 11)
Check handbrake adjustment (Chapter 8, Sec 13)
Check front wheel alignment (Chapter 10, Sec 12)
Check headlamp beam alignment (Chapter 9, Sec 17)
Examine all steering and suspension joints and brakes for wear (Chapter 10, Sec 11)
Renew contact points (Chapter 4, Sec 2)
Clean underside and make good protective coating (Chapter 12, Sec 2)

Every 24 000 miles (38 000 km) or two years – whichever comes first

Renew brake hydraulic fluid by bleeding (Chapter 8, Sec 12)
Renew coolant (antifreeze mixture) (Chapter 2, Sec 2)
Renew transmission oil (Chapter 6, Sec 2)

Topping up with engine oil

Checking a tyre pressure

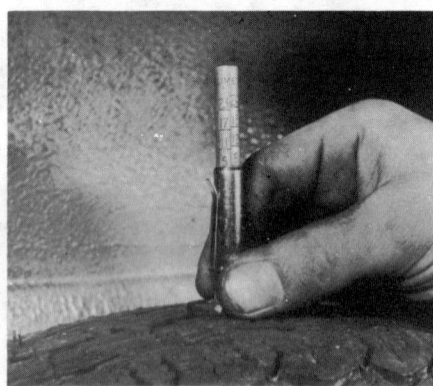

Checking tyre tread depth

Topping up washer fluid reservoir

Topping up coolant expansion tank

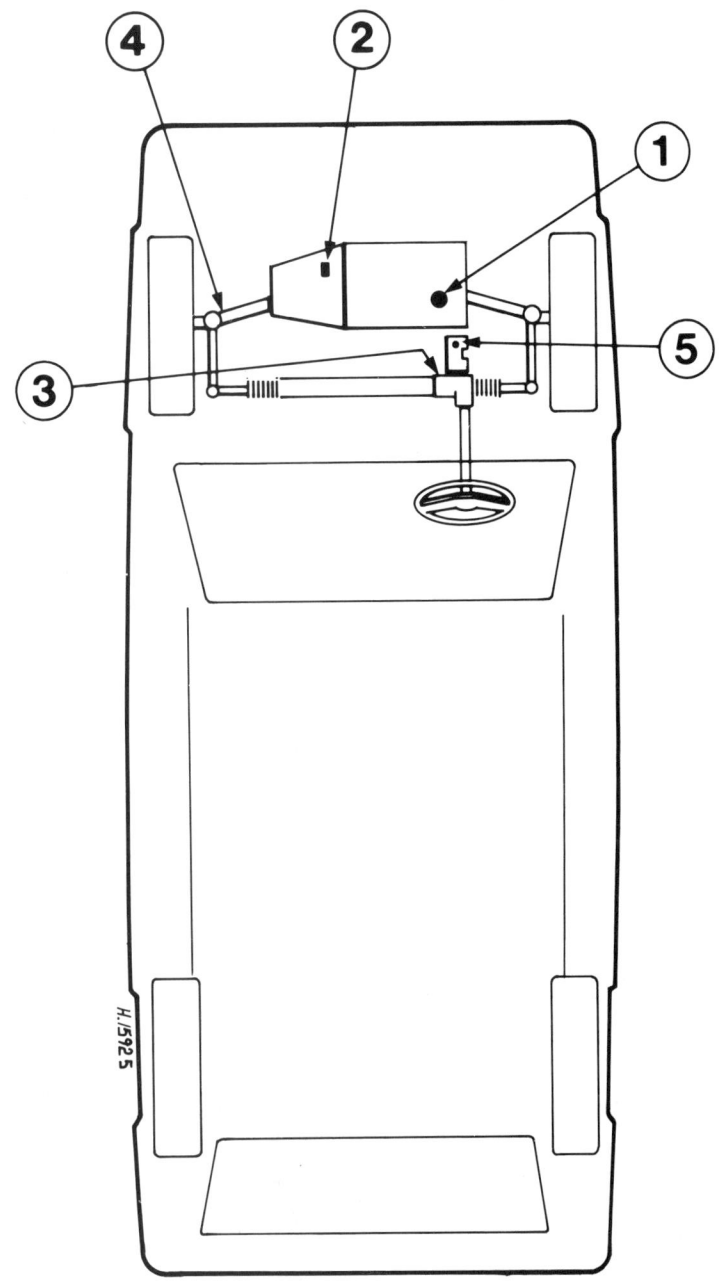

H./5925

Recommended lubricants and fluids

Component or system	Lubricant type
Engine (1)	SAE 15W/40 multigrade engine oil (or equivalent multigrade engine oil having a viscosity rating compatible with temperatures in the vehicle operating area – see manufacturer's handbook)
Transmission (2)	SAE 80W/90 gear oil (not EP)
Steering gear (3)	Molybdenum disulphide grease
Driveshaft CV joint (4)	Molybdenum disulphide grease
Brake fluid reservoir (5)	DOT 3 Hydraulic fluid to FMVSS 116

Fault diagnosis

Introduction

The vehicle owner who does his or her own maintenance according to the recommended schedules should not have to use this section of the manual very often. Modern component reliability is such that, provided those items subject to wear or deterioration are inspected or renewed at the specified intervals, sudden failure is comparatively rare. Faults do not usually just happen as a result of sudden failure, but develop over a period of time. Major mechanical failures in particular are usually preceded by characteristic symptoms over hundreds or even thousands of miles. Those components which do occasionally fail without warning are often small and easily carried in the vehicle.

With any fault finding, the first step is to decide where to begin investigations. Sometimes this is obvious, but on other occasions a little detective work will be necessary. The owner who makes half a dozen haphazard adjustments or replacements may be successful in curing a fault (or its symptoms), but he will be none the wiser if the fault recurs and he may well have spent more time and money than was necessary. A calm and logical approach will be found to be more satisfactory in the long run. Always take into account any warning signs or abnormalities that may have been noticed in the period preceding the fault – power loss, high or low gauge readings, unusual noises or smells, etc – and remember that failure of components such as fuses or spark plugs may only be pointers to some underlying fault.

The pages which follow here are intended to help in cases of failure to start or breakdown on the road. There is also a Fault Diagnosis Section at the end of each Chapter which should be consulted if the preliminary checks prove unfruitful. Whatever the fault, certain basic principles apply. These are as follows:

Verify the fault. This is simply a matter of being sure that you know what the symptoms are before starting work. This is particularly important if you are investigating a fault for someone else who may not have described it very accurately.

Don't overlook the obvious. For example, if the vehicle won't start, is there petrol in the tank? (Don't take anyone else's word on this particular point, and don't trust the fuel gauge either!) If an electrical fault is indicated, look for loose or broken wires before digging out the test gear.

Cure the disease, not the symptom. Substituting a flat battery with a fully charged one will get you off the hard shoulder, but if the underlying cause is not attended to, the new battery will go the same way. Similarly, changing oil-fouled spark plugs for a new set will get you moving again, but remember that the reason for the fouling (if it

wasn't simply an incorrect grade of plug) will have to be established and corrected.

Don't take anything for granted. Particularly, don't forget that a 'new' component may itself be defective (especially if it's been rattling round in the boot for months), and don't leave components out of a fault diagnosis sequence just because they are new or recently fitted. When you do finally diagnose a difficult fault, you'll probably realise that all the evidence was there from the start.

Electrical faults

Electrical faults can be more puzzling than straightforward mechanical failures, but they are no less susceptible to logical analysis if the basic principles of operation are understood. Vehicle electrical wiring exists in extremely unfavourable conditions – heat, vibration and chemical attack – and the first things to look for are loose or corroded connections and broken or chafed wires, especially where the wires pass through holes in the bodywork or are subject to vibration.

All metal-bodied vehicles in current production have one pole of the battery 'earthed', ie connected to the vehicle bodywork, and in nearly all modern vehicles it is the negative (–) terminal. The various electrical components – motors, bulb holders etc – are also connected to earth, either by means of a lead or directly by their mountings. Electric current flows through the component and then back to the battery via the bodywork. If the component mounting is loose or corroded, or if a good path back to the battery is not available, the circuit will be incomplete and malfunction will result. The engine and/or gearbox are also earthed by means of flexible metal straps to the body or subframe; if these straps are loose or missing, starter motor, generator and ignition trouble may result.

Assuming the earth return to be satisfactory, electrical faults will be due either to component malfunction or to defects in the current supply. Individual components are dealt with in Chapter 9. If supply wires are broken or cracked internally this results in an open-circuit, and the easiest way to check for this is to bypass the suspect wire temporarily with a length of wire having a crocodile clip or suitable connector at each end. Alternatively, a 12V test lamp can be used to verify the presence of supply voltage at various points along the wire and the break can be thus isolated.

If a bare portion of a live wire touches the bodywork or other earthed metal part, the electricity will take the low-resistance path thus formed back to the battery: this is known as a short-circuit. Hopefully a short-circuit will blow a fuse, but otherwise it may cause burning of the insulation (and possibly further short-circuits) or even a fire. This is why it is inadvisable to bypass persistently blowing fuses with silver foil or wire.

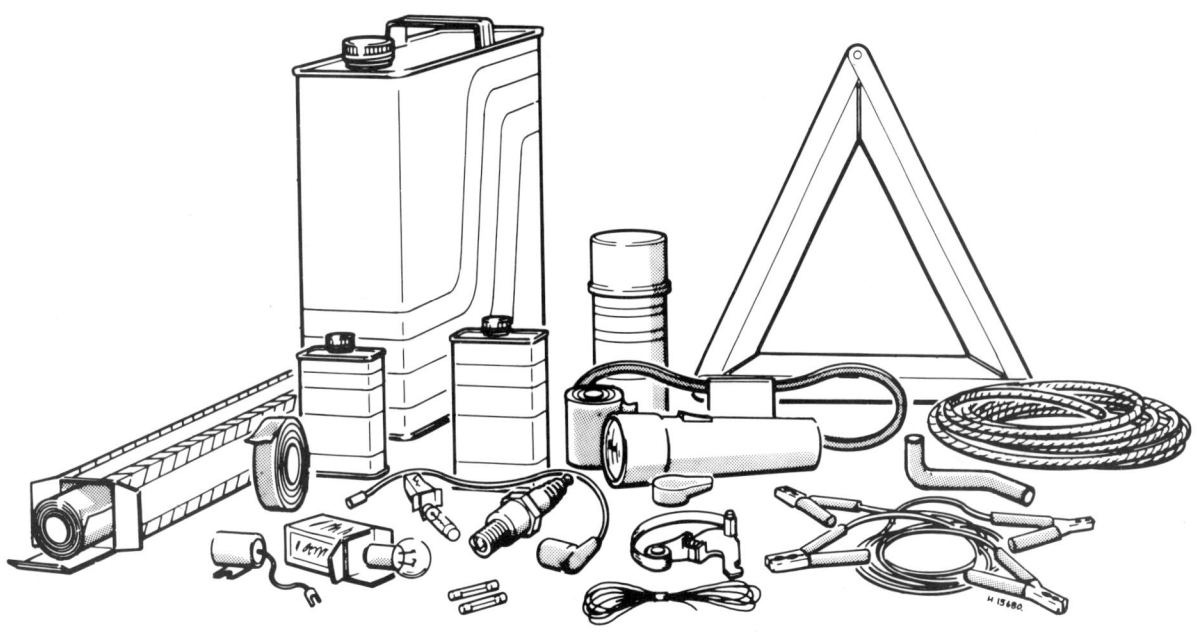

Carrying a few spares can save you a long walk!

Spares and tool kit

Most vehicles are supplied only with sufficient tools for wheel changing; the *Maintenance and minor repair* tool kit detailed in *Tools and working facilities,* with the addition of a hammer, is probably sufficient for those repairs that most motorists would consider attempting at the roadside. In addition a few items which can be fitted without too much trouble in the event of a breakdown should be carried. Experience and available space will modify the list below, but the following may save having to call on professional assistance:

Spark plugs, clean and correctly gapped
HT lead and plug cap – long enough to reach the plug furthest from the distributor
Distributor rotor, condenser and contact breaker points
Drivebelt(s) – emergency type may suffice
Spare fuses
Set of principal light bulbs
Tin of radiator sealer and hose bandage
Exhaust bandage
Roll of insulating tape
Length of soft iron wire
Length of electrical flex
Torch or inspection lamp (can double as test lamp)
Battery jump leads
Tow-rope
Ignition waterproofing aerosol
Litre of engine oil
Sealed can of hydraulic fluid
Emergency windscreen
'Jubilee' clips
Tube of filler paste

If spare fuel is carried, a can designed for the purpose should be used to minimise risks of leakage and collision damage. A first aid kit and a warning triangle, whilst not at present compulsory in the UK, are obviously sensible items to carry in addition to the above.

When touring abroad it may be advisable to carry additional spares which, even if you cannot fit them yourself, could save having to wait while parts are obtained. The items below may be worth considering:

Clutch and throttle cables
Cylinder head gasket
Alternator brushes
Tyre valve core

One of the motoring organisations will be able to advise on availability of fuel etc in foreign countries.

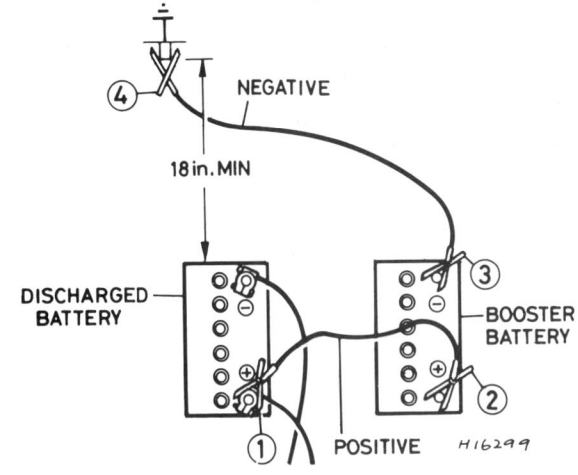

Jump start lead connections for negative earth – correct leads in order shown

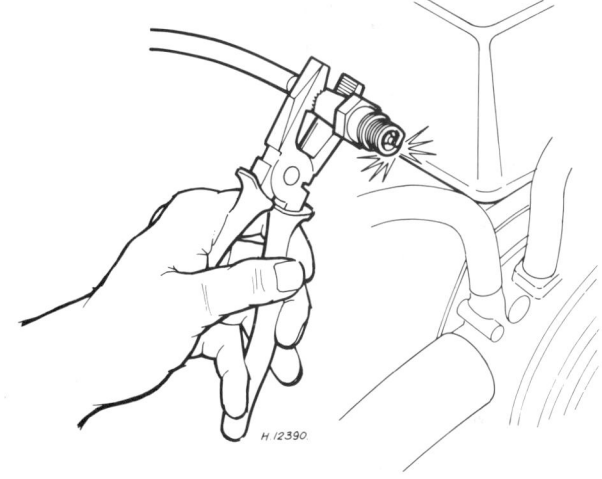

Crank engine and check for spark. Note use of insulated tool to hold lead

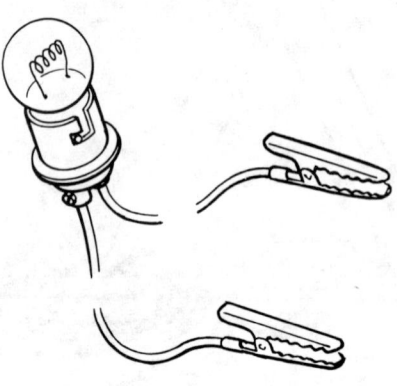

A simple test lamp is useful for checking electrical faults

Engine will not start

Engine fails to turn when starter operated
Flat battery (recharge, use jump leads, or push start)
Battery terminals loose or corroded
Battery earth to body defective
Engine earth strap loose or broken
Starter motor (or solenoid) wiring loose or broken
Ignition/starter switch faulty
Major mechanical failure (seizure)
Starter or solenoid internal fault (see Chapter 9)

Starter motor turns engine slowly
Partially discharged battery (recharge, use jump leads, or push start)
Battery terminals loose or corroded
Battery earth to body defective
Engine earth strap loose
Starter motor (or solenoid) wiring loose
Starter motor internal fault (see Chapter 9)

Starter motor spins without turning engine
Flat battery
Starter motor pinion sticking on sleeve
Flywheel gear teeth damaged or worn
Starter motor mounting bolts loose

Engine turns normally but fails to start
Damp or dirty HT leads and distributor cap (crank engine and check for spark)
Dirty or incorrectly gapped distributor points (if applicable)
No fuel in tank (check for delivery at carburettor)
Excessive choke (hot engine) or insufficient choke (cold engine)
Fouled or incorrectly gapped spark plugs (remove, clean and regap)
Other ignition system fault (see Chapter 4)
Other fuel system fault (see Chapter 3)
Poor compression (see Chapter 1)
Major mechanical failure (eg camshaft drive)

Engine fires but will not run
Insufficient choke (cold engine)
Air leaks at carburettor or inlet manifold
Fuel starvation (see Chapter 3)
Ballast resistor defective, or other ignition fault (see Chapter 4)

Engine cuts out and will not restart

Engine cuts out suddenly – ignition fault
Loose or disconnected LT wires
Wet HT leads or distributor cap (after traversing water splash)
Coil or condenser failure (check for spark)
Other ignition fault (see Chapter 4)

Engine misfires before cutting out – fuel fault
Fuel tank empty
Fuel pump defective or filter blocked (check for delivery)
Fuel tank filler vent blocked (suction will be evident on releasing cap) – not N. American cars with sealed cap
Carburettor needle valve sticking
Carburettor jets blocked (fuel contaminated)
Other fuel system fault (see Chapter 3)

Engine cuts out – other causes
Serious overheating
Major mechanical failure (eg camshaft drive)

Engine overheats

Ignition (no-charge) warning light illuminated
Slack or broken drivebelt – retension or renew (Chapter 2)

Ignition warning light not illuminated
Coolant loss due to internal or external leakage (see Chapter 2)
Thermostat defective
Low oil level
Brakes binding
Radiator clogged externally or internally
Electric cooling fan not operating correctly
Engine waterways clogged
Ignition timing incorrect or automatic advance malfunctioning
Mixture too weak

Note: *Do not add cold water to an overheated engine or damage may result*

Low engine oil pressure

Gauge reads low or warning light illuminated with engine running
Oil level low or incorrect grade
Defective gauge or sender unit
Wire to sender unit earthed
Engine overheating
Oil filter clogged or bypass valve defective
Oil pressure relief valve defective
Oil pick-up strainer clogged
Oil pump worn or mountings loose
Worn main or big-end bearings

Note: *Low oil pressure in a high-mileage engine at tickover is not necessarily a cause for concern. Sudden pressure loss at speed is far more significant. In any event, check the gauge or warning light sender before condemning the engine.*

Engine noises

Pre-ignition (pinking) on acceleration
Incorrect grade of fuel
Ignition timing incorrect

Distributor faulty or worn
Worn or maladjusted carburettor
Excessive carbon build-up in engine

Whistling or wheezing noises
Leaking vacuum hose
Leaking carburettor or manifold gasket
Blowing head gasket

Tapping or rattling
Incorrect valve clearances
Worn valve gear

Worn timing chain
Broken piston ring (ticking noise)

Knocking or thumping
Unintentional mechanical contact (eg fan blades)
Worn drivebelt
Peripheral component fault (generator, coolant pump etc)
Worn big-end bearings (regular heavy knocking, perhaps less under load)
Worn main bearings (rumbling and knocking, perhaps worsening under load)
Piston slap (most noticeable when cold)

Chapter 1 Engine

Contents

Crankcase ventilation system	3
Cylinder head – dismantling and decarbonising	19
Cylinder head – removal and refitting	5
Engine – complete dismantling	18
Engine – complete reassembly	22
Engine – dismantling (general)	16
Engine – initial start up after overhaul or major repair	26
Engine – method of removal	12
Engine – removing ancillary components	17
Engine ancillary components – refitting	23
Engine mountings – removal and refitting	9
Engine oil and filter	2
Engine reassembly (general)	21
Engine/transmission – reconnection	24
Engine/transmission – refitting	25
Engine/transmission – removal downwards	13
Engine/transmission – removal upwards	14
Engine/transmission – separation	15
Examination and renovation	20
Fault diagnosis – engine	27
General description	1
Major operations possible without removing the engine	4
Oil pump – removal and refitting	10
Piston/connecting rods – removal and refitting	7
Sump pan – removal and refitting	6
Timing chain and sprockets – removal and refitting	8
Valve clearances – adjustment	11

Specifications

Type

Four cylinder, in-line, water cooled, overhead valve. Transversely front mounted

General

Bore	65.0 mm (2.54 in)
Stroke	68.0 mm (2.65 in)
Displacement	903 cc
Compression ratio	9.0 : 1
Maximum power (DIN)	45 bhp (33.1 kW) at 5600 rev/min
Maximum torque (DIN)	47 lbf ft (63.76 Nm) at 3000 rev/min
Compression pressure	9.3 to 10.35 bar (135 to 150 lbf/in^2)
Pressure difference between cylinders	0.69 bar (10 lbf/in^2)
Firing order	1 – 3 – 4 – 2 (No. 1 at timing end)

Cylinder block and crankcase

Material	Cast iron
Bore diameter	65.000 to 65.050 mm (2.5591 to 2.5610 in)
Diameter of camshaft bearing bores in crankcase:	
Timing gear end:	
Grade B	50.500 to 50.510 mm (1.9882 to 1.9886 in)
Grade C	50.510 to 50.520 mm (1.9886 to 1.9890 in)
Grade D	50.700 to 50.710 mm (1.9960 to 1.9964 in)
Grade E	50.710 to 50.720 mm (1.9964 to 1.9968 in)
Centre	46.420 to 46.450 mm (1.8275 to 1.8287 in)
Flywheel end	35.921 to 32.951 mm (1.4142 to 1.4154 in)
Maximum cylinder bore taper	0.015 mm (0.0006 in)
Maximum cylinder bore ovality	0.015 mm (0.0006 in)

Pistons and piston rings

Piston diameter:	
A	64.940 to 64.950 mm (2.5566 to 2.5570 in)
C	64.960 to 64.970 mm (2.5574 to 2.5578 in)
E	64.980 to 64.990 mm (2.5582 to 2.5586 in)
Oversizes	0.2, 0.4, 0.6 mm (0.008, 0.016, 0.023 in)
Piston clearance in bore	0.050 to 0.070 mm (0.0020 to 0.0028 in)
Piston ring groove width:	
Top	1.785 to 1.805 mm (0.0703 to 0.0711 in)
Second	2.015 to 2.035 mm (0.0793 to 0.0801 in)
Bottom	2.015 to 2.035 mm (0.0793 to 0.0801 in)
Piston ring thickness:	
Top	1.728 to 1.740 mm (0.0680 to 0.0685 in)
Second	1.978 to 1.990 mm (0.0779 to 0.0784 in)
Bottom	3.925 to 3.937 mm (0.1545 to 0.1550 in)
Piston ring groove clearance:	
Top	0.045 to 0.077 mm (0.0018 to 0.0030 in)
Second	0.025 to 0.057 mm (0.0010 to 0.0022 in)
Bottom	0.020 to 0.052 mm (0.0008 to 0.0020 in)
Piston ring end gap	0.20 to 0.35 mm (0.0079 to 0.0138 in)
Oversize piston rings	0.2, 0.4, 0.6 mm (0.008, 0.016, 0.023 in)
Gudgeon pin diameter:	
Grade 1	19.970 to 19.974 mm (0.7862 to 0.7863 in)
Grade 2	19.974 to 19.978 mm (0.7863 to 0.7865 in)
Grade 3	19.978 to 19.982 mm (0.7865 to 0.7866 in)
Oversize	0.2 mm (0.008 in)

Crankshaft

Journal diameter	50.785 to 50.805 mm (1.9994 to 2.0002 in)
Standard main bearing shell thickness	1.832 to 1.837 mm (0.0721 to 0.0723 in)
Undersizes	0.25, 0.50, 0.76, 1.0 mm (0.010, 0.020, 0.030, 0.039 in)
Main bearing running clearance	0.028 to 0.073 mm (0.0011 to 0.0029 in)
Thrust washer thickness:	
Standard	2.310 to 2.360 mm (0.0909 to 0.0929 in)
Oversize	2.437 to 2.487 mm (0.0959 to 0.0979 in)
Crankshaft endfloat	0.06 to 0.26 mm (0.0024 to 0.0102 in)
Crankpin diameter	39.985 to 40.005 mm (1.5741 to 1.5750 in)
Standard big-end shell bearing thickness	1.807 to 1.813 mm (0.0712 to 0.0714 in)
Undersizes	0.25, 0.50, 0.76, 1.0 mm (0.010, 0.020, 0.030, 0.039 in)
Big-end bearing running clearance	0.026 to 0.071 mm (0.0010 to 0.0028 in)

Camshaft

Diameter of camshaft journals:	
Timing end	37.975 to 38.000 mm (1.4951 to 1.4961 in)
Centre	43.333 to 43.358 mm (1.7060 to 1.7070 in)
Flywheel end	30.975 to 31.000 mm (1.2194 to 1.2205 in)
Bush reamed diameters:	
*Timing gear end	38.025 to 38.050 mm (1.4971 to 1.4981 in)
Centre	43.404 to 43.424 mm (1.7088 to 1.7096 in)
Flywheel end	31.026 to 31.046 mm (1.2215 to 1.2223 in)
* Supplied reamed to size	
Cam lobe height	5.6 mm (0.22 in)

Cam followers

Bore in crankcase	14.010 to 14.028 mm (0.5516 to 0.5523 in)
Outside diameter of cam follower	13.982 to 14.000 mm (0.5505 to 0.5512 in)
Oversizes	0.05 to 0.10 mm (0.002 to 0.004 in)
Cam follower running clearance	0.010 to 0.046 mm (0.0004 to 0.0018 in)

Cylinder head and valves

Material	Light alloy
Maximum distortion	0.05 mm (0.002 in)
Valve guide bore in head	12.950 to 12.977 mm (0.5099 to 0.5109 in)
Valve guide outside diameter	13.010 to 13.030 mm (0.5122 to 0.5130 in)
Valve guide oversize	0.05, 0.10, 0.25 mm (0.002, 0.004, 0.01 in)
Inside diameter of valve guide	7.022 to 7.040 mm (0.2765 to 0.2772 in)
Guide fit in head (interference)	0.033 to 0.080 mm (0.0013 to 0.0032 in)
Valve stem diameter	6.982 to 7.000 mm (0.2748 to 0.2756 in)
Maximum clearance (valve stem to guide)	0.022 to 0.058 mm (0.0009 to 0.0023 in)
Valve seat angle	44° 55' to 45° 05'
Valve face angle	45° 25' to 45° 35'
Valve head diameter:	
Inlet	29.0 mm (1.1417 in)
Exhaust	26.0 mm (1.0236 in)
Contact band (valve to seat)	1.3 to 1.5 mm (0.0512 to 0.0591 in)
Valve clearance:	
Inlet	0.15 mm (0.006 in)
Exhaust	0.20 mm (0.008 in)
For timing check	0.60 mm (0.024 in)

Valve timing:	Up to 1983	1983 on
Inlet		
Opens	17° BTDC	7° BTDC
Closes	43° ABDC	36 ° ABDC
Exhaust	Up to 1983	1983 on
Opens	57° BBDC	38° BBDC
Closes	3° ATDC	5° ATDC

Lubrication system

Oil pump type	Gear, driven by shaft from camshaft
Tooth tip to body clearance	0.05 to 0.14 mm (0.0020 to 0.0055 in)
Gear endfloat	0.020 to 0.105 mm (0.0008 to 0.0041 in)
Oil pressure at normal operating temperature and average road/engine speed	2.94 to 3.92 bar (42 to 57 lbf/in^2)
Oil capacity (with filter change):	
To engine number 6263501	3.5 litres (6.2 pints)
From engine number 6263502 (with miniature type filter)	3.3 litres (5.8 pints)

Torque wrench settings

	Nm	lbf ft
Cylinder head bolts:		
Stage 1	30	22
Stage 2	59	43.5
Camshaft sprocket bolt	49	36
Main bearing cap bolts	69	51
Big-end bearing cap bolts	41	30
Crankshaft pulley nut	98	72
Flywheel bolts	44	32
Rocker pedestal nuts	18	25

1 General description

The engine is of four cylinder, overhead valve type, mounted transversely with the transmission and supported on flexible mountings.

The cylinder head is of light alloy construction with the valves being operated by rocker arms and pushrods from the camshaft which is located within the crankcase.

The cylinder head is of crossflow type having the inlet and exhaust manifolds on opposite sides.

A three bearing crankshaft is used and the camshaft is driven by a Duplex chain and sprockets.

The oil pump is located within the sump pan and is driven by a shaft geared to the camshaft as is the distributor.

A pressure relief valve fitted in the lubrication system controls the maximum oil pressure when the oil is cold. Any surplus oil is returned to the sump. To warn the driver should loss of oil pressure occur, a pressure switch is fitted to the main oil gallery to indicate low oil pressure.

Oil is drawn from the sump through a gauze screen in the oil strainer, and is drawn up the pickup pipe and into the oil pump. From the oil pump it passes to the oil pressure relief valve and then to the oil filter.

Through passages the oil passes from the filter through the crankshaft to the main and big-end bearings. From the main gallery, which also supplies the camshaft bearings, a return pipe takes the oil back to the sump.

From the centre camshaft bearing oil is fed to the overhead rocker gear, returning via two oilways to the camshaft to lubricate the tappets and thereafter to the sump.

The pistons are made from anodised aluminium and have solid skirts. Two compression and one oil control ring are fitted. The gudgeon pin is a press fit in the connecting rod little end. Renewable steel backed bearing shells are fitted to the big-ends.

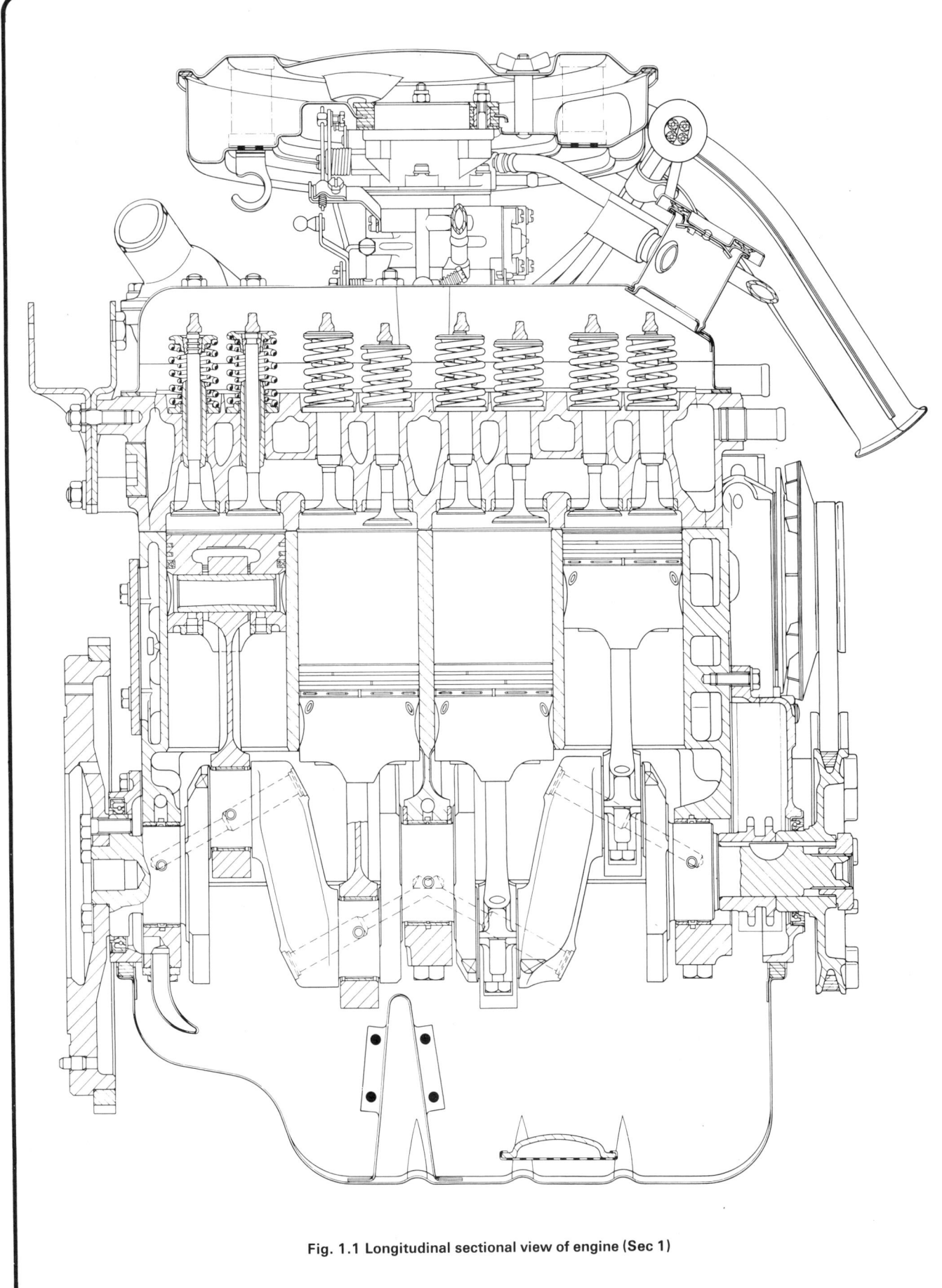

Fig. 1.1 Longitudinal sectional view of engine (Sec 1)

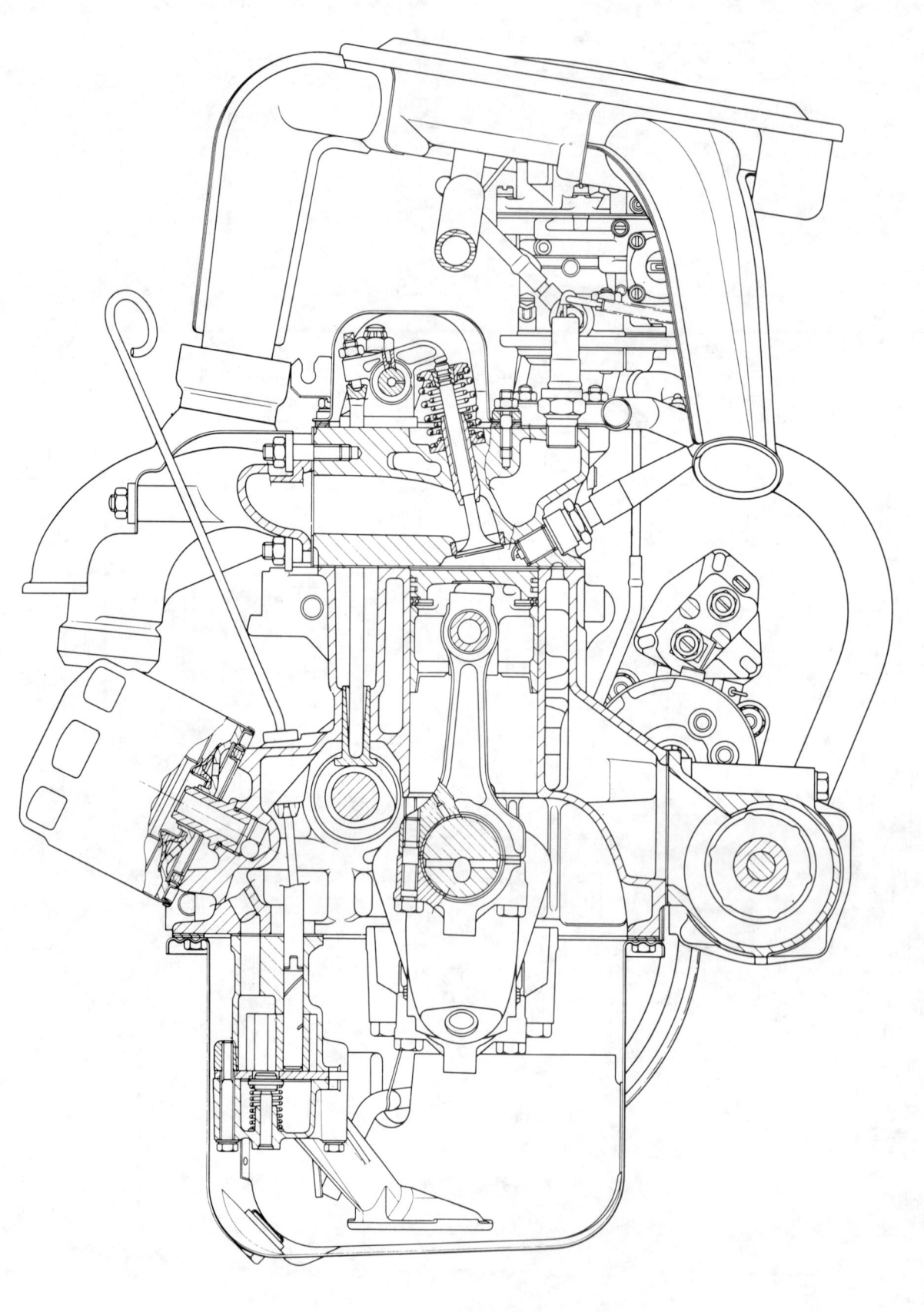

Fig. 1.2 Cross-sectional view of engine (Sec 1)

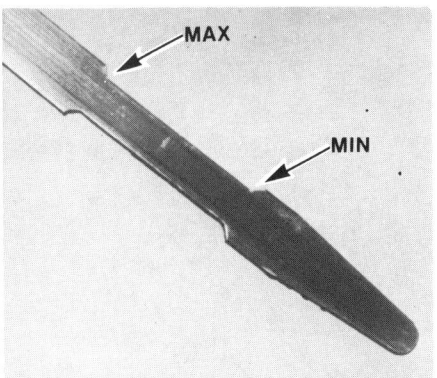

2.2 Engine oil dipstick

2.3 Sump drain plug

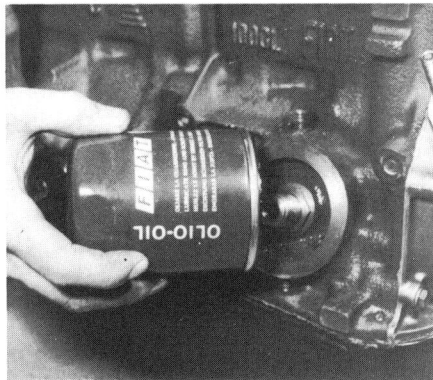

2.6 Fitting oil filter

2 Engine oil and filter

1   Check the engine oil level, preferably when the engine is cold.
2   Withdraw the dipstick, wipe it clean, re-insert it and then withdraw it for the second time. The oil level should be between the MIN and MAX marks. Add oil as necessary through the rocker cover oil filler cap. One litre of oil will raise the oil level from the MIN to MAX marks (photo).
3   At the specified intervals, renew the engine oil and filter. Drain the oil when hot into a suitable bowl by unscrewing the drain plug from the sump pan (photo).
4   The oil will drain more quickly if the filler cap and dipstick are withdrawn.
5   While the oil is draining, unscrew and discard the oil filter cartridge. If it is stuck tight, unscrew it with an oil filter wrench. If one is not available, drive a screwdriver through the filter casing and use it as a lever to unscrew it.
6   Smear the rubber seal of the new filter with engine oil and screw the filter into position using hand pressure only (photo).
7   Once the oil has finished draining, refit the drain plug.
8   Fill the engine with the specified quantity of oil of the recommended grade.
9   Start the engine. The oil pressure warning lamp may take a few seconds to go out. This is normal and is due to the new filter having to fill with oil.
10 Switch off and check the oil level. Top up the oil to the MAX mark.
11 Once the engine has been run to operating temperature, check the tightness of the oil filter cartridge using hand pressure.

3 Crankcase ventilation system

1   This system is designed to draw vapour which has collected in the crankcase (as the result of piston ring gas blow-by and oil fumes) and to direct it into the intake manifold for burning in the normal combustion process.
2   The components of the system consist of the connecting hoses and a valve. Periodically clean the valve and hoses. The evidence of sludge (emulsified oil) in the hoses or on the underside of the oil filler cap will indicate that the intake air is too cold and the air cleaner should be turned to its winter setting (see Chapter 3).

4 Major operations possible without removing the engine

1   The following operations are possible without the need to remove the engine:

Removal and refitting of the cylinder head assembly
Removal and refitting of the sump pan
Removal and refitting of the pistons and connecting rods
Removal and refitting of the timing chain and gears
Removal and refitting of the engine mountings
Removal and refitting of the oil pump

2   Obviously, before any major work can be carried out on the engine, the spare wheel must be removed.

5 Cylinder head – removal and refitting

Removal
1   For safety reasons disconnect the battery negative and positive terminals, in that order.
2   Refer to Chapter 2 and drain the cooling system.
3   Refer to Chapter 3 and remove the carburettor, air cleaner and spacer block.
4   Undo and remove the five nuts and washers securing the exhaust manifold and hot air ducting to the cylinder head.
5   Detach the cable from the temperature indicator sender unit.
6   Refer to Chapter 4 and remove the distributor and spark plug leads.
7   Refer to Chapter 2 and remove the thermostat housing from the cylinder head.
8   Remove the clips connecting the coolant hoses to the cylinder head, just above the support bracket.
9   Note the electrical cable connections to the rear of the alternator and disconnect them.
10 Undo the three mountings and lift away the alternator.
11 Unscrew the four nuts securing the rocker cover to the top of the cylinder head and lift away the spring washers and metal packing pieces. Remove the rocker cover and cork gasket.
12 Unscrew the four rocker pedestal securing nuts in a progressive manner. Lift away the four nuts and spring washers and ease the valve rocker assembly from the cylinder head studs.
13 Remove the pushrods, keeping them in the relative order in which they were removed. The easiest way to do this is to push them through a sheet of thick paper or thin card in the correct sequence.
14 Unscrew the cylinder head securing bolts half a turn at a time in the reverse order to that shown in Fig. 1.3 – don't forget the one within

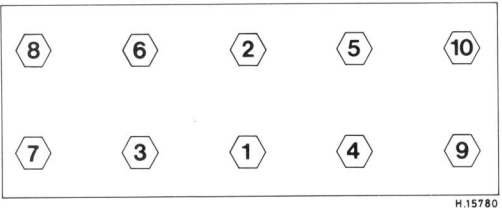

Fig. 1.3 Cylinder head bolt tightening sequence (Sec 5)

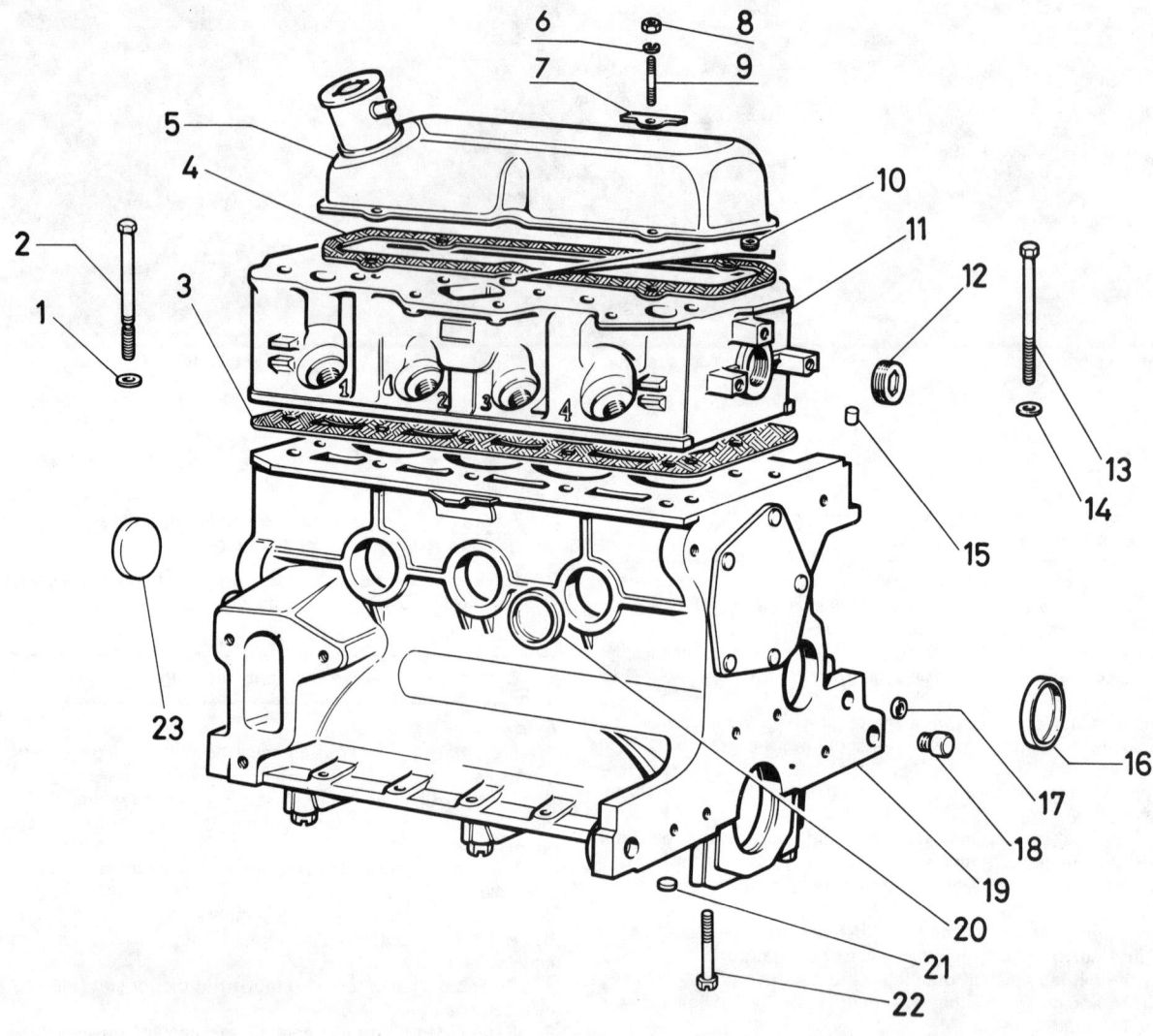

Fig. 1.4 Cylinder head, block and crankcase (Sec 5)

1	Washer	7	Plate	13	Cylinder head bolt	19	Cylinder block
2	Cylinder head bolt	8	Nut	14	Washer	20	Plug
3	Head gasket	9	Stud	15	Dowel	21	Plug
4	Rocker cover gasket	10	Plug	16	Plug	22	Bolt
5	Rocker cover	11	Cylinder head	17	Plug	23	Plug
6	Washer	12	Plug	18	Dowel		

the inlet manifold. When all the bolts are no longer under tension they may be screwed off the cylinder head one at a time. This will also release a section of the cooling system pipe secured by two of the bolts. All the bolts have washers.

15 The cylinder head may now be lifted off. If the head is jammed, try to rock it to break the seal. Under no circumstances try to prise it apart from the cylinder block with a screwdriver or cold chisel as damage may be done to the faces of the head or block. If the head will not readily free, turn the engine over by the flywheel as the compression in the cylinders will often break the cylinder head joint. If this fails to work, strike the head sharply with a plastic headed hammer, or with a wooden hammer, or with a metal hammer with an interposed piece of wood to cushion the blows. Under no circumstances hit the head directly with a metal hammer as this may cause the casting to fracture. Several sharp taps with the hammer, at the same time pulling upwards, should free the head. Lift the head off and place on one side. For details of cylinder head decarbonising and dismantling, refer to Section 19.

Refitting

16 After checking that both the cylinder block and cylinder head mating surfaces are perfectly clean, generously lubricate each cylinder with engine oil.

17 Always use a new cylinder head gasket as the old gasket will be compressed and not capable of giving a good seal.

18 Never smear grease on the gasket as, when the engine heats up, the grease will melt and may allow compression leaks to develop.

19 The cylinder head gasket cannot be fitted incorrectly due to its asymmetrical shape, but the word ALTO should be uppermost in any event.

20 The locating dowels should be refitted to the front right and left-hand side cylinder head securing bolt holes.

21 Carefully fit the cylinder head gasket to the top of the cylinder block (photo).

22 Lower the cylinder head onto the gasket, taking care not to move the position of the gasket.

23 Fit the cylinder head securing bolts and tighten all finger-tight.

5.21 Cylinder head gasket

5.23B Coolant pipe located under cylinder head bolts
1   Bolts
2   Coolant temperature switch

One bolt is located within the inlet manifold. Refit the water temperature sending unit and note that part of the water pipe cooling system, the copper pipe portion, is secured to the cylinder head bolts adjacent to the sender unit (photos).

24 Tighten the cylinder head securing bolts in a progressive manner in the order shown in Fig. 1.3 to the specified torque.

25 With the cylinder head in position, fit the pushrods in the same order in which they were removed. Ensure that they locate properly in the stems of the tappets and lubricate the pushrod ends before fitment (photo).

26 Unscrew the rocker arm adjuster screws as far as they will go.

27 Fit the rocker gear over the four studs in the cylinder head and lower onto the cylinder head. Make sure the ball ends of the rockers locate in the cups of the pushrods.

28 Fit the four nuts and washers in the rocker shaft pedestal studs and tighten in a progressive manner to the torque wrench setting given in the Specifications. Adjust the valve clearances (see Section 11).

29 Fit the exhaust manifold, thermostat housing and alternator, also the rocker cover (photo).

30 Fit the carburettor, air cleaner and distributor.

31 Reconnect all hoses and electrical leads, including the battery.

32 Refill the cooling system.

5.25 Fitting pushrods

5.23A Cylinder head bolt in inlet manifold

5.29 Fitting rocker cover

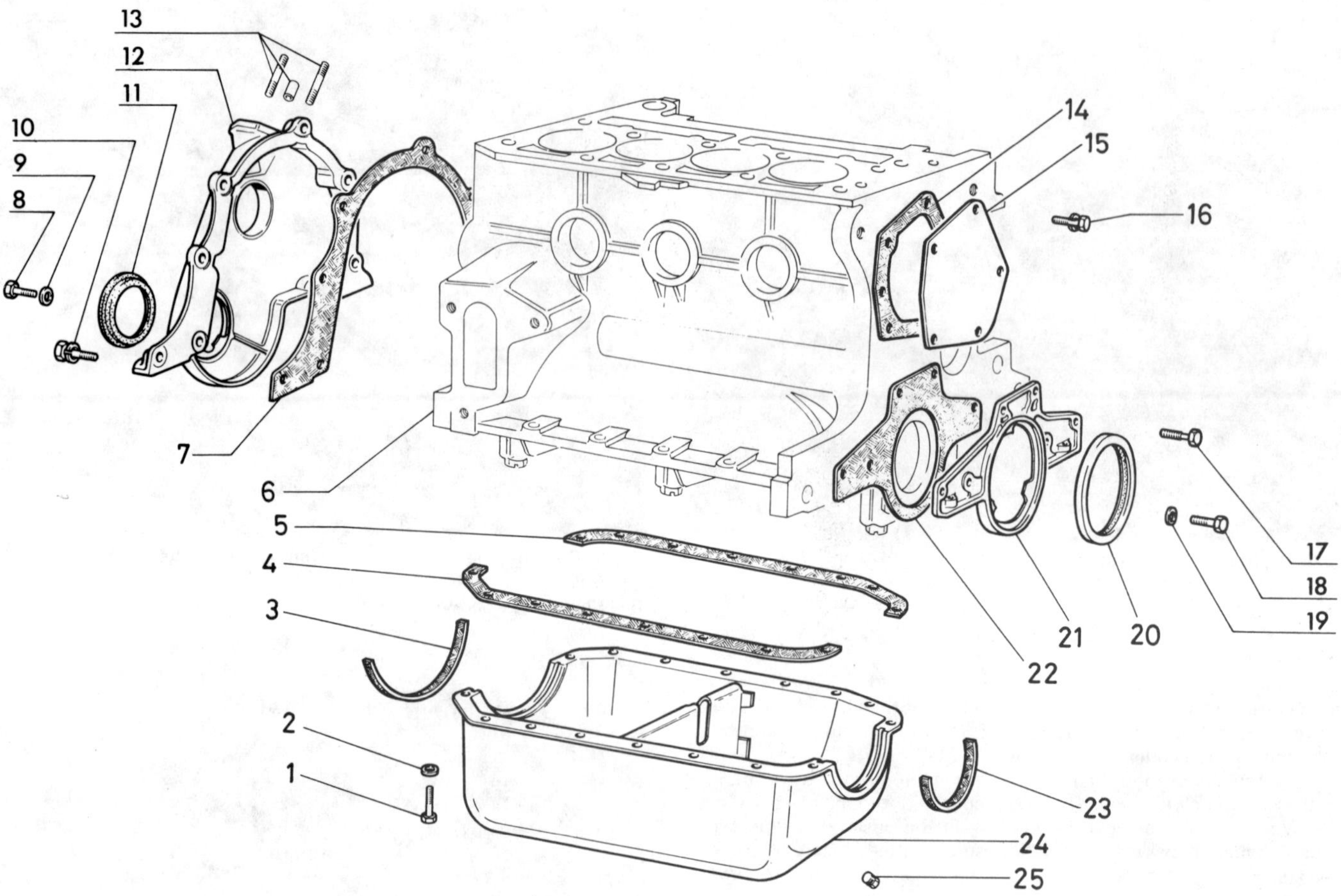

Fig. 1.5 Timing cover, sump pan and oil seals (Sec 6)

1 Sump bolt	8 Bolt	14 Gasket	20 Oil seal
2 Washer	9 Washer	15 Cover	21 Seal carrier
3 Gasket	10 Bolt and washer	16 Bolt and washer	22 Carrier gasket
4 Gasket	11 Oil seal	17 Bolt	23 Gasket
5 Gasket	12 Timing cover	18 Bolt	24 Sump
6 Cylinder block	13 Dowels and bush for	19 Washer	25 Drain plug
7 Timing cover gasket	fuel pump		

6 Sump pan – removal and refitting

Removal

1   Drain the engine oil.
2   To remove the engine oil sump pan, undo and remove the four nuts and twelve securing bolts and lift away the sump. If it has stuck on the gasket, carefully tap the side of the mating flange to break the seal. Recover the joint washer and remove any signs of old jointing compound. Note the cork inserts in the recesses at either end of the sump.

Refitting

3   Fit the cork inserts at each end of the sump pan. If necessary, trim the ends of the cork until they are just proud of the pan flange. Using some thick grease, stick the gasket side strips to the crankcase. Make sure that all old gasket and dirt has been cleaned from the mating surfaces (photo).
4   Apply a blob of gasket cement at the ends of the side gaskets at the points of overlap of the end inserts.
5   Offer up the sump pan, screw in and tighten the bolts and nuts progressively (photos).
6   Refill with oil.

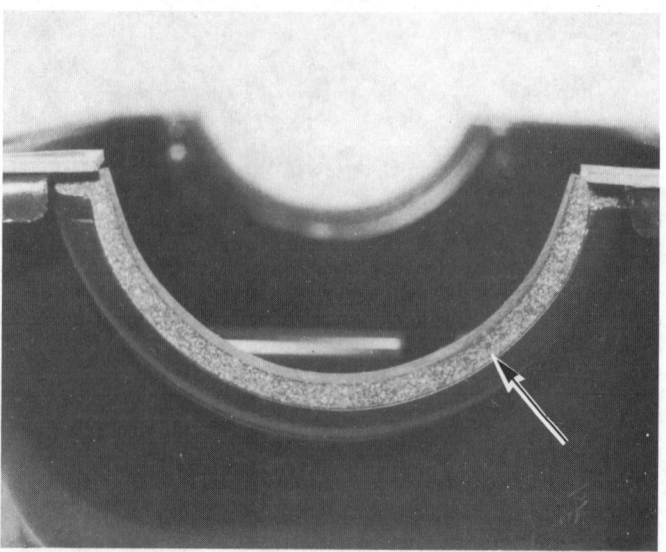

6.3 Sump pan sealing strip

6.5A Fitting sump pan

6.5B Sump pan bolts, washer and nut (timing cover stud)

6   To remove the shell bearings, press the bearing opposite the groove in both the connecting rod and the connecting rod caps and the bearings will slide out easily.
7   Keep the shells with their original cap or rod if the bearings are not being renewed.
8   Withdraw the pistons and connecting rods upwards and ensure they are kept in the correct order for replacement in the same bore.
9   Dismantling the pistons is described in Section 20.
10 Lay the piston and connecting rod assemblies in the correct order ready for refitting into their respective bores (photo).

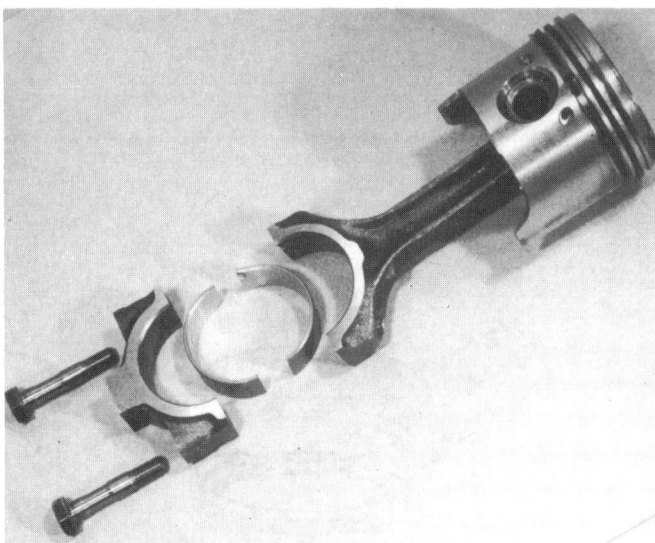

7.10 Piston/connecting rod components

11 With a wad of clean non-fluffy rag wipe the cylinder bores clean.
12 Position the piston rings so that their gaps are 120° apart and then lubricate the rings.
13 Wipe clean the connecting rod half of the big-end bearing and the underside of the shell bearing. Fit the shell bearing in position with its locating tongue engaged with the corresponding groove in the connecting rod.
14 Fit a piston ring compressor to the top of the piston, making sure it is tight enough to compress the piston rings.
15 Using a piece of fine wire double check that the little jet hole in the connecting rod is clean.
16 The pistons, complete with connecting rods, are fitted to their bores from above. The number stamped on the connecting rod must face away from the camshaft; the arrow on the piston crown towards the timing cover.
17 As each piston is inserted into its bore ensure that it is the correct piston/connecting rod assembly for the particular bore and that the connecting rod is the right way round. Lubricate the piston well with clean engine oil.
18 With the base of the piston ring compressor resting on the cylinder block, apply the wooden handle of a hammer to the piston crown, strike the hammer head with the hand and drive the piston/rod into its bore (photo).
19 Draw the rod, complete with shell bearing down onto its crankpin.
20 Generously lubricate the crankpin journals with engine oil, and turn the crankshaft so that the crankpin is in the most advantageous position for the connecting rod to be drawn into it.
21 Wipe clean the connecting rod bearing cap and back of the shell bearing and fit the shell bearing in position ensuring that the locating tongue at the back of the bearing engages with the locating groove in the connecting rod cap.
22 Generously lubricate the shell bearing and offer up the connecting rod bearing cap to the connecting rod (photo).
23 Fit the connecting rod bolts and tighten in a progressive manner to the specified torque (photo).

7   Piston/connecting rods – removal and refitting

1   Remove the cylinder head as described in Section 5.
2   Remove the sump pan as described in Section 6.
3   Undo and remove the big-end cap retaining bolts and keep them in their respective order for correct refitting.
4   Check that the connecting rod and big-end bearing cap assemblies are correctly marked. Normally the numbers 1–4 are stamped on adjacent sides of the big-end caps and connecting rods, indicating which cap fits on which rod and which way round the cap fits (number away from camshaft). If no number is found then, with a sharp file, make mating marks across the joint from the rod to the cap. One line for connecting rod No. 1, two for connecting rod No. 2 and so on. This will ensure that there is no confusion later as it is most important that the caps go back in the correct position on the connecting rods from which they were removed. Number 1 piston should be at the timing cover end of the engine.
5   If the big-end caps are difficult to remove they may be gently tapped with a soft-faced hammer.

7.18 Fitting a piston/rod into block

7.22 Fitting a big-end cap

7.23 Tightening a big-end cap bolt

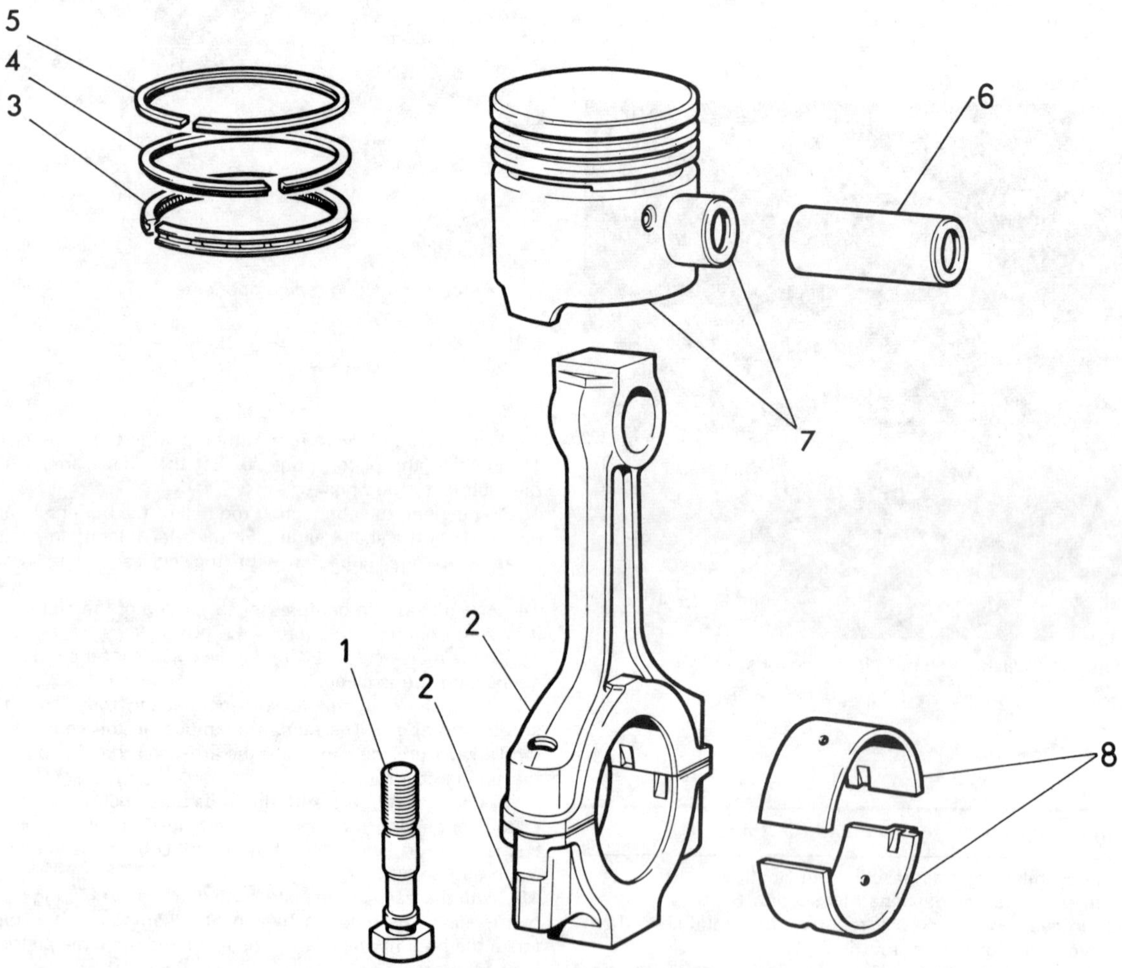

Fig. 1.6 Piston and connecting rod (Sec 7)

1 Bolt
2 Connecting rod
3 Oil control ring
4 Compression ring stepped at base
5 Compression ring marked TOP
6 Gudgeon pin
7 Piston and gudgeon pin assembly
8 Connecting rod bearing halves

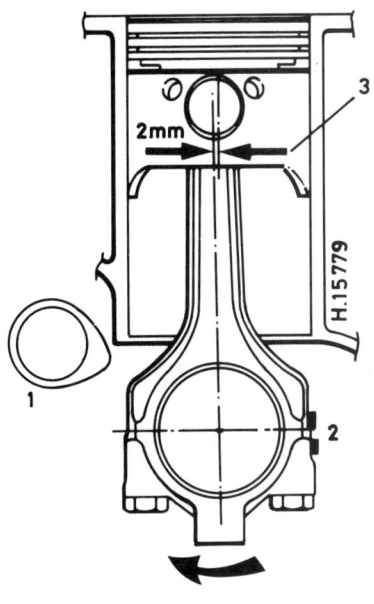

CLOCKWISE ROTATION

Fig. 1.7 Alignment of piston/connecting rod (Sec 7)

1 Camshaft
2 Rod/cap location numbers
3 Gudgeon pin offset

8 Timing chain and sprockets – removal and refitting

Removal

1 Remove the alternator drivebelt as described in Chapter 2.
2 Unscrew and remove the crankshaft pulley nut. To prevent the crankshaft rotating, either select a gear and have an assistant apply the foot brake hard or remove the starter motor and lock the ring gear teeth with a large cold chisel or screwdriver.
3 Disconnect the hoses from the fuel pump.
4 Unbolt and remove the fuel pump with spacer and rod.
5 Support the engine on a hoist or under the sump and disconnect and remove the right-hand mounting. Then unscrew and remove the timing cover bolts. The base of the cover is secured by the front two sump pan studs. Unbolt and lower the front end of the sump. Avoid breaking the gasket. Remove the timing cover.
6 Undo and remove the camshaft sprocket securing bolt; this will also release the fuel pump drive cam from the end of the camshaft. Note the two timing marks on the camshaft and crankshaft sprockets.
7 Using two tyre levers, carefully ease the two sprockets forwards away from the crankcase. Lift away the two sprockets and timing chain.
8 Remove the Woodruff key from the crankshaft nose with a pair of pliers and note how the channel in the pulley is designed to fit over it. Place the Woodruff key in a container, as it is a very small part and can easily become lost.
9 The camshaft sprocket is located on the camshaft by a dowel peg.

Refitting

10 Fit the Woodruff key to the front of the crankshaft.
11 Tap the crankshaft sprocket onto the front of the crankshaft.
12 Turn the sprocket so that the Woodruff key is uppermost.
13 Turn the camshaft until it is in such a position that if the sprocket

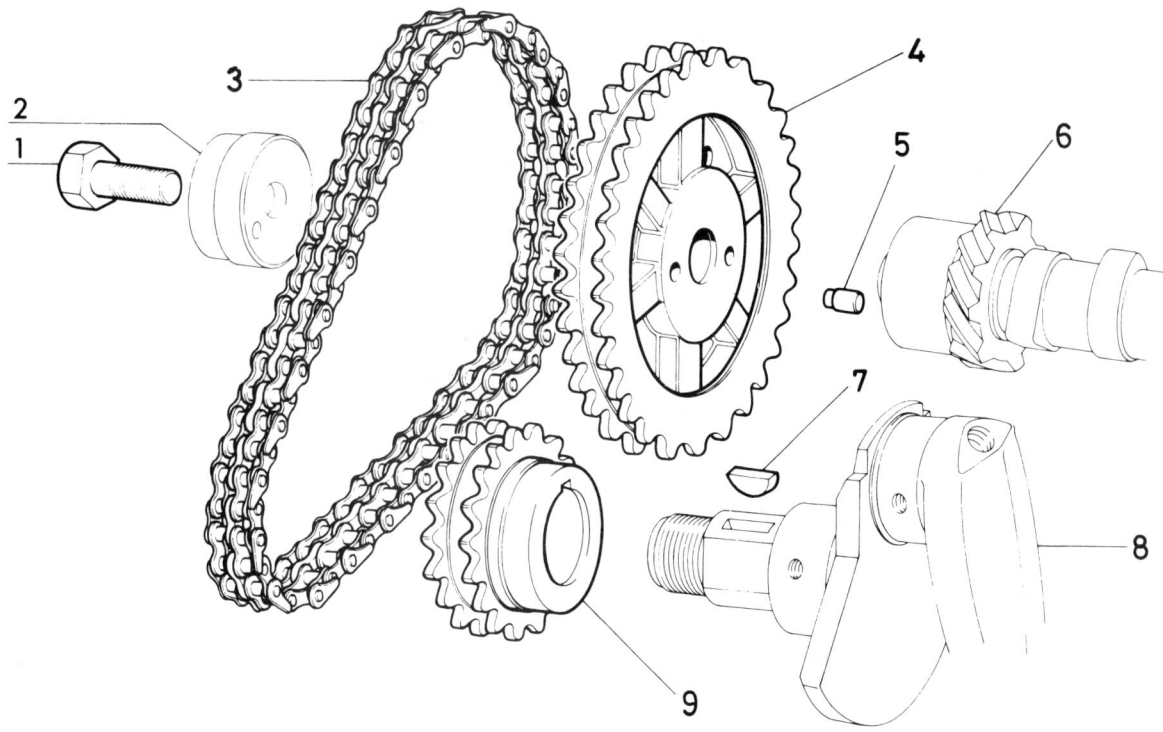

Fig. 1.8 Timing chain and sprockets (Sec 8)

1 Camshaft sprocket retaining bolt	3 Timing chain	5 Camshaft sprocket locating dowel	7 Woodruff key
2 Fuel pump drive cam	4 Camshaft sprocket	6 Camshaft	8 Crankshaft
			9 Crankshaft sprocket

8.13 Timing sprocket marks

were fitted, the dimple timing mark on the sprocket would be furthest from, and in alignment with, the one on the crankshaft sprocket. In this position No 1 piston is at TDC.

14 Engage the timing chain with the teeth of the crankshaft sprocket and then locate the camshaft sprocket within the upper loop of the chain in such a way that when the sprocket is pushed onto the camshaft, the timing marks will be in alignment as previously described. Make sure that the self-tensioning links are on the inside of the chain against the cylinder block.

15 Place the camshaft sprocket onto the camshaft.

16 Secure the camshaft sprocket by fitting the special cam, that drives the fuel pump, on its locating dowel. Fit the camshaft sprocket retaining bolt.

17 Tighten the camshaft sprocket securing bolt to specified torque. At this stage it is worthwhile double-checking the valve timing by rotating the crankshaft one revolution, thus bringing No 4 cylinder to TDC with the mark on the flywheel aligned with the 0° mark in the flywheel housing aperture – see Chapter 4. At this point the marks on the crankshaft and camshaft sprockets should be in alignment with each other, but this time immediately *adjacent* to each other.

18 If the timing cover oil seal showed signs of leaking before engine overhaul the old seal should be removed and a new one fitted.

19 Using a screwdriver, carefully remove the old oil seal, working from the rear of the cover.

20 Fit the new seal making sure it is inserted squarely, and tap home with a hammer.

21 Lubricate the oil seal with engine oil.

22 With all traces of old gasket and jointing compound removed from the timing cover and cylinder block mating faces, smear a little grease onto the timing cover mating face and fit a new gasket in position.

23 Fit the timing cover to the cylinder block and finger tighten the securing bolts, and spring washer. Ensure that the fuel pump pushrod bush is in place in the cover.

24 Wipe the hub of the pulley and carefully place into position on the crankshaft. It should locate on the Woodruff key. It may be necessary to adjust the position of the timing cover slightly in order to centralise the oil seal relative to the pulley hub.

25 Tighten the timing cover securing bolts in a diagonal and progressive manner.

26 Tighten the crankshaft pulley nut to the specified torque again holding the crankshaft against rotation as previously described.

27 Refit the fuel pump and alternator drivebelt.

9 Engine mountings – removal and refitting

1   The engine/transmission flexible mountings can be removed if the power unit is supported under the sump pan or gearbox with a jack or

a hoist is attached to the engine lifting lugs and the weight of the power unit just taken.

2   Unscrew the mounting bracket bolts and remove the mounting (photos).

3   Refit the new mounting and remove the lifting gear.

4   In the unlikely event of all the mountings requiring renewal at the same time, renew them one at a time, never disconnect all the mountings together.

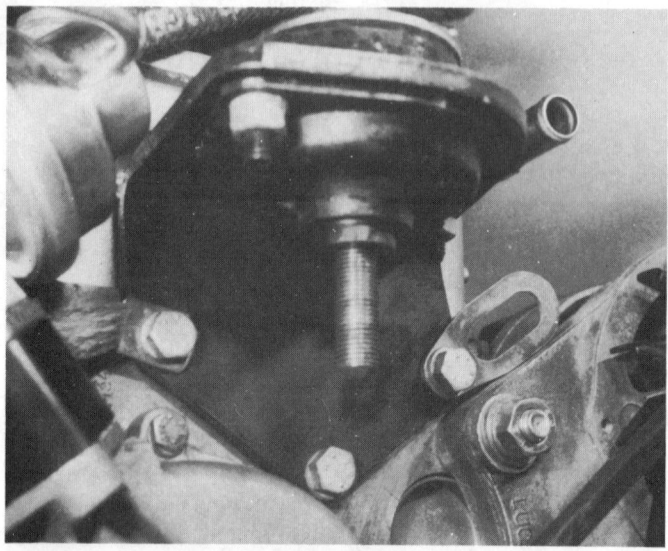

9.2A Right-hand engine mounting

9.2B Left-hand transmission mounting

10 Oil pump – removal and refitting

Removal

1   Remove the sump pan as described in Section 6.

2   Unscrew the two bolts which hold the oil return pipe to the front and centre main bearing caps.

3   Undo and remove the two bolts and spring washers securing the oil pump housing to the underside of the crankcase.

4   Carefully ease the oil pump assembly from the crankcase.

5   Recover the gasket between the oil pump housing and underside of the crankcase.

Refitting

6   Use some grease to stick a new gasket to the oil pump location on the underside of the crankcase (photo).

10.6 Oil pump gasket

10.7 Fitting oil pump

10.8 Tightening oil pump mounting bolt

7 Locate the oil pump driveshaft in the oil pump and then offer up the complete assembly to the crankcase so that the gear teeth on the driveshaft mesh with those on the camshaft (photo).

8 Fit the securing bolts (photo).

9 Fit the oil return pipe.

10 Fit the sump pan.

11 Valve clearances – adjustment

1 Remove the spare wheel and the air cleaner. The engine should be cold.

2 Unbolt and remove the rocker cover.

3 It is important that the clearance is set when the tappet of the valve being adjusted is on the heel of the cam (ie; opposite the peak). This can be done by carrying out the adjustments in the following order, which also avoids turning the crankshaft more than necessary:

Valve fully open	Check and adjust
Valve No. 8 EX	*Valve No. 1 EX*
Valve No. 6 IN	*Valve No. 3 IN*
Valve No. 4 EX	*Valve No. 5 EX*
Valve No. 7 IN	*Valve No. 2 IN*
Valve No. 1 EX	*Valve No. 8 EX*
Valve No. 3 IN	*Valve No. 6 IN*
Valve No. 5 EX	*Valve No. 4 EX*
Valve No. 2 IN	*Valve No. 7 IN*

4 Count the valves from the timing cover end of the engine.

5 Remember, the inlet and exhaust valve clearances are different.

6 Insert the appropriate feeler gauge between the end of the valve stem and the rocker arm. It should be a stiff sliding fit (photo).

11.6 Adjusting a valve clearance

7 If the clearance is incorrect, release the rocker arm adjuster screw locknut using a ring spanner. Turn the adjuster screw using a small open-ended spanner, but tie something to it in case it is inadvertently dropped through one of the pushrod holes.

8 Once the clearance is correct, tighten the locknut without moving the position of the adjuster screw.

9 Repeat the operations on the remaining seven valves.

10 Re-check all the clearances, make sure that the rocker cover gasket is in good condition and fit the rocker cover.

11 Fit the air cleaner and spare wheel.

12 Engine – method of removal

1 Removal of the engine complete with transmission may be carried out in one of two ways.

Downwards

2   The engine/transmission is lowered complete with driveshafts. The front of the car is then raised and the engine/transmission then pulled out from underneath.

Upwards

3   With this method, the driveshafts are disconnected from the final drive and the engine/transmission hoisted upwards out of the engine compartment.

4   The method chosen will depend upon the equipment and assistance available.

13 Engine/transmission – removal downwards

1   Remove the bonnet (Chapter 12).
2   Disconnect the battery.
3   Remove the spare wheel and expansion tank (photo).
4   Drain the cooling system (Chapter 2).
5   Drain the engine oil.
6   Remove the air cleaner (see Chapter 3).
7   Disconnect the accelerator and choke controls from the carburettor; tie them back out of the way.
8   Disconnect the fuel hoses from the fuel pump and plug their open ends. Disconnect the fuel return hose from the carburettor.
9   Disconnect the radiator hoses.
10 Disconnect the heater hoses from the engine.
11 Disconnect the electrical leads from the alternator and the starter motor, and radiator fan motor.
12 Pull the leads from the oil pressure and coolant temperature sender units (photo).
13 Disconnect the coil-to-distributor HT and LT leads, then remove the distributor cap, complete with spark plug leads.
14 Unbolt the exhaust downpipes from the exhaust manifold. It is now preferable to remove the one-piece exhaust system from the car. To do this, disconnect the flexible mountings.
15 Disconnect the clutch operating cable from the clutch release lever.
16 A suitable hoist should be attached to the engine lifting lugs and the weight of the engine/transmission taken on the hoist. Disconnect the engine lower mounting.
17 Working underneath the car, disconnect the speedometer drive cable from the final drive housing.
18 Disconnect the gearchange control rod from the flexible joint at the selector shaft on the gearbox. Swivel the control rod to one side of the car and tie it up, out of the way.
19 Disconnect the electrical leads from the reversing lamp switch on the transmission.

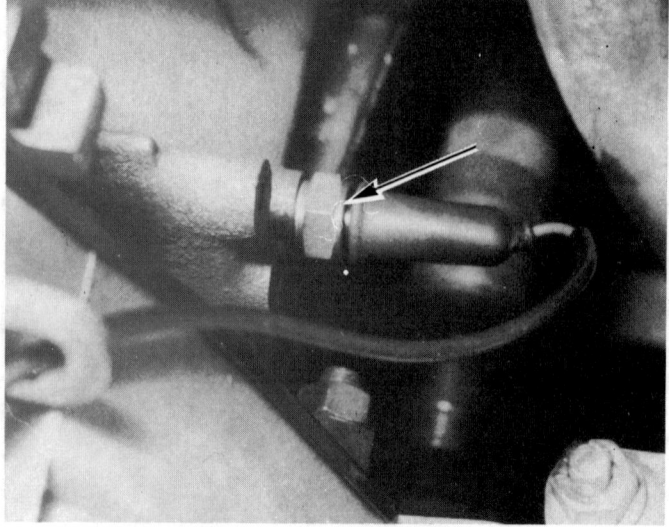

13.12 Oil pressure switch

20 Support the body underframe securely on jacks and axle stands, remove the front wheels and slacken the driveshaft-to-hub nuts. These nuts are very tight and will require a spanner of good length to release them. Have an assistant apply the footbrake to hold the hub stationary.
21 The front end of the car should now be raised and supported so that there is sufficient clearance for the engine to pass under it. This will mean that the engine hoist must also be raised in conjunction with the body jacks.
22 Once the car is raised, make sure that it is really securely supported again on axle stands.
23 Unscrew and remove the previously slackened driveshaft-to-hub nuts.
24 Disconnect both front suspension track control arms from their inboard body brackets. Pull the arms downward.
25 Using a suitable balljoint separator, disconnect the steering tie-rod balljoints from the steering arms.
26 Disconnect the radius rods from the track control arms. Unbolt the brake calipers and tie them up, out of the way.
27 Unbolt the remaining engine mountings from the engine/transmission.
28 From the lower ends of the suspension struts, remove the two

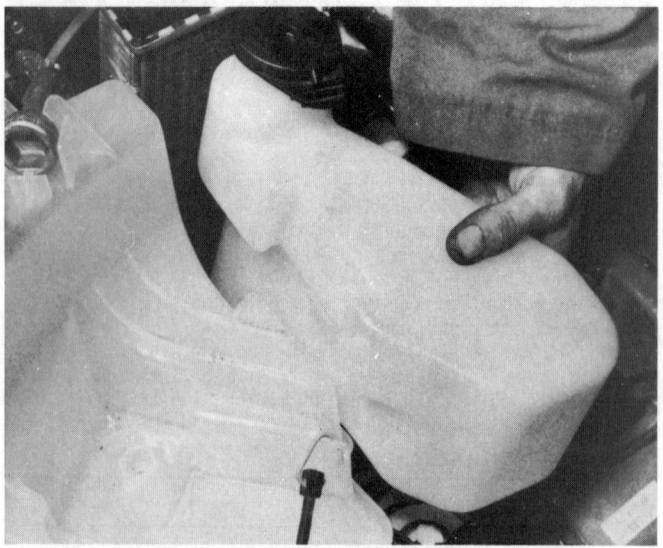

13.3 Removing coolant expansion tank

13.28 Front strut base clamp bolts

pinch bolts and tap the hub carriers downward. The driveshafts can now be pressed or knocked out of the hubs (photo).

29 Make a final check in case any wires or hoses have been overlooked and still require disconnecting, then lower the engine/transmission from the engine compartment.

14 Engine/transmission – removal upwards

1 Carry out the operations described in paragraphs 1 to 19 of the preceding Section.
2 Remove the front roadwheels.
3 Working under the car, unbolt the bottom mounting arm from the transmission and the exhaust pipe. Bend back the locktabs and unbolt the flexible mounting.
4 Raise the front end of the car and remove the front roadwheels.
5 Unbolt the brake calipers and tie them up out of the way, release the hose.
6 Using a balljoint splitter tool, disconnect the tie-rod ends from the steering arms also the track control arm lower balljoints from the hub carriers.
7 Unscrew the bolts which hold the gaiter retainers to the transmission at the inboard ends of the driveshafts. Be prepared for some loss of oil.
8 Disconnect the radius rods from the track control arms.
9 Pull the hub carriers outwards. The strut top flexible mountings will allow the strut to tilt outwards at their bases.
10 Have an assistant support the shafts to prevent them from falling to the floor. Tie them up (photo).

14.10 Driveshafts supported with wire

11 Remove the radiator as described in Chapter 2.
12 Attach a hoist to the engine and take the weight of the engine/transmission.
13 Disconnect the engine and transmission upper mountings.
14 Lift the engine/transmission up and out of the engine compartment.

15 Engine/transmission – separation

1 With the engine/transmission removed from the car, it is best to clean away external dirt and grease before commencing any dismantling.
2 Do this with a water soluble solvent or paraffin, and a stiff brush.
3 To separate the units, first unbolt and remove the starter motor.
4 Unscrew and remove the bolts and take off the cover plate from the lower face of the flywheel housing.

5 Unbolt and remove the engine and transmission mounting brackets.
6 Unscrew the engine to flywheel housing connecting bolts, support the weight of the transmission and withdraw it in a straight line from the engine.
7 Note the positioning dowels. If they are displaced, tap them into their holes now.
8 If the engine was removed downwards, disconnect the driveshafts from the transmission (Chapter 7).

16 Engine – dismantling (general)

1 Stand the engine on a strong bench so as to be at a comfortable working height. Failing this it can be stripped down on the floor, but at least stand it on a sheet of hardboard.
2 During the dismantling process, the greatest care should be taken to keep the exposed parts free from dirt. As the engine is stripped, clean each part in a bath of paraffin.
3 Never immerse parts with oilways in paraffin, e.g. the crankshaft, but to clean, wipe down carefully with a paraffin dampened rag. Oilways can be cleaned out with a piece of wire. If an air line is available, all parts can be blown dry and the oilways blown through as an added precaution.
4 Re-use of old gaskets is false economy and can give rise to oil and water leaks, if nothing worse. To avoid the possibility of trouble after the engine has been reassembled always use new gaskets throughout.
5 Do not throw the old gaskets away as it sometimes happens that an immediate replacement cannot be found and the old gasket is then very useful as a template. Hang up the gaskets on a suitable nail or hook as they are removed.
6 To strip the engine, it is best to work from the top downwards. The engine oil sump proves a firm base on which the engine can be supported in an upright position. When the stage is reached where the pistons are to be removed, turn the engine on its side. Turn the block upside down to remove the crankshaft.
7 Wherever possible, replace nuts, bolts and washers finger-tight from wherever they were removed. This helps avoid later loss and muddle. If they cannot be replaced then lay them out in such a fashion that it is clear from where they came.

17 Engine – removing ancillary components

1 Before basic engine dismantling begins it is necessary to strip it of ancillary components as follows:

Distributor (Chapter 4)
Carburettor and spacer (Chapter 3)
Exhaust manifold and hot air collector (Chapter 3)
Fuel pump (Chapter 3)
Alternator (Chapter 9)
Coolant pump (Chapter 2)
Clutch (Chapter 5)

2 The engine is now stripped of all ancillary components and is ready for major dismantling to begin.

18 Engine – complete dismantling

1 Unbolt and remove the rocker cover.
2 Unscrew the rocker pedestal securing nuts and lift away the rocker assembly.
3 Remove the pushrods, keeping them in their original fitted order.
4 Remove the cylinder head as described in Section 5. Remove the dipstick and guide tube.
5 Turn the engine on its side and unbolt and remove the sump.
6 Remove the piston/connecting rods as described in Section 7.
7 Unscrew and remove the crankshaft pulley nut. To prevent the crankshaft rotating while this is done, either jam the flywheel ring gear or place a block between a crankshaft counterweight and the inside of the crankcase.
8 Unbolt and remove the timing cover.
9 Remove the timing chain and sprockets as described in Section 8.
10 Unbolt and remove the oil pump as described in Section 10.

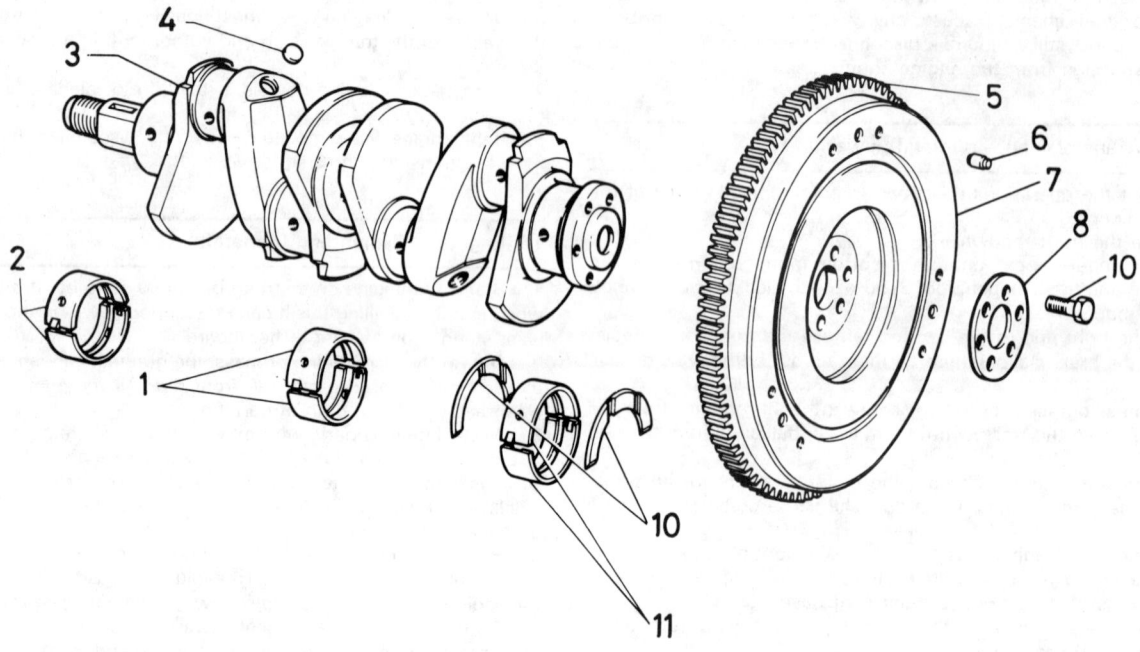

Fig. 1.9 Crankshaft and flywheel (Sec 18)

1	Centre main bearing halves	3	Crankshaft	6	Dowel
2	Main bearing halves -	4	Plug	7	Flywheel
	timing case end	5	Starter ring gear	8	Thrust plate

9	Bolt
10	Thrust washers
11	Main bearing halves -
	flywheel end

11 Undo and remove the camshaft front bearing lock screw. Note that the bearing chamfer faces inwards. The camshaft may now be withdrawn. Take great care to remove the camshaft gently and, in particular, ensure that the cam peaks do not damage the camshaft bearings as the shaft is pulled forwards.

12 Lift out the cam followers and place in order so that they may be refitted in their original positions.

13 Unbolt and remove the flywheel. Jam the ring gear teeth to prevent rotation.

14 Remove the engine rear plate.

15 Turn the cylinder block so that it is standing upside down.

16 Unbolt and remove the crankshaft rear oil seal carrier. Note the sump fixing studs.

17 The main bearing caps should be marked 1, 2 and 3, but if they are not, centre punch them and note which way round they are located.

18 Unscrew the main bearing cap bolts progressively.

19 Remove the bearing caps and half shells. If the shell bearings are to be used again, keep them with their respective caps.

20 Note the semi-circular thrust washers, on either side of the centre main bearing, which control crankshaft endfloat.

21 Lift the crankshaft from the crankcase.

22 Remove the bearing shells from the crankcase and mark them as to position if they are to be used again.

19 Cylinder head – dismantling and decarbonising

1 The exhaust manifold and rocker gear will have been removed from the cylinder head.

2 The valves should now be removed using a universal valve spring compressor.

3 Compress the first valve spring, extract the split cotters. If the valve spring refuses to compress, do not apply excessive force, but remove the compressor and place a piece of tubing on the spring retainer and strike it a sharp blow to release the collets from the valve stem. Refit the compressor and resume operations. The collets should then come out.

4 Gently release the compressor, take off the spring retaining cap, the valve spring and the spring seat. Remove the valve. Keep the valve with its associated components together and in numbered sequence so that they can be returned to their original positions.

5 A small box with divisions is useful for this purpose. Remove and discard the valve stem oil seals.

6 Remove the other valves in a similar way.

7 Bearing in mind that the cylinder head is of light alloy construction and is easily damaged use a blunt scraper or rotary wire brush to clean all traces of carbon deposits from the combustion spaces and the ports. The valve head stems and valve guides should also be freed from any carbon deposits. Wash the combustion spaces and ports down with paraffin and scrape the cylinder head surface free of any foreign matter with the side of a steel rule, or a similar article.

8 If the engine is installed in the car, clean the pistons and the top of the cylinder bores. If the pistons are still in the block, then it is essential that great care is taken to ensure that no carbon gets into the cylinder bores as this could scratch the cylinder walls or cause damage to the piston and rings. To ensure this does not happen, first turn the crankshaft so that two of the pistons are at the top of their bores. Stuff rag into the other two bores or seal them off with paper and masking tape. The waterways should also be covered with small pieces of masking tape to prevent particles of carbon entering the cooling system and damaging the coolant pump.

9 Press a little grease into the gap between the cylinder walls and the two pistons which are to be worked on. With a blunt scraper carefully scrape away the carbon from the piston crown, taking great care not to scratch the aluminium. Also scrape away the carbon from the surrounding lip of the cylinder wall. When all carbon has been removed, scrape away the grease which will now be contaminated with carbon particles, taking care not to press any into the bores. To assist prevention of carbon build-up the piston crown can be polished with a metal polish. Remove the rags or masking tape from the other two cylinders and turn the crankshaft so that the two pistons which were at the bottom are now at the top. Place rag in the cylinders which have been decarbonised, and proceed as just described.

10 Examine the head of the valves for pitting and burning, especially the heads of the exhaust valves. The valve seatings should be examined at the same time. If the pitting on the valve and seat is very

slight, the marks can be removed by grinding the seats and valves together with coarse, and then fine, valve grinding paste.

11 Where bad pitting has occurred to the valve seats it will be necessary to recut them and fit new valves. This latter job should be entrusted to the local agent or engineering works. In practice it is very seldom that the seats are so badly worn. Normally it is the valve that is too badly worn for refitting, and the owner can easily purchase a new set of valves and match them to the seats by valve grinding.

12 Valve grinding is carried out as follows. Smear a trace of coarse carborundum paste on the seat face and apply a suction grinder tool to the valve head. With a semi-rotary motion, grind the valve head to its seat, lifting the valve occasionally to redistribute the grinding paste. When a dull matt even surface is produced on both the valve seat and the valve, wipe off the paste and repeat the process with fine carborundum paste, lifting and turning the valve to redistribute the paste as before. A light spring placed under the valve head will greatly ease this operation. When a smooth unbroken ring of light grey matt finish is produced, on both valve and valve seat faces, the grinding operation is complete. Carefully clean away every trace of grinding compound, take great care to leave none in the ports or in the valve guides. Clean the valves and valve seats with paraffin soaked rag, then with a clean rag, and finally, if an air line is available, blow the valve, valve guides and valve ports clean.

13 Check that all valve springs are intact. If any one is broken, all should be renewed. Check the free height of the springs against new ones. If some springs are not within specifications, replace them all. Springs suffer from fatigue and it is a good idea to renew them even if they look serviceable.

14 Check that the oil supply holes in the rocker arms are clear.

15 The cylinder head can be checked for warping either by placing it on a piece of plate glass or using a straight-edge and feeler blades. If there is any doubt or if its block face is corroded, have it re-faced by your dealer or motor engineering works.

16 Test the valves in their guides for side to side rock. If this is any more than almost imperceptible new guides must be fitted, again a job for your dealer.

17 Commence reassembly by oiling the stem of the first valve and pushing it into its guide which should have been fitted with a new oil seal (photos).

18 Fit the spring seat, the valve spring so that the closer coils are towards the cylinder head and then the spring retaining cap (photos).

19 Compress the valve spring and using a little grease locate the split cotters in the valve stem cut-out (photo).

20 Gently release the compressor, checking to see that the collets are not displaced.

21 Fit the remaining valves in the same way.

22 Tap the end of each valve stem with a plastic or copper-faced hammer to settle the components.

23 The cylinder head is now ready for refitting as described in Section 5.

19.17B Inserting a valve into its guide

19.18A Valve spring lower seat

19.17A Valve stem oil seal

19.18B Valve spring

19.18C Valve spring cap

19.19 Valve spring compressed and split collets located

20 Examination and renovation

1   With the engine stripped down and all parts thoroughly clean, it is now time to examine everything for wear. The following items should be checked and where necessary renewed or renovated as described in the following Sections.

Cylinder block and crankcase

2   Examine the casting carefully for cracks especially around the bolt holes and between cylinders.

3   The cylinder bores must be checked for taper, ovality, scoring and scratching. Start by examining the top of the cylinder bores. If they are at all worn, a ridge will be felt on the thrust side. This ridge marks the limit of piston ring travel. The owner will have a good indication of bore wear prior to dismantling by the quantity of oil consumed and the emission of blue smoke from the exhaust especially when the engine is cold.

4   An internal micrometer or dial gauge can be used to check bore wear and taper against Specifications, but this is a pointless operation if the engine is obviously in need of reboring as indicated by excessive oil consumption.

5   Your engine reconditioner will be able to re-bore the block for you and supply the correct oversize pistons to give the correct running clearance.

6   If the engine has reached the limit for reboring then cylinder liners can be fitted, but here again this is a job for your engine reconditioner.

7   To rectify minor bore wear it is possible to fit proprietary oil control rings. A good way to test the condition of the engine is to have it at normal operating temperature with the spark plugs removed. Screw a compressor tester (available from most motor accessory stores) into the first plug hole. Hold the accelerator fully depressed and crank the engine on the starter motor for several revolutions. Record the reading. Zero the tester and check the remaining cylinders in the same way. All four compression figures should be approximately equal and within the tolerance given in the Specifications. If they are all low, suspect piston ring or cylinder bore wear. If only one reading is down, suspect a valve not seating.

Crankshaft and bearings

8   Examine the crankpin and main journal surfaces for signs of scoring or scratches. Check the ovality of the crankpins at different positions with a micrometer. If more than 0.001 inch (0.025 mm) out of round, the crankpins will have to be reground. They will also have to be reground if there are any scores or scratches present. Also check the journals in the same fashion.

9   Wear in a crankshaft can be detected while the engine is running. Big-end bearing and crankpin wear is indicated by distinct metallic knocking, particularly noticeable when the engine is pulling from low engine speeds. Low oil pressure will also occur.

10 Main bearing and journal wear is indicated by engine rumble increasing in severity as the engine speed increases. Low oil pressure will again be an associated condition.

11 Crankshaft grinding should be carried out by specialist engine reconditioners who will supply the matching undersize bearing shells to give the required running clearance.

12 Inspect the connecting rod big-end and main bearing shells for signs of general wear, scoring, pitting and scratching. The bearings should be matt grey in colour.

13 If a copper colour is evident, then the bearings are badly worn and the surface material has worn away to expose the underlay. Renew the bearings as a complete set.

14 At time of major overhaul it is worthwhile renewing the bearing shells as a matter of routine, even if they appear to be in reasonably good condition.

15 Bearing shells can be identified by the marking on the back of the shell. Standard sized shells are usually marked STD or 0.00. Undersized shells are marked with the undersize such as 0.25 mm.

Connecting rods

16 Check the alignment of the connecting rods visually. If you suspect distortion, have them checked by your dealer or engine reconditioner on the special jig which he will have.

17 The gudgeon pin is an interference fit in the connecting rod small end and removal or refitting and changing a piston is a job best left to your dealer or engine reconditioner. This is owing to the need for a press and jig and careful heating of the connecting rod.

Pistons and piston rings

18 If the cylinders have been rebored, then the reconditioner will supply the oversize pistons, rings and the gudgeon pins. Give the job of fitting the new pistons to the connecting rods to him.

19 Use great care to remove and fit piston rings as they are easily broken if expanded too much. Always remove and fit rings from the crown end.

20 If three old feeler blades are slid behind the piston rings and located at equidistant points, the rings may be removed or fitted without them dropping into the wrong grooves and will reduce the chance of breakage (photo).

21 If the original pistons are being refitted, make sure that the ring grooves and their oil return holes are cleaned out and freed from carbon. A piece of piston ring is a useful tool for this purpose.

22 The three piston rings are as follows:

Top – Thinner compression, marked TOP (photo)
Second – Thicker compression, step at base
Bottom – Oil control

20.20 Removing piston rings

20.22 Piston ring marking

of the flywheel ring gear damaged or worn, but if they are, then the ring gear will have to be renewed.

29 To remove the ring gear, drill a hole between the roots of two teeth taking care not to damage the flywheel and then split the ring with a sharp cold chisel.

30 The new ring gear must be heated to between 180 and 220°C (356 and 428°F). If you do not have facilities for obtaining these temperatures, leave the job to your dealer or engine reconditioner.

31 Where such facilities are available, then the ring gear should be either pressed or lightly tapped gently onto its register and left to cool naturally, when the contraction of the metal on cooling will ensure that it is a secure and permanent fit. Great care must be taken not to overheat the ring gear, as if this happens its temper will be lost. A clutch input shaft pilot bearing is not fitted on this engine.

Camshaft

32 Examine the camshaft bearings for wear, scoring or pitting. If evident then the bearings will have to be renewed. The three bearings are of different sizes and they can be removed and new ones fitted using a bolt, nut and distance pieces. When drawing a new bearing into position, make sure that the oil hole is correctly aligned with the one in the crankcase. The centre and rear bearings require reaming after fitting, the bearing at the timing chain end is supplied ready reamed (photo).

33 The camshaft itself should show no marks or scoring on the journal or cam lobe surfaces. Where evident, renew the camshaft or have it reprofiled by a specialist reconditioner.

34 Check the teeth of the camshaft sprocket for wear. Renew the sprocket if necessary.

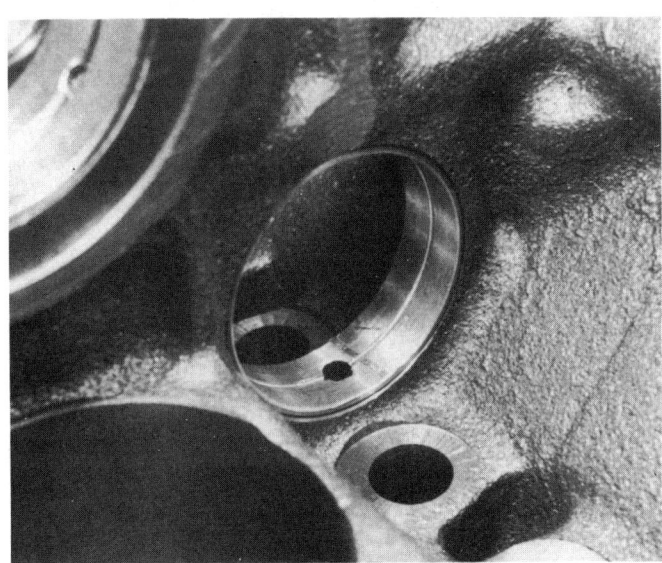

20.32 Camshaft bearing

23 If proprietary wear control rings are to be fitted to overcome bore wear, fit them strictly in accordance with the manufacturer's instructions.

24 Always check the piston ring groove clearance and end gap. Both clearances should be checked with a feeler gauge. Check the end gap when the ring has been pushed squarely down the cylinder bore for two or three inches.

25 If new rings are being used and the cylinder bores have not been rebored, always make sure that the top compression ring has been stepped to prevent it contacting the bore wear ridge.

Flywheel

26 Check the clutch mating surface of the flywheel. If it is deeply scored (due to failure to renew a worn driven plate) then it may be possible to have it surface ground provided the thickness of the flywheel is not reduced too much.

27 If lots of tiny cracks are visible on the surface of the flywheel then this will be due to overheating caused by slipping the clutch or 'riding' the clutch pedal.

28 With a pre-engaged type of starter motor it is rare to find the teeth

Cam followers

35 Examine the bearing surface of the cam followers which lie on the camshaft. Any indentation in this surface or any cracks indicate serious wear and they should be renewed. Thoroughly clean them out, removing all traces of sludge. It is most unlikely that the sides of the cam followers will be worn, but, if they are a very loose fit in their bores and can be readily rocked, they should be discarded and new ones fitted. It is unusual to find worn cam followers and any wear present is likely to occur only at very high mileages.

Timing chain

36 Examine the teeth on both the crankshaft sprocket and the camshaft sprocket for wear. Each tooth forms an inverted 'V' with the sprocket periphery and if worn, the side of each tooth under tension will be slightly concave in shape when compared with the other side of the tooth, ie; one side of the inverted 'V' will be concave when compared with the other. If any sign of wear is present the sprockets must be renewed.

37 Examine the links of the chain for side slackness and particularly
check the self-tensioning links for freedom of movement. Renew the
chain if any slackness is noticeable when compared with a new chain.
It is a sensible precaution to renew the chain at about 30 000 miles
(48 000 km) and at a lesser mileage if the engine is stripped down for
a major overhaul.

Cylinder head

38 This is covered in Section 19 during dismantling and
decarbonising.

Rockers and rocker shaft

39 Thoroughly clean out the rocker shaft. As it acts as the oil
passages for the valve gear, clean out the oil holes and make sure they
are quite clear. Check the shaft for straightness by rolling it on a flat
surface. If it is distorted, renew it (photo).
40 The surfaces of the shaft should be free from any worn ridges
caused by the rocker arms. If any wear is present, renew the rocker
shaft. Wear is likely to have occurred only if the rocker shaft oil holes
have become blocked.
41 Check the rocker arms for wear of the rocker bushes, for wear at
the rocker arm face which bears on the valve stem, and for wear of the
adjusting ball ended screws. Wear in the rocker arm bush can be
checked by gripping the rocker arm tip and holding the rocker arm in
place on the shaft, noting if there is any lateral rocker arm shake. If any

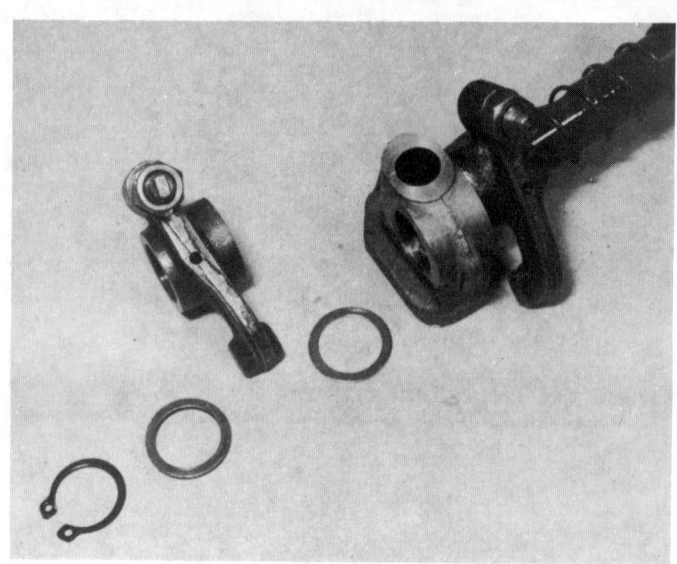

20.39 Rocker shaft components

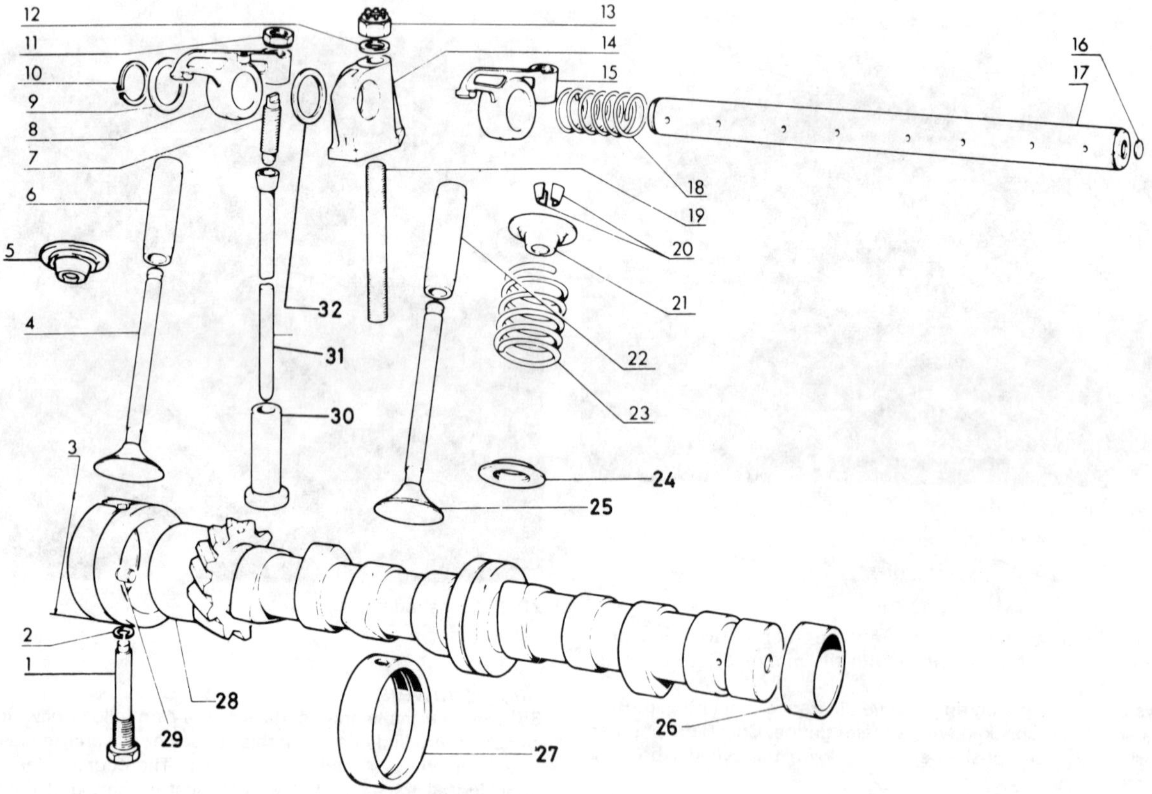

Fig. 1.10 Valve gear (Sec 20)

1 Bush locating bolt	9 Thrust washer	17 Rocker shaft	25 Inlet valve
2 Washer	10 Circlip	18 Spring	26 Bush
3 Bush	11 Locknut	19 Stud	27 Bush
4 Exhaust valve	12 Washer	20 Collets	28 Camshaft
5 Spring	13 Locknut	21 Spring retainer	29 Locating dowel
6 Valve guide	14 Pedestal	22 Valve guide	30 Tappet
7 Adjuster - tappet	15 Rocker	23 Valve spring	31 Pushrod
8 Rocker	16 Plug	24 Spring seat	32 Washer

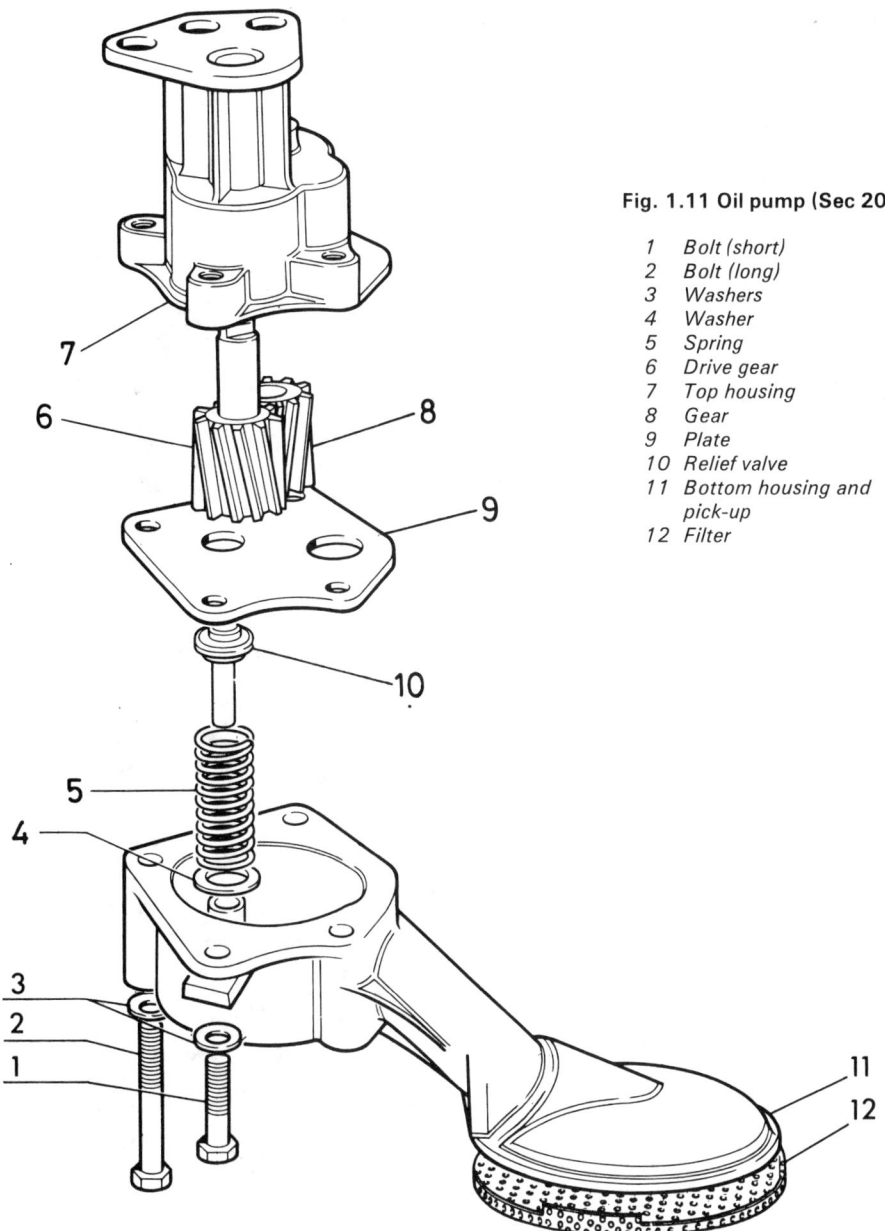

Fig. 1.11 Oil pump (Sec 20)

1   Bolt (short)
2   Bolt (long)
3   Washers
4   Washer
5   Spring
6   Drive gear
7   Top housing
8   Gear
9   Plate
10 Relief valve
11 Bottom housing and
    pick-up
12 Filter

shake is present, and the arm is very loose on the shaft, remedial action must be taken. It is recommended that any worn rocker arm be taken to your local Fiat agent or automobile engineering works to have the old bush drawn out and a new bush fitted.

42 Check the tip of the rocker arm where it bears on the valve head, for cracking or serious wear on the case hardening. If none is present the rocker arm may be refitted. Check the pushrods for straightness by rolling them on a flat surface.

Oil pump

43 Unscrew the four securing bolts which connect the two halves of the pump body.

44 Clean all the components in a bath of paraffin and dry them.

45 Inspect the gears for wear or damage and then check for wear in the following way.

46 Insert a feeler blade between the tooth peak and the body. This should be between 0.05 and 0.14 mm (0.0019 and 0.0055 in).

47 Now place a straight edge across the body flange and check for gear endfloat. This should be between 0.020 and 0.105 mm (0.0008 and 0.0041 in). Where the clearances exceed the specified limits, renew the pump.

48 Check that the oil pressure relief valve spring is in good condition and not deformed.

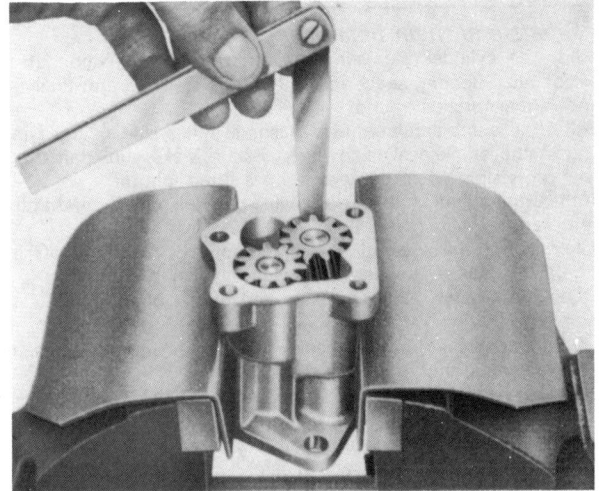

Fig. 1.12 Checking oil pump gear clearance (Sec 20)

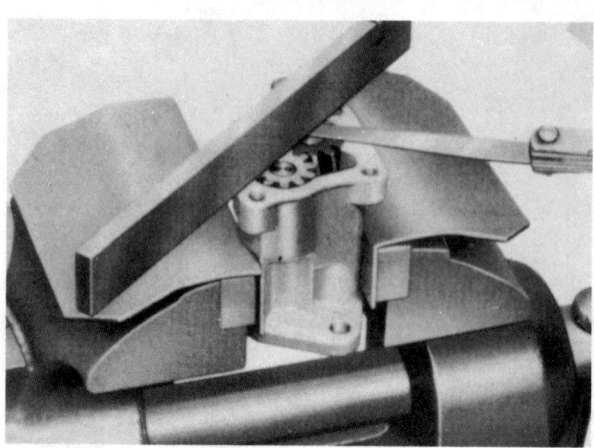

Fig. 1.13 Checking oil pump gear endfloat (Sec 20)

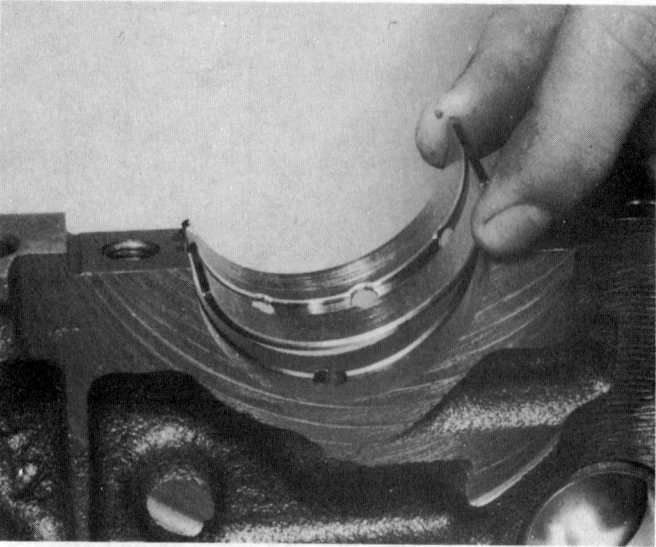

22.1 Crankshaft main bearing shell

22.2 Crankshaft thrust washer

22.4A Oiling crankshaft bearing shells

Oil seals and gaskets
49 It is recommended that all gaskets and oil seals are renewed at major engine overhaul. Sockets are useful for removing or refitting oil seals. An arrow is moulded onto some seals to indicate the rotational direction of the component which it serves. Make sure that the seal is fitted the correct way round to comply with the arrow.

21 Engine reassembly (general)

1 To ensure maximum life with minimum trouble from a rebuilt engine, not only must every part be correctly assembled, but everything must be spotlessly clean, all the oilways must be clear, locking washers and spring washers must always be fitted where indicated and all bearing and other working surfaces must be thoroughly lubricated during assembly. Before assembly begins renew any bolts or studs whose threads are in any way damaged; whenever possible use new spring washers.
2 Apart from your normal tools, a supply of non-fluffy rag, an oil can fitted with engine oil, a supply of new spring washers, a set of new gaskets and a torque wrench should be collected together.

22 Engine – complete reassembly

Crankshaft and main bearings
1 With the cylinder block inverted on the bench, wipe out the crankcase shell bearing seats and fit the half shells so that their tabs engage in the notches (photo).
2 Stick the semi-circular thrust washers either side of the centre bearing in the crankcase using thick grease. Make sure that the oil grooves are visible when the washers are fitted (photo).
3 If the original bearing shells are being refitted, make sure that they are returned to their original positions.
4 Liberally oil the bearing shells and lower the crankshaft into position. Make sure that it is the correct way round (photos).
5 Wipe out the main bearing caps and fit the bearing shells into them.
6 Oil the crankshaft journals and fit the main bearing caps, the correct way round and in proper sequence.
7 Replace the main bearing cap bolts and screw them up finger tight (photo).
8 Test the crankshaft for freedom of rotation. Should it be very stiff to turn, or possess high spots, a most careful inspection must be made, preferably by a skilled mechanic with a micrometer to trace the cause of the trouble. It is very seldom that any trouble of this nature will be experienced when fitting the crankshaft.

22.4B Fitting crankshaft

22.9 Tightening main bearing cap bolt

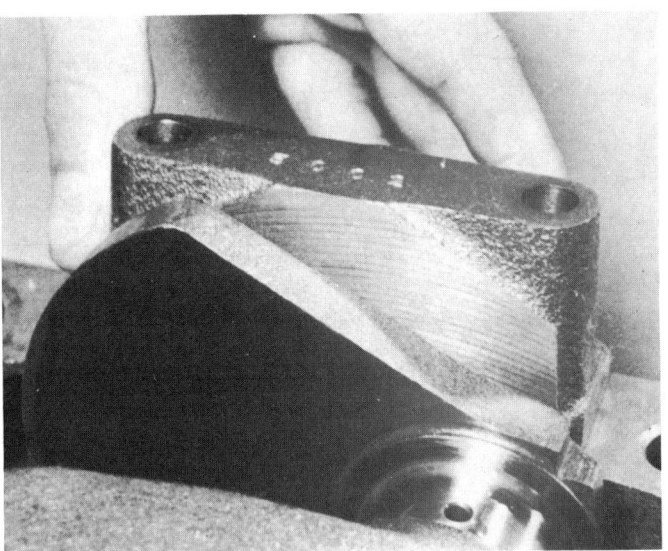

22.7 Fitting main bearing cap

22.10 Checking crankshaft endfloat

9   Tighten the main bearing bolts to the specified torque wrench setting (photo).

10 Using a dial gauge or feeler blades inserted between a thrust washer and the crankshaft; check the crankshaft endfloat. If it exceeds the specified limit, the thrust washers can be changed for thicker ones (photo).

11 Bolt on the crankshaft rear oil seal carrier using a new gasket. The carrier should have been fitted with a new oil seal and the seal lips greased (photos).

12 Fit the engine rear plate (photo).

Flywheel

13 Offer the flywheel to the crankshaft. With pistons 1 and 4 at TDC the dimple on the flywheel must be uppermost (towards top of engine) so it will only fit one way.

14 Screw in and tighten the bolts to the specified torque. The crankshaft may be held against rotation by either jamming the starter ring gear or placing a block of wood between one of the crankshaft webs and the inside of the crankcase (photo).

22.11A Fitting crankshaft rear oil seal retainer and gasket

22.11B Crankshaft rear oil seal and retainer fitted

Camshaft

15 Oil the cam followers and return them to their original positions (photo).

16 Oil the camshaft bearings and insert the camshaft, taking great care not to damage the bearings with the cam lobes. Fit the front bearing, chamfer inwards (photos).

17 Screw in the camshaft front bearing lock screw.

Oil pump

18 Refit the oil pump and oil tube as described in Section 10.

Timing chain and sprockets

19 Fit the timing chain and sprockets as described in Section 8. Fit the Woodruff key to the crankshaft nose.

20 Using a new gasket, fit the timing chain cover, but leave the bolts finger tight (photo).

21 Apply grease to the lips of the timing cover oil seal and then push the crankshaft pulley into position.

22 Move the timing cover if necessary so that the pulley hub is centralised in the oil seal and then tighten the cover bolts.

23 Screw on the crankshaft pulley nut and tighten to the specified torque. Hold the crankshaft against rotation either by jamming the starter ring gear or by placing a block of wood between a crankshaft web and the inside of the crankcase (photo).

22.12 Engine end plate

22.15 Cam followers

22.14 Tightening flywheel bolt

22.16A Fitting camshaft front bearing

22.16B Fitting camshaft

22.23 Tightening the crankshaft pulley nut

22.16C Camshaft front bearing lockbolt

Piston/connecting rods

24 Fit these as described in Section 7.

Sump pan

25 Fit the sump pan as described in Section 6.

Cylinder head

26 Stand the engine upright and fit the cylinder head as described in Section 5.

27 Insert the pushrods in their original fitted order.

28 With the rocker arm adjuster screws fully unscrewed, locate the rocker gear and screw on the fixing nuts.

29 Adjust the valve clearances as described in Section 11.

30 Locate a new gasket in position and fit the rocker cover (photo).

31 Screw on a new oil filter (Section 2).

22.20 Fitting timing cover

22.30 Rocker cover nut

23 Engine ancillary components – refitting

1   Refer to Chapter 5 and refit the clutch, making sure to centralise the driven plate.
2   Fit the coolant pump as described in Chapter 2. Fit the thermostat housing if it was removed noting the air cleaner mounting bracket on the housing studs (photo).
3   Fit the alternator and drivebelt as described in Chapter 9.
4   Refer to Chapter 3 and fit the exhaust manifold and hot air collector, the carburettor and spacer and the fuel pump.
5   Fit the distributor as described in Chapter 4. Fit the oil dipstick guide tube (photos).

24 Engine/transmission – reconnection

1   Support the weight of the transmission and offer it squarely to the engine. The splined input shaft should pass easily through the hub of the driven plate, provided the plate has been centralised as described in Chapter 5. It may be necessary to align the splines with the hub grooves, in which case have an assistant turn the crankshaft pulley

23.5B Dipstick guide tube bracket

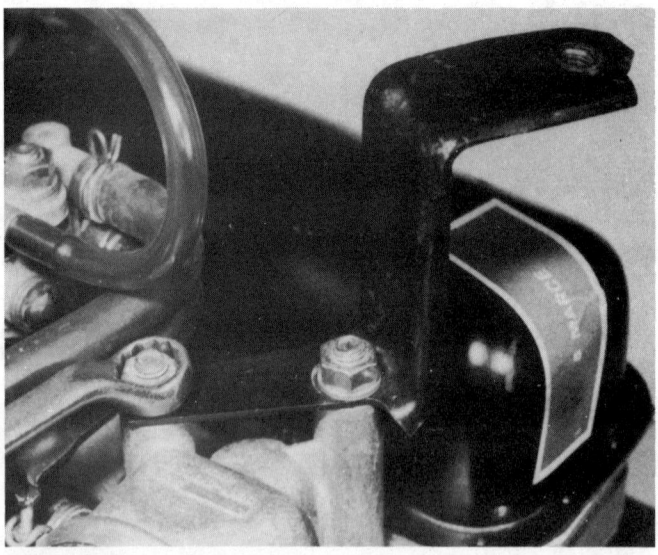

23.2 Air cleaner support bracket

24.1 Coupling engine/transmission

23.5A Dipstick guide tube

24.2 Flywheel housing upper bolts and lifting lugs

nut. The alignment dowels will make the connection stiff, so drawing the engine and transmission together with two connecting bolts will ease it (photo).

2   Once the engine and transmission are fully engaged, insert and tighten the connecting bolts, locate the lifting eyes (photo).

3   Bolt on the flywheel housing cover plate and the mounting brackets.

4   Bolt on the starter motor.

25 Engine/transmission – refitting

1   The refitting operations are reversals of those described in either Section 13 or 14 according to the method of removal employed.

2   However, observe the following special points.

3   When lowering the unit into the engine compartment, make sure that the lifting chains are so adjusted that the transmission end is inclined downwards at a steep angle (45°). Otherwise the transmission will not pass under the left-hand side member. This is to allow the sump pan to clear the right-hand engine mounting bracket (photo).

25.3 Refitting engine/transmission from above

4   Tighten the engine mounting and front suspension (disconnected) bolts to the specified torque when the hoist has been removed and the weight of the car is again on its roadwheels.

5   Fill the cooling system.

6   Fill the engine with oil.

7   Replenish lost transmission oil.

8   Reconnect the battery.

9   Adjust the clutch pedal as described in Chapter 5.

26 Engine – initial start up after overhaul or major repair

1   Make sure that the battery is fully charged and that all lubricants, coolant and fuel are replenished.

2   If the fuel system has been dismantled it will require several revolutions of the engine on the starter motor to pump the petrol up to the carburettor.

3   Turn the carburettor throttle speed screw through one complete turn to increase the idle speed in order to offset the initial stiffness of new engine internal components.

4   As soon as the engine fires and runs, keep it going at a fast idle speed and bring it up to normal working temperature.

5   As the engine warms up there will be odd smells and some smoke from parts getting hot and burning off oil deposits. The signs to look for are leaks of water or oil which will be obvious.

6   Check also the exhaust pipe and manifold connections as these do not always 'find' their exact gas tight position until the warmth and vibration have acted on them and it is almost certain that they will need tightening further. This should be done, of course, with the engine stopped.

7   When normal running temperature has been reached, adjust the engine idle speed as described in Chapter 3.

8   Stop the engine and wait a few minutes to see if any lubricant or coolant is dripping out when the engine is stationary.

9   Road test the car to check that the timing is correct and that the engine is giving the necessary smoothness and power. Do not race the engine – if new bearings and/or pistons have been fitted it should be treated as a new engine and run in at a reduced speed for the first 500 km (300 miles).

10   After the first 1000 km (600 miles) the cylinder head bolts must be retightened in the following way.

11   Remove the spare wheel, air cleaner and rocker cover. Unscrew the first bolt (Fig. 1.3) through one quarter of a turn and then tighten it to the specified torque. Repeat the operations on the remaining bolts (one at a time).

12   Check and adjust the valve clearances.

13   Refit the rocker cover, air cleaner and spare wheel.

Fault diagnosis appears overleaf

27 Fault diagnosis – engine

Symptom	Reason(s)
Engine fails to turn when starter control operated	
No current at starter motor	Flat or defective battery
	Loose battery leads
	Defective starter solenoid or switch or broken wiring
	Engine earth strap disconnected
Current at starter motor	Jammed starter motor drive pinion
	Defective starter motor
Engine turns but will not start	
No spark at spark plug	Ignition leads or distributor cap damp or wet
	Ignition leads to spark plugs loose
	Shorted or disconnected low tension leads
	Dirty, incorrectly set, or pitted contact breaker points
	Faulty condenser
	Defective ignition switch
	Ignition leads connected wrong way round
	Faulty coil
	Contact breaker point spring earthed or broken
No fuel at carburettor float chamber or at jets	No petrol in petrol tank
	Vapour lock in fuel line (in hot conditions or at high altitude)
	Blocked float chamber needle valve
	Fuel pump filter blocked
	Choked or blocked carburettor jets
	Faulty fuel pump
Engine stalls and will not restart	
Excess of petrol in cylinder or carburettor flooding	Too much choke allowing too rich a mixture to wet plugs
	Float damaged or leaking or needle not seating
	Float lever incorrectly adjusted
No spark at spark plug	Ignition failure – sudden
	Ignition failure – misfiring precedes total stoppage
	Ignition failure – in severe rain or after traversing water splash
No petrol at jets	No petrol in petrol tank
	Petrol tank breather choked
	Sudden obstruction in carburettor
	Water in fuel system
Engine misfires or idles unevenly	
Intermittent spark at spark plug	Ignition leads loose
	Battery leads loose on terminals
	Battery earth strap loose on body attachment point
	Engine earth lead loose
	Low tension leads on coil loose
	Low tension lead to distributor loose
	Dirty or incorrectly gapped plugs
	Dirty, incorrectly set, or pitted contact breaker points
	Tracking across inside of distributor cover
	Ignition too retarded
	Faulty coil
Fuel shortage at engine	Mixture too weak
	Air leak in carburettor
	Air leak at inlet manifold to cylinder head, or inlet manifold to carburettor
Lack of power and poor compression	
Mechanical wear	Burnt out valves
	Sticking or leaking valves
	Weak or broken valve springs
	Worn valve guides or stems
	Worn pistons and piston rings
Fuel/air mixture leaking from cylinder	Burnt out exhaust valves
	Sticking or leaking valves
	Worn valve guides and stems
	Weak or broken valve springs
	Blown cylinder head gasket (accompanied by increase in noise)
	Worn pistons and piston rings
	Worn or scored cylinder bores

Symptom	Reason(s)
Incorrect adjustments	Ignition timing wrongly set Contact breaker points incorrectly gapped Incorrect valve clearances Incorrectly set spark plugs Carburation too rich or too weak
Carburation and ignition faults	Dirty contact breaker points Fuel filter blocked Air filter blocked Distributor automatic advance and retard mechanisms not functioning correctly Faulty fuel pump giving top end fuel starvation
Excessive oil consumption	Excessively worn valve stems and valve guides Worn piston rings Worn pistons and cylinder bores Excessive piston ring gap allowing blow-by Piston oil return holes choked
Oil being lost due to leaks	Leaking oil filter gasket Leaking rocker cover gasket Leaking timing gear cover gasket Leaking sump gasket Loose sump plug
Unusual noise from engine Excessive clearances due to mechanical wear	Worn valve gear (noisy tapping from rocker box) Worn big-end bearing (regular heavy knocking) Worn timing chain and gears (rattling from front of engine) Worn main bearings (rumbling and vibration) Worn crankshaft (knocking, rumbling and vibration)
Pinking on acceleration	Fuel octane rating too low Ignition timing over-advanced Carbon build-up in cylinder head Valve timing incorrect (after rebuild) Mixture too weak Overheating

Chapter 2 Cooling and heating systems

Contents

Coolant pump – overhaul	10	Drivebelt – tensioning, removal and refitting	7
Coolant pump – removal and refitting	9	Electric cooling fan and switch	6
Coolant temperature switch	8	Fault diagnosis – cooling system	12
Cooling mixtures	3	Heater – removal and refitting	11
Cooling system – draining, flushing and refilling	2	Radiator – removal and refitting	5
Description and maintenance	1	Thermostat – removal, testing and refitting	4

Specifications

System type .... Thermo-syphon with pump assistance. Front-mounted radiator, thermostat, expansion tank

Thermostat
Starts to open .... 85°C (185°F)
Fully open .... 89°C (192°F)

Fan thermostatic switch
Cuts-in .... 90 to 94°C (194 to 201°F)
Cuts-out .... 85 to 89°C (185 to 192°F)

Pressure cap rating .... 0.98 bar (14 lbf/in²)

Coolant capacity .... 5.2 litres (9.2 pints)

Torque wrench settings

	Nm	lbf ft
Coolant temperature switch	30	22
Coolant pump cover nuts	27	20
Coolant pump mounting bolts	25	18

1 Description and maintenance

1 The cooling system is of the 'no loss' type and incorporates a belt-driven pump, a front-mounted radiator with thermo-switch for the electric cooling fan, and a remotely sited coolant expansion tank.
2 A thermostat is located on the right-hand end of the cylinder head.
3 The car interior heater is supplied with coolant from the engine cooling system.
4 A fresh air type ventilation system is employed.
5 Maintenance consists of checking the coolant level in the expansion tank, periodically inspecting the condition and security of

the hoses and their clips and checking the condition and tension of the pump drivebelt (Section 7).
6 In theory, the addition of coolant to the expansion tank should never be required as none is ever lost. If anything more than very infrequent topping up with a small quantity of coolant is required, check for leaks. If none is found, the loss may be due to an internal leak in the engine (faulty gasket or porous block), but this will usually be detected by water on the dipstick or a rise in the engine oil level. Always check the coolant level when the engine is cold. If topping up is necessary, use antifreeze mixture made up in similar strength to the original.
7 At the intervals specified in Routine Maintenance, renew the coolant mixture.

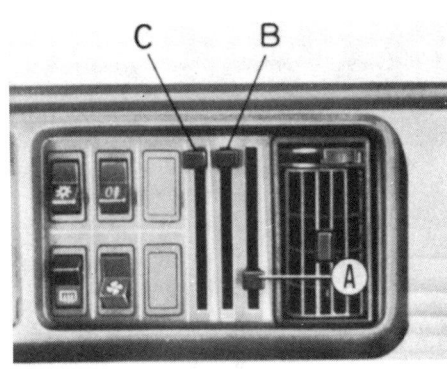

Fig. 2.1 Heater controls (Sec 1)

A Temperature C Air volume
B Direction of flow

2 Cooling system – draining, flushing and refilling

1   Move the heater temperature control lever to HOT.
2   Disconnect the hose which runs from the expansion tank to the radiator and allow the coolant to drain.
3   Unscrew and remove the caps from the radiator and expansion tank.
4   Disconnect the coolant hose from the rear of the coolant pump and allow the coolant to drain. If the coolant is to be used again, catch it in a clean container (photo).
5   If the coolant has been renewed regularly then it should run clear from the hose without any sign of rust or sediment. If this is the case, the system may be refilled as soon as the hoses are reconnected.
6   If the system has been neglected, then it should be flushed through by placing a cold water hose in the radiator top hose connection until the water comes out clean. In extreme cases a chemical descaler may be needed. This should be used strictly in accordance with the manufacturer's instructions. If the radiator is clogged, remove it (Section 5), invert it and then reverse flush it.
7   To fill the cooling system, check that the hoses are secure and pour the coolant mixture (see Section 3) slowly into the radiator filler neck, until it is brim full (photo).
8   Fill the expansion tank to the mark indicated on it using a similar mixture to that poured into the radiator. Push the connecting hose into the expansion tank cap (photo).

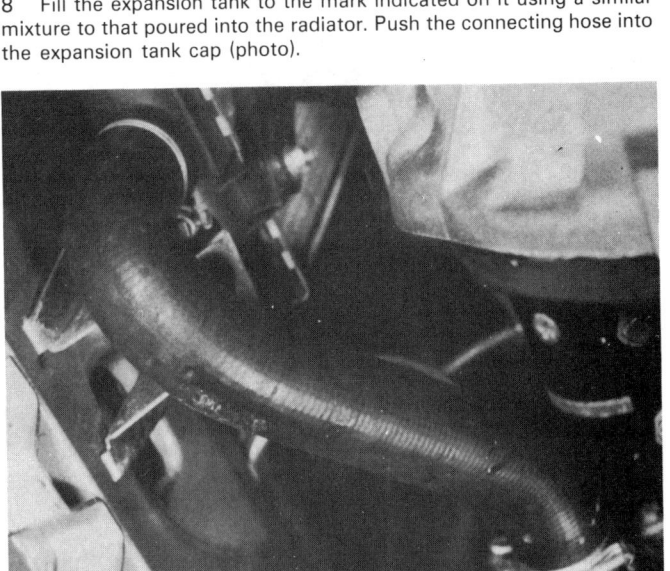

2.4 Hose, radiator to coolant pump

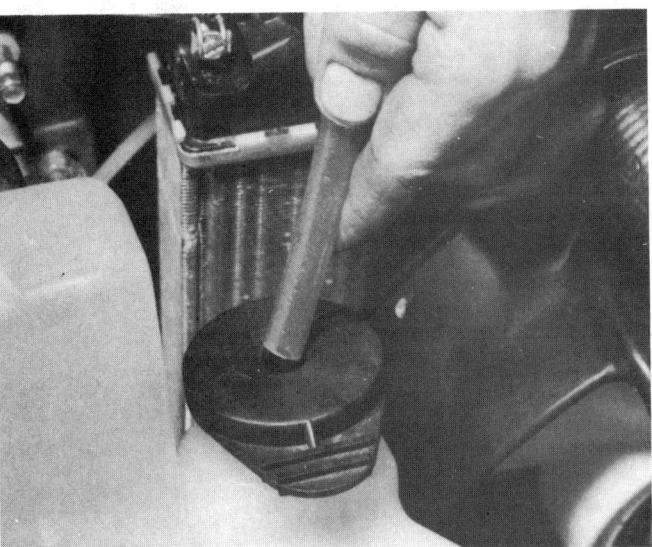

2.7 Filling the radiator

2.8 Expansion tank hose

9   Refit the radiator cap.
10 Start the engine and run it at a fast idle until bubbles no longer appear to rise through the coolant in the expansion tank.
11 Switch off the ignition, allow the engine to cool and top up the expansion tank if necessary to the full mark.

3 Coolant mixtures

1   Plain water should never be used in the engine cooling system. Apart from giving protection against freezing, an antifreeze mixture protects the engine internal surfaces and components against corrosion. This is especially important in respect of the alloy cylinder head.
2   Always use a top quality glycol based antifreeze which is suitable for alloy engines.
3   Ideally, a 50% mixture of antifreeze and soft or demineralised water should be used to maintain maximum protection against freezing and corrosion. On no account use less than 25% antifreeze.

4 Renew the coolant at the specified intervals as the inhibitors contained in the antifreeze gradually lose their effectiveness.
5 Even when operating in climates where antifreeze is not necessary, never use plain water, but add a corrosion inhibitor to it.

4 Thermostat – removal, testing and refitting

1 The purpose of the thermostat is to prevent coolant circulating during engine cold start and warm up. This is achieved by means of its heat-sensitive plate valve.
2 If the engine appears to take a long time to warm up or the heater is not very effective, suspect a defective thermostat.
3 To remove the thermostat, first drain the cooling system and then disconnect the hoses from the thermostat housing (photo).
4 Unbolt and remove the thermostat housing complete (photo).
5 Unfortunately, the thermostat is integral with the housing. If faulty, the complete assembly must be renewed.
6 Test the thermostat for correct functioning by suspending the assembly on a string in a saucepan of cold water together with a thermometer. Heat the water and note the temperature at which the thermostat begins to open. Check with Specifications.

7 Discard the thermostat if it opens too early or too late and also if the valve does not open fully.
8 Allow the thermostat to cool down and check if the valve seats fully.
9 Refitting is a reversal of removal. Always use a new flange gasket.

5 Radiator – removal and refitting

1 Drain the cooling system.
2 Disconnect the hoses and the thermostatic switch leads from the radiator (photos).
3 Unscrew the two fixing bolts from the radiator top clamp and remove the clamp (photo).
4 Lift the radiator complete with fan, up and out of the bottom insulators (photo).
5 The fan assembly may be unbolted and removed from the radiator.
6 Aluminium/plastic radiators cannot be repaired, only renewed. On some models, a copper core is used which can be soldered. It is recommended that radiator repair is left to a professional radiator repairer.

4.3 Thermostat housing

5.2A Radiator top hose

4.4 Removing the thermostat housing

5.2B Front coolant hose and pipe

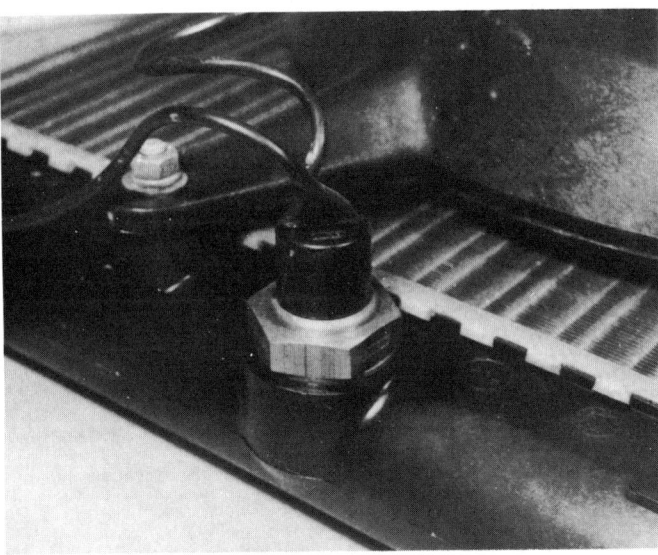

5.2C Radiator thermostatic switch

5.3 Radiator fixing clamp

5.4 Removing radiator/fan

7   With the radiator removed, take the opportunity to brush or blow away (using compressed air) flies and dirt from the radiator fins.
8   If the radiator and expansion pressure caps are old, they may be tested at your dealers and if faulty renewed with ones of similar pressure rating.
9   Refit the radiator and fill the cooling system as described in Section 2.

6   Electric cooling fan and switch

1   The electric cooling fan only operates when the coolant temperature has reached a specified level and cuts-out again once the coolant temperature has dropped.
2   Control of the fan is carried out by means of a thermostatic switch screwed into the radiator lower tank.
3   The fan, motor and supporting shroud may be removed as an assembly after disconnecting the electrical leads and mounting nuts (photo).

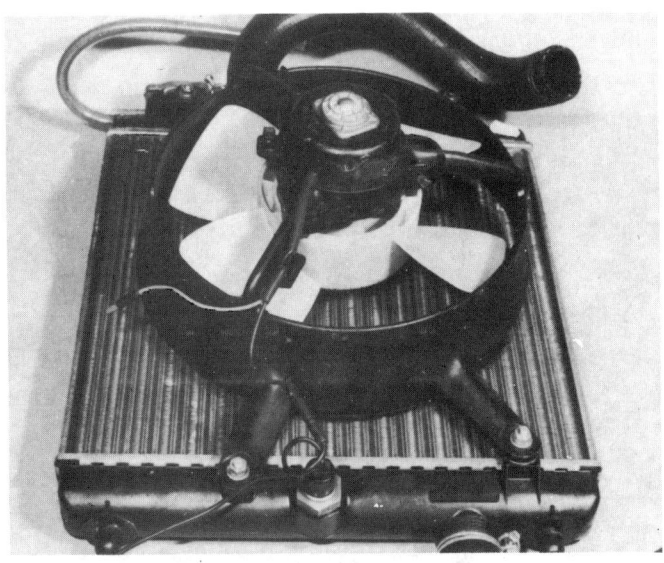

6.3 Radiator, fan and shroud

4   The fan is held to the motor shaft by a nut.
5   If the thermostatic switch is removed, always fit a new sealing washer and avoid overtightening.
6   The cooling fan will normally only come on when the car is held up in a traffic jam or has been idling for an extended period. If it comes on at other times, this will be due to overheating because of lack of coolant or a slack or broken drivebelt to the coolant pump.

7   Drivebelt – tensioning, removal and refitting

1   The vee drivebelt drives the coolant pump and alternator.
2   Regularly inspect the condition of the belt. It should not be frayed or show any sign of cracking.
3   Check the belt tension by applying finger pressure at the centre of the top run of the belt. The belt should deflect by 10.0 mm (0.394 in) (photo).
4   If it is slack, release the mounting nuts and the adjuster elongated hole nut. Pull the alternator away from the engine then retighten and check the tension again.
5   If the belt must be renewed, slacken the mounting and adjuster hole nut and push the alternator fully in towards the engine. Slip the belt from the pulleys. If this is difficult to do because of the tightness of the belt, turn the crankshaft pulley nut with a spanner while prising the belt over and off the rim of one of the other pulleys. Use this method to fit the new unstretched belt (photo).
6   Tension the belt as described earlier and if it is a new belt, check its tension again after a few miles of running.

Fig. 2.2 Drivebelt (Sec 7)

A   Pressure point for tension   C   Mounting bolt
B   Adjuster bolt

8   Coolant temperature switch

1   This is located on the cylinder head just above number one spark plug.
2   If the engine coolant temperature exceeds a predetermined level, a warning lamp on the instrument panel lights up.
3   Failure to operate correctly should be checked first by making sure that the warning lamp bulb is not blown and that the wiring is secure. If these are in order, renew the switch by unscrewing it from the cylinder head and screwing in a new switch.

9   Coolant pump – removal and refitting

1   Drain the cooling system.
2   Disconnect the hoses from the rear of the pump.
3   Remove the drivebelt as described in Section 7.
4   Unbolt and remove the pump (photo).
5   Refitting is a reversal of removal. Tension the drivebelt, fill the cooling system as described in Section 2.

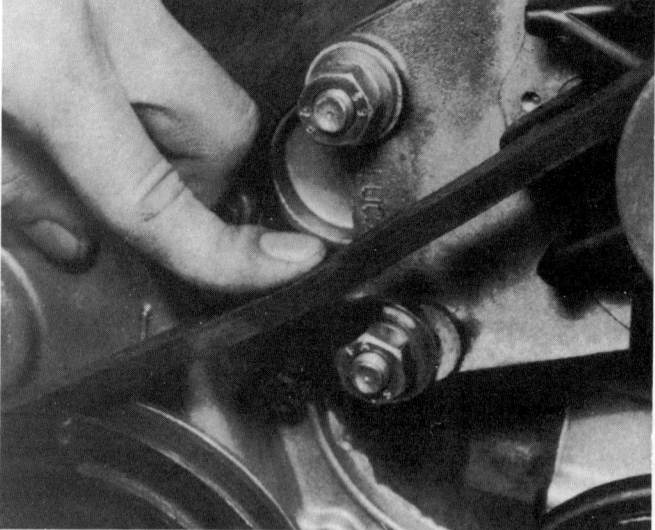

7.3 Checking the drivebelt tension

9.4 Removing the coolant pump

10   Coolant pump – overhaul

1   If the pump has been in service for a considerable mileage, then it will probably be more economical to purchase a new pump rather than renew the bearings and seals on the old one.
2   If only the seals are to be renewed, then proceed in the following way, after removing the pump from the car.

Up to 1983

3   Unscrew the nuts and separate the two halves of the pump.
4   The main problem is now withdrawing the impeller from the pump shaft. A special tool is available (A.40026) to do this job, but a suitable

7.5 Fitting the drivebelt

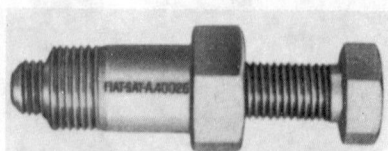

Fig. 2.3 Impeller withdrawal tool (Sec 10)

10 To reassemble start by inserting the new bearing seals in their grooves by each bearing. Fit the circlip to the shaft, then the shouldered ring, bearings, spacer and lockwasher. Fit the shaft and bearing assembly into the cover. Fit the stop screw. Press on the pulley.

11 Fit the new gland (seal), seating it in its location in the cover.

12 When fitting the impeller, it is imperative that the final installed position will give the specified clearance between impeller and pump cover of between 0.8 and 1.2 mm (0.03 and 0.05 in).

13 In order to achieve this, support the pulley end of the pump shaft and press on the impeller in stages. Locate the pump cover and gasket and check the clearance through the opening in the side of the pump.

1984 on

14 The impeller on later pumps is not threaded, so the following dismantling procedure must be followed.

15 Remove the pump cover and joint gasket.

16 Support the pulley and press the shaft from it.

17 Extract the staked screw which holds the bearing.

18 Drive out the bearing/impeller from the pump body using a piece of tubing (photo).

Fig. 2.4 Removing impeller from coolant pump shaft (Sec 10)

1 Pump body	3 Puller
2 Impeller	

substitute can be made up if two bolts with the correct threads can be obtained and the larger one drilled and tapped. Screw the outer bolt into the impeller and then turn the inner bolt to force the pump shaft out of the impeller.

5 Take out the bearing stop screw.

6 From the impeller end, press the shaft with the bearings out of the cover half of the housing.

7 Press the shaft out of the bearings and pulley, taking off the spacer, the circlip, the shouldered ring, and the lockwasher.

8 Do not immerse the bearings in cleaning fluid. They are 'sealed'. Liquid will get in, but a thorough clean will be impracticable, and it will be impossible to get new grease in.

9 Check all the parts. Get a new main seal, two bearing seals and a new gasket. Scrape all water deposits out of the housing and off the impeller.

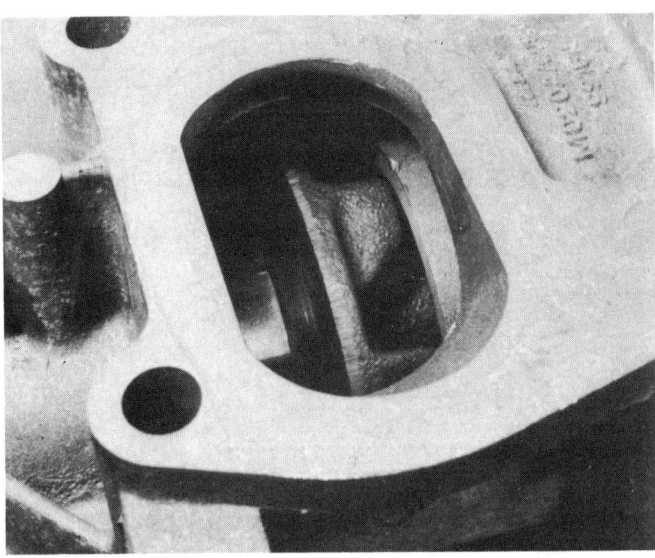

10.18 Coolant pump showing the impeller

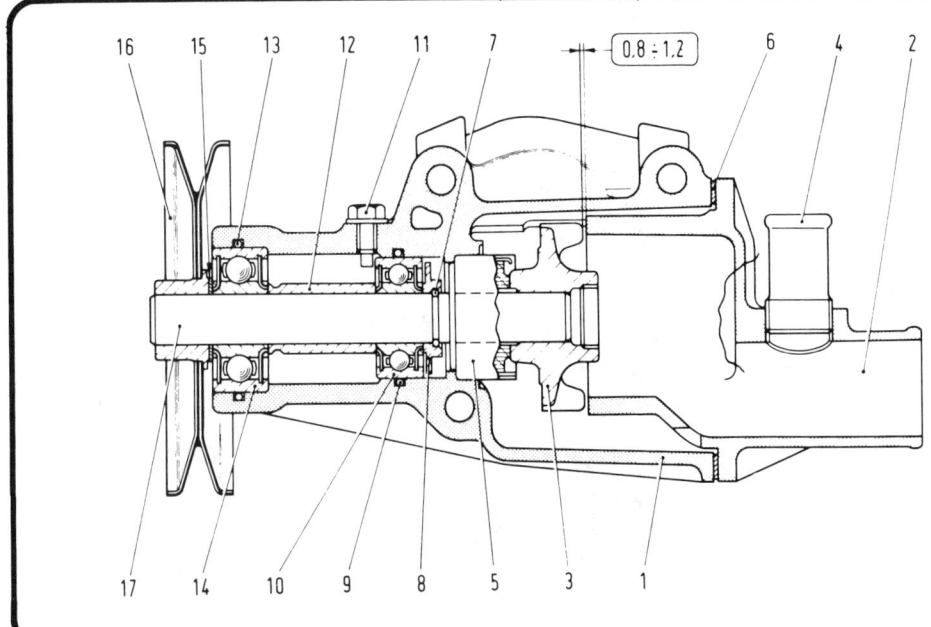

Fig. 2.5 Sectional view of coolant pump (Sec 10)

1 Pump body
2 Pump cover
3 Impeller
4 Connector for hose from outlet to pump
5 Seal
6 Gasket
7 Circlip
8 Bearing shoulder washer
9 Inner seal
10 Inner bearing
11 Bearing retaining screw and lock washer
12 Spacer
13 Outer seal
14 Outer bearing
15 Lock washer
16 Pulley
17 Pump shaft

0.8 ÷ 1.2

19 Support the impeller and press the shaft from it.
20 Renew the seals and shaft bearing.
21 When reassembling, press the pulley onto the pump shaft so that the shaft projects between 1.0 and 1.2 mm (0.04 and 0.05 in).
22 Press or drive the bearing/shaft into the pump housing until the bearing screw holes are aligned. Fit the screw and stake.
23 Support the end of the shaft and fit the impeller as described in paragraphs 12 and 13.

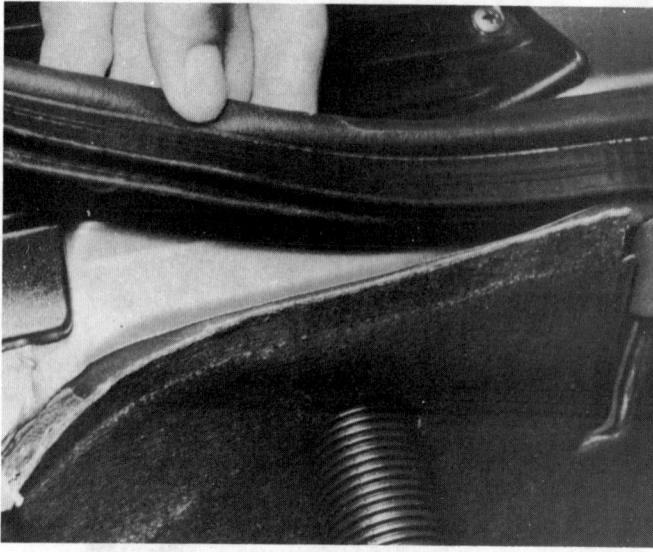

11.4A Removing the rubber seal from the bonnet edge

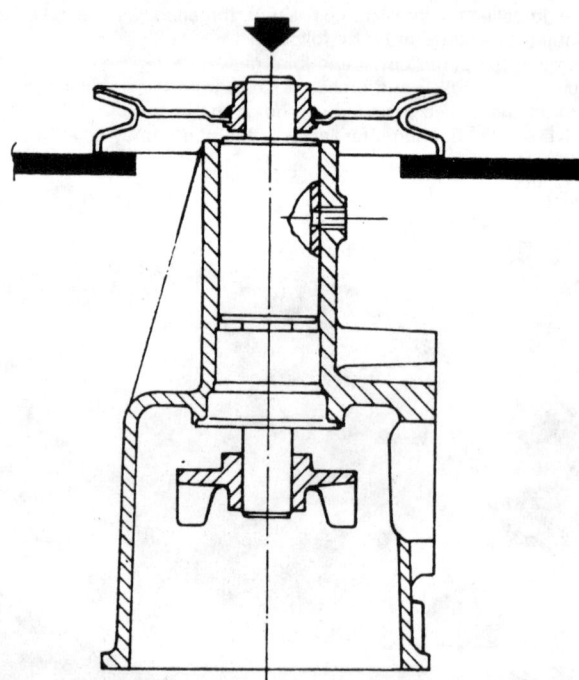

Fig. 2.6 Pressing coolant pump shaft from pulley (Sec 10)

11.4B Withdrawing the insulation from the heater air intake

11 Heater – removal and refitting

1 Remove the instrument panel (Chapter 9) and then drain the cooling system (Section 2).
2 Disconnect the battery and remove it.
3 Unbolt the wiper motor (Chapter 9) and lay to one side.
4 Pull away the insulating material from around the heater air intake, feed the material over the fuse box (photos).
5 Disconnect the heater hoses from the right-hand side of the heater (photo).
6 Disconnect the heater control cable clamps and cables from the heater (photos).
7 Unscrew the heater mounting bolts on the engine compartment bulkhead (photo).
8 Working inside the car, extract the fixing screws from the right-hand side of the control lever bracket on the facia panel (photo).
9 Withdraw the heater on the engine compartment side while an assistant guides the control lever assembly through the hole in the facia panel.
10 The heater casing spring clips may be prised off and the casing sections separated for access to the matrix and blower motor (photos).
11 Reassembly and refitting are reversals of removal and dismantling.

11.5 Hose connections at the heater

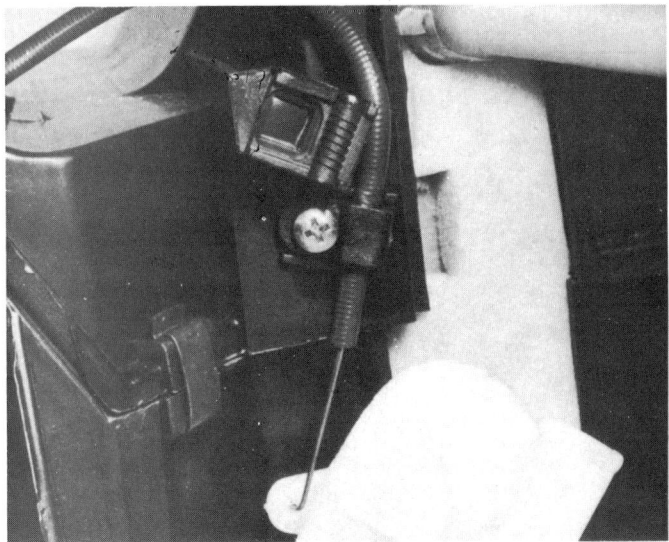

11.6A Heater coolant valve control cable

11.6B Heater air volume control flap cable

11.7 Heater mounting nut at engine compartment rear bulkhead

11.8 Heater control levers

11.10A Heater casing section clip

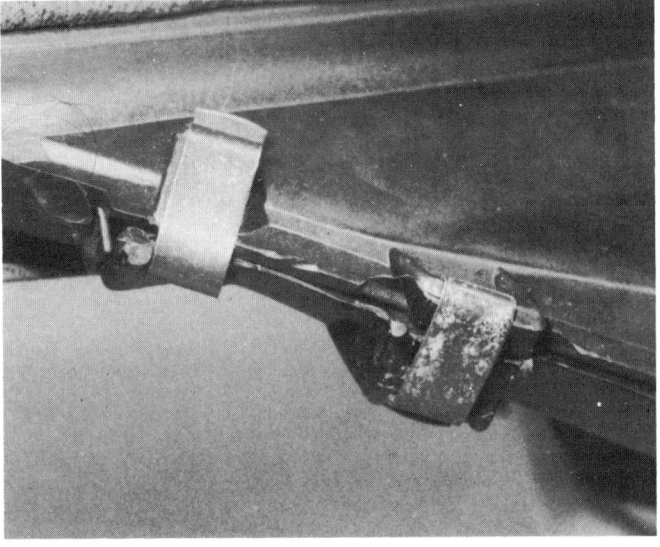

11.10B Heater casing section clip

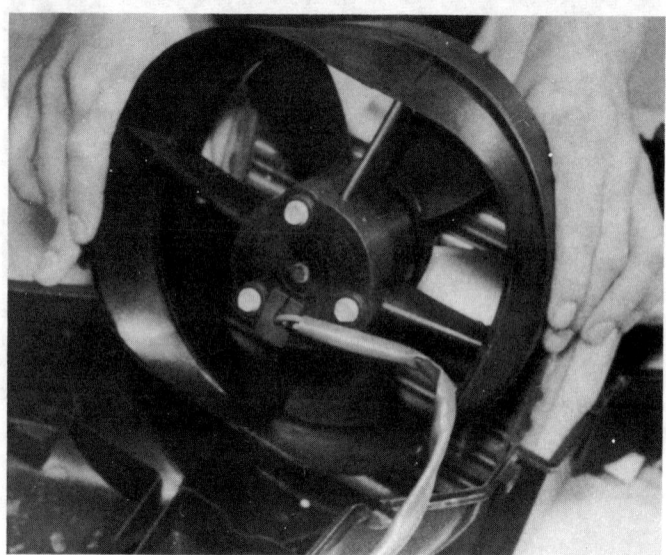

11.10C Heater blower motor and fan

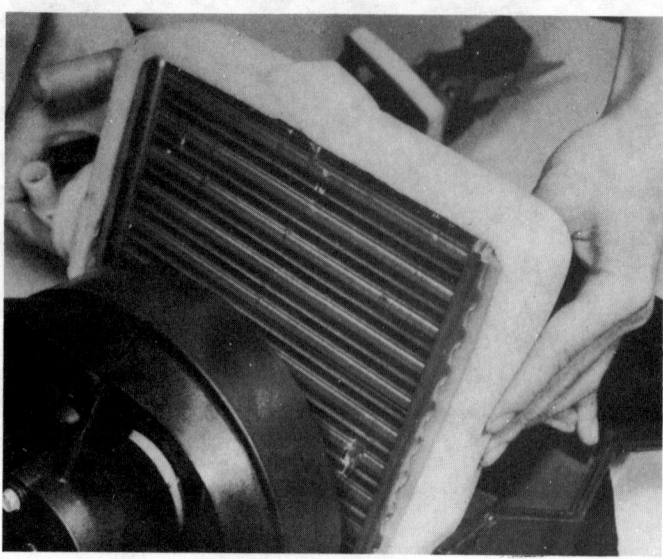

11.10D Withdrawing the heater matrix

12 Fault diagnosis – cooling system

Symptom	Reason(s)
Overheating	Insufficient coolant in system
	Pump ineffective due to slack drivebelt
	Radiator blocked either internally or externally
	Kinked or collapsed hose causing coolant flow restriction
	Thermostat not working properly
	Engine out of tune
	Ignition timing retarded or auto advance malfunction
	Cylinder head gasket blown
	Engine not yet run-in
	Exhaust system partially blocked
	Engine oil level too low
	Brakes binding
Engine running too cool	Faulty or incorrect thermostat
Loss of coolant	Loose hose clips
	Hoses perished or leaking
	Radiator leaking
	Filler/pressure cap defective
	Blown cylinder head gasket
	Cracked cylinder block or head
Heater gives insufficient output	Engine overcooled (see above)
	Heater matrix blocked
	Heater controls maladjusted or broken
	Heater control valve jammed or otherwise defective

Chapter 3 Fuel system

Contents

Accelerator pedal and linkage 13	Fault diagnosis – fuel system 16
Air cleaner – servicing, removal and refitting 2	Fuel pump – cleaning 3
Carburettor – description and maintenance 9	Fuel pump – removal and refitting 5
Carburettor – idle speed and mixture adjustment 10	Fuel pump – testing 4
Carburettor – overhaul 12	Fuel pump (non-sealed type) – overhaul 6
Carburettor – removal and refitting 11	Fuel tank – removal and refitting 8
Choke control cable – adjustment and renewal 14	Fuel tank transmitter – removal and refitting 7
Description and maintenance 1	Manifold and exhaust system 15

Specifications

System type .... Mechanical fuel pump, downdraught fixed jet carburettor

Fuel tank capacity (including reserve) .... 35.0 litres (7.7 gal)

Carburettor calibration (dimensions in mm)

Type	**Weber 32 ICEV**
Venturi	22.0
Auxiliary venturi	3.5
Main jet	1.12
Air bleed jet	1.60 (1.70 – 1983 on)
Emulsion tube	F86 (F89 – 1983 on)
Slow running jet	0.50 (0.47 – 1983 on)
Air idle jet	1.10
Pump jet	0.40
Pump discharge orifice	0.40
Power fuel jet	1.30
Power air jet	1.40
Power mixture jet	2.0
Fuel inlet needle valve	1.50
One-way	1.70
Mixture	1.50
Accelerator pump fuel ejection for every ten strokes	4.0 to 5.0 cc
Float setting	10.50 to 11.0

Type .... **Solex C32 DISA**
    Venturi 22
    Auxiliary venturi 3.4
    Main jet .... 1.20 (1.175 – 1983 on)
    Air bleed jet .... 2.0 (1.90 – 1983 on)
    Emulsion tube N93
    Slow running jet .... 0.47 (0.50 – 1983 on)
    Air idle jet .... 1.0 (1.20 – 1983 on)
    Pump jet 0.50
    Pump discharge orifice 0.50
    Power jet 0.90
    Power mixture jet 2.00
    Needle valve 1.60
    Accelerator pump fuel injection for every ten strokes .... 4.0 to 5.0 cc
    Float setting .... 2.0 to 3.0

Idle speed .... 700 to 800 rev/min

CO level at idle .... 2 to 3%

1 Description and maintenance

1   The fuel system consists of a fuel tank located inboard of the right, rear roadwheel, a mechanically-operated fuel pump, a downdraught carburettor and air cleaner.
2   Maintenance consists of renewing the air cleaner element and cleaning the fuel pump at the specified intervals, as described later in this Chapter.

2 Air cleaner – servicing, removal and refitting

1   Open the bonnet and unscrew the wing nuts from the lid of the air cleaner.
2   Lift off the lid and take out the element and discard it (photo).
3   Wipe out the casing. Fit the new element and replace the lid.
4   Winter and summer positions are provided so that the air intake spout can draw air in from the front of the car or from around the

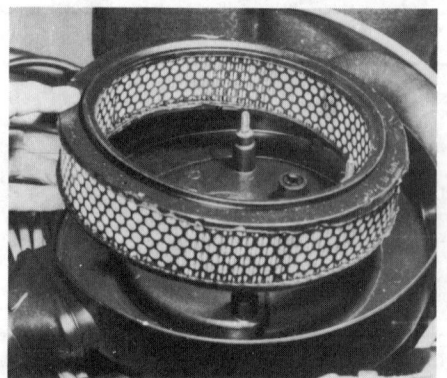

2.2 Air cleaner element

2.4A Air cleaner cold air intake

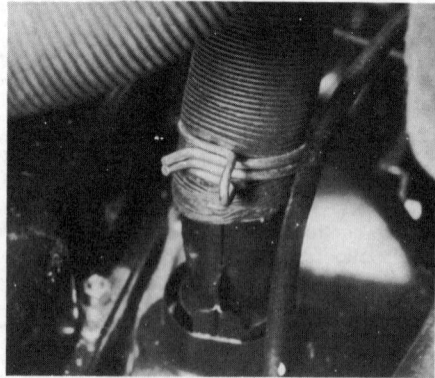

2.4B Air cleaner hot air intake

2.4C Air cleaner summer setting

2.4D Air cleaner winter setting

exhaust manifold according to ambient air temperature. If the outside temperature is above 13°C (55°F) then align the 'Sun' symbol with the arrow on the air intake spout. If the outside temperature is below 13°C (55°F) then align the 'Snowflake' symbol with the arrow on the spout. Unbolt the cover and turn it to do this (photos).

5   To remove the air cleaner, take out the filter element as previously described.

6   Disconnect the warm air intake hose and unscrew the cleaner casing mounting nuts. Lift the casing away. Note the vent hose attached (photos).

7   Refitting is a reversal of removal. Make sure that the flange sealing gaskets are in good condition (photo).

---

3   Fuel pump – cleaning

---

1   If the fuel pump is not of the sealed type, unscrew the cover mounting screw and lift away the screw, sealing gasket and cover.

2   Lift out the filter gauze from the pump upper body.

3   Inspect the filter gauze for sediment and, if dirty, clean it with petrol and a soft brush.

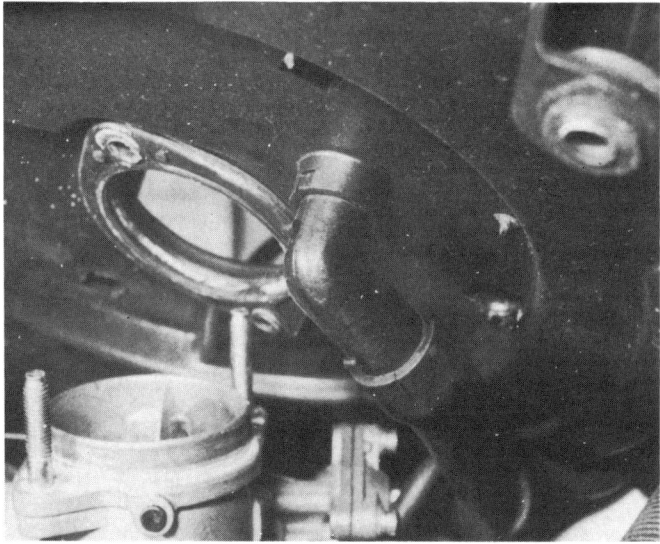

2.6C Underside of air cleaner casing

2.6A Air cleaner casing and mounting nuts

2.7 Air cleaner lower mounting flange

2.6B Air cleaner casing mounting bracket bolt

4   Check the condition of the gasket and renew it if it has hardened or distorted.

5   Replacement is the reverse sequence to removal. Tighten the centre screw just sufficiently to ensure a fuel-tight joint.

---

4   Fuel pump – testing

---

1   If the fuel pump is suspected of faulty operation, disconnect the fuel inlet hose from the carburettor and place its open end in a container.

2   Disconnect the LT lead which runs from the ignition coil to the distributor.

3   Have an assistant turn the ignition key to the 'start' position to rotate the crankshaft through a few revolutions. While the engine is turning, observe the end of the disconnected hose. The fuel should be ejected in regular, well defined spurts. If this does not happen and fuel is known to be in the tank, the pump must be removed and overhauled as described in the following Sections.

5 Fuel pump – removal and refitting

1   Disconnect the fuel lines from the pump (photo).
2   Undo and remove the two pump securing nuts and spring washers. Carefully lift away the fuel pump. Recover the two paper gaskets, spacer, pump actuating pushrod and bush from the pushrod bore (photo).
3   Refitting the fuel pump is the reverse sequence to removal, but care is necessary to use the right thickness of gasket (photo).
4   With the pushrod in its fully retracted position the end of the pushrod should project between 1.0 and 1.5 mm (0.039 and 0.059 in) beyond the spacer outer gasket. The projection can be altered by fitting a gasket of alternative thickness from the sizes available.

6 Fuel pump (non-sealed type) – overhaul

Note: *If the pump is of sealed type, overhaul is not possible.*
1   With the fuel pump removed from the engine, clean away external dirt and grease.
2   Unscrew the centre bolt and remove the pump cover.
3   Remove the filter gauze.
4   Mark the upper and lower flanges of the pump that are adjacent to each other so that they may be refitted in their original positions.
5   Undo and remove the six screws and spring washers which hold the two halves of the pump body together. Separate the two halves with great care, ensuring that the diaphragm does not stick to either of the two flanges. This also releases the spacer between the two halves of the pump.
6   To release the diaphragm, depress the centre and turn it 90°. This will release the diaphragm pull rod from the stirrup in the operating link, and its associated spring.
7   Do not remove the rocker arm and pivot from the body base unless there are signs of excessive wear – in which case it would probably be more economical to obtain an exchange pump.
8   To remove the valve assemblies from the body centre section they must be prised out carefully past the stakes which locate them. Remove the sealing ring fitted behind each valve. On some later models the valves are not available as separate spares. Instead, the complete upper half of the pump must be renewed if a valve is faulty.
9   A fuel pump repair kit is available which will contain all the renewable items.
10 Reassembly of the pump is the reverse sequence of removal. Take care to ensure that the valves are correctly assembled to the upper housing.

7 Fuel tank transmitter – removal and refitting

1   Access to the tank transmitter can be obtained by lowering the tank as described in the following Section.
2   Disconnect the fuel lines and electrical leads and release the transmitter securing ring.
3   Withdraw the unit taking care not to damage the float or arm.
4   When refitting check that the sealing ring is in good condition.

8 Fuel tank – removal and refitting

1   Syphon as much fuel as possible from the fuel tank into a safe, sealable container.
2   Working within the car, remove the right-hand trim panel as described in Chapter 12 to give access to the fuel filler hose. Disconnect the hose.
3   Working under the car, unscrew the mounting nuts from the tank flange and carefully lower the tank (photo).
4   Disconnect the fuel lines and electrical leads from the tank transmitter unit.
5   Remove the tank.
6   If the tank was removed for cleaning, remove the transmitter unit and using several changes of paraffin, shake it vigorously, rinsing finally with petrol.

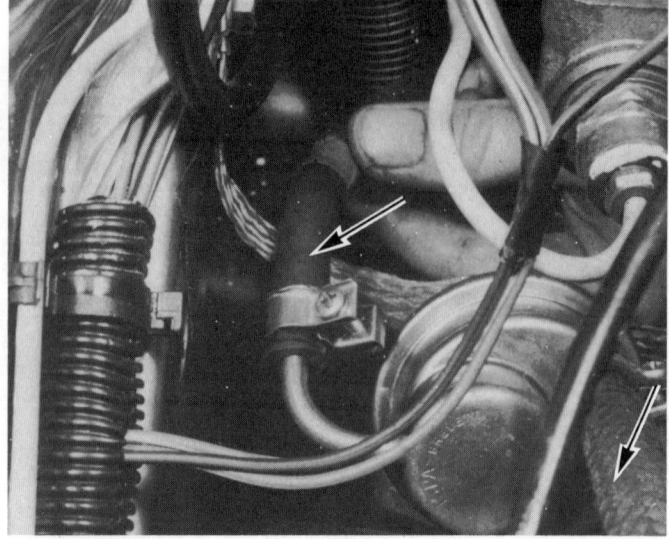

5.1 Fuel pump hoses

5.2 Fuel pump spacer block and operating rod

5.3 Fuel pump mounting nuts

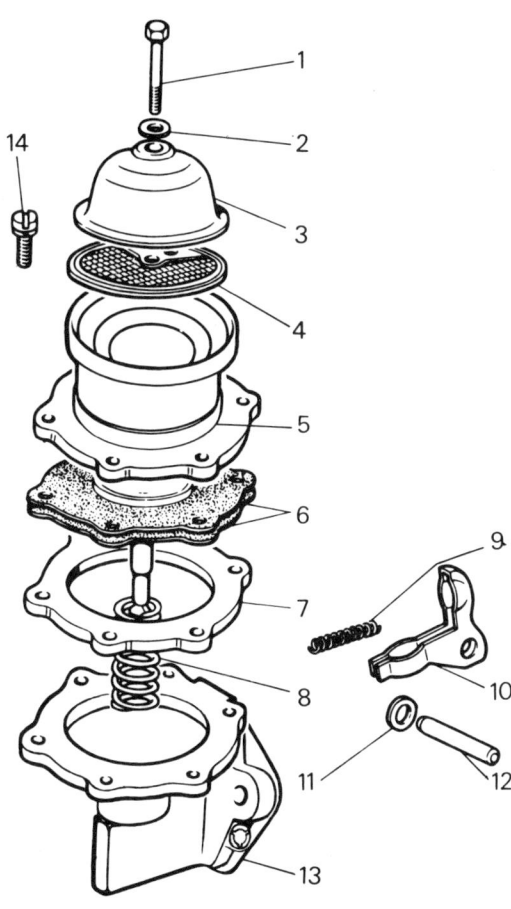

Fig. 3.1 Exploded view of fuel pump (Sec 6)

1	Cover screw	9	Rocker arm spring
2	Flat washer	10	Rocker arm
3	Pump cover	11	Shoulder washer
4	Filter	12	Rocker arm shaft
5	Upper body	13	Lower body
6	Diaphragm	14	Upper and lower bodies
7	Spacer		attachment screw
8	Diaphragm spring		

7   If the tank requires repair, leave this to the professionals, usually radiator repairers. *Never attempt to weld or solder a fuel tank unless it has been thoroughly steamed out to remove all explosive vapour.*
8   Refitting is a reversal of removal. Note the upper section of filler pipe under the rear wing (photo).

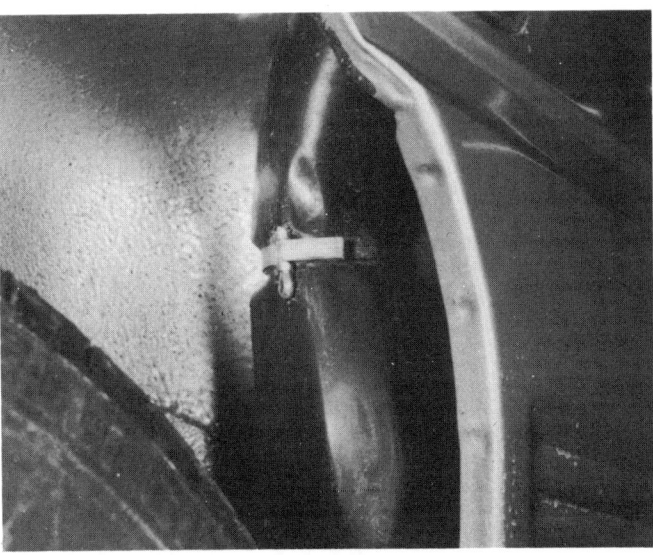

8.8 Fuel tank filler pipe protective sleeve

9   Carburettor – description and maintenance

1   The carburettor is of single venturi, manual choke, downdraught type of either Weber or Solex manufacture (photos).
2   Both carburettors are of fixed jet type with an accelerator pump and coolant-heated throttle block.
3   Normal maintenance consists of keeping the exterior clean and the pivots and linkage oiled.
4   On Weber units a filter is incorporated at the fuel inlet. Periodically unscrew the filter plug, extract the filter gauze and brush it clean in some fuel.

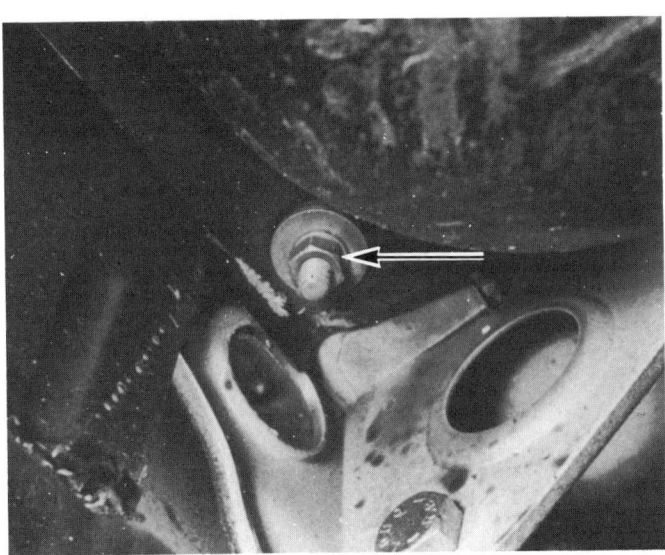

8.3 Fuel tank flange nut

9.1A Solex carburettor showing coolant hose nozzles

9.1B Solex carburettor showing accelerator pump

Fig. 3.2 Weber 32 ICEV carburettor (Sec 9)

9.1C Solex carburettor showing choke linkage

10 Carburettor – idle speed and mixture adjustment

1   Under normal circumstances the only adjustment required is to set the idle speed when the engine is at normal operating temperature.
2   Turn the throttle speed screw until the engine is running smoothly and evenly.
3   If a tachometer can be connected, then set the idle speed to the specified figure.
4   If the fuel mixture setting is obviously too rich, this will be indicated by black exhaust and sooty spark plugs. If the fuel mixture is too weak, this will be indicated by a white deposit on the inside of the exhaust pipe and on the spark plug electrodes. There may also be a tendency for the engine to stall. Under these circumstances carry out the following adjustment.
5   Remove the tamperproof plug from the lower flange of the carburettor body to expose the mixture screw (photos).
6   With the engine at normal operating temperature and idling, turn the mixture screw until the highest idle speed is obtained. Now turn the screw in until the speed just starts to drop. Turn the screw back a fraction if necessary to smooth the running. Obviously, if a tachometer

9.1D Solex carburettor showing choke unloader

10.5A Solex adjusting screws

1   Idle speed   2   Mixture (fitted with
                                              tamperproof cap)

10.5B Mixture screw with tamperproof cap removed

11.4 Disconnecting fuel hose from carburettor

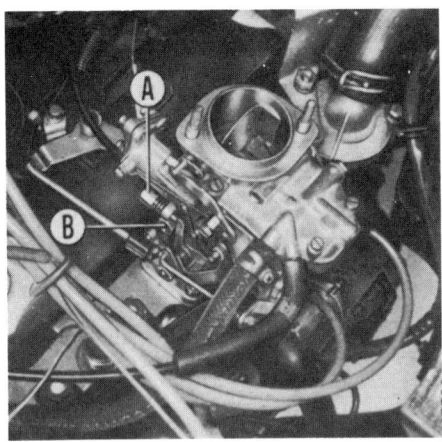

Fig. 3.3 Typical idle speed screw (A) and mixture screw (B) (Sec 10)

11.5 Removing carburettor
1   Spacer   2   Inlet manifold

is available for connecting to the engine then the points of highest idle speed and drop can be more easily established.

7   If an exhaust gas analyser is available, connect it in accordance with the manufacturer's instructions and adjust the mixture screw until the exhaust gas CO emission level is at the specified level.

8   Finally adjust the idle speed to specified level.

11 Carburettor – removal and refitting

1   Remove the air cleaner as described in Section 2.

2   Disconnect the coolant hoses from the carburettor throttle valve plate block. Tie them up high to avoid coolant loss.

3   Disconnect the throttle and choke controls from the carburettor.

4   Disconnect the fuel hoses from the carburettor. Identify them in respect of flow and return or they may be confused when reconnecting. Plug the open ends (photo).

5   Unscrew the carburettor mounting nuts and lift the unit from the cylinder head (photo).

6   Refitting is a reversal of removal. Renew the flange gasket and adjust the choke and throttle controls as described in Sections 13 and 14.

12 Carburettor – overhaul

1   Overhaul should be limited to the following operations. If more extensive work is required, for example, to renew the valve plate spindles or bushes, then such a generally worn carburettor is best renewed or a good secondhand unit obtained.

2   With the carburettor removed and cleaned externally, extract the top cover securing screws and remove the cover.

3   As the cover is partially lifted off disconnect the link rod (Weber) or tension spring (Solex) connecting the valve plate levers.

4   Mop out the float bowl.

5   The various jets and air bleeds may be unscrewed and cleaned by blowing air through them. Never attempt to probe a jet with wire. In extreme conditions of blockage, a nylon bristle may be used.

6   Take the opportunity to compare the jets with those listed in the Specifications in case a previous owner has substituted any of incorrect size. The jets are clearly marked, but a magnifying glass will be required to see some of them.

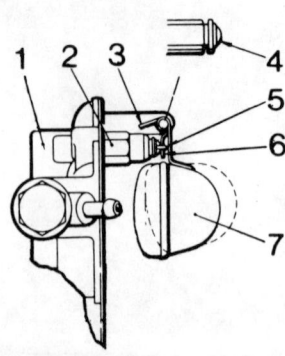

Fig. 3.4 Weber float setting diagram (Sec 12)

1   Carburettor top cover   5   Valve hook
2   Fuel inlet needle valve   6   Tang
3   Float stroke stop   7   Metal type float
4   Valve ball

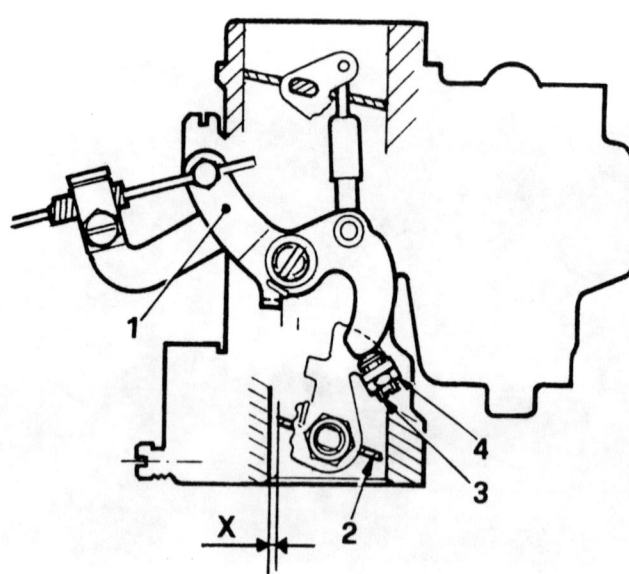

Fig. 3.5 Fast idle adjustment diagram (Sec 12)

1   Control lever   4   Locknut
2   Throttle valve plate   X   Throttle valve plate gap
3   Fast idle screw

7   Obtain a repair kit for your particular carburettor. This will contain all the necessary gaskets, seals and other renewable items.
8   On a carburettor which has been in service for a long time, it will be worthwhile renewing the fuel inlet needle valve. To do this, very carefully tap out the float pivot pin (Weber) or release the spring clip and slide the float from its rod (Solex).
9   Withdraw the needle from the valve and then unscrew the valve body. Note the soft metal sealing washer.
10   Locate the new sealing washer and screw in the valve body. Tighten firmly but do not overdo it or the threads in the carburettor top cover will strip. On the other hand, if it is not tightened enough, fuel will leak past the sealing washer and bypass the needle and cause the carburettor to flood.
11   Refit the float and check the float setting. To do this, hold the top cover vertically on Weber carburettors so that the float arm just contacts the ball of the needle valve. With a flange gasket held in position, measure between the nearest point on the float and the

surface of the gasket. This should be between 10.5 and 11.0 mm (0.41 and 0.43 in). If it requires adjustment, bend the tab which bears on the needle valve.
12   On Solex carburettors, the float to flange dimension should be between 2.0 and 3.0 mm (0.079 to 0.118 in). If adjustment is required, do not bend the float, but alter the thickness of the sealing washer used under the fuel inlet valve.
13   Extract the screws from the accelerator pump cover and remove the cover. If the diaphragm is in anything but perfect condition, renew it.
14   The pump stroke can be adjusted if the locknut is released and the adjuster nut turned to give an ejection of between 4 and 5 cc of fuel for every ten strokes of the pump rod. Obviously the fuel bowl will have to be filled and a measuring glass required for this test.
15   Close the choke valve plate by pulling the control lever (1) (Fig. 3.5). The throttle valve plate should be open so that the gap (X) is between 0.75 and 0.80 mm (0.030 and 0.032 in). Measure with a wife of known diameter. If adjustment is required release the locknut (4) and turn the fast idle screw (3) (Fig. 3.5).
16   Once the carburettor is reassembled, refit it to the engine. Starting will take longer than usual unless the float bowl has been filled from an outside supply.
17   With the choke control fully out, start the engine. Check the fast idle speed. If necessary, this can be adjusted to the specified level by releasing the locknut and turning the fast idle screw.
18   Now run the engine to normal operating temperature and check the idle speed and mixture adjustment.

13   Accelerator pedal and linkage

1   The accelerator pedal is of pendant type which actuates the carburettor throttle lever using a cable.
2   The cable should be adjusted by means of the nuts at the end fitting at the carburettor. The adjustment should provide only the slightest amount of free movement. Check that with the accelerator pedal fully depressed, the throttle lever is fully back against its stop on the carburettor (valve plates fully open).
3   To remove the accelerator cable, fully release the cable adjustment and disconnect the cable from the throttle quadrant at the carburettor, a ball and socket type connector is used (photos).
4   Working under the instrument panel inside the car, unhook the cable from the fork at the top of the pedal arm (photo).
5   Release the bulkhead grommet and withdraw the cable.
6   Fitting the new cable is a reversal of removal. Adjust as described earlier in this Section.

13.3A Throttle cable end fitting

13.3B Throttle cable bracket clip

14.1 Choke cable at carburettor
1   Outer cable clamp   2   Inner cable trunnion swivel

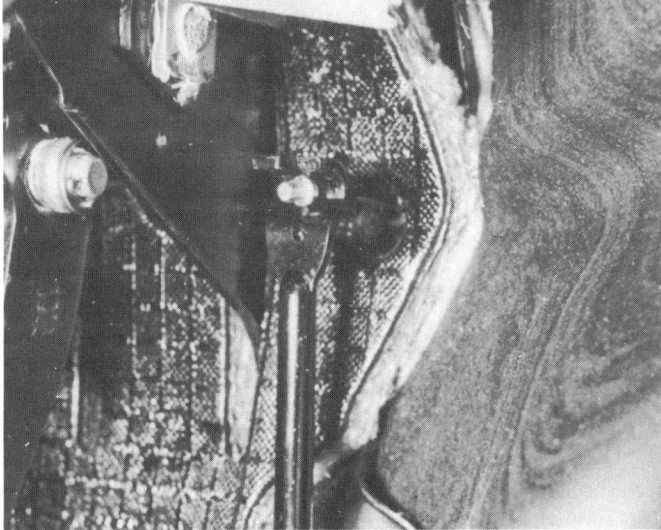

13.4 Accelerator pedal and cable end fitting

14 Choke control cable – adjustment and renewal

1   The choke cable is attached to the choke butterfly valve lever by means of a swivel trunnion. The outer conduit is clamped to a bracket (photo).

2   To set the cable correctly, release the pinch-bolt on the trunnion at the carburettor and make sure that the choke valve plate (strangler) is in the fully open position. Push the choke control fully in and then withdraw it about 3.0 or 4.0 mm. Tighten the trunnion pinch-bolt. This method of setting will ensure that with the control pushed fully in, the choke valve plate is fully open.
3   To renew the inner cable, release it from the carburettor and withdraw it into the car. Smear the new cable with grease before sliding it into the conduit.
4   The conduit can be removed if it is unclamped from the carburettor and released from the facia (claw type fitting).
5   Withdraw it through the bulkhead after releasing the sealing grommet.

15 Manifolds and exhaust system

1   The intake manifold is integral with the cylinder head, with a spacer fitted between the head and the carburettor.
2   Always use a new gasket on each side of the spacer.
3   The exhaust manifold is bolted to the side of the cylinder head and has a hot air collector attached to it from where the air cleaner draws air for the carburettor during low temperature operation (photos).
4   Always use a new gasket when fitting the exhaust manifold (photo).
5   The exhaust system is in separate sections incorporating front pipe and silencer assemblies.

15.3A Exhaust manifold hot air collector

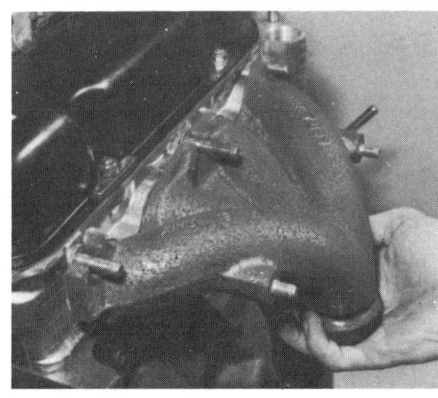

15.3B Exhaust manifold

15.4 Exhaust manifold gasket

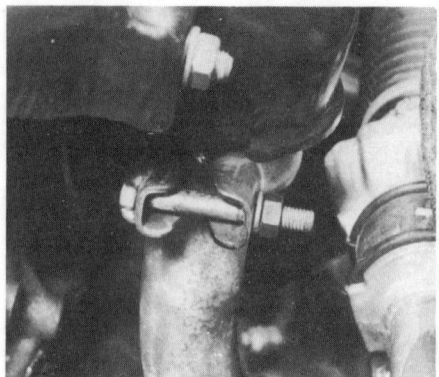

15.6A Exhaust downpipe connection from side

15.6B Exhaust flexible mounting

15.6C Exhaust flexible mounting

15.7A Exhaust downpipe clamp from underneath

15.7B Exhaust pipe clamp

6   If only one section of the system requires renewal, it is recommended that the complete exhaust is withdrawn from under the car to make separation easier. Do this by disconnecting the downpipe from the manifold and releasing the flexible mountings (photos).
7   When reassembling the system, do not tighten the clamps until the exhaust has been attached to the car. Once the pipe and silencer have been correctly aligned and they are not likely to knock against any adjacent suspension or body components, fully tighten the clamps (photos).

16 Fault diagnosis – fuel system

Unsatisfactory engine performance and excessive fuel consumption are not necessarily the fault of the fuel system or carburettor. In fact they more commonly occur as a result of ignition and timing faults. Before acting on the following it is necessary to check the ignition system first. Even though a fault may lie in the fuel system it will be difficult to trace unless the ignition is correct. The faults below, therefore, assume that this has been attended to first (where appropriate).

Symptom	Reason(s)
Smell of petrol when engine is stopped	Leaking fuel lines or unions Leaking fuel tank
Smell of petrol when engine is idling	Leaking fuel line unions between pump and carburettor Overflow of fuel from float chamber due to wrong level setting, ineffective needle valve or punctured float
Excessive fuel consumption for reasons not covered by leaks or float chamber faults	Worn jets Over-rich setting Sticking mechanism Dirty air cleaner element Sticking air cleaner thermostatic mechanism

Symptom	Reason(s)
Difficult starting, uneven running, lack of power, cutting out	One or more jets blocked or restricted Float chamber fuel level too low or needle valve sticking Fuel pump not delivering sufficient fuel Faulty solenoid fuel shut-off valve (if fitted) Induction leak
Difficult starting when cold	Choke control incorrectly set Insufficient use of manual choke Weak mixture
Difficult starting when hot	Excessive use of manual choke Accelerator pedal pumped before starting Vapour lock (especially in hot weather or at high altitude) Rich mixture
Engine does not respond properly to throttle	Faulty accelerator pump Blocked jet(s) Slack in accelerator cable
Engine idle speed drops when hot	Defective temperature compensator Overheated fuel pump
Engine runs on	Faulty fuel cut-off valve

Chapter 4 Ignition system

Contents

Condenser – testing and renewal 5
Contact breaker – points servicing 2
Distributor – overhaul 7
Distributor – removal and refitting 6
Dwell angle – checking 3

Fault diagnosis 10
General description 1
Ignition coil 8
Ignition timing 4
Spark plugs and high tension leads 9

Specifications

Type .... Battery, coil, mechanical breaker distributor

Firing order .... 1 – 3 – 4 – 2 (No 1 at timing end of engine)

Distribtuor
Make .... Marelli or Ducellier
Rotor rotational direction .... Clockwise
Contact breaker gap .... 0.37 to 0.43 mm (0.014 to 0.017 in)
Dwell angle .... 52 to 58°

Ignition timing
Static or with vacuum advance hose disconnected and engine idling at
specified speed .... 5° BTDC

Ignition advance
Centrifugal .... 30 to 34°
Vacuum .... 10 to 14°

Spark plugs
Type
    Marelli .... CW7 LPR
    Champion .... RN 9Y
    Bosch .... WR 7 D
Electrode gap .... 0.7 to 0.8 mm (0.029 to 0.031 in)

Ignition coil
Types
    Marelli .... BE 200 B
    Bosch .... K 12 V
    Pol-Mot .... BE 200 B
    O.E.M. .... G 52 S

Condenser capacity .... 0.225 to 0.275 mF

1 General description

For the engine to run correctly it is necessary for an electrical spark to ignite the fuel/air mixture in the combustion chamber at exactly the right moment in relation to engine speed and load. The ignition system is based on feeding low tension current to the coil where it is converted to high tension current. This high voltage is powerful enough to jump the spark plug gap in the cylinders under high pressures, providing that the system is in good condition and that all adjustments are correct.

The ignition system is divided into two circuits, the low tension circuit and the high tension circuit.

The low tension (sometimes known as the primary) circuit consists of the battery; lead to the control box; lead to the ignition switch; lead from the ignition switch to the low tension or primary coil windings, to the contact breaker points and condenser in the distributor.

Measuring plug gap. A feeler gauge of the correct size (see ignition system specifications) should have a slight 'drag' when slid between the electrodes. Adjust gap if necessary

Adjusting plug gap. The plug gap is adjusted by bending the earth electrode inwards, or outwards, as necessary until the correct clearance is obtained. Note the use of the correct tool

Normal. Grey-brown deposits, lightly coated core nose. Gap increasing by around 0.001 in (0.025 mm) per 1000 miles (1600 km). Plugs ideally suited to engine, and engine in good condition

Carbon fouling. Dry, black, sooty deposits. Will cause weak spark and eventually misfire. Fault: over-rich fuel mixture. Check: carburettor mixture settings, float level and jet sizes; choke operation and cleanliness of air filter. Plugs can be re-used after cleaning

Oil fouling. Wet, oily deposits. Will cause weak spark and eventually misfire. Fault: worn bores/piston rings or valve guides; sometimes occurs (temporarily) during running-in period. Plugs can be re-used after thorough cleaning

Overheating. Electrodes have glazed appearance, core nose very white – few deposits. Fault: plug overheating. Check: plug value, ignition timing, fuel octane rating (too low) and fuel mixture (too weak). Discard plugs and cure fault immediately

Electrode damage. Electrodes burned away; core nose has burned, glazed appearance. Fault: pre-ignition. Check: as for 'Overheating' but may be more severe. Discard plugs and remedy fault before piston or valve damage occurs

Split core nose (may appear initially as a crack). Damage is self-evident, but cracks will only show after cleaning. Fault: pre-ignition or wrong gap-setting technique. Check: ignition timing, cooling system, fuel octane rating (too low) and fuel mixture (too weak). Discard plugs, rectify fault immediately

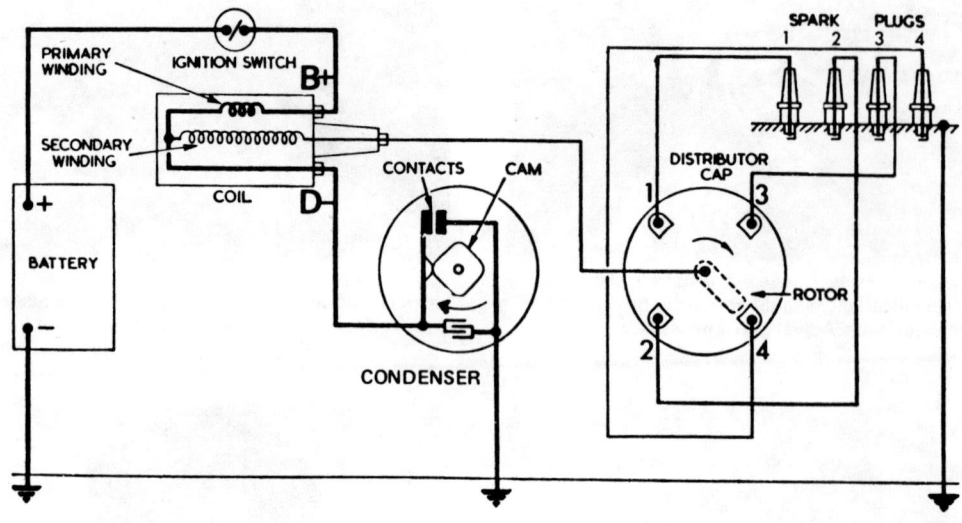

Fig. 4.1 Schematic diagram of ignition system (Sec 1)

The high tension circuit consists of the high tension or secondary coil windings, the heavy ignition lead from the centre of the coil to the centre of the distributor cap, the rotor arm, and the spark plug leads and spark plugs.

The system functions in the following manner. High tension voltage is generated in the coil by the interruption of the low tension circuit. The interruption is effected by the opening of the contact breaker points in this low tension circuit. High tension voltage is fed from the centre of the coil, via the carbon brush in the centre of the distributor cap, to the rotor arm of the distributor.

The rotor arm revolves at half engine speed inside the distributor cap, and each time it comes in line with one of the four metal segments in the cap, which are connected to the spark plug leads, the opening of the contact breaker points causes the high tension voltage to build up, jump the gap from the rotor arm to the appropriate metal segment, and so via the spark plug lead to the spark plug, where it finally jumps the spark plug gap before going to earth.

The ignition is advanced and retarded automatically, to ensure the spark occurs at just the right instant for the particular load at the prevailing engine speed.

The ignition advance is controlled mechanically and by vacuum. The mechanical governor mechanism consists of two weights, which move out from the distributor shaft as the engine speed rises, owing to centrifugal force. As they move outwards they rotate the cam relative to the distributor shaft, and so advance the spark. The weights are held in position by two springs and it is the tension of the springs which is largely responsible for correct spark advancement.

Vacuum control is by means of a diaphragm unit and hose to the carburettor venturi.

2 Contact breaker – points servicing

1   At the intervals specified in Routine Maintenance, check the condition of the contact breaker points.

2   Unclip and take off the distributor cap and place it to one side.

3   Remove the rotor, this may be of push-on type or held by two screws according to make of distributor.

4   With the thumb nail, prise back the movable contact arm and examine the faces of the points. If they are burnt, pitted or eroded, they must be removed and renewed. If they are in good condition then just clean them by drawing a fuel-moistened cloth between them.

Ducellier

5   To remove the points, first unscrew the terminal screw and remove it together with the washer under its head. Remove the low tension cable from the terminal, together with the condenser cable.

6   Unscrew and remove the contact breaker locking screw.

7   Lift away the contact breaker points.

Marelli

8   Remove the distributor cap, rotor and spark shield.

9   Disconnect the LT lead from the spade terminal inside the body (photo).

10 Extract the two screws and remove the vacuum unit by unhooking the connecting link (photo).

11 Extract the E-clip from the top of the distributor shaft, remove the shims (photos).

12 Remove the complete top bearing and contact points assembly to the bench.

13 Extract the circlip from the movable arm pivot post. Prise the arm upwards (photos).

14 Extract the circlip from the fixed arm post on the underside of the baseplate.

15 Unscrew the fixed arm Allen type adjuster screw and lift off the fixed arm (photo).

16 It is not recommended that the faces of the points are dressed smooth on an oil stone or abrasive paper as it is impossible to maintain the correct face contour. Obtain new points, clean their faces with methylated spirit, apply a drop of oil to the pivot and fit them.

2.9 LT lead and terminal

2.10 Removing distributor vacuum unit

2.11A Distributor shaft and contact arm pivot circlips

2.11B Removing distributor shaft shims

2.13A Distributor top bearing assembly

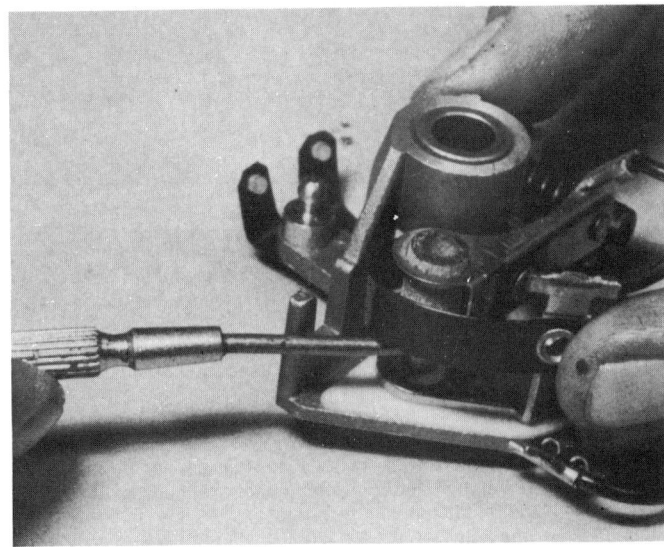

2.13B Removing moveable contact arm

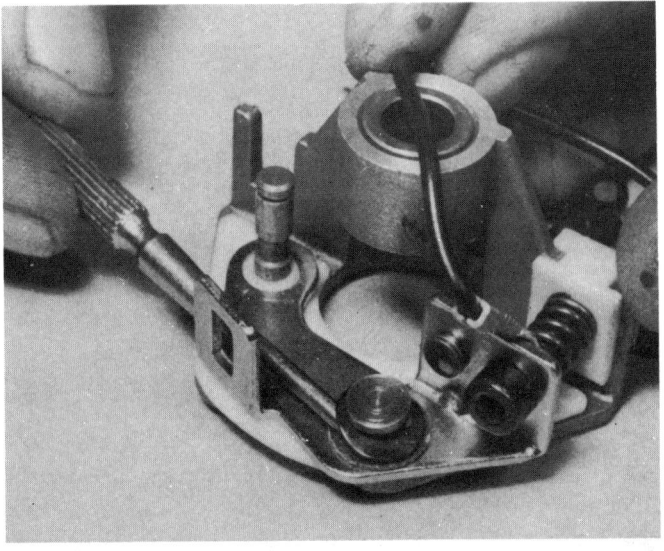

2.15 Fixed contact arm

17 Turn the crankshaft pulley nut until the rubbing block of the movable contact arm is on one of the high points of the distributor shaft cam.
18 Move the fixed arm until the points gap is as specified using a feeler blade. Tighten the arm fixing screw without altering the gap.
19 Check the contact end of the rotor arm. If this is eroded, renew it.
20 Check the distributor cap for cracks, or erosion of the interior contacts.
21 The carbon brush in the centre of the cap should be free to slide and not be too worn, otherwise renew the cap.
22 Fit the rotor and cap.
23 Check the dwell angle as described in the following Section.

3 Dwell angle – checking

1 On modern engines, setting the contact breaker gap in the distributor using feeler gauges must be regarded as a basic adjustment only. For optimum engine performance, the dwell angle must be checked. The dwell angle is the number of degrees through which the distributor cam turns during the period between the instance of closure and opening of the contact breaker points. Checking the dwell angle not only gives a more accurate setting of the contact breaker gap but also evens out any variations in the gap which could be caused by wear in the distributor shaft or its bushes, or difference in height of any of the cam peaks.
2 The angle should be checked with a dwell meter connected in accordance with the maker's instructions. Refer to the Specifications for the correct dwell angle. If the dwell angle is too large, increase the points gap, if too small, reduce the points gap.
3 The dwell angle should always be adjusted before checking and adjusting the ignition timing.
4 On Marelli distributors, the points gap is adjustable externally using an Allen key.

4 Ignition timing

1 At the intervals specified in Routine Maintenance, or if new contact points have been fitted, check the ignition timing in one of the following ways.
2 Remove the spare wheel and pull the rubber plug from the clutch bell housing.

Static method
3 Turn the crankshaft pulley nut or engage a gear, jack up the front of the car and turn a front roadwheel until the timing mark on the flywheel is aligned with the 5° BTDC mark on the edge of the bell housing aperture (photo).

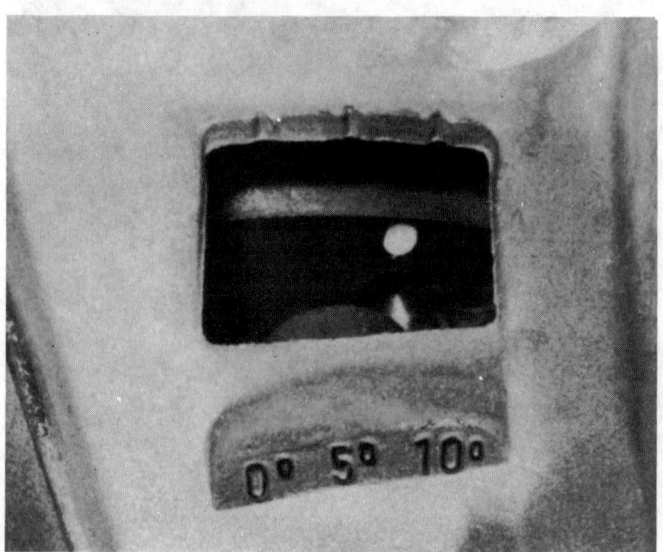

4.3 Flywheel timing mark and scale

4 Remove the distributor cap and check that the contact points are just about to open. If not, release the distributor clamp nut and turn the distributor until the desired position is obtained (photo).
5 A more accurate method of determining the point of opening is to connect a test bulb between the distributor LT terminal and earth. Switch on the ignition, release the distributor clamp plate nut and turn the distributor until the test bulb just goes out indicating that the points have just separated.
6 Switch off the ignition, fit the distributor cap and tighten the clamp plate nut.

Dynamic method
7 This should be regarded as the more accurate method, but will require the use of a stroboscope connected in accordance with the manufacturer's instructions. Disconnect the distributor vacuum hose.
8 The flywheel and bell housing timing marks may be highlighted with a dab of quick-drying white paint.
9 With the engine running at idle speed, point the stroboscope at the timing marks. They should appear stationary with the flywheel mark opposite the specified housing mark.
10 If the marks are not in alignment, release the distributor clamp plate nut and rotate the distributor until they align.
11 Tighten the clamp plate nut.
12 The correct functioning of the centrifugal advance mechanism may be checked if the engine speed is increased. Then the timing marks should move away from each other.
13 Having completed the adjustment of the ignition timing, replace the distributor vacuum hose and check the security of all ignition leads.

4.4 Distributor clamp plate and securing nut

5 Condenser – testing and renewal

1 The purpose of the condenser (sometimes known as capacitor) is to ensure that when the contact breaker points open there is no sparking across them which would weaken the spark and cause rapid deterioration of the points.
2 The condenser is fitted in parallel with the contact breaker points. If it develops a short circuit, it will cause ignition failure as the points will be prevented from interrupting the low tension circuit.
3 If the engine becomes very difficult to start or begins to misfire whilst running and the breaker points show signs of excessive burning, then suspect the condenser has failed. A further test can be made by separating the points by hand with the ignition switched on. If this is accompanied by a bright spark at the contact points it is indicative that the condenser has failed.
4 Without special test equipment the only sure way to diagnose condenser trouble is to replace a suspected unit with a new one and note if there is any improvement.

Chapter 4 Ignition system

5   To remove the condenser from the distributor, release the screw which secures it to the distributor body (Marelli) or baseplate (Ducellier). Release the condenser lead from the LT terminal (photo).
6   When fitting the condenser it is vital to ensure that the fixing screw is secure and the condenser tightly held. The lead must be secure on the terminal with no chance of short circuiting.

6.10 Fitting distributor

5.5 Condenser

6   Distributor – removal and refitting

1   The distributor driveshaft is driven from the upper end of the oil pump driveshaft which is geared to the camshaft.
2   Turn the crankshaft (by means of the pulley nut or by engaging a gear, raising a front roadwheel and turning the wheel) until number one position is at TDC on the compression stroke. This can be established by removing No 1 spark plug and placing the finger over the hole and feeling the compression being generated. This can also be determined by aligning the timing marks and removing the distributor cap and checking that the rotor contact end is pointing at number one spark plug contact in the distributor cap. If it is pointing at number four, turn the crankshaft one revolution.
3   Mark the alignment of the contact end of the rotor with the distributor body and the setting of the distributor pedestal in relation to the cylinder head.
4   Unscrew the clamp plate nut.
5   Disconnect the distributor cap and lay it to one side complete with the HT leads. Disconnect the LT lead.
6   Pull the distributor up and out of the cylinder head.
7   If the oil pump driveshaft is displaced, simply push it back into position. It has no set position. The oil pump driveshaft can be removed if necessary by pushing a tapered piece of soft wood into the hole in the gear and pulling the shaft out.
8   Before the distributor can be refitted, No. 1 piston must be set to TDC on the compression stroke as described in the first part of paragraph 2.
9   Hold the distributor over its mounting hole with the pedestal mark aligned with the one on the cylinder head, and the contact end of the rotor opposite the one made on the distributor body rim.
10 Push the distributor into position. The rotor may need a very slight turn to engage the shaft splines as the distributor is pushed downwards (photo).
11 Align the distributor mounting pedestal to cylinder head marks and fit the clamp plate nut.
12 Reconnect the LT lead and fit the distributor cap and clip it with the retaining springs.
13 Start the engine and check the ignition timing as described in Section 4.

7   Distributor – overhaul

1   Apart from the contact points the other parts of a distributor which deteriorate with age and use, are the cap and the rotor.
2   The cap must have no flaws or cracks and the four HT terminal contacts should not be severely corroded. The centre spring-loaded carbon contact is replaceable. If in any doubt about the cap buy a new one.
3   The rotor deteriorates minimally but with age the metal conductor may corrode. It should not be cracked or chipped and the metal conductor must not be loose. If in doubt renew it. Always fit a new rotor if fitting a new cap. Assuming the cover and rotor have been removed, proceed with dismantling as follows:
4   Release the low tension and condenser cables from the terminal on the contact set, then remove the contact set by releasing the retaining screws.
5   If it is necessary to remove the centre shaft from the distributor body, use a small parallel pin punch to drive out the pin securing the collar to the bottom of the centre shaft. Recover the washer from under the collar and slide out the centre shaft.
6   Check the contact breaker points as described in Section 2.
7   Examine the balance weights and pivot pins for wear (photo). Also examine the shaft and bushes.

7.7 Distributor counterweights and springs

8   If these components are worn, it will normally be more economical to renew the complete distributor.

9   Reassembly is a straightforward reversal of the dismantling process, but there are several points which should be noted.

10   Lubricate the balance weights and other parts of the mechanical advance mechanism, and the distributor centre shaft, with engine oil during assembly. Do not oil excessively but ensure these parts are adequately lubricated.

11   Check the action of the weights in the fully advanced and fully retarded positions and ensure they are not binding.

12   Finally, set the contact breaker gap to the correct clearance (refer to Section 2).

8   Ignition coil

1   Coils normally last the life of the car. The most usual reason for a coil to fail is after being left with the ignition switched on but the engine not running. There is then constant current flowing, instead of the intermittent flow when the contact breaker is opening. The coil then overheats, and the insulation is damaged (photo).

2   The contact breaker points should preferably not be flicked without a lead from the coil centre to some earth, otherwise the opening of the points will give a HT spark which, finding no proper circuit, could break down the insulation in the coil. When connecting a timing light for setting the ignition, this should come from the switch side of the coil, the coil itself being disconnected.

3   Unless an ohmmeter is available, testing the coil should be left to your dealer or auto electrician, or by substitution of a new coil.

8.1 Coil location

9   Spark plugs and high tension leads

1   Correctly functioning spark plugs are essential for efficient engine operation.

2   At the intervals specified in Routine Maintenance, the plugs should be removed, cleaned and re-gapped.

3   To remove the plugs, open the bonnet and pull the HT leads from them. Grip the rubber end fitting, not the lead, otherwise the connection to the cable end fitting may fracture.

4   Brush out any accumulated dirt or grit from the spark plug recesses in the cylinder head otherwise it may drop into the combustion chamber when the plug is removed.

5   Unscrew the spark plugs with a deep socket or box spanner. Do not allow the tool to tilt otherwise the ceramic insulator may be cracked or broken.

6   Examination of the spark plugs will give a good indication of the condition of the engine.

7   If the insulator nose of the spark plug is clean and white with no deposits, this is indicative of a weak mixture, or too hot a plug (a hot plug transfers heat away from the electrode slowly, a cold plug transfers heat away quickly).

8   The plugs fitted as standard are specified at the beginning of this Chapter. If the tip and insulator nose are covered with hard black looking deposits, then this is indicative that the mixture is too rich. Should the plug be black and oily, then it is likely that the engine is fairly worn, as well as the mixture being too rich.

9   If the insulator nose is covered with light tan to greyish brown deposits, then the mixture is correct and it is likely that the engine is in good condition.

10   If there are any traces of long brown tapering stains on the outside of the white portion of the plug, then the plug will have to be renewed. These stains show that there is a faulty joint between the plug body and the insulator and compression is being allowed to leak away.

11   Before cleaning a spark plug, wash it in fuel to remove oily deposits.

12   Although a wire brush can be used to clean the electrode end of the spark plug, this method of cleaning can cause metal conductance paths across the nose of the insulator and it is therefore to be preferred that an abrasive powder type cleaning machine is used. Such machines are available quite cheaply from motor accessory stores or you may prefer to take the plugs to your dealer who will not only be able to clean them, but also to check the sparking efficiency of each plug under compression.

13   The spark plug gap is of considerable importance as, if it is too large or too small, the size of the spark and its efficiency will be seriously impaired.

14   For the best results, the spark plug gap should be set in accordance with the Specifications at the beginning of this Chapter.

15   To measure the gap, use a feeler gauge and then open or close the gap as necessary by bending the outer electrode. Special plug gapping and electrode bending tools are available for the purpose. *Never* bend the centre electrode or the ceramic insulator will crack.

16   Before refitting the spark plugs, wash each one again thoroughly using clean fuel in order to remove all trace of abrasive powder and then apply a smear of grease to the plug threads.

17   Screw each plug in by hand. This will ensure that there is no chance of cross-threading.

18   Tighten the plugs to the specified torque. If a torque wrench is not available, just lightly tighten each plug. It is better to under-tighten rather than strip the threads from the light alloy cylinder head.

19   When reconnecting the spark plug leads make sure that they are refitted in their correct order 1 – 3 – 4 – 2 (No. 1 being at the timing end).

20   The spark plug leads require no routine attention other than being kept clean by wiping them regularly.

21   In order to minimise corrosion, in the distributor cap lead sockets, smear the HT cable end fittings with a light coating of petroleum jelly.

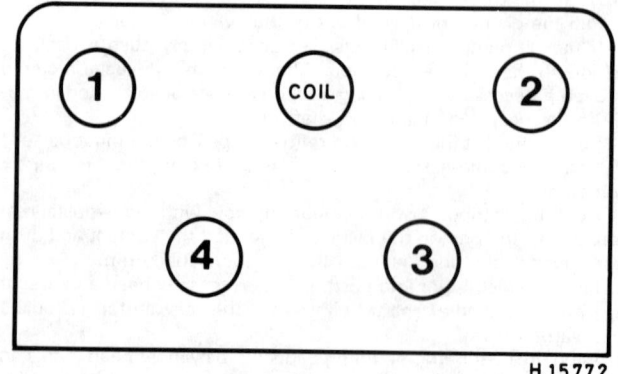

H.15772

Fig. 4.2 Distributor cap lead connections viewed from oil filler cap (Sec 9)

10 Fault diagnosis – ignition system

Symptom	Reason(s)
Engine fails to start	Loose battery connections
	Discharged battery
	Oil on contact points
	Disconnected ignition leads
	Faulty condenser
Engine starts and runs but misfires	Faulty spark plug
	Cracked distributor cap
	Cracked rotor arm
	Worn advance mechanism
	Incorrect spark plug gap
	Incorrect contact points gap
	Faulty condenser
	Faulty coil
	Incorrect timing
	Poor engine/transmission earth connections
Engine overheats, lacks power	Seized distributor weights
	Incorrect ignition timing

Chapter 5 Clutch

Contents

Clutch – adjustment 2
Clutch – inspection 6
Clutch – refitting 8
Clutch – removal 5
Clutch cable – renewal 3

Clutch pedal – removal and refitting 4
Clutch release mechanism 7
Fault diagnosis – clutch 9
General description 1

Specifications

Type .... Single dry plate, diaphragm spring, cable actuation

Driven plate diameter .... 170.0 mm (6.69 in)

Release bearing type .... Sealed ball

Torque wrench settings	**Nm**	**lbf ft**
Clutch cover to flywheel	15	11
Release fork lockbolt	27	20

1 General description

The vehicle is fitted with a single dry plate diaphragm clutch. The unit consists of a steel cover which is dowelled and bolted to the face of the flywheel and contains the pressure plate, pressure plate diaphragm spring and fulcrum rings.

The clutch disc is free to slide along the splined gearbox input shaft and is held in position between the flywheel and the pressure plate by the pressure of the pressure plate spring. Friction lining material is riveted to the clutch disc and it has a spring cushioned hub to absorb transmission shocks.

The circular diaphragm spring is mounted on shouldered pins and held in place in the cover by two fulcrum rings and rivets.

The clutch is actuated by cable.

Unlike in-line engines and gearboxes, the shaft through the clutch into the gearbox does not have a spigot bearing in the end of the crankshaft.

2 Clutch – adjustment

1 At the cable connection to the clutch release lever at the bellhousing is the cable adjuster nut.
2 The nut should be turned until the clutch pedal is level with the brake pedal. The clutch is now correctly adjusted. The release bearing is of the type which is in constant contact with the fingers of the diaphragm spring.

3 Clutch cable – renewal

1 Working within the engine compartment, unscrew the cable

3.1 Clutch cable at transmission

adjuster nut and disconnect the cable from the clutch release lever. Release the cable from the bracket (photo).
2 Working within the car, disconnect the clutch cable from the pedal arm. Do this by extracting the clip and pulling the cable end fitting off its pivot pin.

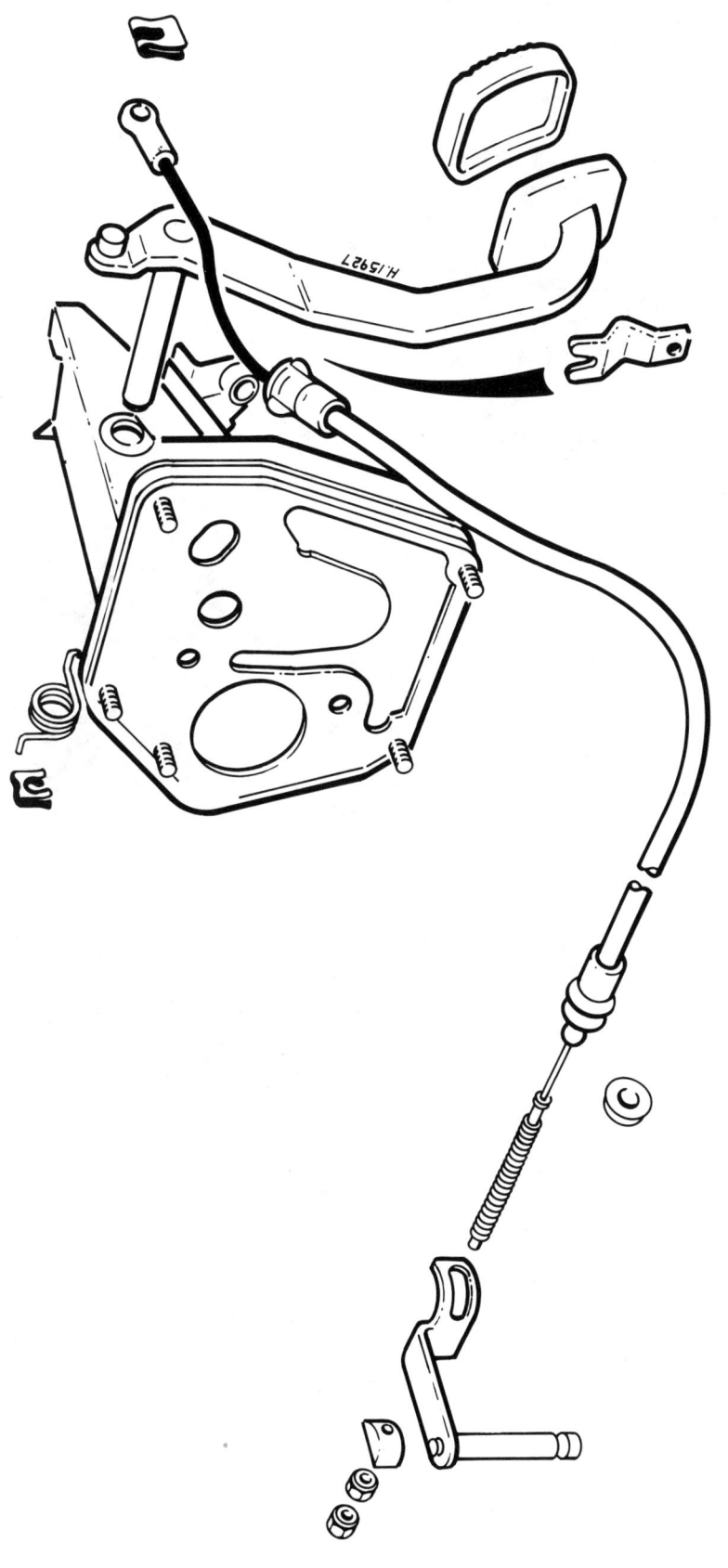

H.15927

Fig. 5.1 Clutch cable and pedal components (Sec 3)

3.3 Clutch cable retaining fork at bulkhead

3   Release the cable retainer from the bulkhead by unbolting the forked type plate (photo).
4   Withdraw the cable into the car interior.
5   Refit the new cable by reversing the removal operations.
6   Adjust the cable as described in Section 2.

4   Clutch pedal – removal and refitting

1   Working inside the car, disconnect the clutch cable from the pedal by prising off the spring clip and sliding the cable end fitting off the pivot pin.
2   From the end of the pedal cross-shaft, remove the spring clip and withdraw the pedal/shaft assembly. Note the torsion spring which is located on the cross-shaft and the location of the spring ends.
3   Refitting is a reversal of removal, smear the cross-shaft with grease before fitting.

5   Clutch – removal

1   Access to the clutch is obtained after removing the transmission as described in Chapter 6.
2   The need for clutch renewal is usually indicated by slipping becoming evident when climbing a gradient and increasing the engine speed does not bring about a corresponding increase in road speed.
3   Unscrew the clutch cover bolts a turn at a time until the pressure of the diaphragm spring is relieved, then remove the bolts.
4   Remove the cover from its flywheel dowels and catch the driven plate (friction disc) as it drops out.

6   Clutch – inspection

1   Examine the diaphragm spring for cracks and wear steps on the ends of the spring fingers due to rubbing of the release bearing. If these problems are evident renew the cover. Even if the cover assembly appears to be in good condition, but has been in service for a high mileage it is recommended that it is renewed.
2   If the friction linings on the driven plate have worn down to, or nearly down to, the rivet heads, renew the plate.
3   Any evidence of oil staining or contamination of the inside of the bellhousing will indicate a leaking oil seal either from the rear end of the crankshaft or from the front end (input shaft) of the gearbox. This must be rectified immediately.

4   Do not attempt to re-line the driven plate or dismantle the pressure plate cover, but purchase new components.
5   Check the surface of the flywheel as described in Chapter 1, Section 20.
6   Check the clutch release mechanism as described in the next Section.

7   Clutch release mechanism

1   Whenever work is being carried out on the clutch, always check the release mechanism and bearing. If the clutch has covered a high mileage, it will be worthwhile renewing the release bearing at the same time as the clutch (photo).

7.1 Clutch release bearing and fork

2   The release lever return spring should be unhooked and the release bearing unclipped from the release fork.
3   If the bearing is noisy when spun with the fingers, renew it.
4   Any shake in the release fork pivot shaft can only be rectified by renewing the shaft bushes.
5   The release bearing is of sealed type and lubricated for life. Never attempt to clean it by immersing it in solvent.

8   Clutch – refitting

1   Clean the flywheel and pressure plate faces free from dirt, oil or protective grease.
2   Place the driven plate against the flywheel so that the greater projecting hub is furthest from the flywheel (photo).
3   Locate the pressure plate cover on the flywheel dowels and screw in the retaining bolts finger tight.
4   The driven plate must now be centralised in order that the clutch (input) shaft will pass though its hub when the transmission is offered to the engine. As the nose of the input shaft does not run in a bearing or bush in the crankshaft rear flange, the normal alignment tool cannot be used. Instead, centralise the driven plate hub within the tips of the diaphragm spring fingers by eye or by cutting a paper disc to fit within the tips of the fingers and having a hole, at its centre, of the same diameter as the driven plate hub.
5   Adjust the position of the driven plate by sliding it up or down or sideways until it is aligned centrally.
6   Tighten the cover bolts evenly and progressively to the specified torque (photo).
7   Apply a smear of grease to the release bearing guide sleeve and the input shaft splines within the bellhousing.
8   Fit the transmission as described in Chapter 6.

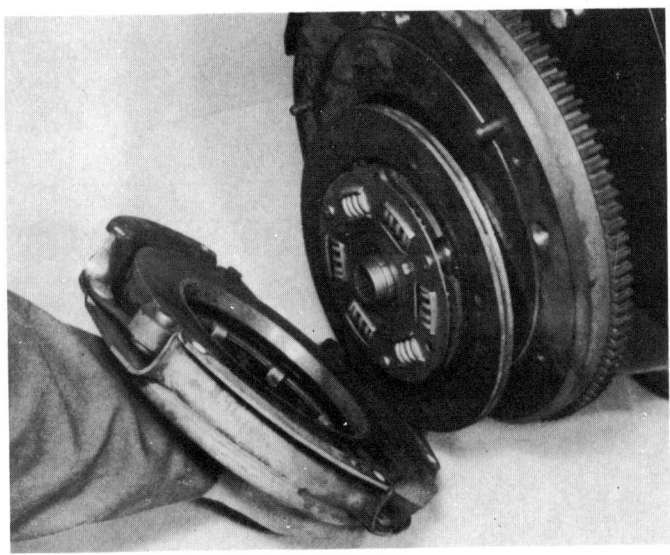

8.2 Clutch driven plate and pressure plate cover

8.6 Tightening a clutch cover bolt

9 Fault diagnosis – clutch

Symptom	Reason(s)
Judder when taking up drive	Loose engine or gearbox mountings Badly worn friction linings or contaminated with oil Worn splines on gearbox input shaft or driven plate hub
*Clutch spin (failure to disengage) so that gears cannot be meshed	Incorrect release bearing to pressure plate clearance Rust on splines (may occur after vehicle standing idle for long periods) Damaged or misaligned pressure plate assembly Cable stretched or broken
Clutch slip (increase in engine speed does not result in increase in vehicle road speed – particularly on gradients)	Incorrect release bearing to pressure plate finger clearance Friction linings worn out or oil contaminated
Noise evident on depressing clutch pedal	Dry, worn or damaged release bearing Incorrect pedal adjustment Weak or broken pedal return spring Excessive play between driven plate hub splines and input shaft splines
Noise evident as clutch pedal released	Distorted driven plate Broken or weak driven plate cushion coil springs Incorrect pedal adjustment Weak or broken clutch pedal return spring Distorted or worn input shaft Release bearing loose on retainer hub

*This condition may also be due to the driven plate being rusted to the flywheel or pressure plate. It is possible to free it by applying the handbrake, engaging top gear and operating the starter motor. If really badly corroded, then the engine will not turn over, but in the majority of cases the driven plate will free. Once the engine starts, rev it up and slip the clutch several times to clear the rust deposits.

Chapter 6 Transmission

Contents

Differential – overhaul 8
Fault diagnosis – transmission 10
Gearchange lever and linkage – removal, refitting and
adjustment 3
General description 1
Inspection of components 6
Maintenance 2
Shaft geartrains – overhaul 7
Transmission – reassembly 9
Transmission – removal and refitting 4
Transmission – removal of main assemblies 5

Specifications

Type

Comfort	Four forward speeds and reverse
Super	Five forward speeds and reverse

Ratios

1st	3.909 : 1
2nd	2.055 : 1
3rd	1.342 : 1
4th	0.964 : 1
5th	0.723 : 1
Reverse	3.615 : 1
Final drive	5.455 : 1

Oil capacity .... 2.36 litres (4.15 Imp pints)

Torque wrench settings

	Nm	lbf ft
Selector fork lock bolts	18	13
Crownwheel bolts	69	51
Gearshaft nuts (main and secondary shaft)	122	90
Flywheel housing to engine bolts	80	59
Flywheel housing to gearcase bolts	45	33
Driveshaft inboard gaiter flange bolts	1.0	0.7
Final drive tapered roller bearing cap bolts	25	18

1 General description

The transmission (gearbox and final drive) is mounted in line with the engine.

Four speeds and reverse are provided on the Comfort and five speeds and reverse on the Super.

Synchromesh is provided on all forward speeds. On 1st and 2nd it is of baulk ring type, while on 3rd, 4th and 5th it is of Porsche spring segment type.

The gearchange lever is floor-mounted, operating through rod linkage.

2 Maintenance

1 At the intervals specified in Routine Maintenance and with the transmission cold and the car standing on level ground, unscrew and remove the oil filler/level plug. If oil just starts to dribble out then the

oil level is correct. If it does not, add oil of the correct grade to bring it up to level. Refit the plug (photo).

2   At the intervals specified in Routine Maintenance drain the transmission oil hot by removing the filler/level plug and the drain plug. When the oil has ceased dripping, refit the drain plug and refill the transmission with the correct grade and quantity of oil. Screw in and tighten the filler/level plug.

3   Gearchange lever and linkage – removal, refitting and adjustment

1   Access to the gearchange lever ball cup, spring and clamp may be obtained by sliding the bellows up the lever.
2   The connecting pivot pin can be removed after the cover has been removed from the underside of the lever beneath the car.
3   On some models, the gearchange linkage incorporates two adjustable rods. Set the linkage in the following way.
4   Position the gearchange lower relay lever parallel to the plane of the relay lever support.
5   Set the gearchange shaft lever in neutral.
6   Release the locknut and alter the length of the adjustable rod (A) until the external control lever connects with the upper relay lever.
7   Place the gearchange lever in neutral.
8   Release the locknut and alter the length of the adjustable rod (B) until the external control lever connects with the gear control rod.

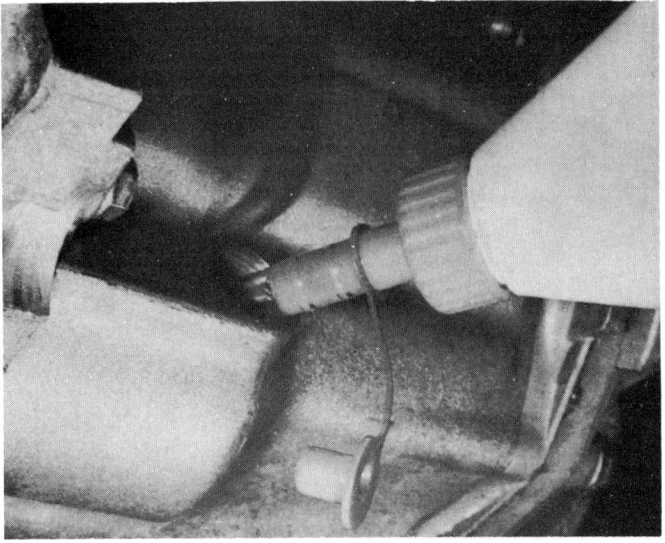

2.1 Topping up transmission oil

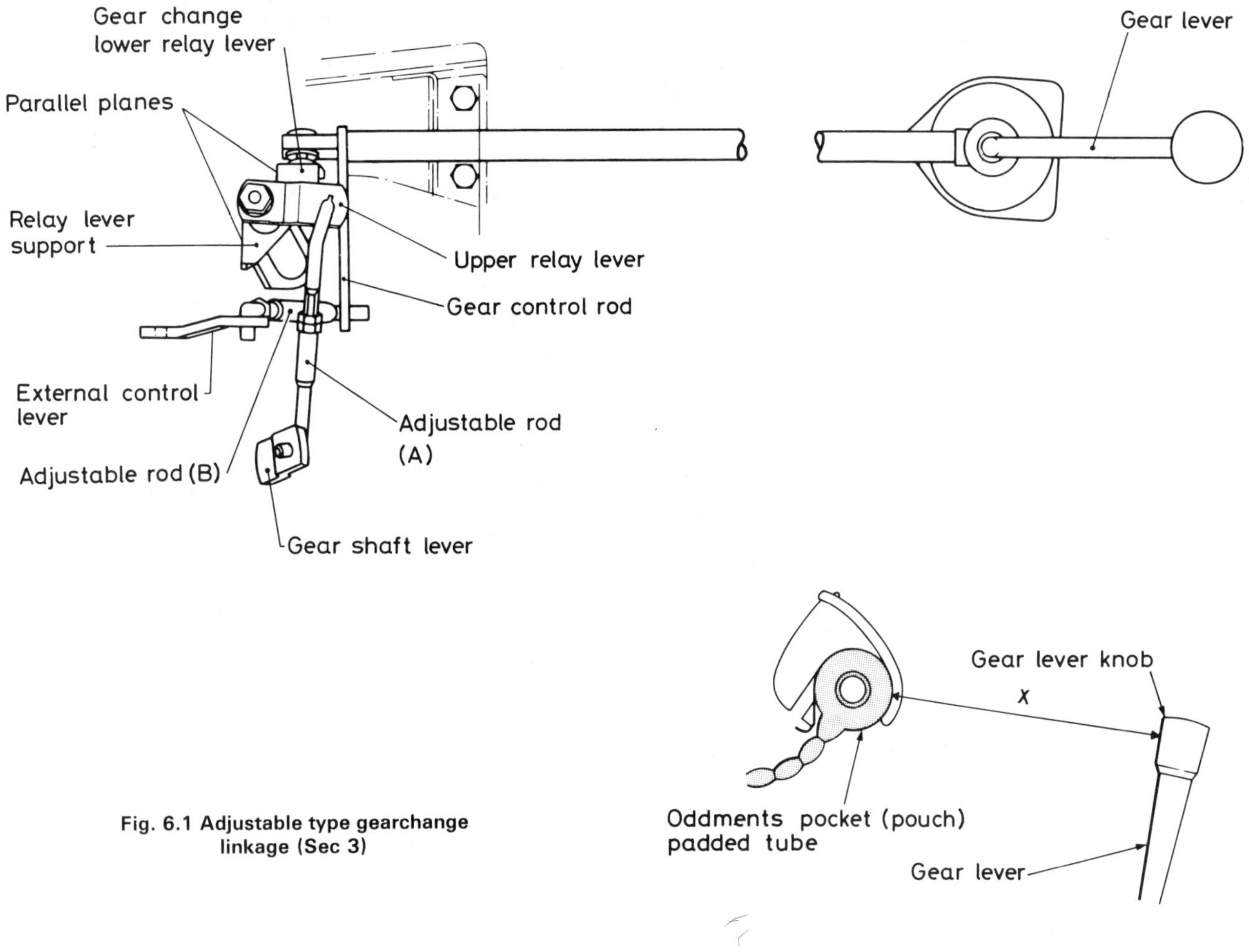

Fig. 6.1 Adjustable type gearchange
linkage (Sec 3)

Gear change lower relay lever
Parallel planes
Relay lever support
Upper relay lever
Gear control rod
External control lever
Adjustable rod (B)
Adjustable rod (A)
Gear shaft lever
Gear lever

Gear lever knob
X
Oddments pocket (pouch) padded tube
Gear lever

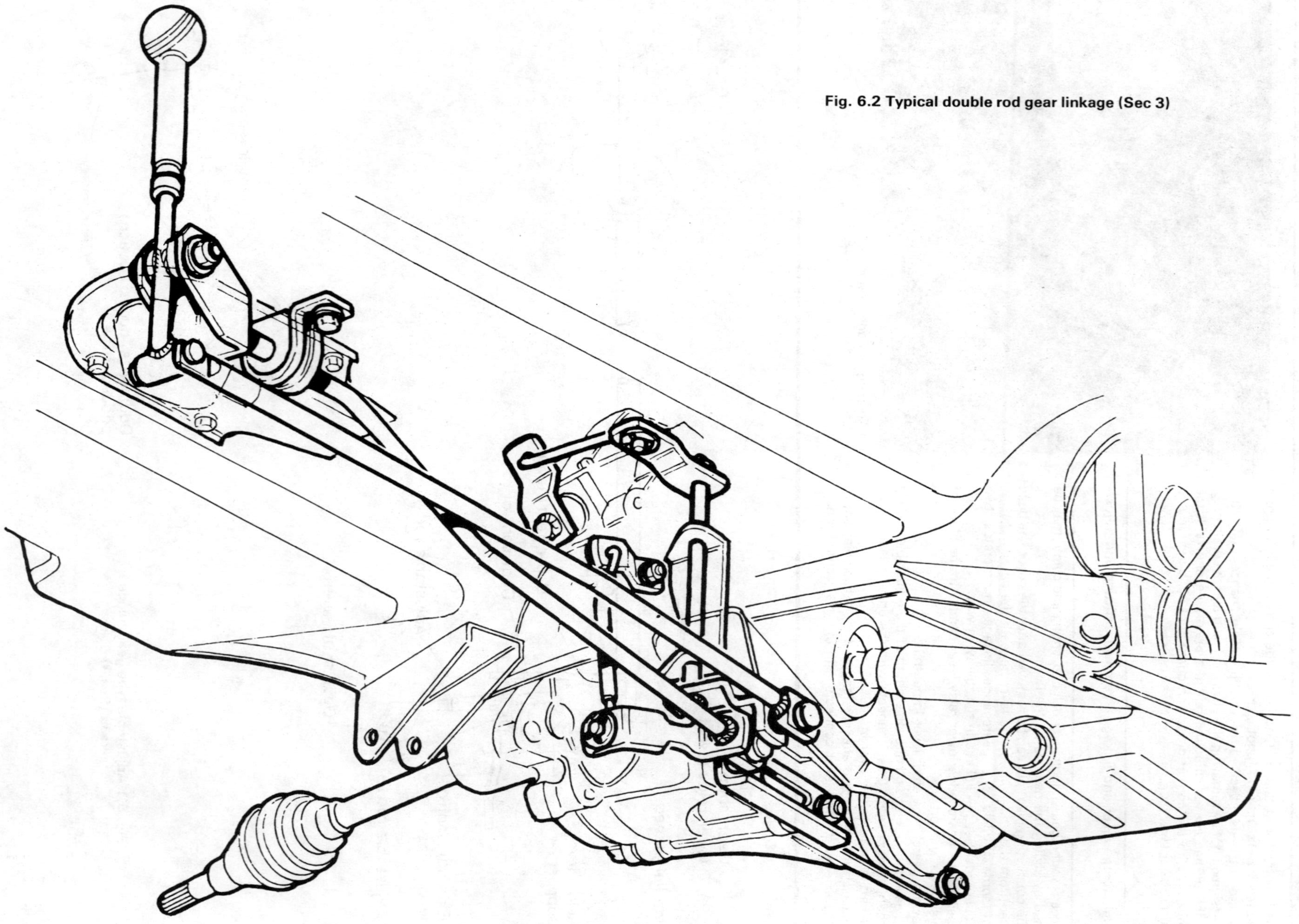

Fig. 6.2 Typical double rod gear linkage (Sec 3)

9 Working inside the car, check that the distance (X) from the gear lever knob to the padded tube of the front parcels shelf is between 170.0 and 200.0 mm (6.7 and 7.9 in).

10 On other models, the linkage is of single or double rod welded type without provision for adjustment (photos).

3.10A Welded type gearchange link rods

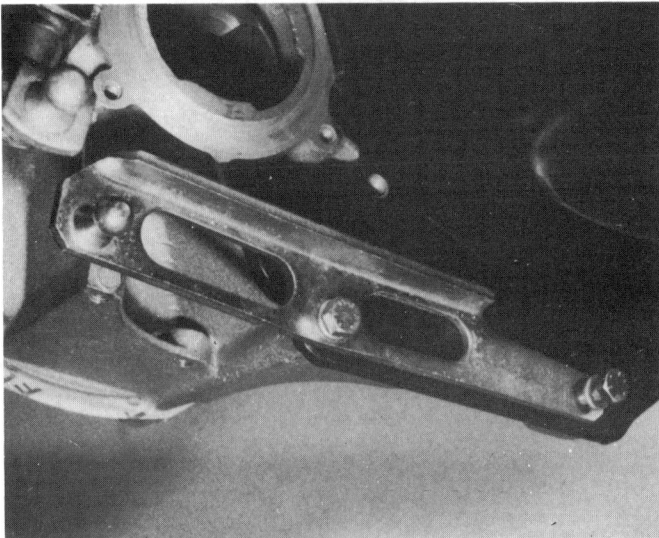

3.10B Gearchange rod ball stud support

4.6 Transmission lower mounting arm. Bolt locktab arrowed

8 Disconnect the leads and unbolt and remove the starter motor.

9 Raise the front of the car, support securely and remove the front roadwheels.

10 Unbolt the brake calipers and tie them up out of the way.

11 Using a balljoint splitter tool, disconnect the tie-rod ends from the steering arms. Also disconnect the suspension lower track control arm balljoints from the hub carriers. Disconnect the radius rods from the control arms.

12 Unbolt and remove the cover plate from the base of the flywheel housing. One bolt is very high up by the driveshaft opening.

13 Disconnect the clutch operating cable from the release lever on the transmission.

14 Unscrew the bolts which hold the gaiter retainers to the transmission at the inboard ends of the driveshafts. Even though the transmission has been drained, be prepared for some loss of oil.

15 Disconnect the brake flexible hoses from their suspension strut retainers. Then pull the hub carriers outwards within the flexibility of the strut top mountings until the driveshafts drop out of the transmission. Have an assistant support the driveshafts from impact on the floor.

16 Be prepared for some loss of oil.

17 Support the weight of the engine on a jack or with a hoist.

18 Unscrew the flywheel housing to engine connecting bolts.

19 Place a trolley jack under the transmission and disconnect the transmission top mounting.

4 Transmission – removal and refitting

1 This Section describes removal of the transmission leaving the engine in the car. Removal together with the engine for later separation is described in Chapter 1.

2 Drain the transmission oil.

3 Open the bonnet. Remove the spare wheel.

4 Disconnect the speedometer drive and the leads from the reversing lamp switch on the transmission.

5 Disconnect the gearchange linkage. Do this by prising off the link rod ball ends and spring clip noting the fitted sequence of the bushes.

6 Still working under the car, unbolt the bottom mounting arm from the transmission and exhaust pipe. Bend back the lock tabs and unbolt the flexible mounting (photo).

7 Disconnect the exhaust downpipe from the manifold.

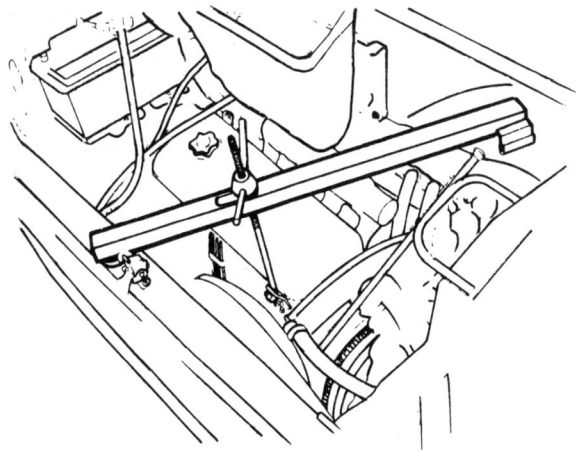

Fig. 6.3 Tool for supporting engine (Sec 4)

20 The transmission is now ready for removal, check that everything has been disconnected.

21 Working within the engine compartment and with an assistant gently lowering the transmission jack, pull the transmission from the engine and lower it to the floor.

22 Refitting is a reversal of removal, but if the clutch has been disturbed, make sure that it has been centralised as described in Chapter 5.

23 Check the clutch adjustment, refill the transmission with oil, apply the footbrake two or three times to bring the pads up against the discs.

24 Use self-locking grips to connect the gear link rod balls and sockets (photo).

4.24 Using grips to connect gearchange link rods

5 Transmission – removal of main assemblies

1 With the transmission removed, clean away external dirt and grease using paraffin and a stiff brush or a water-soluble solvent.

2 Remove the clutch release bearing from the bellhousing.

3 Disconnect the gearchange selector link rod.

4 Unscrew the bolts which connect the bellhousing and gearcase. Note that one bolt is inside the bellhousing.

5 Unbolt the detent spring plate and extract the springs and balls. The blue painted spring is at the reverse lamp switch end.

6 Stand the gearbox upright on the bellhousing flange.

7 Unbolt the rear cover to expose the 5th speed gears and synchromesh (five-speed) or shaft circlips (four-speed).

8 Unbolt the pressed steel cover to expose the gear bias springs.

9 Unscrew the nut and withdraw the gear engagement lever from the reverse spring cap. Note the master spline so that the lever can only be fitted in one position. Note also that the closer coiled spring is on the right-hand side.

10 Unbolt the gear selector lever from its dog. It will only go in one position as the shaft has a square shank.

11 Using an Allen key, extract the lock screw and pull out the speedometer driven gear.

12 Unscrew and remove the reverse lamp switch.

Four-speed units

13 On four-speed units, extract the circlips from the ends of the shafts.

Five-speed units

14 On five-speed units, lock two gears simultaneously by moving the selector dogs with a screwdriver inserted through the bias spring aperture.

15 Relieve the staking on the shaft nuts and unscrew them (normal RH thread).

16 Unscrew the 5th speed selector fork lock bolt.

17 From the mainshaft pull off 5th speed gear, the synchromesh unit selector fork and gear bush.

18 Pull 5th speed gear from the secondary shaft.

All units

19 Pull the gearcase upwards and at the same time have an assistant tap the ends of the shafts downwards with a plastic or copper-faced hammer which will release the bearings and allow the casing to be removed.

20 Unbolt the reverse idler lockplate and draw out the reverse idler gear and shaft, reverse selector shaft and fork or 5th/reverse selector shaft as applicable.

21 Unscrew the selector fork lock bolts and withdraw 1st/2nd and 3rd/4th selector shafts. Remove the selector forks.

22 Note that the 1st/2nd selector fork is closest to the bellhousing. Note also that the three adjacent shaft notches are furthest from the bellhousing (photo).

23 Retrieve the large interlock plungers from the casing passages and the smaller one from its hole in the 3rd/4th selector shaft.

24 Withdraw both shaft/geartrains simultaneously, meshed together.

25 Lift out the final drive/differential.

26 Remove the small magnet from the casing.

27 If necessary, remove the bearings from the casing, using a puller or tubular drift.

28 If necessary, the differential flanges can be unbolted (photo).

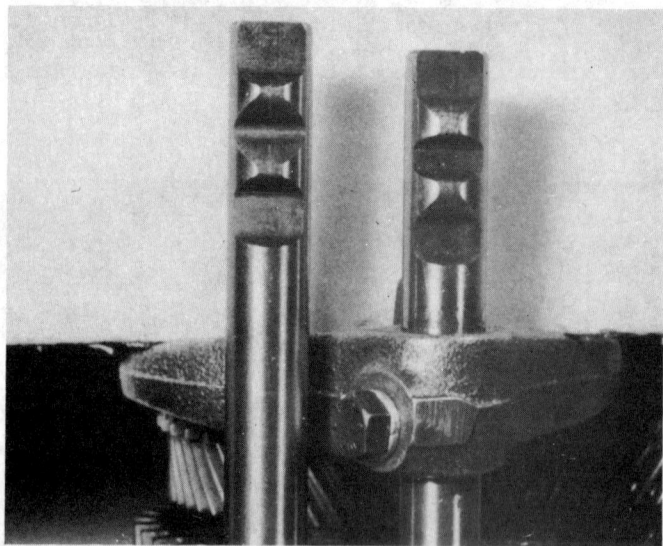

5.22 Selector shaft notches and 3rd/4th selector fork

5.28 Differential flange

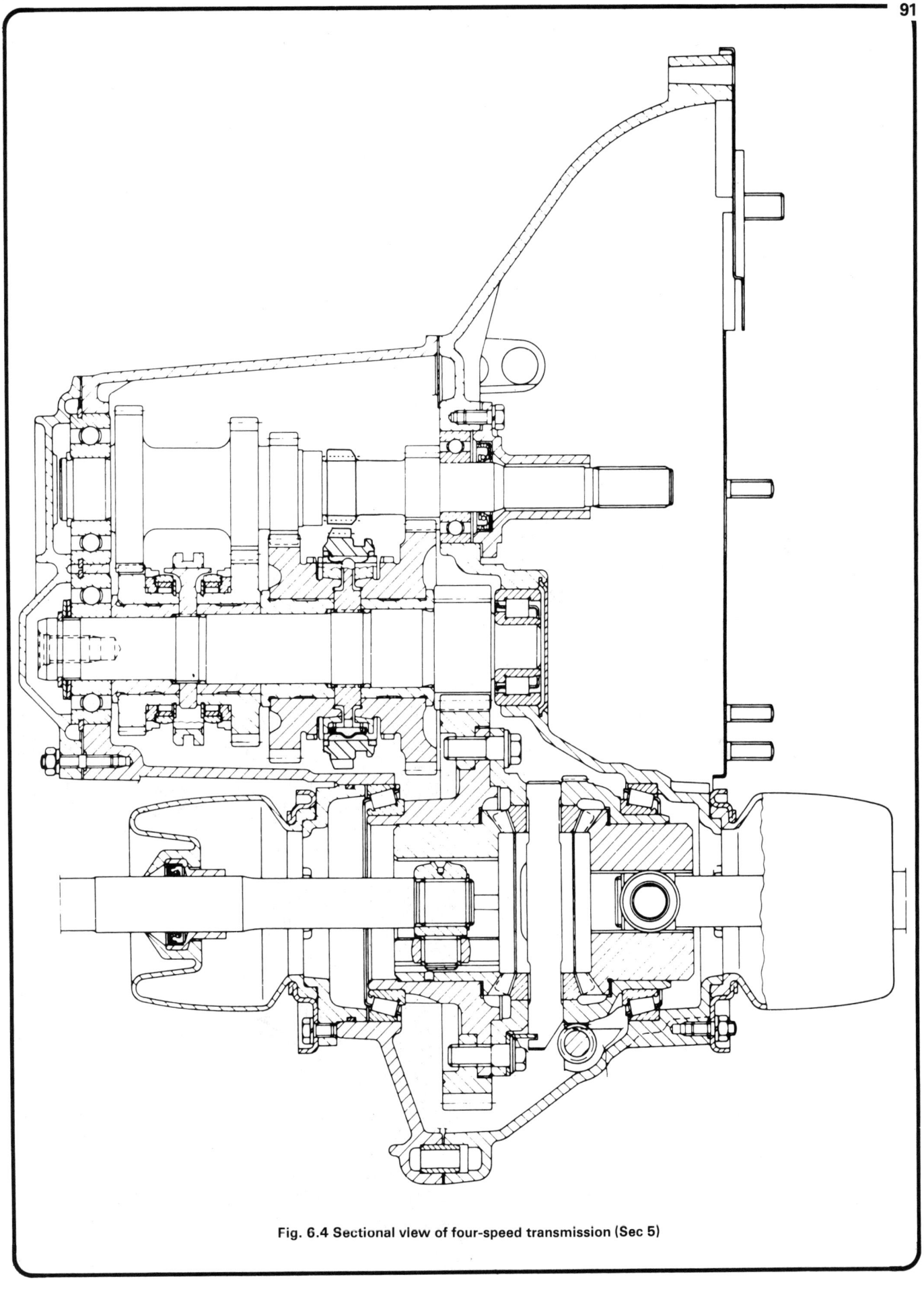

Fig. 6.4 Sectional view of four-speed transmission (Sec 5)

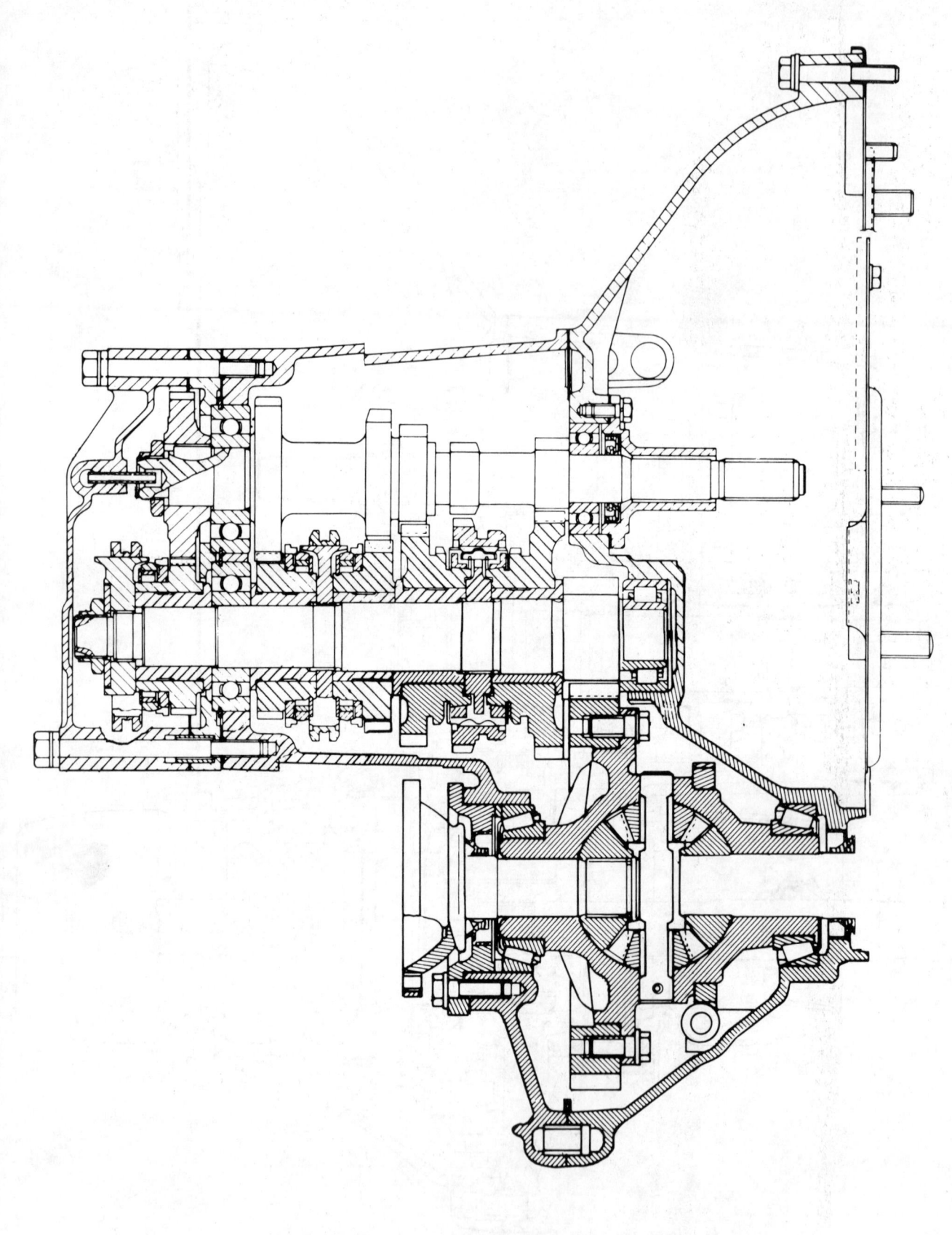

Fig. 6.5 Sectional view of five-speed transmission (Sec 5)

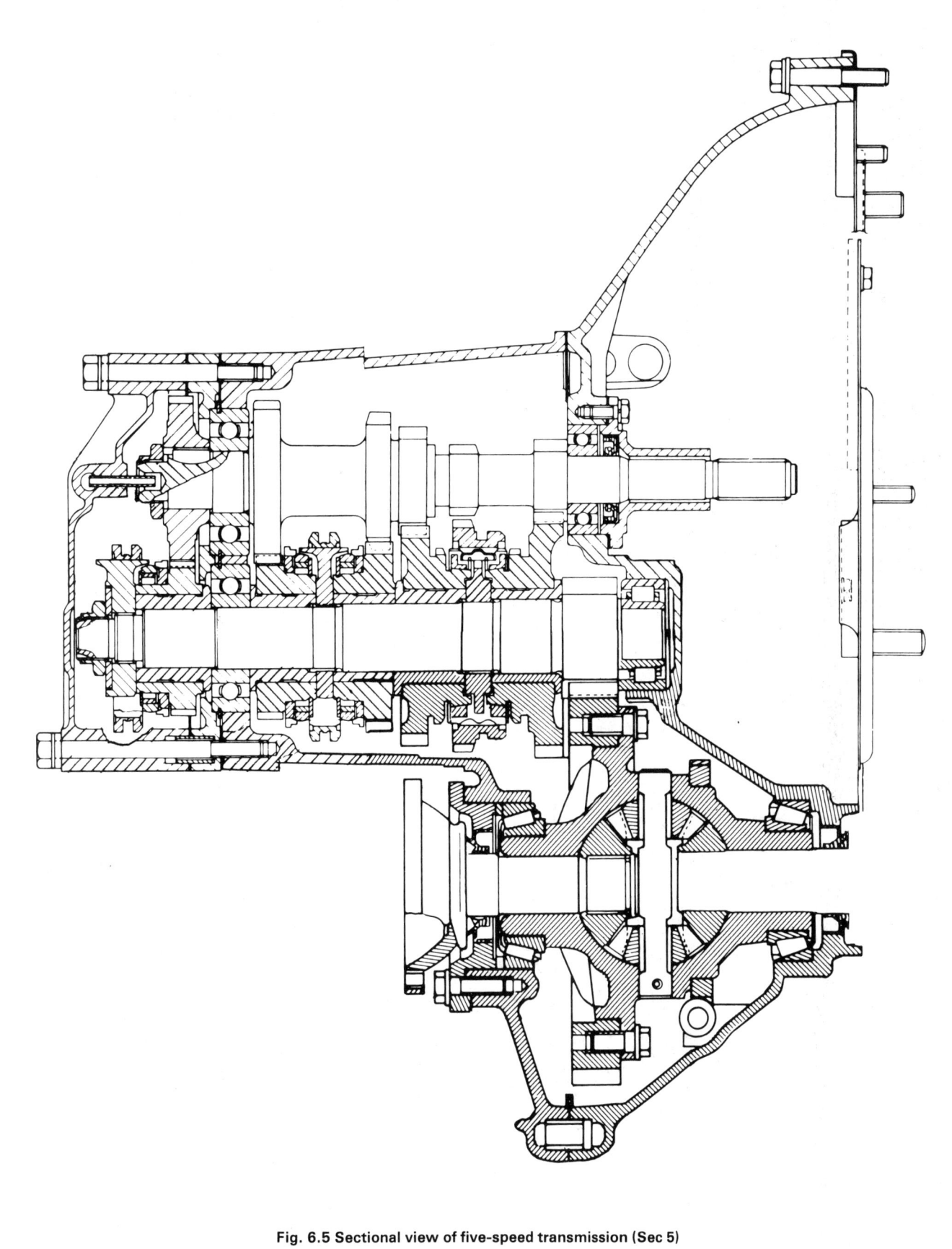

Fig. 6.5 Sectional view of five-speed transmission (Sec 5)

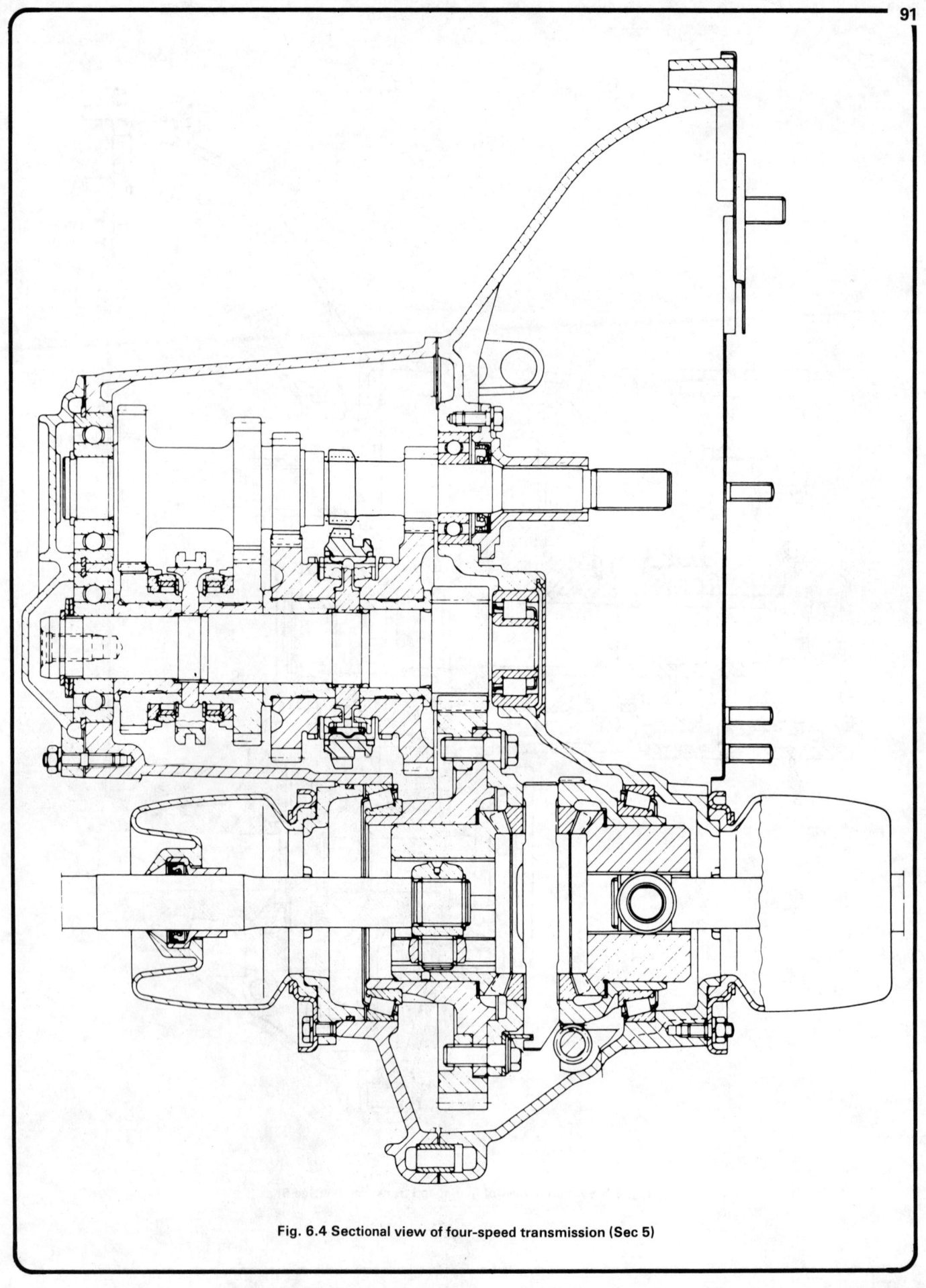

Fig. 6.4 Sectional view of four-speed transmission (Sec 5)

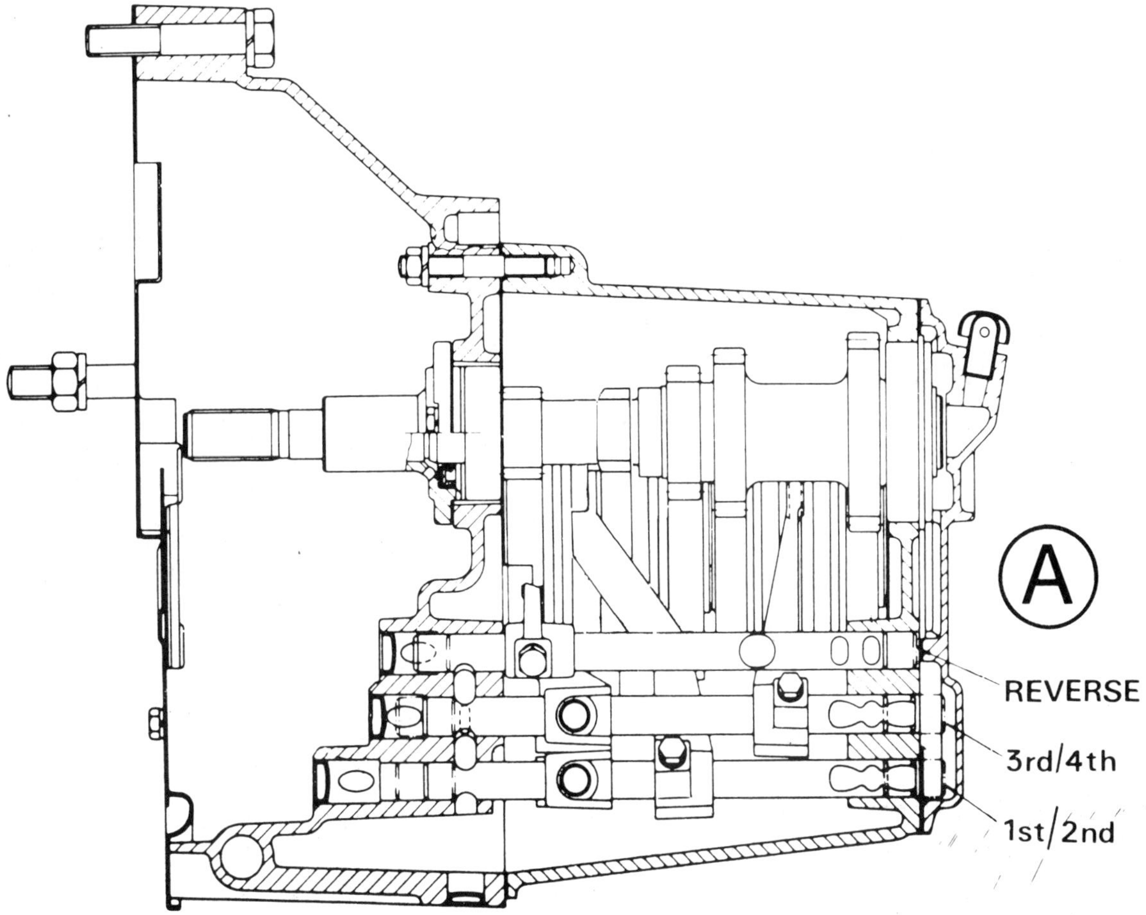

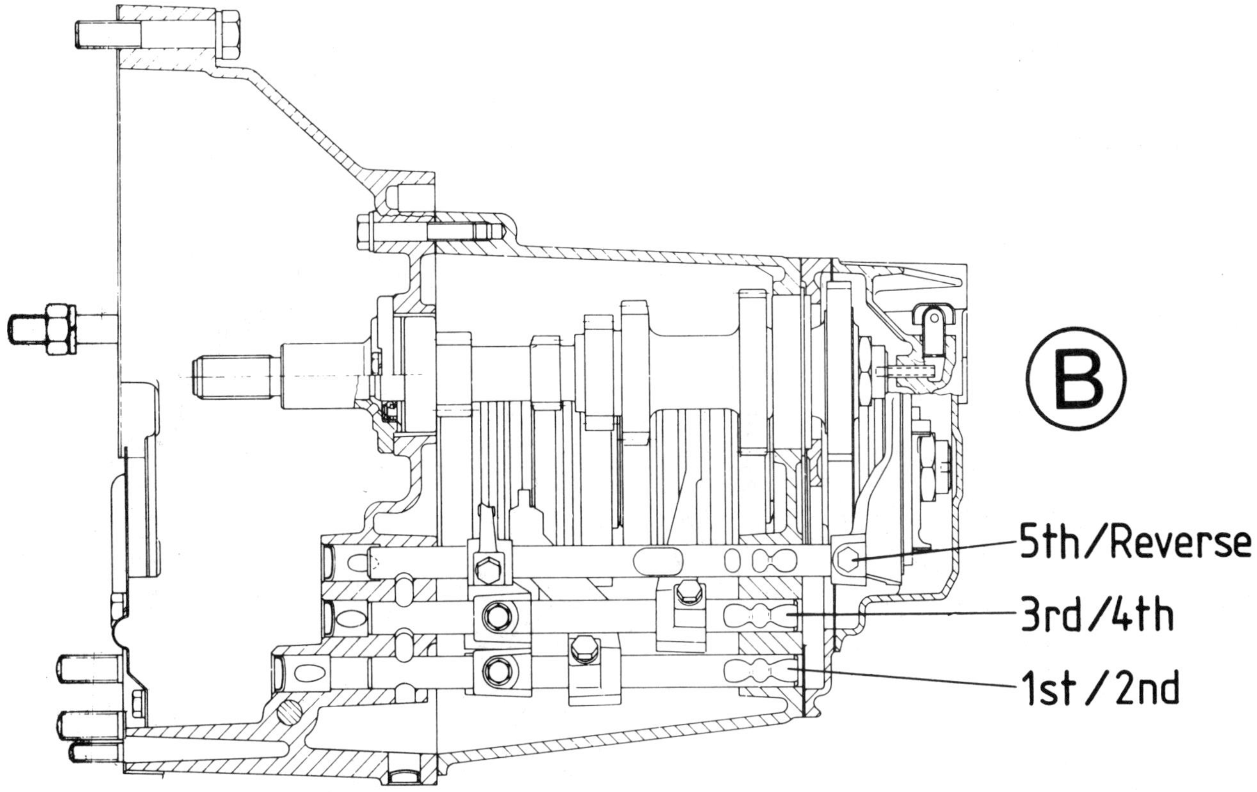

REVERSE

3rd/4th

1st/2nd

5th/Reverse

3rd/4th

1st/2nd

Fig. 6.6 Location of selector shafts (Sec 5)

1 Four-speed   *b Five-speed*

Gear engagement lever   Gear selector lever

Fig. 6.7 Four-speed transmission (Sec 5)

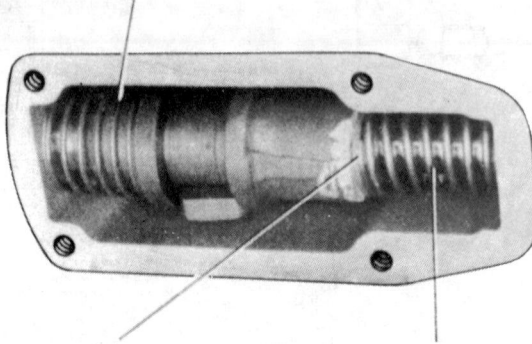

1st and 2nd gear bias spring

Reverse spring cap   Reverse gear bias spring

Fig. 6.8 Location of bias springs (Sec 5)

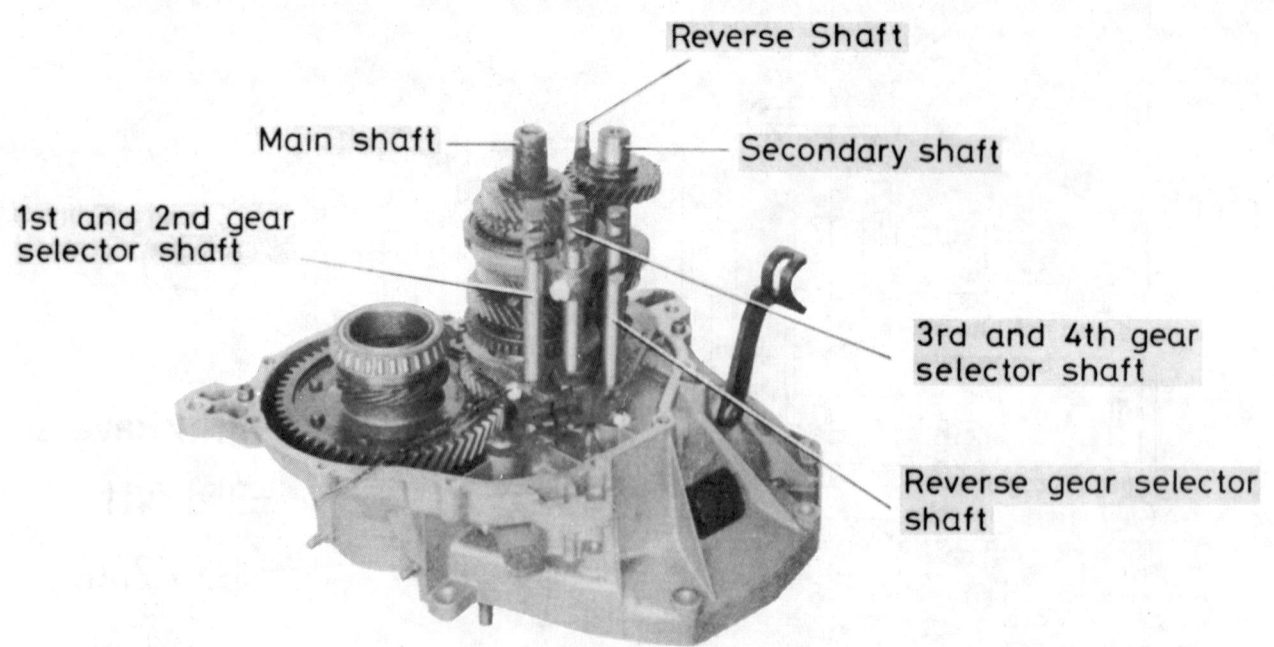

Main shaft

Reverse Shaft

Secondary shaft

1st and 2nd gear
selector shaft

3rd and 4th gear
selector shaft

Reverse gear selector
shaft

Fig. 6.9 Gearcase removed from four-speed transmission (Sec 5)

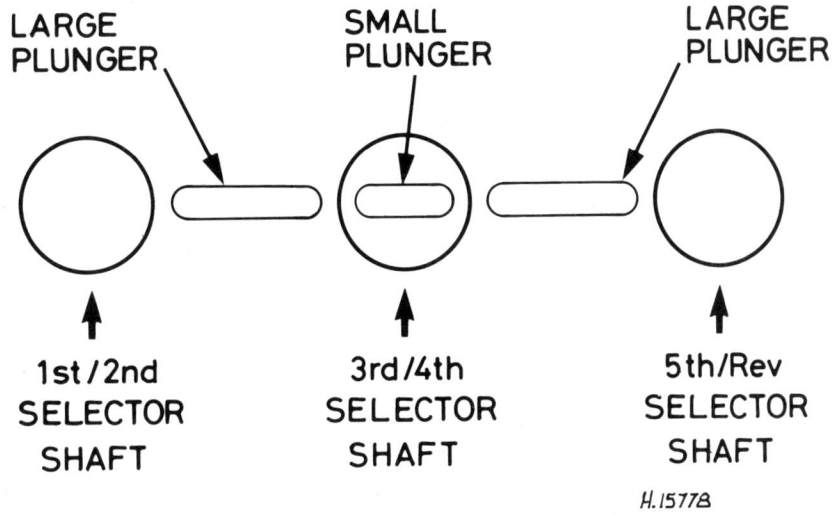

Fig. 6.10 Location of selector shaft interlock plungers (Sec 5)

6 Inspection of components

1   Check all the components for signs of damage. All the gear teeth should be smooth and shiny, without any chips. The ball and rollers of the bearings should be unblemished.

2   The tracks of the final drive taper roller bearings, still in the casing, should be a smooth, even colour without any mark. Should either the rollers or the tracks be marked at all, the complete bearing must be renewed. In this case, the outer tracks must be extracted from the casing, and the rollers with the inner tracks pulled off the differential cage halves.

3   Check the synchromesh baulk rings for signs of wear. Check their fit in their respective gears. If the gears are being renewed, the synchromesh units should also be renewed. One point easy to miss in examining the gears is fracture of the small ends of the teeth that are on the outside of the synchro-ring, and are an extension of the teeth for the dog clutch to engage. If any of these are chipped, the gear must be renewed.

4   Check the casings for cracks. If there are leaks at a plug, it must be renewed. This must be tapped carefully into place, sufficient to expand it but not enough to distort it too much. If a new plug is not available, or its security is in doubt after fitting, it can be secured in place with a layer of epoxy resin, two part adhesive, round its rim. This type of adhesive requires 24 hours to set fully at ambient temperature, but can be used in a few hours if heated in an oven.

5   Renew seals and gaskets at each dismantling.

6   Check the movement of the selector rods in their bores in the casing. They should move freely but without appreciable sideplay . Inspect the sliding surfaces of the selector forks for wear or damage.

7 Shaft geartrains – overhaul

Secondary shaft

1   Only the bearing can be renewed on this shaft. Use a puller or press to remove and refit it (photo).

Mainshaft

2   All components can be removed from the mainshaft using hand pressure only, with the exception of the bearing, for which a puller will be required.

3   Keep the dismantled components in the exact order and same way round as they were originally fitted.

4   A worn synchromesh unit is best renewed complete – especially if there has been a history of noisy gearchanging – or if the synchromesh could be easily 'beaten'.

5   With all parts clean, renewed (where necessary) and lightly lubricated, assemble the mainshaft in the following sequence (photo).

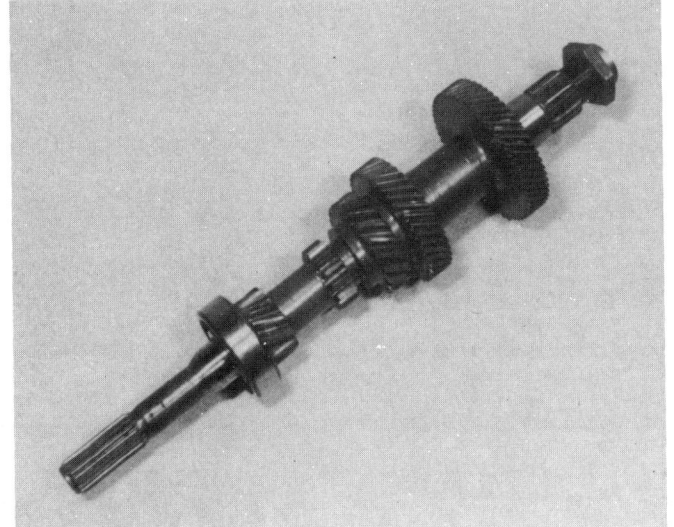

7.1 Secondary shaft (five-speed)

7.5 Mainshaft (five-speed)

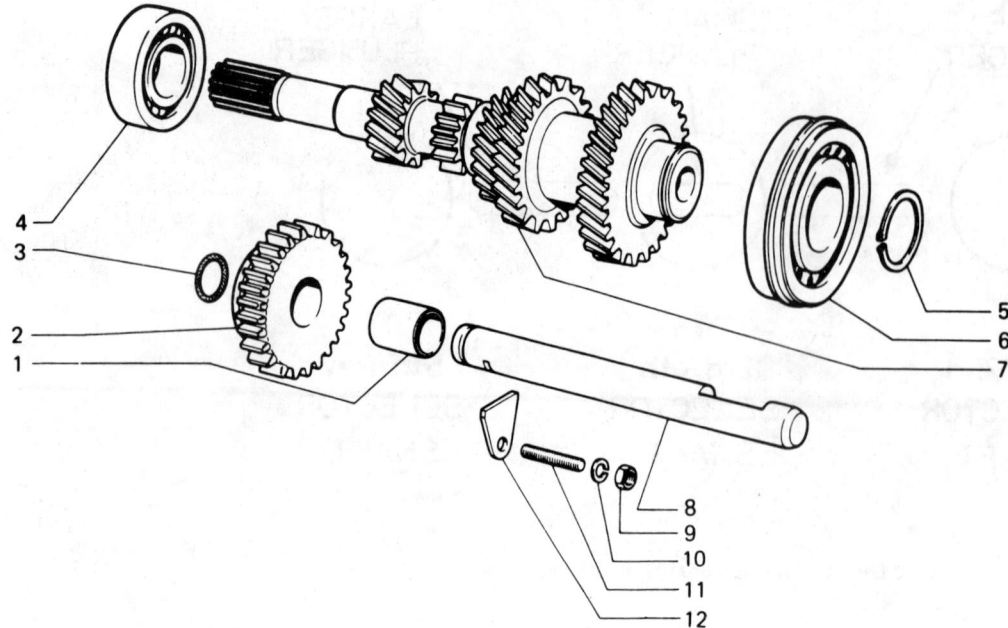

Fig. 6.11 Secondary and reverse shafts (Sec 7)

1   Bush
2   Reverse idler gear
3   Oil seal
4   Bearing
5   Circlip
6   Bearing
7   Input shaft/gear assembly
8   Idler shaft
9   Nut
10 Lockwasher
11 Stud
12 Lockplate

Fig. 6.12 Mainshaft components (four-speed) (Sec 7)

1   Bearing
2   Pinion gear to final drive (crownwheel)
3   Bush
4   1st speed gear
5   Synchroniser (baulk ring)
6   Spring ring
7   1st/2nd synchro sleeve with reverse gear
8   1st/2nd synchro hub
9   Sliding key
10 Spring ring
11 Synchroniser (baulk ring)
12 2nd speed gear
13 Bush
14 Bush
15 3rd speed gear
16 Synchroniser ring
17 Drive spring
18 Snap ring
19 3rd/4th synchro sleeve
20 3rd/4th synchro hub
21 Snap ring
22 Sliding key
23 Synchroniser ring
24 4th speed gear
25 Bush
26 Bearing
27 Belleville washer
28 Belleville washer
29 Circlip

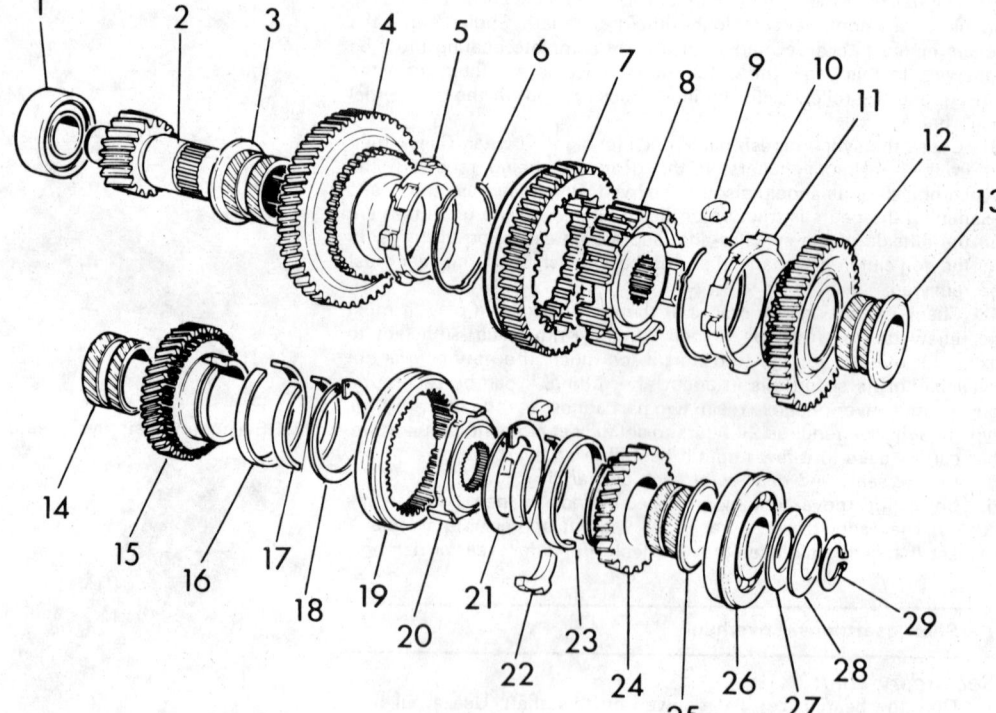

6   Slide on the 1st speed gear bush (photo).
7   Fit the 1st speed gear (photo).
8   Fit the 1st/2nd synchro sleeve/reverse gear with baulk rings. The sleeve groove must be towards the shaft pinion gear (photos).
9   Fit 2nd speed gear (photo).
10 Warm and fit 2nd and 3rd gear bushes followed by 3rd speed gear (photos).
11 Fit 3rd/4th synchro hub so that the completely circular oil groove is towards 3rd speed gear. Fit 3rd/4th synchro sleeve (photos).

12 Warm and fit the bush together with 4th speed gear (photo).
13 The shafts are now ready for assembling into the casing as described in Section 9.

8   Differential – overhaul

1   The speedometer drivegear can be removed from the differential case using a drift (photo).

7.6 1st speed gear bush on mainshaft

7.7 1st speed gear on mainshaft

7.8A 1st/2nd synchro sleeve with reverse gear

7.8B Fitting baulk ring to mainshaft

7.9 Fitting 2nd speed gear to mainshaft

7.10A 2nd speed gear bush

7.10B 3rd speed gear bush

7.10C 3rd speed gear

7.11A 3rd/4th synchro hub

7.11B 3rd/4th synchro sleeve

7.12 4th speed gear and bush

8.1 Differential and speedo drive gear

8.2A Crownwheel bolts

8.2B Differential planet gear pinion shaft lockplate

8.2C Differential dismantled

8.2D Removing differential planet gears

8.3 Differential side gear and thrustwasher

2   Unscrew the crownwheel bolts and separate the two halves of the differential cage and the crownwheel. The lockplate for the pinion shaft will also be released (photo). Remove the planet gears.
3   Take out the bevel side gears and thrust washers (photo).
4   Remove the tapered roller bearings if to be renewed.

5   Reassembly is a reversal of the dismantling procedure. Tighten the bolts in diagonal sequence to the specified torque. If new bearings are being fitted, drive them into place carefully and evenly, applying the drift to the inner tracks. Set the preload of these bearings as described in Section 9.

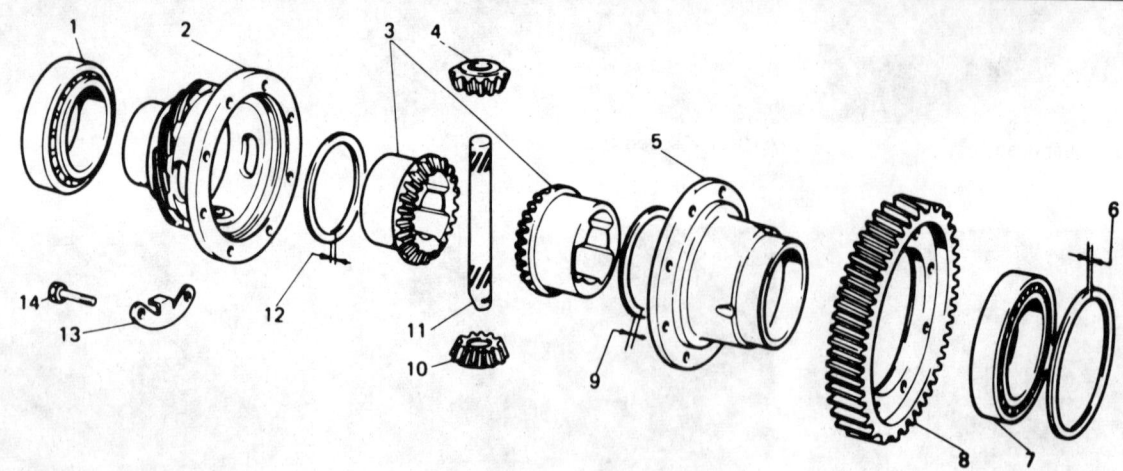

Fig. 6.13 Differential/final drive components (Sec 8)

1	Differential case bearing	5	Differential half case	9	Thrust washer	12	Thrust washer
2	Differential half case	6	Spacer	10	Pinion bevel gear	13	Lockplate
3	Side gears	7	Differential case bearing	11	Pinion gear shaft	14	Bolt
4	Pinion gear	8	Crownwheel				

9.2A Shaft bearings in casing

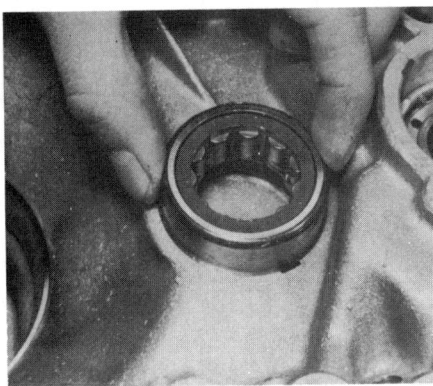

9.2B Shaft bearing in casing

9.3 Fitting magnet

9 Transmission – reassembly

1   As work proceeds, oil the components liberally with gear oil.
2   Fit the shaft bearings to the casings (photos).
3   Fit the magnet (photo).
4   Lower the differential/final drive into position, with speedometer drivegear uppermost (photo).
5   Mesh the geartrains together and fit them simultaneously into the casing (photo).
6   Locate the selector shaft interlock plungers in the casing as shown in Fig. 6.10. A pencil magnet is useful for this (photo).
7   Locate the 1st/2nd and 3rd/4th selector forks in their synchro sleeve grooves.
8   Fit the 1st/2nd and 3rd/4th selector shafts passing them through the holes in the forks. Make sure that the small interlock plunger is in its hole in the 3rd/4th selector shaft (photo).
9   Screw in and tighten the fork locking bolts (photos).

9.4 Differential/final drive in casing

9.5 Fitting geartrains

9.6 Using a magnet to fit interlock plunger

9.8 Interlock plunger in 3rd/4th selector shaft

9.9A Tightening 3rd/4th selector fork lockbolt

9.9B Tightening 1st/2nd selector fork lockbolt

9.10 Reverse idler gear and shaft O-ring arrowed

9.13 Reverse idler shaft lockplate and bolt

10 Fit a new O-ring to the reverse idler shaft and fit the shaft and reverse idler gear (photo).

11 Fit the reverse selector fork (photo).

12 Fit 5th/reverse selector shaft.

13 Fit the reverse idler shaft lockplate (photo).

14 Bolt reverse selector fork to its shaft (photo).

15 If the differential bearings have been renewed, the bearing preload must now be calculated and adjusted by means of shims. This sounds very complicated, but in fact means that when the bearing cover is bolted down, it must exert just enough pressure to give the bearings the specified preload.

16 To do this work, a suitable depth gauge will be required. First, measure the depth of the bearing cover recess. Second, measure the projection of the cover's machined section (O-ring removed). Subtract one dimension from the other and add 0.08 mm (0.003 in). This is the thickness of the shim required. Where a depth gauge is not available, shims can be inserted into the housing recess until, when the bearing cover plate is fitted (and resting under its own weight), there is a gap between the plate and the edge of the bearing recess of between 0.08

9.14 Tightening reverse selector fork lockbolt

and 0.12 mm (0.003 and 0.005 in). This method is not so accurate and will require the purchase of unnecessary shims.

17 If necessary, fit a new oil seal to the differential bearing cover.

18 Fit a new O-ring to the bearing cover and bolt it down, using a new paper gasket.

19 Lower the casing over the geartrains. Use a piece of tubing if necessary to tap the casing down around the shaft bearings. Always use a new flange gasket.

20 Screw in and tighten the casing bolts, noting the one inside the bellhousing (photo).

Five-speed units

21 Fit 5th speed gear to the secondary shaft (photo).

22 Fit 5th speed gear, the synchro unit, the selector fork and the gear bush as an assembly to the mainshaft. Note the Belleville washer on the synchro hub (photo).

23 Select two gears simultaneously to lock up the geartrains. This is

9.11 Reverse selector fork

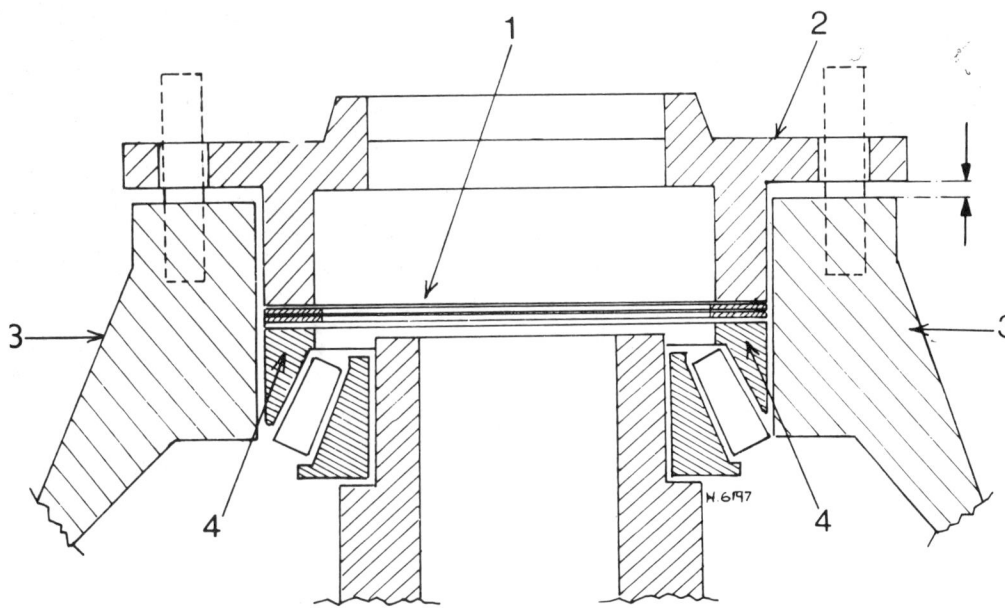

Fig. 6.14 Location of differential bearing preload adjusting shims (Sec 9)

1 Shims
2 Bearing cover plate
3 Final drive housing
4 Bearing outer track

9.20 Casing bolt inside bellhousing

9.21 Fitting 5th speed gear to secondary shaft

9.22 5th speed gear, fork and synchro being fitted to mainshaft

9.24A Tightening secondary shaft nut

9.24B Staking shaft nut

9.25 5th speed selector fork lockbolt

done by pushing up the 1st/2nd selector shaft by means of its dog, then pushing down the 5th/reverse fork.

24 Screw on two new shaft nuts, tighten to the specified torque and stake the nuts into the shaft grooves (photos).

25 Return the gears to neutral and then fit the 5th/reverse fork lock bolt (photo).

Four-speed units

26 Fit the two Belleville washers, their outer rims next to each other on the end of the shaft.

27 Fit the circlip. To get into its groove against the considerable pressure of the pair of washers, the latter must be compressed by a clamp. The end of the shaft is internally threaded, and the bolts fixing

the transmission to the engine are the same thread. Select a socket just large enough to span the shaft but press on the circlip. The bolts are a bit long, so another socket makes a handy distance piece to use up the extra length of bolt. Screw in the bolt to push the two washers and the circlip down the shaft, watching carefully at the gap in the circlip to see when it is lined up with the groove in the shaft. Tap the circlip, which is trapped by the socket, with a small screwdriver, to push it into the groove. Release the press.

All units

28 Fit the speedometer driven gear and its lockscrew. Screw in the reverse lamp switch (photos).
29 Reassemble the gear engagement lever, reverse spring cap and coil springs (photos).
30 Bolt on the pressed steel cover noting the 5th speed gear resistor spring. Always use a new cover gasket (photos).
31 Using a new gasket, bolt on the rear cover (photo).
32 Fit the detent balls and springs and bolt on the retaining plate (photos).
33 Reconnect the gearcasing and bellhousing.
34 Fit the gearchange selector link rod (photos).
35 Fit the clutch release bearing into the bellhousing.

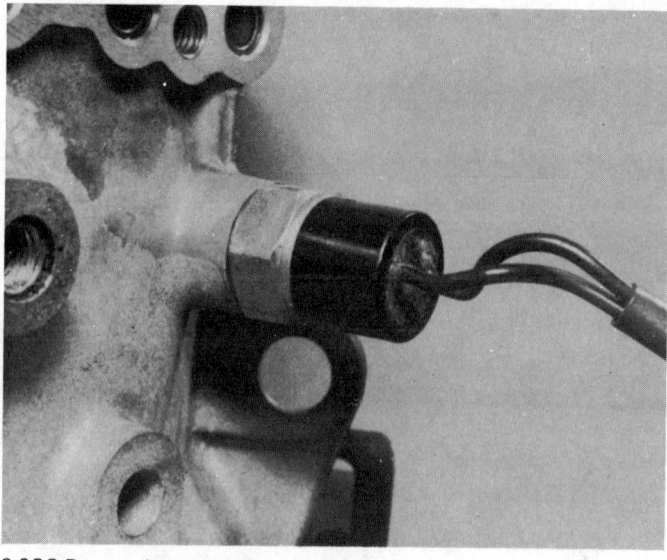

9.28C Reverse lamp switch

9.28A Speedo driven gear

9.29A Fitting gear engagement lever

9.28B Speedo driven gear lockscrew

9.29B Gear engagement lever shaft nut

9.29C Gear selector lever and fixing nut

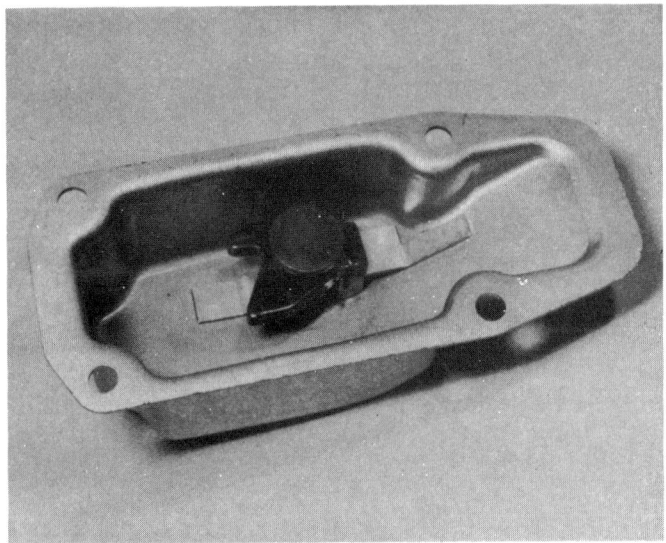

9.30A Pressed steel cover and 5th gear pawl and resistor spring

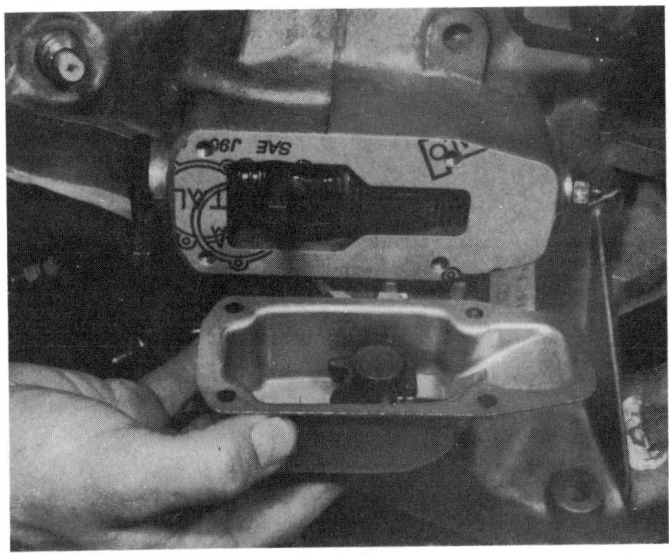

9.30B Fitting pressed steel cover and gasket

9.31 Fitting end cover and gasket

9.32A Detent balls

9.32B Detent springs

9.32C Detent spring retaining plate

9.34A Selector link rod

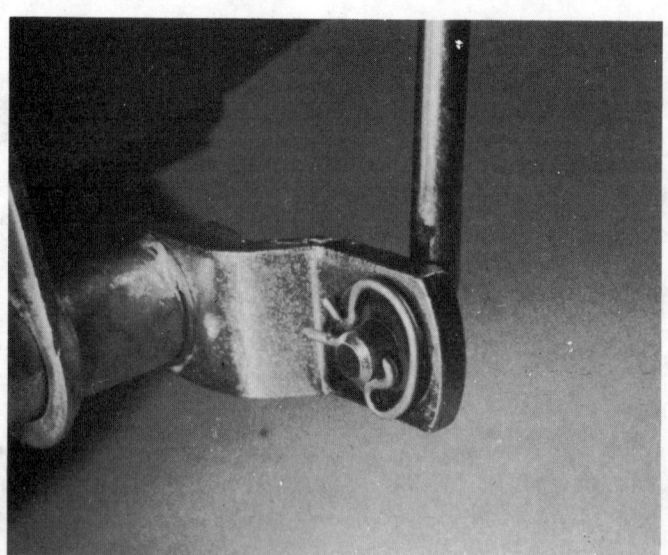

9.34B Selector link rod securing clip

10 Fault diagnosis – transmission

Symptom	Reason(s)
Weak or ineffective synchromesh	Synchro baulk rings worn, split or damaged Synchromesh units worn, or damaged
Jumps out of gear	Gearchange mechanism worn Synchromesh units badly worn Selector fork badly worn
Excessive noise	Incorrect grade of oil in gearbox or oil level too low Gearteeth excessively worn or damaged Intermediate gear thrust washers worn allowing excessive end play Worn bearings
Difficulty in engaging gears	Clutch pedal adjustment incorrect
Noise when cornering	Wheel bearing or driveshaft fault Differential fault

Note: *It is sometimes difficult to decide whether it is worthwhile removing and dismantling the gearbox for a fault which may be nothing more than a minor irritant. Gearboxes which howl, or where the synchromesh can be 'beaten' by a quick gearchange, may continue to perform for a long time in this state. A worn gearbox usually needs a complete rebuild to eliminate noise because the various gears, if re-aligned on new bearings, will continue to howl when different wearing surfaces are presented to each other. The decision to overhaul therefore, must be considered with regard to time and money available, relative to the degree of noise or malfunction that the driver has to suffer.*

Chapter 7 Driveshafts, hubs, wheels and tyres

Contents

Driveshaft – removal and refitting 3
Driveshaft joints – renewal 4
Fault diagnosis 8
Front hub bearings – renewal 5

General description 1
Maintenance 2
Rear hub bearings – renewal 6
Roadwheels and tyres 7

Specifications

Driveshaft .... Open shaft with constant velocity ball and cage type joint at outboard end and tripod needle roller joint at inboard end

Hub bearings .... Double row sealed in hub

Roadwheels
Type .... Pressed steel or alloy (option)
Size .... 4.00 x 13

Tyres
Type .... Radial ply or Denovo (option)
Size .... 135 x 13
Pressures:
    Front .... 1.8 bar (26 lbf/in^2)
    Rear .... 2.0 bar (29 lbf/in^2)

Torque wrench settings

	Nm	lbf ft
Driveshaft end nut	196	144
Hub to axle flange bolts	20	15
Inboard joint gaiter retainer bolt	1.0	0.7
Suspension lower arm balljoint to hub carrier	35	26
Suspension strut base clamp bolts	35	26
Tie-rod end ball stud nut	34	25
Caliper mounting bolts	48	35

1 General description

The driveshafts are of open type and transmit power from the transmission to the front roadwheels.

At the inboard end of the shaft a tripod type joint is fitted which incorporates needle bearings.

The outboard joint is a ball and cage type constant velocity joint.

The front and rear hub bearings are of twin track ball type. New bearings are only supplied complete with hub and attachment flange as sealed units.

The roadwheels are of pressed-steel type and the tyres of radial ply construction.

Alloy wheels are available as an option on certain models.

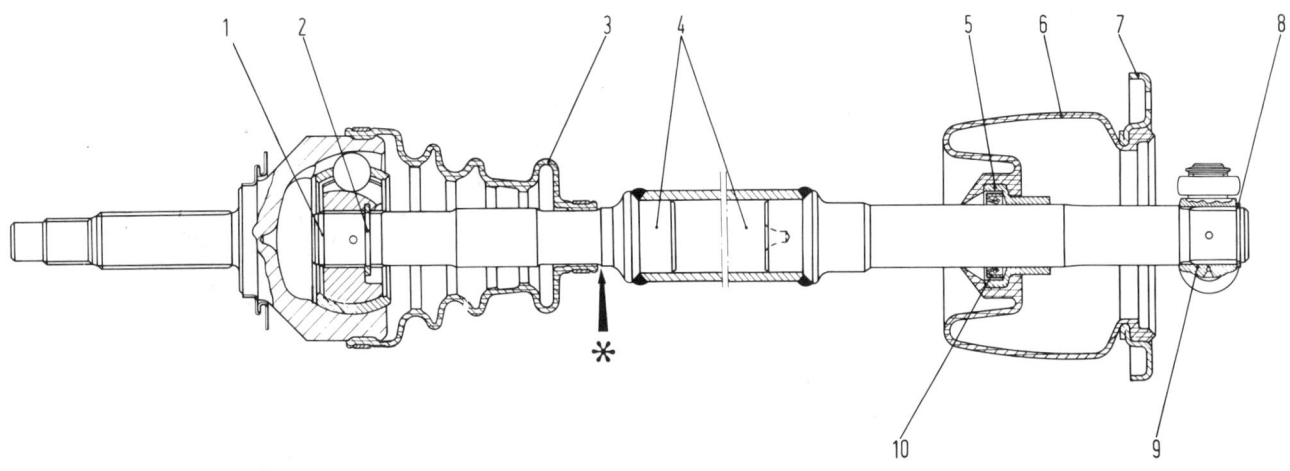

Fig. 7.1 Sectional view of driveshaft (Sec 1)

1	Outboard (CV) joint	4	Driveshaft
2	Circlip	5	Bush
3	Gaiter	6	Gaiter

7	Gaiter retaining flange	10	Seal
8	Circlip		
9	Tripod joint	*Abutment shoulder for gaiter	

2 Maintenance

1   This is largely visual and should be carried out at the intervals specified in Routine Maintenance.

2   Raise the front roadwheels and turn them slowly while examining the gaiters on the joints for splits or signs of leaking lubricant. Extend the gaiters with the fingers to ensure that there are no splits at the base of the pleats.

3   If the gaiter is found to be damaged then the joint must be dismantled as described in Section 4. All the old lubricant must be removed and the gaiter discarded. Fresh lubricant should be applied and a new gaiter fitted.

4   Also at the specified intervals, raise each roadwheel in turn (handbrake off), grip the top and bottom of the tyre and attempt to rock the wheel. Provided the front hub nut has been correctly tightened any movement will be due to worn bearings. Noise when cornering will be due to the same reason. There is no nut or adjustment on the rear hub and any movement will be due to wear.

3 Driveshaft – removal and refitting

1   Raise the appropriate roadwheel and support the car securely under the sill front jacking point.

2   Remove the roadwheel.

3   Have an assistant apply the footbrake hard and release the driveshaft nut using a long wrench bar as it is very tight.

4   Unbolt the brake caliper and tie it up out of the way, do not strain the flexible hose.

5   Using a balljoint splitter tool, disconnect the tie-rod end from the steering arm as described in Chapter 10.

6   Remove the nut and washer from the end of the driveshaft.

7   Clean dirt and grease from around the driveshaft inboard gaiter (photo).

8   Place a suitable oil container (tray or bowl) under the inboard end of the driveshaft and unscrew the gaiter retainer fixing bolts. Pull back the gaiter and allow the oil to drain (photo).

9   Unscrew the bolts which secure the hub carrier to the clamp at the base of the front suspension strut.

10 Again using the splitter tool, disconnect the suspension balljoint just below the hub carrier. Disconnect the radius rod from the track control arm.

11 Pull the stub axle carrier outwards. The inboard end of the driveshaft will now release from the transmission with some loss of oil.

12 Push the splined outboard end of the driveshaft out of the hub carrier. If it is tight use the centre screw of a three-legged extractor to persuade it.

13 Remove the driveshaft to the bench.

14 Refit by reversing the removal operations. Tighten all nuts and

3.7 Driveshaft inboard gaiter

3.8 Driveshaft inboard gaiter retainer disconnected

bolts to the specified torque. To tighten the driveshaft nut, have an assistant apply the footbrake hard. If a torque wrench of suitable range is not available, use a socket with a long wrench bar (457.2 mm – 18.0 in) and tighten fully. Stake the nut into the groove.

15 Fit the roadwheel and top up the transmission oil.

4 Driveshaft joints – renewal

Tripod joint

1   Obtain a repair kit. This is in fact a new tripod complete with needle rollers and tracks.

2   Extract the circlip and pull the tripod from the shaft or press the shaft from the tripod (photos).

3   If the object of dismantling was to renew the gaiter, pull the old one from the shaft now. Detach the flange (photos).

4   Fit the new gaiter and its retainer followed by the tripod joint and circlip. As this joint is lubricated by oil from the transmission, no supplementary greasing or oiling is required. A bush and oil seal arrangement is used to prevent any oil seepage along the shaft at the gaiter contact area (photos).

4.2C Removing tripod joint

4.2A Tripod joint exposed

4.3A Removing joint gaiter

4.2B Extracting tripod joint circlip

4.3B Removing gaiter retainer

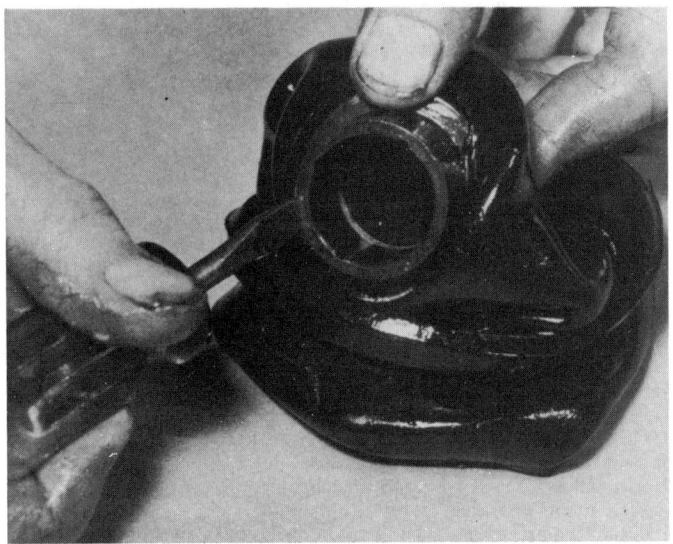

4.4A Prising out gaiter bush

4.5A CV joint circlip (arrowed)

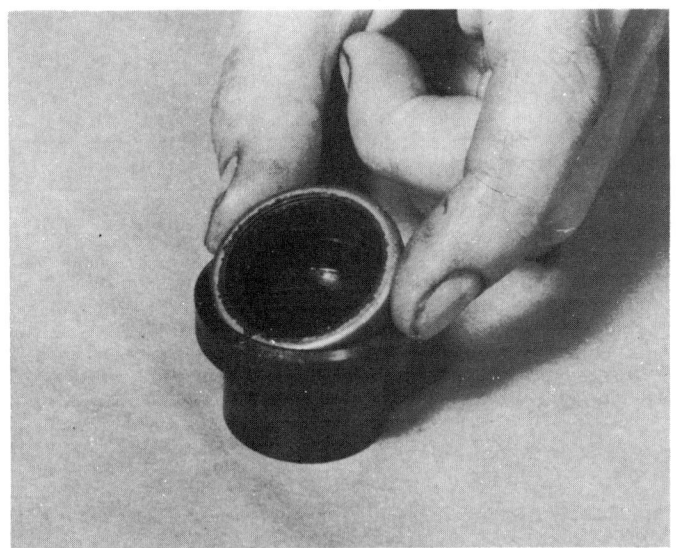

4.4B Gaiter bush oil seal

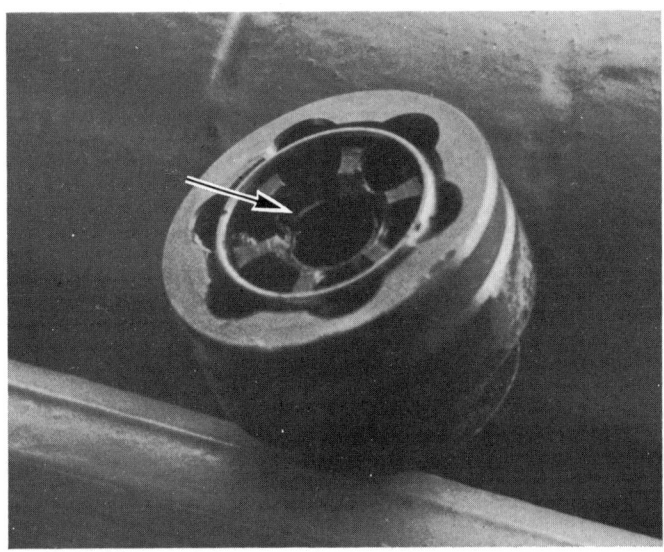

4.5B CV joint circlip (arrowed with shaft withdrawn)

Constant velocity joint

5   Release the gaiter retaining band and pull the gaiter away from the joint. Extract the circlip and withdraw the shaft from the joint (photos).
6   If the object of dismantling was to renew the gaiter, do this now. If the old gaiter had been operating in a split condition unnoticed for some time, wipe away all the old grease, and dismantle the joint for cleaning. To do this, swivel the ball cage through 90° and withdraw it complete with balls. The balls are a slight snap fit in the cage. Once they are removed, the inner and outer cage members can be separated, but mark the cage sides so that they can be refitted in their original position. Pack the joint with either the grease contained in the sachet supplied with the repair kit or 55g (2.0 oz) of molybdenum disulphide grease (photos).
7   Secure the joint with a circlip and draw the gaiter into position. Finally fit the retaining band.

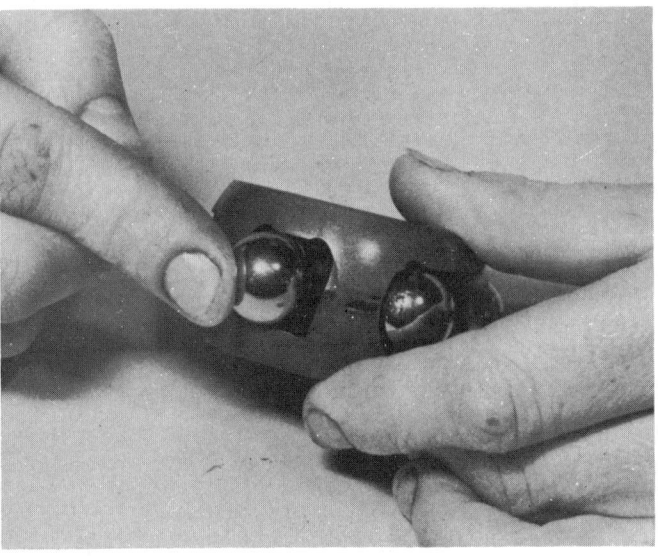

4.6A CV joint balls and cages

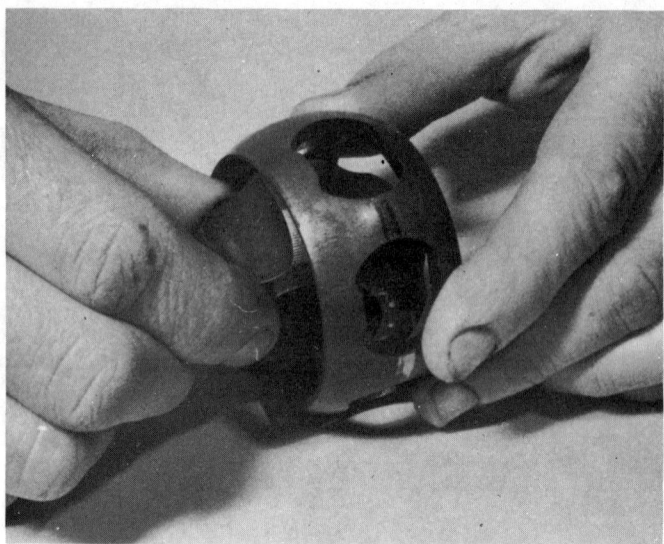

4.6B Separating CV joint inner and outer cages

6   Remove the nut and washer from the end of the driveshaft.
7   Unscrew the bolts which secure the hub carrier to the clamp at the base of the front suspension strut.
8   Again using the splitter tool, disconnect the suspension balljoint just below the hub carrier. Disconnect the radius rod.
9   Pull the hub carrier downwards and outwards, at the same time pressing the driveshaft out of it in an inward direction. If the driveshaft will not release from the carrier, press it out using the centre screw from a three-legged puller.
10 Unscrew the brake disc fixing bolt and roadwheel alignment stud. Remove the disc. Unbolt the hub/flange assembly.
11 Unfortunately, this is as far as dismantling can go. The bearings can only be renewed complete with hub and flange as these components incorporate the bearing tracks and are supplied as a complete assembly.
12 Fit the new hub/flange to the stub axle carrier. Fit the brake disc.
13 Offer the hub carrier onto the outboard end of the driveshaft and loosely screw on the nut with washer.
14 Reconnect the hub carrier to the clamp at the base of the suspension strut and to the suspension lower control arm balljoint.
15 Reconnect the tie-rod end balljoint to the steering arm. Tighten the nut to the specified torque.
16 Refit the brake caliper and tighten the bolts to the specified torque wrench setting. Reconnect the radius rod.
17 Have an assistant apply the footbrake hard while the driveshaft nut is tightened to the specified torque. In the absence of a suitable torque wrench, use a socket with a wrench bar 18.0 in long and tighten fully.
18 Stake the nut into the shaft groove.
19 Fit the roadwheel and lower the car to the floor.

5   Front hub bearings – renewal

1   Raise the appropriate roadwheel and support the car securely under the sill front jacking point.
2   Remove the roadwheel.
3   Have an assistant apply the footbrake hard and unscrew the driveshaft nut using a long wrench bar as it is very tight.
4   Unbolt the brake caliper and tie it up out of the way. Release the brake hose from the suspension strut if necessary.
5   Using a balljoint splitter tool, disconnect the tie-rod end from the steering arm as described in Chapter 10.

6   Rear hub bearings – renewal

1   Raise the rear wheel and remove it. Make sure that the car is supported securely.
2   Unscrew the brake drum fixing bolt and the roadwheel alignment spigot and pull off the brake drum. It may need tapping off with a copper or plastic-faced hammer.
3   Remove the brake shoes as described in Chapter 8.
4   Unscrew the bolts which hold the hub to the axle tube end flange.

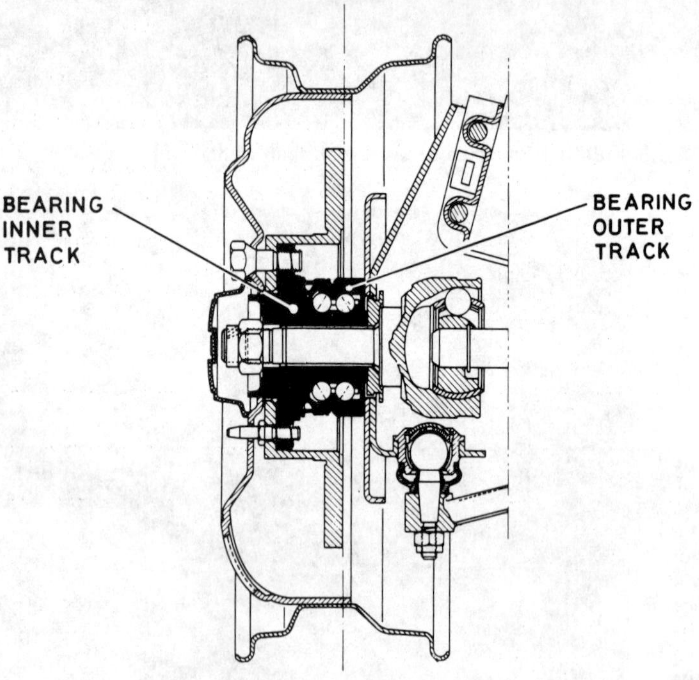

BEARING INNER TRACK

BEARING OUTER TRACK

INNER TRACK

OUTER TRACK

Fig. 7.2 Sectional view of front hub (Sec 5)

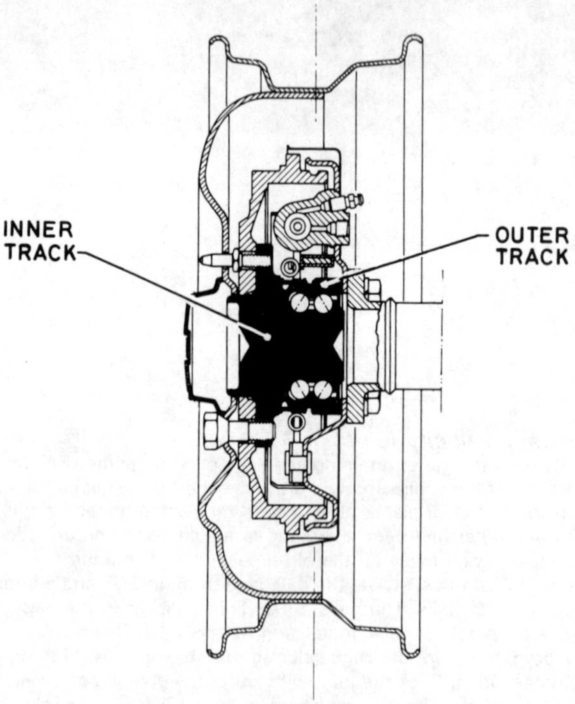

Fig. 7.3 Sectional view of rear hub (Sec 6)

6.5 Rear hub showing cut-out to accept shoe adjusters

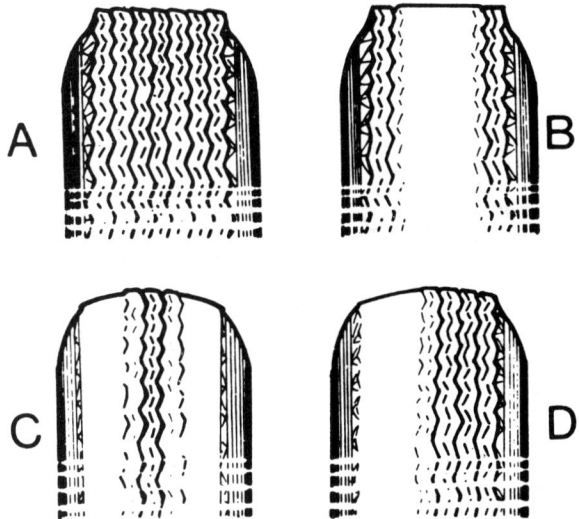

Fig. 7.4 Tyre tread wear patterns and causes (Sec 7)

5   Withdraw the hub/bearing assembly (photo).
6   If the bearings are worn, then a complete hub assembly will be required as the parts are supplied only as a complete sealed assembly.
7   Bolt the bearing/hub with brake backplate to the axle flange. Fit the brake shoes and drum.
8   Fit the roadwheel and lower the car.

A   'Feathering due to incorrect toe-in
B   Over inflation
C   Under inflation
D   Wear due to incorrect camber, worn wheel bearings and fast cornering

7   Roadwheels and tyres

1   Pressed steel roadwheels are fitted as standard equipment using bolts to retain them. Alloy wheels with larger or Denovo tyres may be optionally specified.
2   Periodically, remove the wheels, clean the inside and outside, and make good any rusty patches.
3   Keep the wheel retaining bolts lightly greased and tighten them fully after fitting the wheel.
4   Keep the tyres inflated to specified pressure and inspect the treads and sidewalls regularly for cuts, blisters or damage.
5   If the wheels and tyres have been balanced on the car, they should not be moved from their original positions, nor their location on the hub be altered; paint one bolt hole on the wheel, and the matching one on the hub flange, before removing the wheel or the original balance will be lost at time of refitting.
6   If the wheels have been balanced off the car, they may be moved to even out the tread wear. With the radial tyres fitted as original equipment, however, only move them from front to rear and rear to front on the same side of the car. *Do not change them from side to side.*

7   If the spare wheel is introduced into the tyre rotational scheme, mark it as to which side it is fitted and from which side the 'new' spare came from. Keep the wheels to that side of the car in future movements.
8   It is recommended that the wheel is re-balanced after a puncture is repaired and at halfway through the life of the tyre (perhaps 15 000 miles (24 000 km) approximately) when loss of tread rubber due to wear may have altered the original balance.
9   Tyre tread wear characteristics are illustrated. Apart from those shown, if parts of the tread are scooped out or flattened, this may be caused by out of balance wheels or repeated heavy brake applications, causing the wheels to lock.
10   Bulges or blisters on the tyre sidewalls may be caused by striking kerbs or mounting the kerb at anything more than a walking pace.
11   Scrubbing the tyres can occur where the roadwheel steering angles are incorrect on steering lock. This may be due to the lengths of the tie-rods being unequal.
12   Some tyres have tread wear indicator bars moulded into them. Renew the tyres when the bars appear. On other tyres, renew them when or before the tread depth is worn down to a minimum of 1.0 mm over the complete tread width.

8   Fault diagnosis – driveshafts, hubs, wheels and tyres

Symptom	Reason(s)
Vibration	Driveshaft bent Worn universal joints Out-of-balance roadwheels
'Clonk' on taking up drive or on overrun	Worn universal joints Worn splines on shaft, hub carrier or differential side gears Loose driveshaft nut Loose roadwheel bolts
Noise or roar especially when cornering	Worn hub bearings Incorrectly tightened hub flange or driveshaft nuts

Chapter 8 Braking system

Contents

Brake pedal – removal and refitting	15
Caliper – removal, overhaul and refitting	5
Disc pads – inspection and renewal	3
Fault diagnosis	16
Front disc – inspection and renovation or renewal	6
General description	1
Handbrake – adjustment	13
Handbrake cable – renewal	14
Hydraulic rigid pipes and flexible hoses – inspection and renewal	11
Hydraulic system – bleeding	12
Maintenance	2
Master cylinder – removal, overhaul and refitting	9
Pressure regulating valve	10
Rear drum – inspection and renovation or renewal	7
Rear hydraulic wheel cylinder – removal, overhaul and refitting	8
Rear shoe linings – inspection and renewal	4

Specifications

System type .... Four-wheel dual circuit hydraulic, discs front, drums rear. Handbrake mechanical on rear wheels

Disc brakes
Diameter	227.0 mm (8.9 in)
Thickness	10.70 to 10.90 mm (0.42 to 0.43 in)
Minimum regrind thickness	9.70 mm (0.38 in)
Minimum wear thickness	9.0 mm (0.35 in)
Minimum pad friction material thickness	1.5 mm (0.059 in)
Caliper cylinder diameter	48.0 mm (1.89 in)

Drum brakes
Drum internal diameter	185.24 to 185.53 mm (7.298 to 7.310 in)
Maximum refinishing diameter	186.33 mm (7.34 in)
Maximum wear limit	186.83 mm (7.36 in)
Minimum shoe friction lining thickness	1.5 mm (0.059 in)
Wheel cylinder bore diameter	15.875 mm (0.63 in)

Torque wrench settings
	Nm	lbf ft
Caliper mounting bolts	48	35
Flexible hose to caliper	27	20
Master cylinder mounting nuts	25	18
Master cylinder stop screw	8	6

1 General description

The braking system is of four wheel dual circuit, hydraulic type. Disc brakes are fitted at the front with drum brakes at the rear.

A pressure regulating valve is located in the rear hydraulic circuit to limit pressure to the rear wheels during heavy pedal applications and so prevent rear wheel lock up and skidding.

The handbrake operates through cables to the rear brakes.

All brakes are self-adjusting.

2 Maintenance

1 Although a low hydraulic fluid level indicator is fitted, the level should still be checked through the translucent reservoir on the master cylinder at the weekly service check (photos).

2 The fluid should rarely need topping up and then only with a small quantity to replace the fluid displaced by wear of the pads and linings.

3 Always use fluid for topping up which has been stored in an airtight container as the fluid is hygroscopic and therefore absorbs moisture readily from the atmosphere.

4 Regularly check all hoses and brake lines for leakage.

5 At the specified intervals, check the disc pads and shoe linings for wear as described later in this Chapter. When carrying out this work, check for fluid seepage from the caliper or wheel cylinder hydraulic seals.

6 Renew the hydraulic fluid in the braking system by bleeding, as described in Section 12, at the intervals specified in Routine Maintenance.

3 Disc pads – inspection and renewal

1 Jack up the front of the car and remove the roadwheels.

2 Inspect the thickness of the friction material on each pad. If it is 1.5 mm (0.059 in) or less, the pads must be renewed.

3 To remove the pads, extract the spring clips and slide out the tapered locking blocks. The upper block has taper outboard (photo).

4 Lift the cylinder body from the disc and withdraw the pads, one from each side of the disc. Remove the anti-rattle springs (photos).

5 Brush away any dust and dirt from the caliper, taking care not to inhale the dust – this contains asbestos and is thus potentially injurious to health.

2.1A Brake fluid reservoir level warning switch

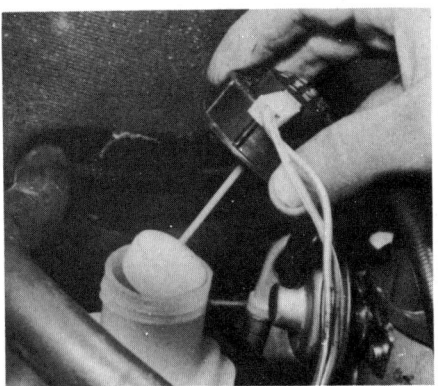

2.1B Brake fluid reservoir cap, switch and float

3.3 Disc pad spring clip and locking block

3.4A Removing caliper cylinder

3.4B Removing disc pad and anti-rattle spring

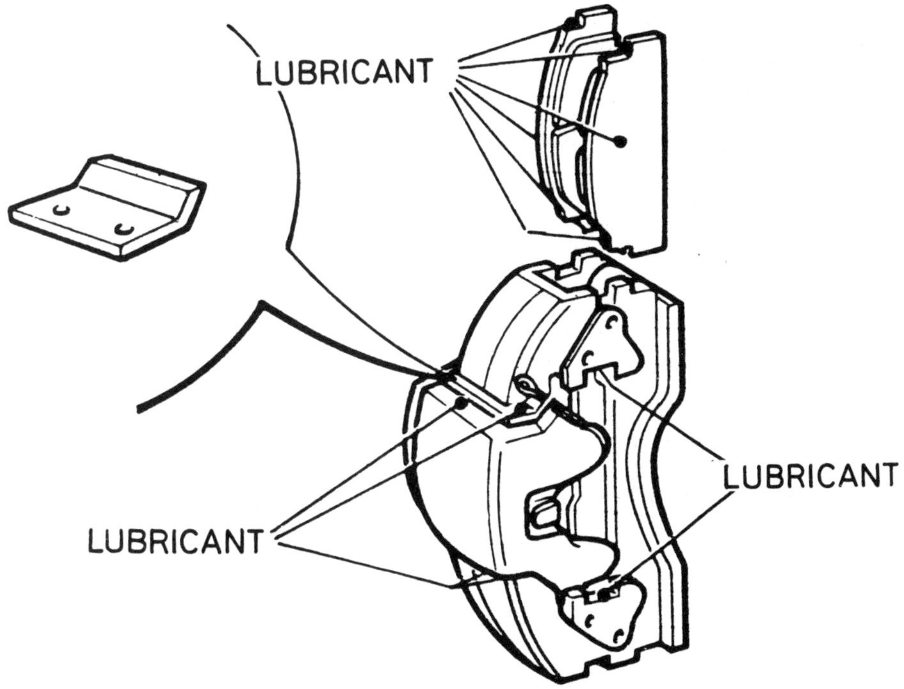

LUBRICANT

LUBRICANT

LUBRICANT

Fig. 8.1 Caliper and disc pad application areas (Sec 3)

6   As the new pads are thicker than the old ones, the caliper piston must be depressed into its cylinder to accommodate them. This will cause the fluid level to rise in the reservoir. Anticipate this by syphoning some out beforehand, but take care not to let it drip onto the paintwork – it acts as an effective paint stripper!

7   Apply a smear of anti-seize lubricant to the points indicated on the caliper and pads.

8   Refit the anti-rattle springs, the pads (friction lining-to-disc), the cylinder body, the locking blocks and the retaining clips.

9   Refit the roadwheel and apply the footbrake hard, several times, to bring the pads into contact with the brake disc.

10 Renew the pads on the opposite brake. The pads should always be renewed in axle sets.

11 Top up the fluid reservoir.

---

4   Rear shoe linings – inspection and renewal

---

1   Jack up the rear of the car and remove the roadwheels.

2   Fully release the handbrake.

3   Unscrew and remove the drum securing bolts. One of these is a long locating spigot for the roadwheel (photo).

4   Pull off the drum. If it is tight, clean off the rust at its joint with the hub flange, and apply a little penetrating fluid. Two bolts may be screwed into the drum securing bolt holes if necessary and the drum thus eased off the hub. The securing bolt holes are tapped for this purpose (photo).

5   Brush away all the dust and dirt from the shoes and operating mechanism, taking care not to inhale it.

6   The friction linings fitted as original equipment are of the bonded type and the rivet heads normally used as a guide to wear are not, of course, fitted. However, if the thickness of the friction linings is down to 1.5 mm (0.059 in), or less, the shoes must be renewed. Always purchase new or factory relined brake shoes.

7   Before removing the brake shoes, note the way in which the shoes are positioned, with respect to leading and trailing ends (the end of the shoe not covered by lining material). Note also into which holes in the shoe web the return springs are connected. Sketch the shoes or mark the holes in the new shoes with quick drying paint if you are doubtful about remembering (photo).

8   Undo the steady springs by depressing them with a pair of pliers to disengage the slot from the pin (photos).

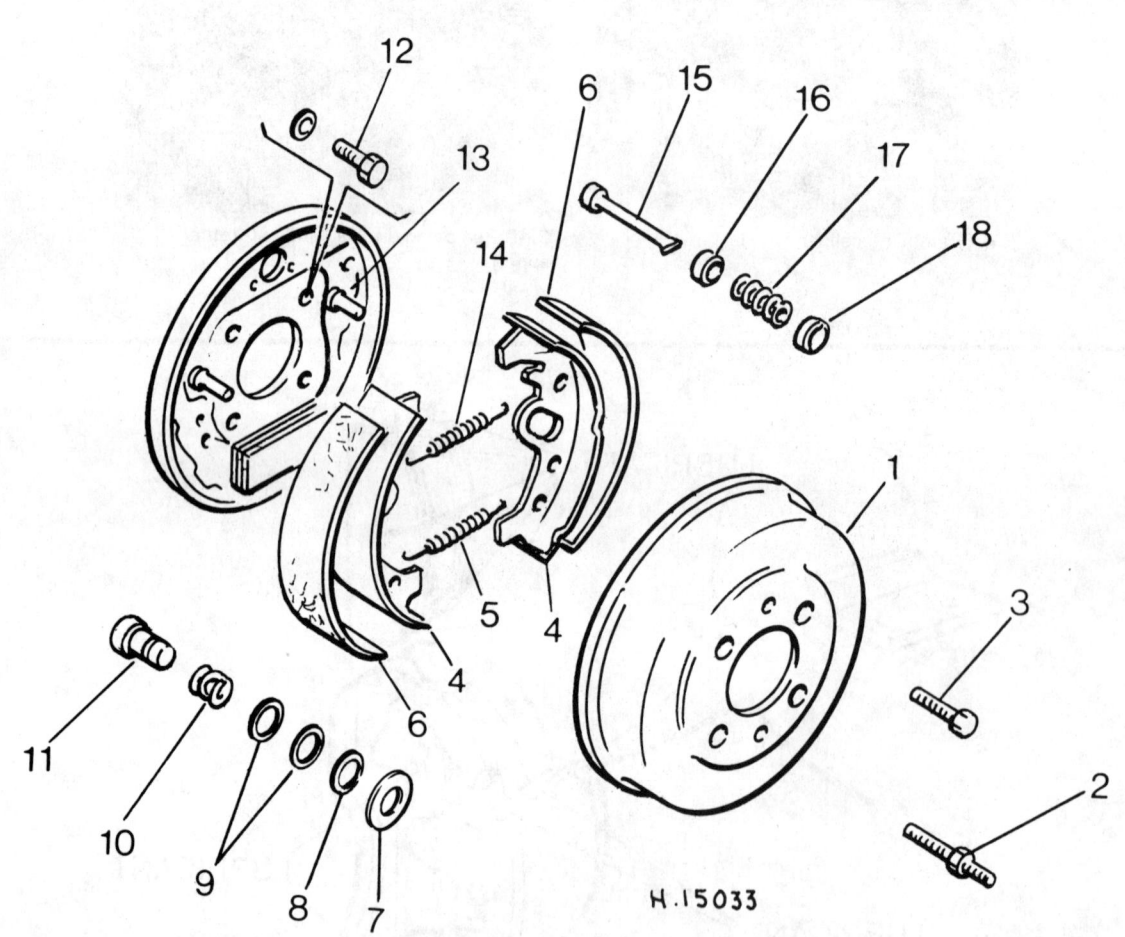

Fig. 8.2 Rear brake components (Sec 4)

1 Drum	6 Linings	10 Self adjuster spring	15 Steady pin
2 Spigot bolt	7 Retaining plate	11 Bush	16 Inner cup
3 Drum bolt	8 Washer	12 Backplate fixing bolts	17 Steady spring
4 Brake shoes	9 Self adjuster friction	13 Backplate	18 Spring retainer
5 Lower pull-off spring	washers	14 Top pull-off spring	

H.15033

4.3 Unscrewing drum retaining bolt

4.8A Shoe steady spring clip

4.4 Removing brake drum

4.8B Releasing shoe steady spring clip

4.7 Drum brake assembly

9   Pull the trailing shoe (the one nearest the rear of the car) from its slot in the wheel cylinder piston. Pull the lower end of the shoe out of the anchor block and then work the shoe up the self-adjuster post. Note that cut-outs are provided in the rear face of the axle flange to accommodate the self-adjuster head when drawing the shoe off the pivot post (photo).

10 Once the shoe is off the self-adjuster post it can be allowed to move towards the other shoe and the return springs disconnected using a pair of pliers.

11 New shoes are supplied complete with the self-adjusters riveted to them (photos).

12 If the hydraulic cylinder needs overhaul, now is the time with the shoes out of the way, especially if there is evidence of fluid leakage.

13 When reassembling the new shoes with the adjusters, and the shoes to the brakes, put a slight smear of grease on all the working surfaces for the adjusters, the bottom shoe pivot, and the steady springs, but not where the shoe sits on the hydraulic cylinder piston.

14 Fit the new leading shoe with the return springs attached. Connect the trailing shoe to the return springs and pull it across until the shoe can be pushed down onto the self-adjuster pivot post. Wriggle the shoe down and work the shoe into place. Check that the shoe strut is in position.

4.9A Shoe upper return spring and strut

4.9B Shoe lower return spring and anchor block

4.11 Drum brake components

15 Fit the shoe steady pins and spring clips, using pliers to depress and engage the clips.
16 Before refitting the drum, clean it out and examine it for grooves or scoring (refer to Section 7).
17 Using a soft-faced mallet, tap the shoes in towards the centre of the hub. They will move against the pressure of the self-adjuster coil springs and permit the brake drum to be fitted. This should now be done and the bolts screwed in.
18 Refit the roadwheel and apply the footbrake two or three times, to position the shoes close to the drum.
19 Renew the shoes on the opposite brake in a similar way.
20 The handbrake should be automatically adjusted by the action of the shoe adjuster. If the handbrake control lever has excessive travel, refer to Section 13 for separate adjusting instructions.

5 Caliper – removal, overhaul and refitting

Note: *Purchase a repair kit in advance of overhaul.*
1 Jack up the front roadwheel and remove it.
2 Brush away all dirt from the caliper assembly and the flexible pipe, particularly the fixing bracket and union at the inboard end of the flexible pipe.
3 Have ready a container suitable to catch the brake fluid, and sheets of clean newspaper on which to put parts.
4 Take out the spring clips and locking blocks, and take the caliper off the support bracket.
5 Disconnect the hydraulic flexible pipe at the under wing support bracket and cap both pipe ends. It may help to prevent loss of fluid if the vent in the reservoir cap is sealed with adhesive tape, to create a vacuum.
6 Remove the caliper to the bench or other work surface, and clean it thoroughly.
7 Depress the piston until the dust excluding boot can be removed.
8 Now apply air pressure to the flexible hose and eject the piston. Quite a low pressure is required for this, such as can be generated with a hand or foot operated pump.
9 Pick out the piston seal from its groove in the cylinder. Use a sharp probe, but take care to avoid scratching the cylinder bore.
10 Examine the surface of the piston and cylinder bore. If either is corroded, scored or shows metal-to-metal rubbed areas, the complete assembly should be renewed.

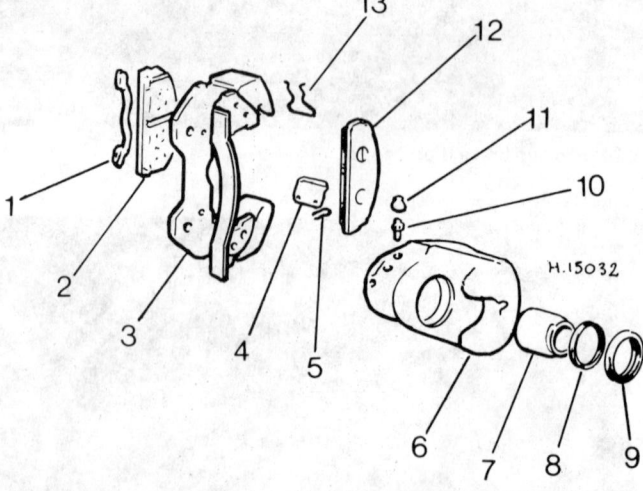

Fig. 8.3 Components of a disc brake caliper (Sec 5)

1 Pad anti-rattle spring	8 Seal
2 Pad	9 Dirt excluder
3 Support bracket	10 Bleed nipple
4 Tapered locking block	11 Bleeder dust cap
5 Spring clip	12 Pad
6 Caliper cylinder body	13 Spring clip for caliper
7 Piston	

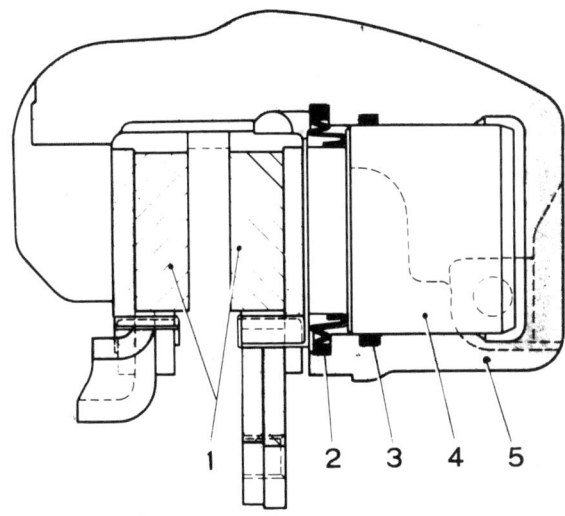

Fig. 8.4 Sectional view of disc caliper (Sec 5)

1 Pads
2 Dust excluder
3 Piston seal

4 Piston
5 Caliper body

11 If the components are in good condition, discard the oil seals, clean the piston and cylinder and fit the new seal for the piston. This is included in the repair kit. Use the fingers only to manipulate it into its groove.

12 Lubricate the piston with clean hydraulic fluid and insert it partially into the cylinder.

13 Fit the new dust excluding boot to its projecting end, push the piston fully into the cylinder and engage the dust excluder with the rim of the cylinder.

14 Refit the caliper, reconnect the flexible hose, then bleed the front hydraulic circuit (refer to Section 12).

6 Front disc – inspection and renovation or renewal

1 Whenever the front disc pads are being checked for wear, take the opportunity to inspect the discs for deep scoring or grooving. After a high mileage, the disc may become reduced in thickness away from the extreme outer edge of the disc. If this wear is rapid, it is possible that the friction pads are of too hard a type.

2 If the disc has evidence of many tiny cracks, these may be caused by overheating due to a seized caliper piston in the 'applied' position.

3 The foregoing conditions may be corrected by regrinding the disc

provided that the thickness of the disc is not reduced below that specified by such action. Alternatively, fit a new disc.

4 To remove a disc, take off the caliper and pads as described in Section 3. Tie the caliper up, out of the way. Unbolt and remove the caliper support bracket (photo).

5 Unscrew the disc fixing screw and roadwheel locating spigot and withdraw the disc (photos).

6 Sometimes a disc may be found to have excessive run-out. This can be checked with a dial gauge or by inserting feeler blades between the disc and a fixed point and turning it by hand. Repositioning the disc in relation to the hub may bring it within tolerance by cancelling out the distortion. If not, renew the disc.

7 Refitting is a reversal of removal.

7 Rear drum – inspection and renovation or renewal

1 Whenever the rear brake linings are being checked for wear, take the opportunity to inspect the internal surfaces of the brake drums.

2 If the drums are grooved or deeply scored, they may be reground, provided that their new internal diameter will not then exceed the specified dimension. If it will, or the drum is cracked, it must be renewed.

3 Removal and refitting of a brake drum is described in Section 4.

8 Rear hydraulic wheel cylinder – removal, overhaul and refitting

Note: *Purchase a repair kit in advance of overhaul*

1 If fluid seepage is observed from the ends of the rear wheel cylinder when the brake drum has been removed, the seals are leaking and immediate action must be taken.

2 Although the cylinder can be dismantled without taking it from the backplate, this is not recommended owing to the possibility of under wing dirt and mud dropping onto the components as work proceeds.

3 Remove the brake shoes, as described in Section 4.

4 Disconnect the hydraulic line from the wheel cylinder and cap the open end of the pipe. It may help to reduce the loss of fluid if the vent hole in the reservoir cap is taped over to create a vacuum.

5 Unscrew and remove the setscrews which hold the cylinder to the backplate and withdraw the cylinder. Prise off the rubber dust excluding boots.

6 Apply gentle air pressure from a hand or foot operated pump to eject the pistons and spring.

7 Inspect the piston and cylinder bore surfaces for scoring or evidence of metal-to-metal rubbing areas. If these are found, discard the assembly and purchase a new one.

8 If the components are in good condition, note which way round the lips are fitted, then discard the seals and boots and wash the pistons and cylinder bore in clean hydraulic fluid or methylated spirit.

9 Manipulate the new seals into position, using the fingers only for this job.

10 Dip the pistons in clean hydraulic fluid and insert them with the coil spring and washers into the cylinder.

11 Fit the new dust excluding boots.

6.4 Caliper support bracket

6.5A Unscrewing disc fixing screw

6.5B Removing hub/disc

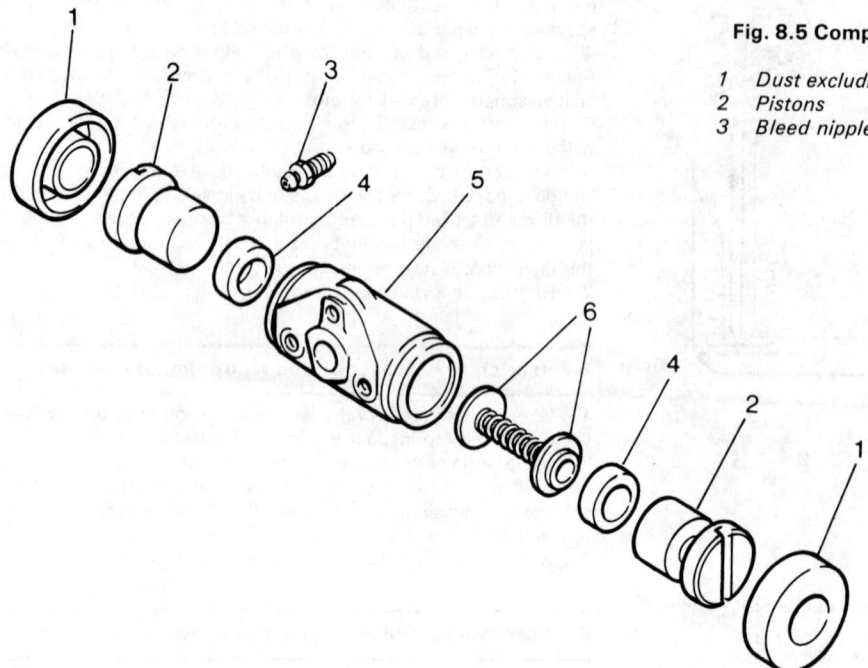

Fig. 8.5 Components of rear wheel cylinder (Sec 8)

1   Dust excluding boots   4   Seals
2   Pistons   5   Cylinder body
3   Bleed nipple   6   Spring and washers

12   Refit the wheel cylinder to the backplate, reconnect the hydraulic pipe, then refit the shoes, the drum and the roadwheel.
13   Bleed the rear hydraulic circuit as described in Section 12.

9   Master cylinder – removal, overhaul and refitting

Note: *Purchase a repair kit in advance of overhaul*
1   The master cylinder is mounted on the engine compartment rear bulkhead (photo).

2   Cover the front wings with polythene sheeting or similar material in case hydraulic fluid spills onto the paintwork of the car during removal of the cylinder.
3   Detach the leads from the terminals on the reservoir cap, then unscrew and remove the cap and float.
4   Unscrew the pipe unions and prise the pipes carefully away from the master cylinder. Cap the open ends of the pipes and catch any fluid leaking from the master cylinder in a suitable container.
5   Unscrew the mounting nuts and withdraw the master cylinder from the bulkhead.

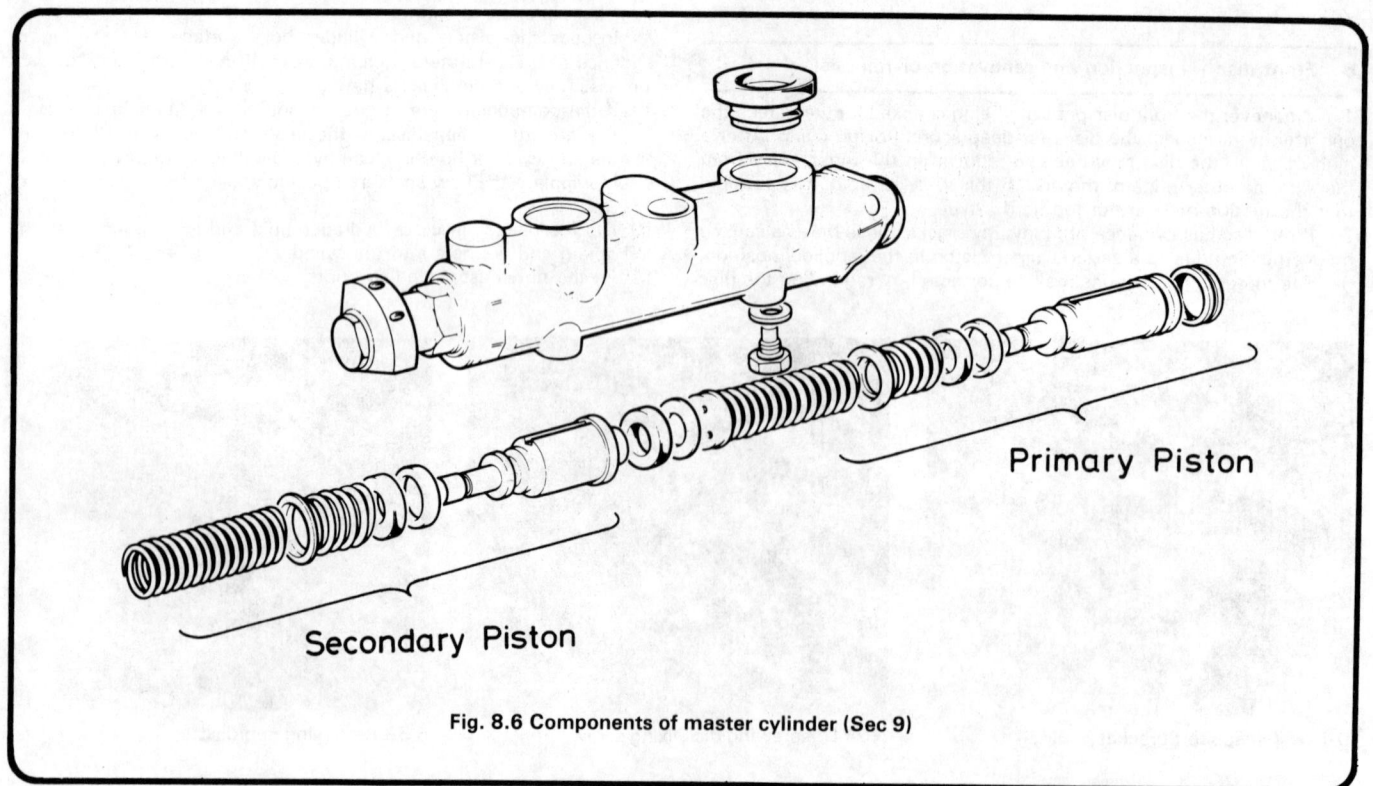

Primary Piston

Secondary Piston

Fig. 8.6 Components of master cylinder (Sec 9)

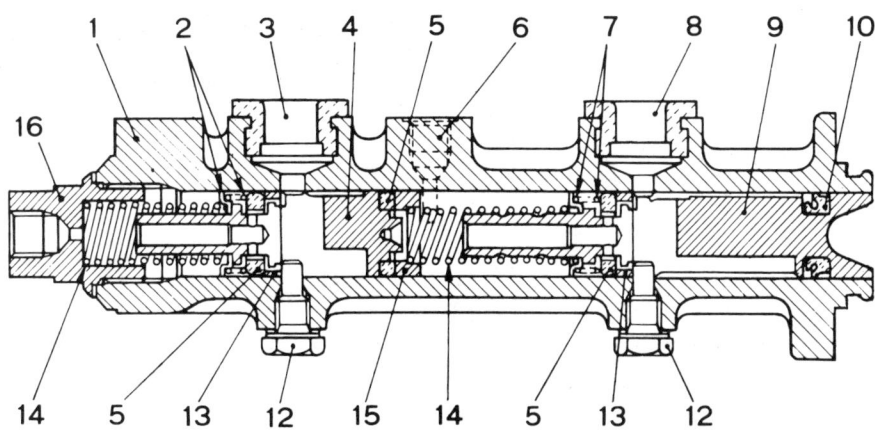

Fig. 8.7 Sectional view of master cylinder (Sec 9)

1	Cylinder body	5	Seal	9	Primary piston	14	Springs
2	Spring and cup	6	Fluid outlet	10	Seal	15	Seal
3	Inlet from reservoir	7	Spring and cup	12	Stop bolts	16	End plug and fluid
4	Secondary piston	8	Inlet from reservoir	13	Spacer		outlet

9.1 Master cylinder

6   Clean away all external dirt and tip out the fluid from the reservoir and cylinder body.

7   The fluid reservoirs need not be removed from the master cylinder but if they are, renew the rubber sealing collars when refitting.

8   Grip the master cylinder in a vice, then unscrew and remove the end plug. Catch the coil spring.

9   Using a thin rod, apply pressure to the end of the primary piston then unscrew and remove the two stop bolts and sealing washers.

10 The internal piston assemblies with seals and springs can now be pushed out of the cylinder body. Keep all the components in their originally fitted sequence and note in which direction the seal lips are located.

11 Inspect the surfaces of the piston and cylinder bore. If scoring or metal-to-metal rubbing areas are evident, renew the master cylinder complete.

12 If the components are in good condition, discard the old seals and manipulate the new ones into position, using the fingers only.

13 Refit by reversing the removal operations; apply pressure to the piston ends so that the stop bolts can be fitted, then tighten the end plug. Make sure that the grooves in the pistons engage in the stop bolts. Apply thread locking fluid to the end plug and use a new copper washer.

14 Bolt the master cylinder to the vacuum servo; reconnect the fluid pipelines and reservoir cap leads.

15 Bleed the complete hydraulic system, as described in Section 12.

10 Pressure regulating valve

1   This device is designed to prevent rear wheel lock up by limiting the pressure to the rear brakes during heavy applications of the foot pedal (photo).

2   If the valve fails to function correctly and the rear wheels are found to lock then the regulator valve must be renewed as it is a sealed unit and cannot be repaired.

10.1 Brake pressure regulator

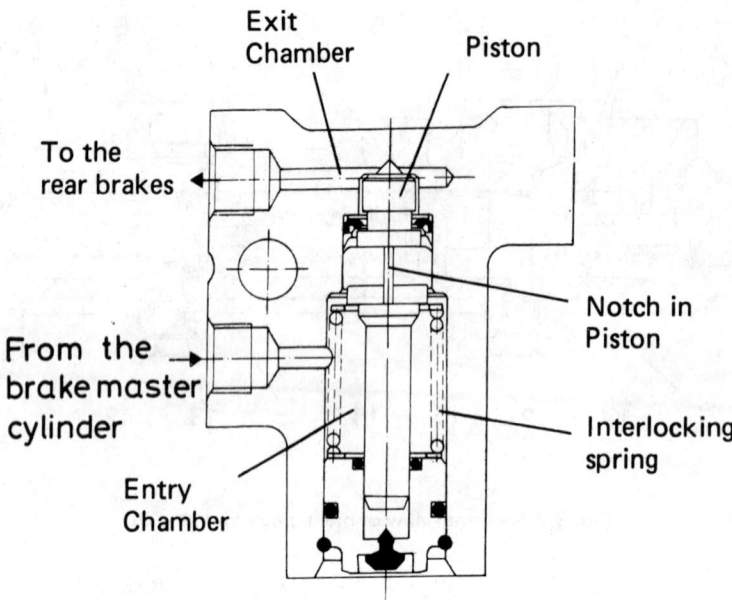

Fig. 8.8 Sectional view of pressure regulating valve (Sec 10)

Labels: Exit Chamber, Piston, To the rear brakes, Notch in Piston, From the brake master cylinder, Interlocking spring, Entry Chamber

11 Hydraulic rigid pipes and flexible hoses – inspection and renewal

Flexible hoses

1   Periodically, all brake pipes, pipe connections and unions should be completely and carefully examined.

2   First examine for signs of leakage where the pipe unions occur. Then examine the flexible hoses for signs of chafing and fraying and, of course, leakage. This is only a preliminary part of the flexible hose inspection, as exterior condition does not necessarily indicate the interior condition, which will be considered later.

3   Flexible hoses are always mounted at both ends in a rigid bracket attached to the body or a sub-assembly. To remove them, it is necessary first of all to unscrew the pipe unions of the rigid pipes which go into them. The hose ends can then be unclipped from the brackets. The mounting brackets, particularly on the body frame, are not very heavy gauge and care must be taken not to wrench them off (photo).

11.3 Brake hose support bracket and retaining clip

4   A flexible hose should be bent double to give a good indication of its condition. The appearance of tiny cracks in the rubber will indicate the need for immediate renewal.

5   Specks of black rubber ejected when bleeding the system will indicate that the hose lining is breaking up and renewal is again called for.

6   When refitting the flexible pipes, check they cannot be under tension, or rub, when the wheels are at the full range of suspension or steering movement.

7   Bleed the system (see Section 12) on completion.

Rigid pipes

8   Inspect the condition of the braking system rigid pipelines at frequent intervals. They must be cleaned off and examined for any signs of dents (or other percussive damage) and rust and corrosion. Rust and corrosion should be scraped off and, if the depth of pitting in the pipes is significant, they will need renewal. This is particularly likely in those areas underneath the car body and along the rear axle where the pipes are exposed to the full force of road and weather conditions.

9   Rigid pipe removal is usually straightforward. The unions at each end are undone, the pipe and union pulled out, and the centre sections of the pipe removed from the body clips where necessary. Underneath the car, exposed unions can sometimes be very tight. As one can use only an open-ended spanner and the unions are not large, burring of the flats is not uncommon when attempting to undo them. For this reason, a self-locking grip wrench is often the only way to remove a stubborn union.

10   Rigid pipes which need renewal can usually be purchased at any garage where they have the pipe, unions and special tools to make them up. All they need to know is the total length of the pipe, the type of flare used at each end with the union, and the length and thread of the union. Fiat is metric, remember.

11   Fitting your new pipes is a straightforward reversal of the removal procedure. If the rigid pipes have been made up, it is best to get all the sets (bends), in them before trying to fit them. Also, if there are any acute bends, ask your supplier to put these in for you on a tube bender. Otherwise, you may kink the pipe and thereby restrict the bore area and fluid flow.

12   Bleed the system (see Section 12) on completion.

12 Hydraulic system – bleeding

1   The two independent circuits are for:

(i)   *The front calipers*
(ii)   *The rear wheel cylinders*

2   If the master cylinder has been disconnected and reconnected then the complete system (both circuits) must be bled.

3   If a component of just one circuit has been disturbed then only that particular circuit need be bled.

4   If the entire system is being bled, the sequence of bleeding should be carried out by starting at the bleed screw furthest from the master cylinder and finishing at the one nearest to it. Unless the pressure bleeding method is being used, do not forget to keep the fluid level in the master cylinder reservoir topped up to prevent air from being drawn into the system which would make any work done worthless.

5   Before commencing operations, check that all system hoses and pipes are in good condition with the unions tight and free from leaks.

6   Take great care not to allow hydraulic fluid to come into contact with the vehicle paintwork as it is an effective paint stripper! Wash off any spilled fluid immediately with cold water.

Bleeding — two-man method

7   Gather together a clean glass jar and a length of rubber or plastic tubing which will be a tight fit on the brake bleed screws.

8   Engage the help of an assistant.

9   Push one end of the bleed tube onto the first bleed screw and immerse the other end in the glass jar containing enough hydraulic fluid to cover the end of the tube.

10 Open the bleed screw one half a turn and have your assistant depress the brake pedal fully then slowly release it. Tighten the bleed screw at the end of each pedal downstroke to obviate any chance of air or fluid being drawn back into the system.

11 Repeat this operation until clean hydraulic fluid, free from air bubbles, can be seen coming through into the jar.

12 Tighten the bleed screw at the end of a pedal downstroke and remove the bleed tube. Bleed the remaining screws in a similar way.

Bleeding — using one-way valve kit

13 There are a number of one-man, one-way, brake bleeding kits available from motor accessory shops. It is recommended that one of these kits is used wherever possible as it will greatly simplify the bleeding operation and also reduce the risk of air or fluid being drawn back into the system, quite apart from being able to do the work without the help of an assistant.

14 To use the kit, connect the tube to the bleed screw and open the screw one half a turn.

15 Depress the brake pedal fully and slowly release it. The one-way valve in the kit will prevent expelled air from returning at the end of each pedal downstroke. Repeat this operation several times to be sure of ejecting all air from the system. Some kits include a translucent container which can be positioned so that the air bubbles can actually be seen being ejected from the system.

16 Tighten the bleed screw, remove the tube and repeat the operations on the remaining brakes.

17 On completion, depress the brake pedal. If it still feels spongy repeat the bleeding operations as air must still be trapped in the system.

Bleeding — using a pressure bleeding kit

18 These kits too are available from motor accessory shops and are usually operated by air pressure from the spare tyre.

19 By connecting a pressurised container to the master cylinder fluid reservoir, bleeding is then carried out simply by opening each bleed screw in turn and allowing the fluid to run out, rather like turning on a tap, until no air is visible in the expelled fluid.

20 By using this method, the large reserve of hydraulic fluid provides a safeguard against air being drawn into the master cylinder during bleeding which may occur if the fluid level in the reservoir is allowed to fall too low.

21 Pressure bleeding is particularly effective when bleeding 'difficult' systems or when bleeding the complete system at time of routine fluid renewal.

All methods

22 When bleeding is completed, check and top up the fluid level in the master cylinder reservoir.

23 Check the feel of the brake pedal. If it feels at all spongy, air must still be present in the system and further bleeding is indicated. Failure to bleed satisfactorily after a reasonable repetition of the bleeding operations may be due to worn master cylinder seals.

24 Discard brake fluid which has been expelled. It is almost certain to be contaminated with moisture, air and dirt making it unsuitable for further use. Clean fluid should always be stored in an airtight container as it absorbs moisture readily (hygroscopic) which lowers its boiling point and could affect braking performance under severe conditions.

13 Handbrake — adjustment

1   The handbrake should be fully applied after pulling it over four or five notches of its ratchet.

2   The handbrake is normally kept in correct adjustment by the action of the rear shoe automatic adjusters. However, after a high mileage, additional adjustment may be required to take up stretch in the cable.

3   To do this, release the locknut at the cable equaliser under the car and turn the adjuster nut as necessary to shorten the travel of the hand control lever (photo).

4   Raise the rear wheels and check that the brakes do not bind with the handbrake fully released.

5   Tighten the cable adjuster locknut.

6   Always keep the cable groove in the equaliser well greased.

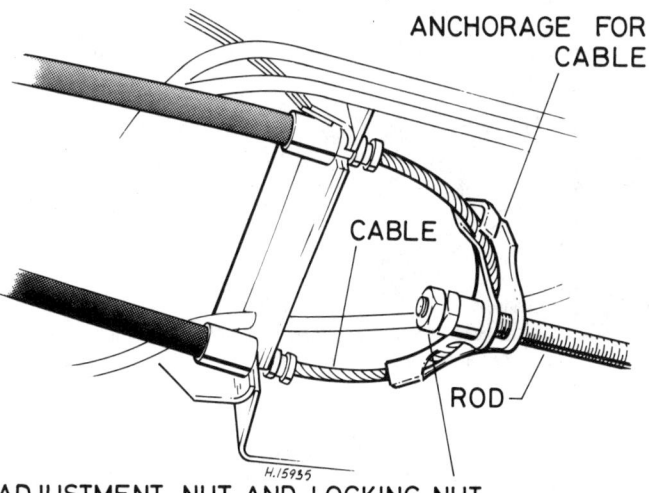

Fig. 8.9 Handbrake cable equaliser (Sec 13)

13.3 Handbrake cable adjuster and equaliser

14 Handbrake cable – renewal

1   Release the handbrake, chock the front wheels and raise the rear of the car and support securely.
2   Unscrew the adjuster nut and locknut and release the equaliser and cable from the primary rod.
3   Remove the rear roadwheels for better access to the brake backplates.
4   Disconnect the handbrake cable end fittings from the shoe actuating levers and the axle tube brackets (photos).

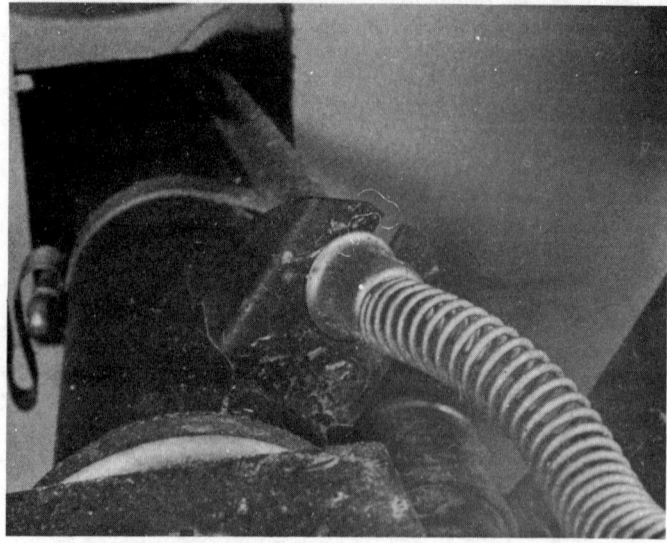

14.4C Handbrake cable axle tube bracket

14.4A Handbrake cable connection to shoe lever

5   Fit the new cable by reversing the removal operations, adjust as described in the preceding Section.
6   Fit the roadwheels and lower the car.

15 Brake pedal – removal and refitting

1   The brake pedal pivots on a cross-shaft with the clutch pedal. Refer to Chapter 5, Section 4 for details of removal and refitting.
2   The master cylinder pushrod is held to the pedal arm by a clevis pin and split pin (photo).

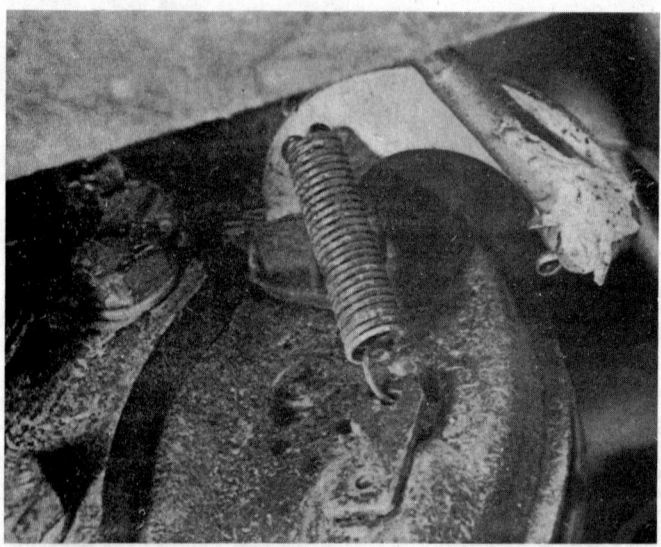

14.4B Handbrake shoe lever spring

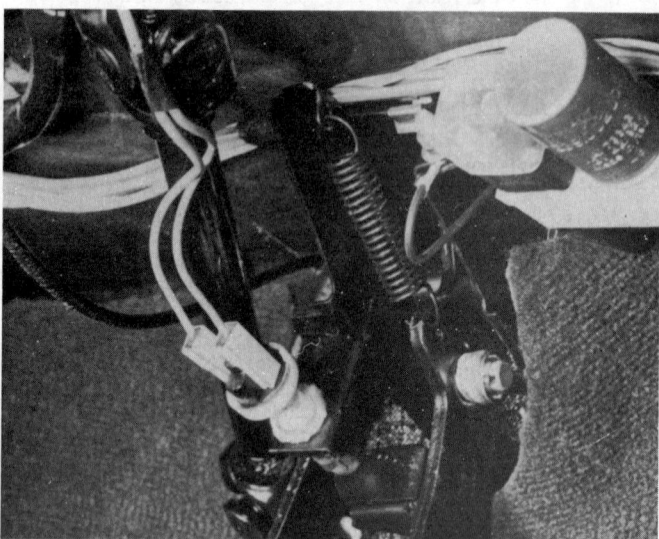

15.2 Pedals, stop lamp switch and relays

16 Fault diagnosis – braking system

Before diagnosing faults from the following chart, check that any braking irregularities are not caused by:
  Uneven and incorrect tyre pressures
  Wear in the steering mechanism
  Defects in the suspension and dampers
  Misalignment of the bodyframe

Symptom	Reason(s)
Stopping ability poor, even though pedal pressure is firm	Linings, discs or drums badly worn or scored One or more wheel hydraulic cylinders seized, resulting in some brake shoes not pressing against the drums (or pads against disc) Brake linings contaminated with oil Wrong type of linings fitted (too hard) Brake shoes wrongly assembled
Car veers to one side when the brakes are applied	Brake pads or linings on one side are contaminated with oil Hydraulic wheel cylinder on one side partially or fully seized A mixture of lining materials fitted between sides Brake discs not matched Unequal wear between sides caused by partially seized wheel cylinders
Pedal feels spongy when the brakes are applied	Air is present in the hydraulic system
Pedal feels springy when the brakes are applied	Brake linings not bedded into the drums (after fitting new ones) Master cylinder or brake backplate mounting bolts loose Severe wear in brake drums causing distortion when brakes are applied Discs out of true
Pedal travels right down with little or no resistance and brakes are virtually non-operative	Leak in hydraulic system resulting in lack of pressure for operating wheel cylinders If no signs of leakage are apparent the master cylinder internal seals are failing to sustain pressure
Binding, juddering, overheating	One or a combination of reasons given above Shoes installed incorrectly with reference to leading and trailing ends Broken shoe return spring Disc out-of-round Drum distorted

Chapter 9 Electrical system

Contents

Alternator – description, maintenance and precautions 4
Alternator – overhaul 6
Alternator – removal and refitting 5
Battery – maintenance 2
Battery – removal and refitting 3
Bulbs – renewal 15
Clock – setting 21
Courtesy lamp, clock, mirror assembly – removal and
refitting 20
Courtesy lamp switch – removal and refitting 13
Fault diagnosis – electrical system 28
Fuses and relays 10
General description 1
Headlamp – removal and refitting 16
Headlamp beam – alignment 17
Heated tailgate window 25

Horn and switch 14
Instrument panel – removal and refitting 18
Modible radio equipment – interference-free installation
(non-Fiat equipment) 27
Radio (Fiat accessory) – fitting 26
Rocker switches – removal and refitting 12
Speedometer cable – renewal 19
Starter motor – description and in-car testing 7
Starter motor – overhaul 9
Starter motor – removal and refitting 8
Steering column switch – removal and refitting 11
Washer system 24
Wiper blade and arm – removal and refitting 22
Wiper motor and linkage – removal and refitting 23
Wiring diagrams – see end of Manual

Specifications

System type .... 12 volt negative earth, alternator, battery, pre-engaged starter motor

Battery .... 32 Ah

Alternator
Make .... Marelli, Femsa or Lucas
Continuous rating 45A
Maximum output 47A

Starter motor
Make .... Marelli or Femsa
Nominal power .... 0.8 kW

Fuses

Number	Circuit protected	Amps
1	Reversing lamp, stop lamp, direction indicator, warning lamps, fuel gauge	8
2	Windscreen wiper, heated rear screen switch, rear wiper	8
3	LH headlamp main beam	8
4	RH headlamp main beam	8
5	LH headlamp dipped beam and rear foglamps	8
6	RH headlamp dipped beam	8
7	Front LH parking and RH tail lamp. Rear number plate lamp, instrument panel illumination	8
8	Front RH parking and LH tail lamps	8
9	Horn, courtesy lamps	16
10	Heated rear tailgate glass and hazard warning lamps	16

Bulbs

	Wattage
Headlamp	45/40
Front parking	5
Front direction indicator	21
Side repeater	4
Rear direction indicator	21
Tail lamp	5
Stop lamp	21
Reversing lamp	21
Rear foglamp	21
Rear number plate	5
Warning and indicator lamps	3

Torque wrench settings

	Nm	lbf ft
Alternator mounting nuts	49	36
Starter motor mounting bolts	25	19

1 General description

The electrical system is of 12 volt negative earth type with battery, alternator and pre-engaged starter.

Circuit fuses are provided.

2 Battery – maintenance

Earlier models

1   The modern battery seldom requires topping up but nevertheless, the electrolyte level should be inspected weekly as a means of providing the first indication that the alternator is overcharging or that the battery casing has developed a leak. The battery plates should always be covered to a depth of 6.0 mm (0.25 in) with electrolyte.

2   When topping up is required, use only distilled water or melted ice from a refrigerator (frosting not ice cubes).

3   Acid should never be required if the battery has been correctly filled from new, unless spillage has occurred.

4   Inspect the battery terminals and mounting tray for corrosion. This is the white fluffy deposit which grows at these areas. If evident, clean it away and neutralise it with ammonia or baking soda. Apply petroleum jelly to the terminals and paint the battery tray with anti-corrosive paint.

5   Keep the top surface of the battery casing dry.

6   An indication of the state of charge of a battery can be obtained by checking the electrolyte in each cell using a hydrometer. The specific gravity of the electrolyte for fully charged and fully discharged conditions at the electrolyte temperature indicated, is listed below.

Fully discharged	Electrolyte temperature	Fully charged
1.098	38°C (100°F)	1.268
1.102	32°C (90°F)	1.272
1.106	27°C (80°F)	1.276
1.110	21°C (70°F)	1.280
1.114	16°C (60°F)	1.284
1.118	10°C (50°F)	1.288
1.122	4°C (40°F)	1.292
1.126	-1.5°C (30°F)	1.296

7   There should be very little variation in the readings between the different cells, but if a difference is found in excess of 0.025 then it will probably be due to an internal fault indicating impending battery failure. This assumes that electrolyte has not been spilled at some time and the deficiency made up with water only.

8   If electrolyte is accidentally spilled at any time, mop up and neutralise the spillage at once. Electrolyte attacks and corrodes metal rapidly; it will also burn holes in clothing and skin. Leave the addition of acid to a battery cell to your dealer or service station as the mixing of acid with distilled water can be dangerous.

9   Never smoke or allow naked lights near the battery; the hydrogen gas which it gives off is explosive.

10 With normal motoring, the battery should be kept in a good state of charge by the alternator and never need charging from a mains charger.

11 However, if the daily mileage is low with much use of starter and electrical accessories, it is possible for the battery to become discharged due to the fact that the alternator is not in use long enough to replace the current consumed.

12 Also as the battery ages, it may not be able to hold its charge and some supplementary charging may be needed. Before connecting the charger, disconnect the battery terminals or better still, remove the battery from the vehicle.

13 Specially rapid 'boost' charges which are claimed to restore the power of the battery in 1 to 2 hours are most dangerous as they can cause serious damage to the battery plates through overheating.

14 While charging the battery note that the temperature of the electrolyte should never exceed 100°F (37.8°C).

Later models

15 These cars are fitted with a maintenance-free type battery which should never need topping up.

16 Regularly inspect the electrolyte level visually through the translucent battery case. Any drop below the minimum level will indicate leakage from the casing.

17 Keep the battery terminals free from corrosion by smearing them with petroleum jelly.

3 Battery – removal and refitting

1   The battery is located within the engine compartment next to the heater air intake (photo).

2   Disconnect the negative lead and then the positive one.

3   Unbolt the battery clamp (photo) and lift the battery out, keeping it level.

4   Refitting is a reversal of removal.

3.1 Battery locations

3.3 Unscrewing battery clamp bolt

5.3 Removing alternator – adjuster and mounting nuts arrowed

4 Alternator – description, maintenance and precautions

1 The alternator may be of Femsa, Lucas or Marelli construction and has an integral voltage regulator.
2 The alternator generates current at much lower revolutions than a dynamo; the battery does not therefore discharge, even under idling or slow motoring conditions.
3 The alternator develops its current in the stationary windings, the rotor carrying this field. The brushes therefore carry only a small current, so they last a long time, and only simple slip rings are needed instead of a commutator.
4 The AC voltage is rectified by a bank of diodes. These also prevent battery discharge through the alternator.

To avoid damage to the alternator, the following precautions should be observed
5 Disconnect the leads from the battery before connecting a mains charger to the battery terminals.
6 Never stop the engine by pulling off one of the battery leads.
7 Disconnect the battery if electric welding is to be carried out on the vehicle.
8 If using booster cables from another battery to start the car, make sure that they are connected positive to positive and negative to negative.
9 Maintenance consists of keeping the outside of the alternator clean, the electrical connections secure and the drivebelt correctly tensioned (refer to Chapter 2).

5 Alternator – removal and refitting

1 Release the alternator adjuster slot and mounting nuts, push the alternator in towards the engine and slip the drivebelt off the pulleys.
2 Disconnect the leads and plugs from the rear face of the alternator.
3 Remove the mounting and adjuster slot nuts and lift the alternator from the engine mounting studs (photo).
4 Refitting is a reversal of removal. Adjust the drivebelt tension as described in Chapter 2.

6 Alternator – overhaul

The alternator normally has a very long and trouble-free life. When a fault does develop (or after a high mileage, when wear in the

bearings is evident), complete renewal with a new or factory rebuilt unit is recommended.
1 With the alternator removed from the car, the brushes can be renewed after removing the rear cover or brush holder and disconnecting or unsoldering the brush leads according to type (photos).
2 Take the opportunity of cleaning the slip rings with a fuel moistened cloth or if severely marked, with very fine glasspaper.

7 Starter motor – description and in-car testing

1 The starter motor may be one of two different makes, both of which are of pre-engaged type.
2 This type of starter motor incorporates a solenoid mounted on top of the starter motor body. When the ignition switch is operated, the solenoid moves the starter drive pinion, through the medium of the shift lever, into engagement with the flywheel starter ring gear. As the solenoid reaches the end of its stroke, and with the pinion by now partially engaged with the flywheel ring gear, the main fixed and moving contacts close and engage the starter motor to rotate the engine.
3 This pre-engagement of the starter drive does much to reduce the wear on the flywheel ring gear associated with inertia type starter motors.
4 If the starter fails, some fault-finding can be done with it still on the car. Check the ignition warning light comes on, and does not go out when the starter is switched on. If it goes out, the fault is probably in the battery. If it stays bright, get an assistant to work the switch, whilst listening to the starter. Listen to find out if the solenoid clicks into position. If it does not, pull the red solenoid wire, and check it with a test bulb. If the wire is live when the key is turned, but the solenoid does not move, take off the starter and remove it to the bench for overhaul.

8 Starter motor – removal and refitting

1 Disconnect the earth lead from the negative terminal of the battery.
2 Disconnect the lead from the starter solenoid and the heavy cable from the battery (photo).
3 Remove the mounting bolts and lift out the starter (photo).
4 Refitting is the reverse of the removal sequence. Make sure the electrical connections are secure.

6.1A Rear cover on Lucas alternator

6.1B Lucas alternator integral regulator

6.1C Alternator brushbox

6.1D Alternator brush removed

8.2 Starter solenoid terminals

8.3 Removing the starter motor

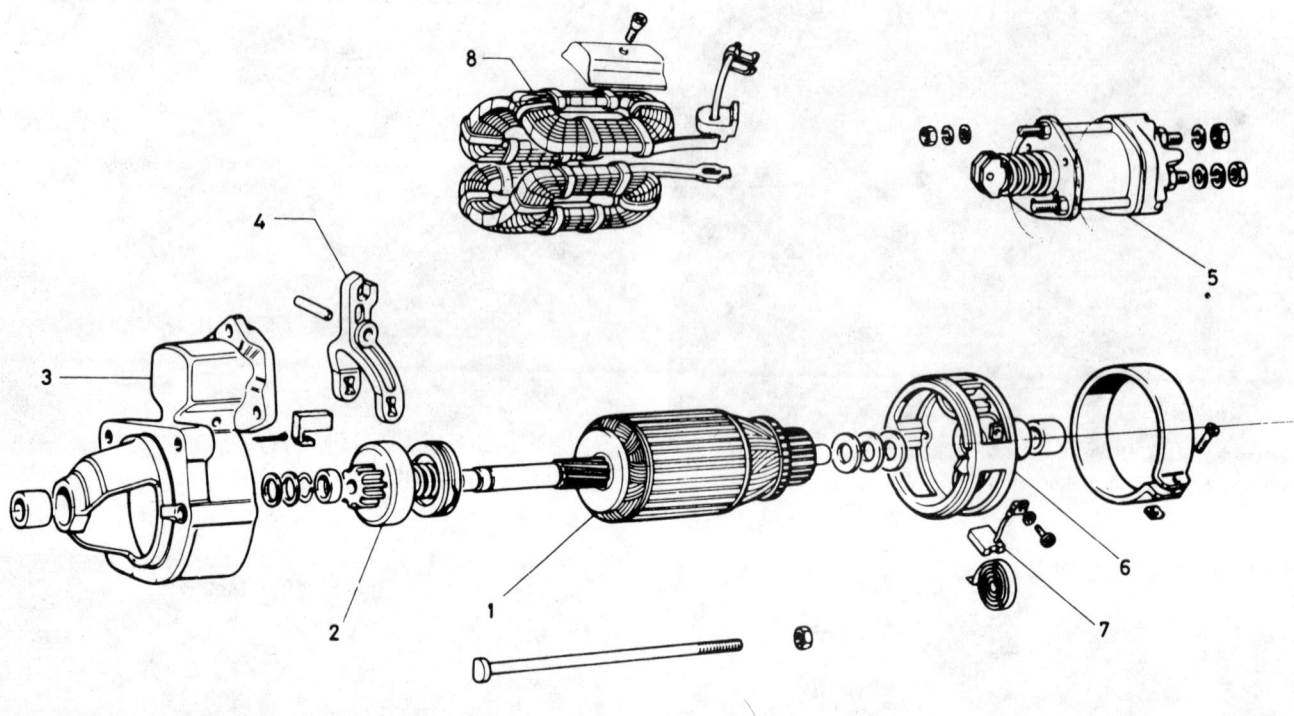

Fig. 9.1 Exploded view of typical starter motor (Sec 9)

1 Armature	3 Drive end bracket	5 Solenoid	7 Brush
2 Drive pinion/clutch	4 Shift lever	6 Brush end plate	8 Field windings

9 Starter motor – overhaul

1 Having removed the starter from the engine, first clean the outside.

2 If the starter has been removed because it will not work, before stripping it, test to see where the defect is, and decide whether to try repairing it, or if it is better to obtain a replacement. Connect a lead from the battery negative terminal to the starter body, using one of the bolts that held it to the engine. Connect the positive battery terminal to the little solenoid terminal. The solenoid should slide the starter's gear along the shaft, but the starter will not turn because there is no power to the motor terminal. Now connect battery power to that terminal. With the solenoid live, the starter should turn after the gear has slid into engagement. If it does not, try the wire direct to the motor's lead on the solenoid terminal nearer the motor main body, on which is the lead into the motor. If the motor now turns it shows that the switch part of the solenoid is faulty.

3 The starter should be dismantled for cleaning and renewing of the brushes whenever its performance deteriorates.

4 Take off the nut on the solenoid, and disconnect the cable from the solenoid to the motor.

5 Remove the nuts and washers on the long studs holding the solenoid to the end frame. Lift off the solenoid, unhooking it from the shift lever.

6 Slacken and slide off the dust cover on the end of the yoke, to uncover the brushes.

7 Disconnect the wire from the field winding to its brush.

8 Hook up the brush springs on the sides of the brush holders, so the load is taken off them.

9 Undo the nuts on the long through bolts holding the whole motor together.

10 Take off the brush-end endplate, and retrieve the one fibre and two steel washers from the end of the armature shaft.

11 Tip the motor pinion end down, and lift the yoke off the armature and pinion end frame.

12 Take out its split pin, and remove the pivot pin for the shift lever,

from the 'waist' of the pinion housing.

13 Take the pinion housing off the assembly of armature, pinion and gear lever.

14 Clean all the parts by wiping. Do not immerse in cleaning liquid, especially the freewheel and the armature bushes in the end frames, as the liquid will get into the freewheel race and the pores of the bushes.

15 Check the condition of the commutator. If it is dirty and blackened, clean it with a rag, dampened with petrol. If the commutator is in good condition, the surface will be smooth and free from pitting or burnt areas, and the insulated segments clearly defined.

16 Scrape the dirt out of the undercut gaps of insulator between the metal segments with a narrow screwdriver.

17 If, after the commutator has been cleaned, pitted and burnt spots are still present, wrap a strip of fine glass paper round the commutator. Rub the patches off while turning the armature so that the rubbing is spread evenly all over. Finally, polish the commutator with metal polish, then clean out the gaps.

18 Clean every part thoroughly when finished and ensure that no rough edges are left as any roughness will cause excessive brush wear.

19 Before reassembly, lubricate the splines of the freewheel with general purpose grease. Use a thin oil on the spiral splines. Use engine oil for the armature bushes, allowing it time to soak in before assembly.

20 Fit the brushes in their guides, but clip them back so that they will clear the commutator by putting the springs on their side. The springs can be hooked into place after the brush endplate has been fitted.

10 Fuses and relays

1 The fuses are located on the engine compartment rear bulkhead (photo).

2 Prise off the fuse block cover for access to the individual fuses.

3 Always renew a fuse with one of similar rating. If the new fuse blows immediately find the reason before renewing again, this is usually due to faulty wiring insulation causing a short circuit.

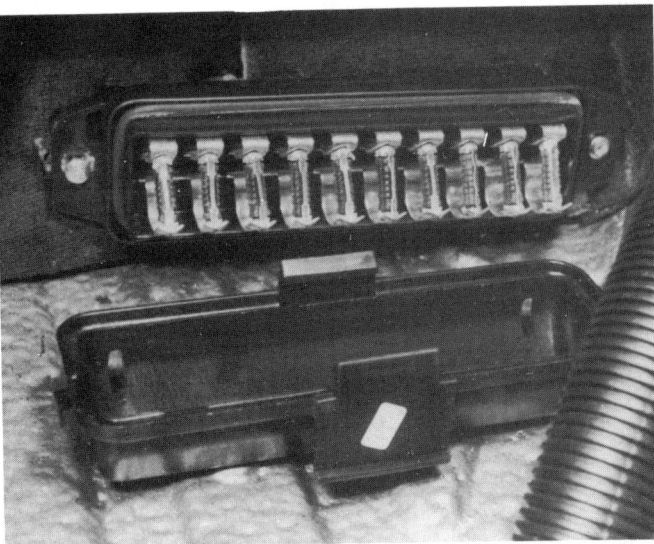

10.1 Fuse box

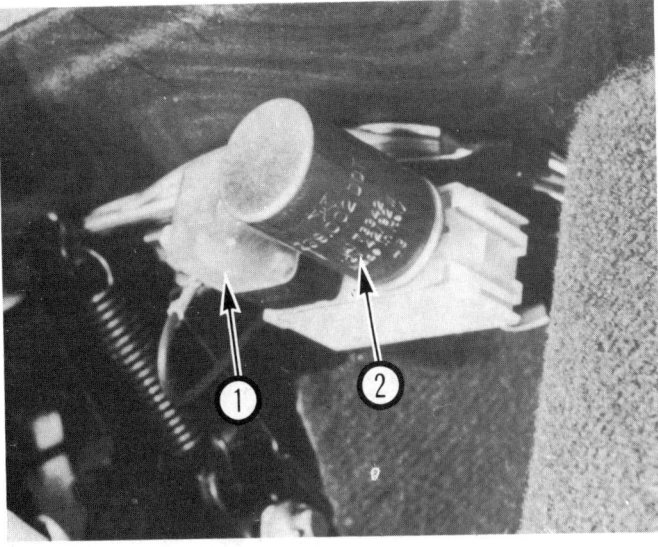

10.4 Relays

1   Heated rear window   *2   Direction indicator*

4   Two relays are located under the facia panel adjacent to the steering column. The cylindrical one is the direction indicator/hazard warning relay, the other one being the heated rear window relay (photo).
5   Rapid flashing of the direction indicators will usually mean that one of the lamp bulbs is broken. If one lamp will not light up, check the earth connection before assuming that the bulb or relay is faulty.

11 Steering column switch – removal and refitting

1   Removal of the steering column combination switch is described in Chapter 10, Section 6.

12 Rocker switches – removal and refitting

1   The easiest way to remove the rocker switches is to withdraw the instrument panel as described in Section 18.
2   From the rear of the switches, pull of the multi-plug and then squeeze the switch retaining tabs and withdraw the switch.
3   Refitting is a reversal of removal.

13 Courtesy lamp switch – removal and refitting

1   Open the door and extract the small screw which holds the switch in the body pillar (photo).
2   Withdraw the switch and disconnect the leads. Tape the leads to the pillar in case they should slip back into the body cavity.
3   Smear the switch contacts with petroleum jelly to prevent corrosion and refit by reversing the removal operations.

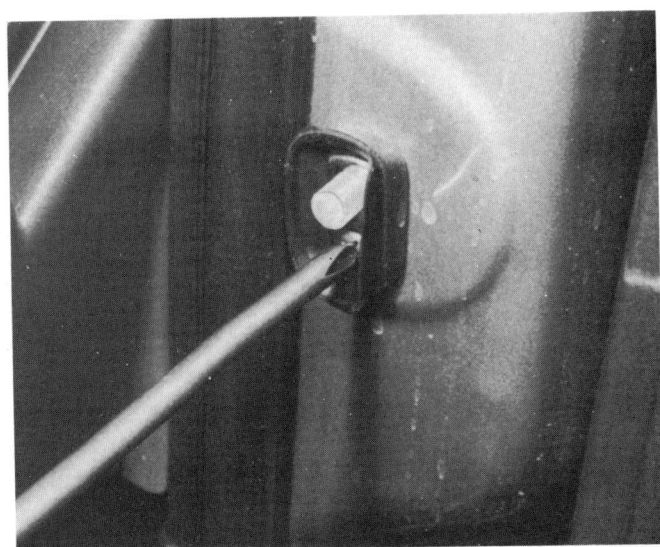

13.1 Extracting courtesy lamp switch screw

14 Horn and switch

1   The horn is located behind the body front panel.
2   The horn switch is mounted in the hub of the steering wheel. Prise out the switch for access to the contacts and coil springs.

15 Bulbs – renewal

Headlamp
1   Pull off the wiring plug from the rear of the headlamp (photo).

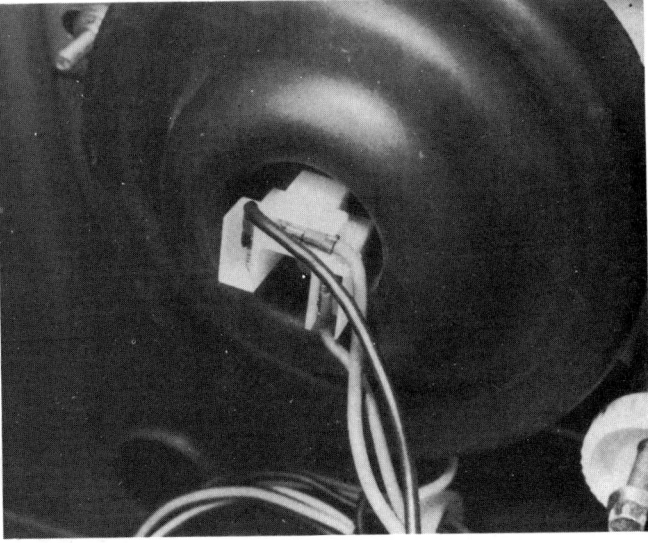

15.1 Headlamp wiring plug

2   Twist the cover on the rear of the headlamp in an anti-clockwise direction and remove it (photo).
3   Depress the tabs on the spring retainer and turn it anti-clockwise (photo).
4   Withdraw the bulb and fit a new one so that the pip on the bulbholder flange engages in the notch in the reflector (photo).
5   Push on the wiring plug and fit the cover.

Front parking lamp

6   Access to this bulb is obtained as described for the headlamp bulb. Pull the bulbholder from the socket in the headlamp reflector (photo).

Front direction indicator lamp

7   Extract the screws and remove the lamp lens (photo).
8   Remove the bayonet type bulb and fit the new one.

Side repeater lamp

9   Should a bulb fail, renew the complete lamp as an assembly. Simply pull the lamp from its hole and disconnect the wiring (photo).

Rear lamp cluster

10   Extract the two fixing screws and withdraw the lamp (photo).
11   Depress the retaining clip to release the bulbholder and to give access to the bayonet type bulbs (photos).

15.2 Headlamp rear cover

15.3 Headlamp bulbholder

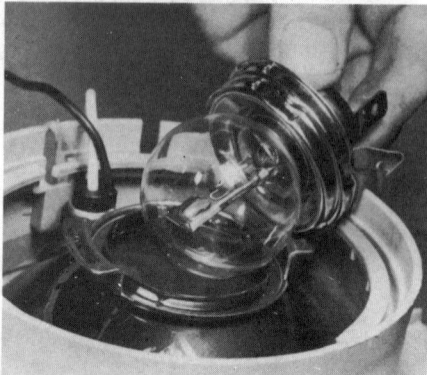
15.4 Removing headlamp bulb

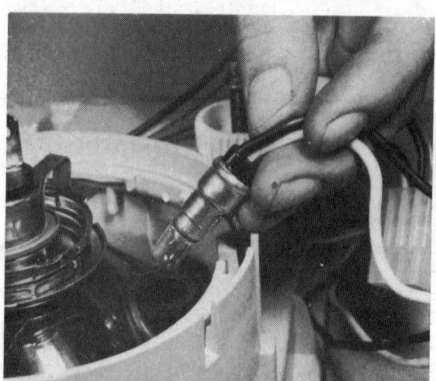
15.6 Front parking lamp bulb

15.7 Front direction indicator lamp

15.9 Side repeater lamp

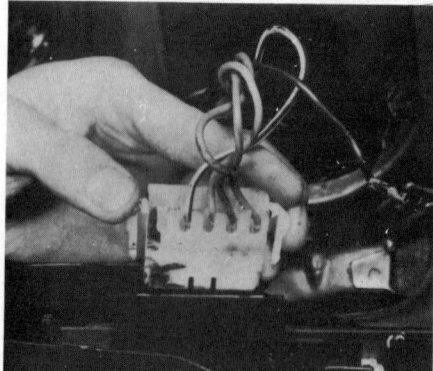
15.10 Rear lamp cluster wiring plug

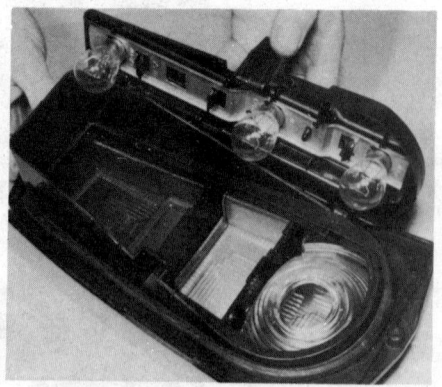
15.11A Rear lamp lens and bulbholder

15.11B View of rear of rear lamp cluster

15.12A Rear number plate lamp

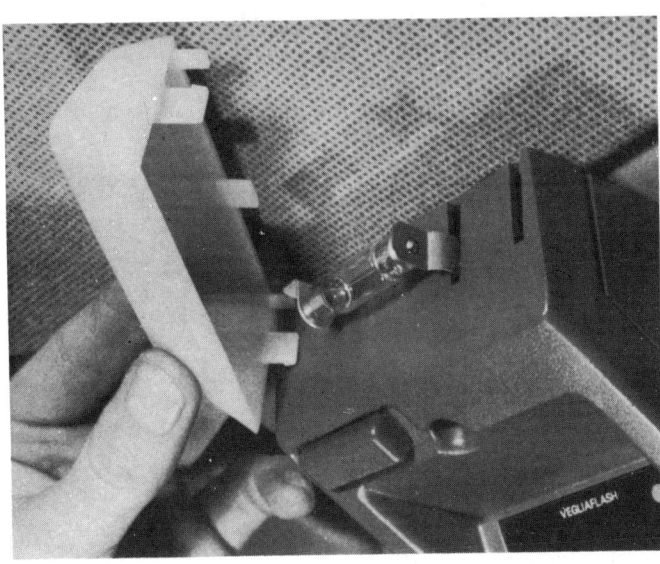
15.13 Courtesy lamp lens and bulb

15.12B Rear number plate bulb

15.14 Instrument panel bulb and holder

Rear number plate lamp
12 The lamp is held in its bumper cut-out by spring clips. Prise the lamp from its hole and then squeeze the two retainers to separate the lens and bulbholder (photos).

Interior lamp
13 Prise off the lamp lens for access to the festoon type bulb (photo).

Instrument panel warning and indicator lamps
14 These are wedge base bulbs located in 'push and twist' type holders. Remove the instrument panel as described in Section 18 for access to the bulbholders (photo).

16 Headlamp – removal and refitting

1 Remove the cover and wiring plug from the rear of the headlamp.
2 Unscrew the three mounting nuts. One of these is difficult to reach and is more easily removed using a box spanner. Withdraw the headlamp unit (photos).
3 Refitting is a reversal of removal.

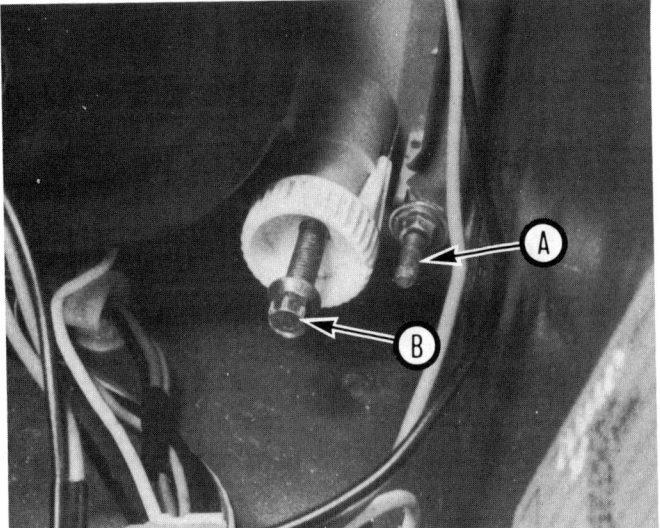
16.2A Headlamp fixing nut (A) and adjuster screw (B)

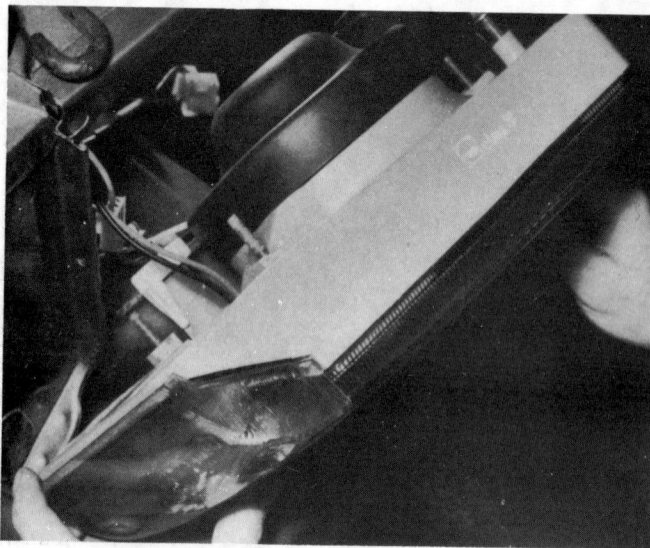

16.2B Removing headlamp

17 Headlamp beam – alignment

1   It is recommended that the headlamp beams are aligned by a garage or service station having optical beam setting equipment, but for owners wishing to do the work themselves, carry out the following procedure.

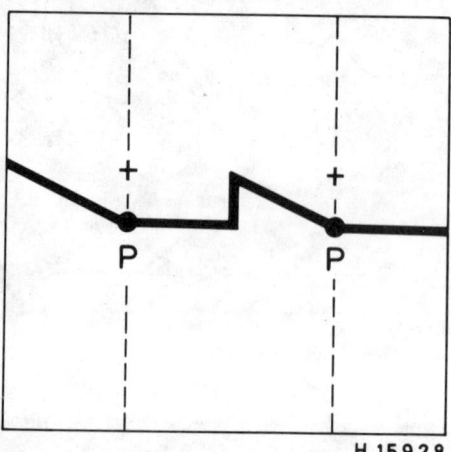

H.15928

Fig. 9.2 Headlamp beam alignment pattern (Sec 17)

+   = headlamp centres   P = dipped beam bright spots

Fig. 9.3 Headlamp beam adjusting screws (Sec 7)

A   Vertical   B   Horizontal

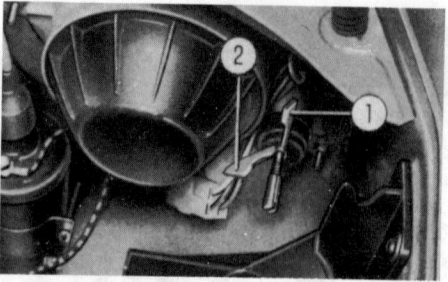

Fig. 9.4 Headlamp beam leveller (Sec 17)

1   Light load position   2   Heavy load position

2   Place the car on level ground, with its tyres correctly inflated, facing a wall at a distance of 5.0 m (16.4 ft) from the wall.
3   Mark the wall with crosses to represent the headlamp centres and then switch on dipped beams.
4   The bright points of the lamps should be 50.0 mm (1.9 in) below the marks on the wall.
5   Adjust as necessary using the screws provided.
6   To compensate for varying loads, a headlamp beam levelling lever is provided at each lamp.

18 Instrument panel – removal and refitting

1   Disconnect the battery.
2   Remove the steering wheel as described in Chapter 10.
3   Pull off the heater control knobs. These are very tight on the levers, but it will ease removal if they are bent to the right and their anchor tabs relieved with a thin screwdriver.
4   Extract the three screws from under the lower edge of the instrument panel (photo).

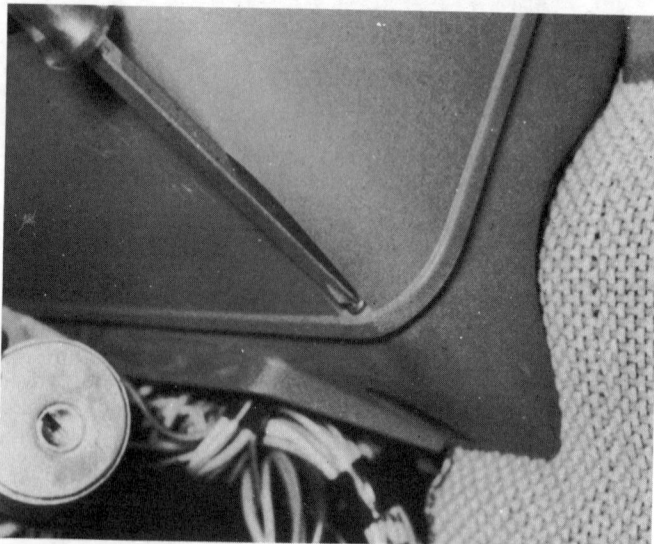

18.4 Extracting instrument panel screw

5   Pull the instrument panel towards you until the speedometer cable can be disconnected from the head. Do this by squeezing the plastic cable retainer and pulling (photo).
6   Disconnect the wiring plugs, but making sure to note their positions first.
7   Remove the instrument panel (photo).
8   The individual instruments may be removed from the rear of the panel after releasing the fixing screws or nuts (photo).
9   Refitting is a reversal of removal.

18.5 Withdrawing instrument panel

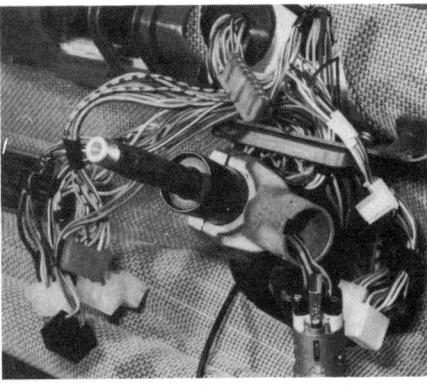
18.7 Instrument panel and associated items removed

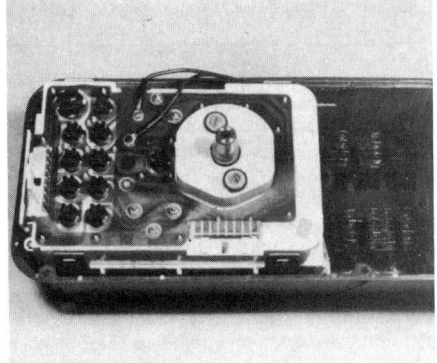
18.8 Rear view of instrument panel

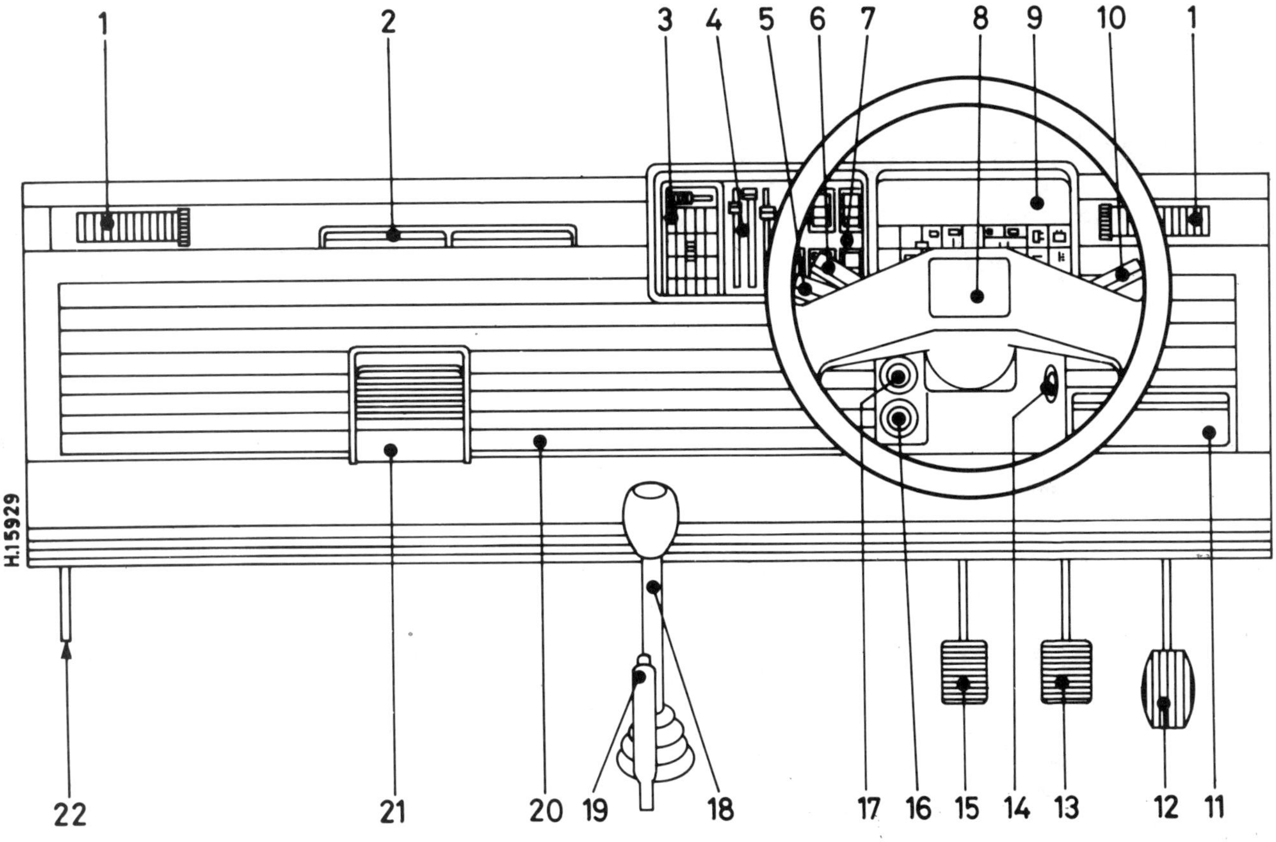

H.15929

Fig. 9.5 Controls and instruments (Sec 18)

1 Fresh air vents	9 Instrument panel	16 Windscreen washer control
2 Demister vents	10 Windscreen wiper control	17 Choke control
3 Adjustable air vents	11 Radio housing	18 Gearchange lever
4 Heater control levers	12 Accelerator pedal	19 Handbrake control lever
5 Headlamp dip lever	13 Brake pedal	20 Parcels shelf
6 Direction indicator lever	14 Ignition switch	21 Ashtray
7 Rocker switch panel	15 Clutch pedal	22 Bonnet release
8 Horn control		

19 Speedometer cable – renewal

1 Working at the transmission, unscrew the speedometer cable knurled nut.
2 Working inside the car, withdraw the instrument panel as described in the preceding Section and disconnect the cable from the speedometer by squeezing the plastic retaining collar and pulling the cable (photo).
3 Withdraw the cable through the bulkhead grommet.
4 Refitting the new cable is a reversal of removal. Do not make any of the cable bends sharper than the original ones.

19.2 Speedometer cable connector

20 Courtesy lamp, clock, mirror assembly – removal and refitting

1 Disconnect the battery.
2 The assembly is held above the windscreen by a single screw (photos).

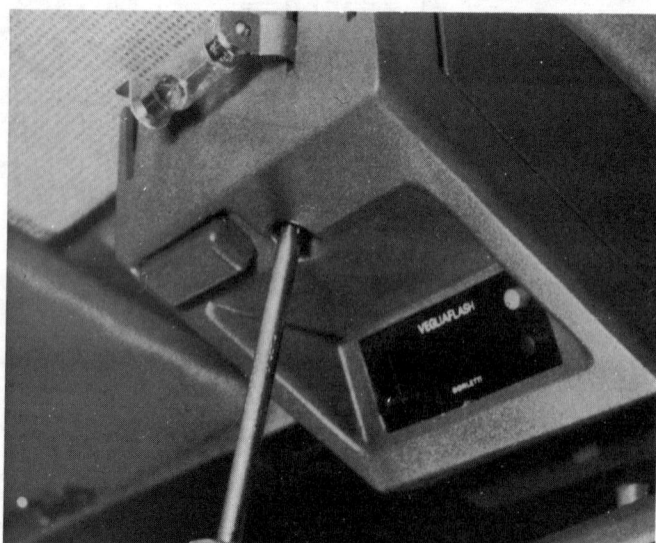

20.2A Clock/courtesy lamp fixing screw

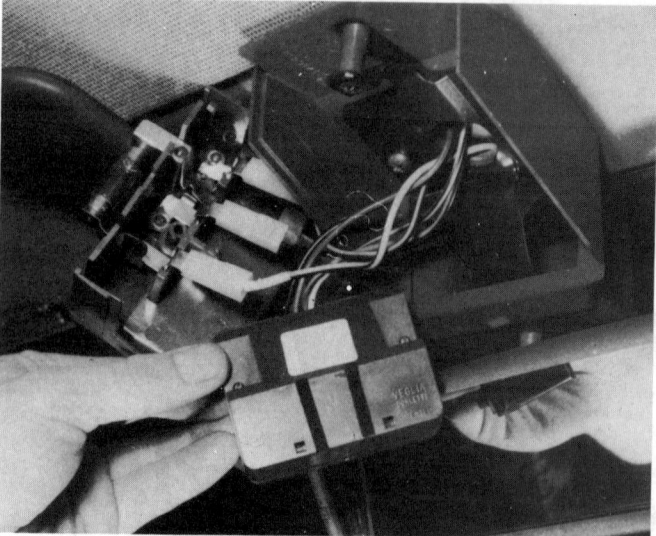

20.2B Clock/courtesy lamp removed

21 Clock – setting

1 The optional digital type clock displays the time when the ignition key is turned to MAR.
2 To set the hours, depress button C then button A and release it at the correct time. Press button C three times to display hours and minutes.
3 To set the minutes, depress button C twice, then button A and release it at the correct time. Press button C twice to display hours and minutes.
4 To set the seconds, depress button C three times. Hold button A depressed to zero the seconds and then release it to start seconds. Press button C to display hours and minutes.

H.15930

Fig. 9.6 Digital clock control buttons (Sec 21)

22 Wiper blade and arm – removal and refitting

1 Pull the arm away from the glass and depress the blade locking tab with the thumb nail and slide the blade from the arm (photo).
2 The arm is a push fit on the wheel box spindle. Before pulling it off, it is worthwhile sticking a piece of masking tape along the blade on the glass as a guide to alignment when refitting (photo).

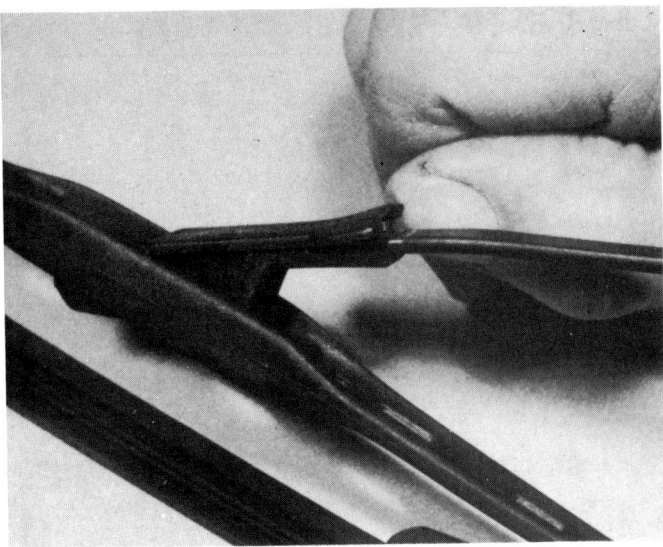

22.1 Disconnecting wiper blade from arm

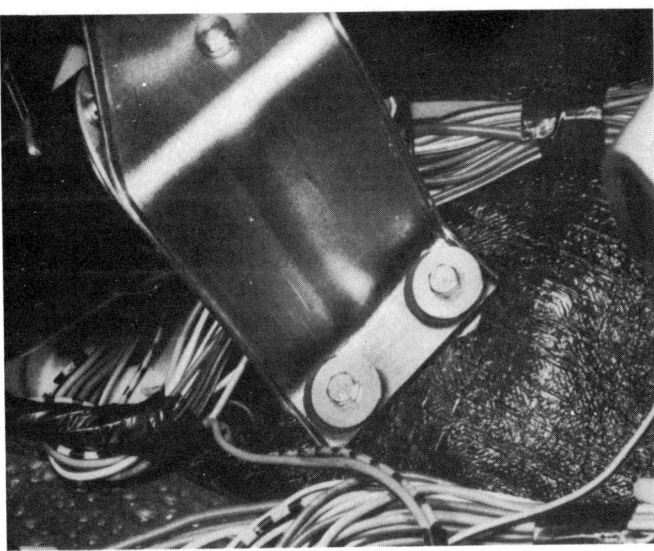

23.3A Windscreen wiper support bracket

22.2 Removing wiper arm

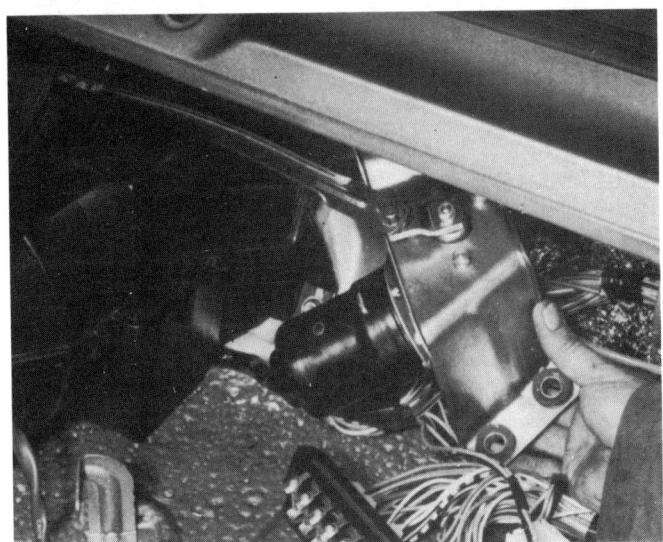

23.3B Removing wiper assembly

23 Wiper motor and linkage – removal and refitting

Windscreen

1   Remove the wiper arm and blade as described in the preceding Section.
2   Working within the engine compartment, pull out the insulating strip from the bulkhead to expose the wiper motor.
3   Disconnect the wiring plug and then release the motor mounting and wheelbox mounting. Withdraw the motor and linkage from the scuttle (photos).
4   Refitting is a reversal of removal.

Tailgate

5   Remove the blade and arm using the same method as for the windscreen wiper.
6   Open the tailgate and remove the cover from the wiper motor.
7   Unbolt the assembly and wheelbox spindle nut and withdraw the unit until the connecting plug can be disconnected (photo).
8   Refitting is a reversal of removal.

23.7 Tailgate wiper motor

24 Washer system

1   The washer fluid reservoir is located within the engine compartment and doubles as a support for the spare wheel (photo).
2   The reservoir incorporates two independent pumps, one for the windscreen and one for the tailgate.
3   The washer jets should strike the glass towards the top of the arc swept by the blade. To adjust, twist the nozzle and then turn the screw (A) with a small screwdriver.

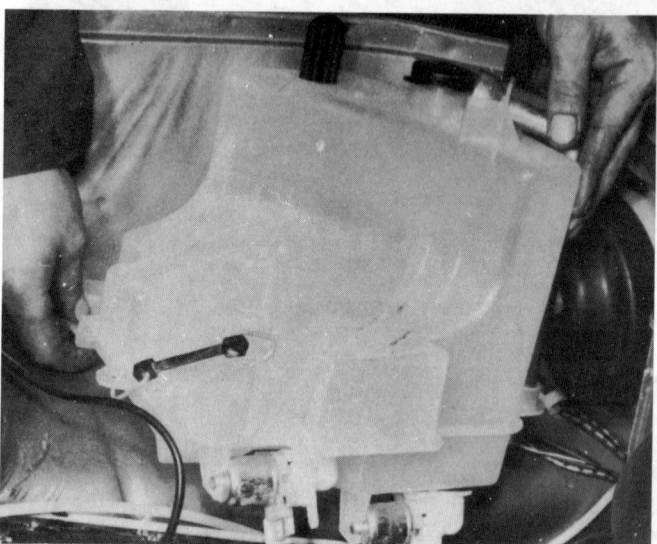

24.1 Removing washer fluid reservoir

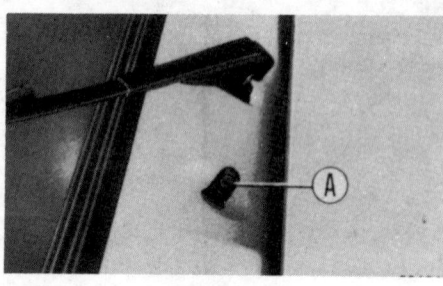

Fig. 9.7 Windscreen washer jet (Sec 24)

A   Screw

25 Heated tailgate window

1   To prevent damage to the elements of the heated rear window, observe the following precautions:

   (a)   Clean the interior surface of the glass with a damp cloth or chamois leather, rubbing in the direction that the elements run
   (b)   Avoid scratching the elements with rings on the fingers or contact with articles in the luggage compartment
   (c)   Do not stick adhesive labels over the elements

2   Should the element be broken, it can be repaired using a conductive silver paint, without the need to remove the glass from the window.
3   The paint is available from many sources and should be applied with a soft brush to a really clean surface. Use two strips of masking tape as a guide to the thickness of the element to be repaired.
4   Allow the new paint to dry thoroughly before switching the heater on.

26 Radio (Fiat accessory) – fitting

1   A radio console is available as a Fiat accessory for fitting into the facia panel or as a centre console (photo).

Aerial and power leads

2   Working within the engine compartment, release the fuse box and move it to one side.
3   Partially remove the weatherstrip and then cut a hole (22.0 mm diameter) on the front pillar in accordance with the diagram (Fig. 9.8).

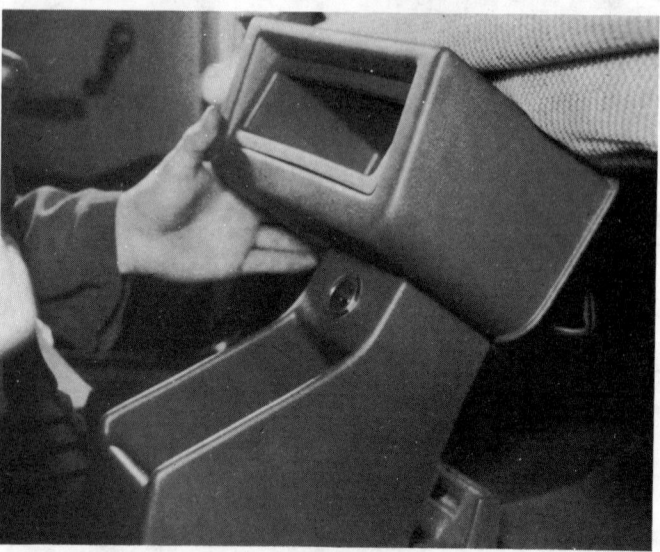

26.1 Centre console

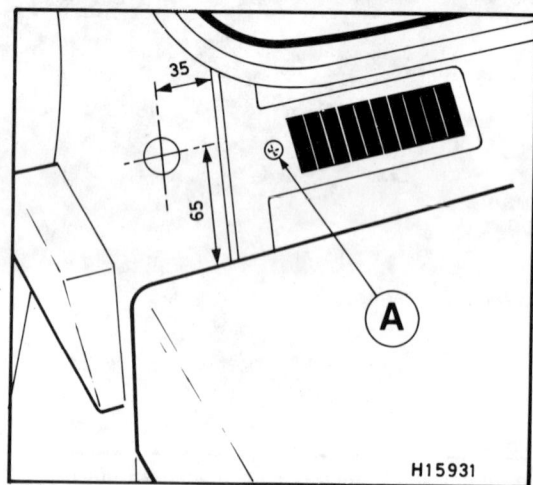

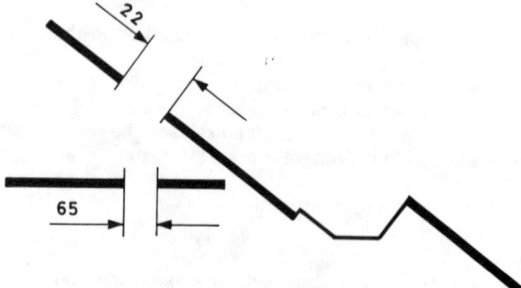

Fig. 9.8 Aerial mounting hole (Sec 26)

Dimensions in mm   *A   Air grille screw*

4   Working through the hole just made, cut another hole (12.0 mm diameter) on the pillar box section.
5   Remove the air intake grille (A).
6   Remove the side vent (B) (Fig. 9.9).
7   Fit the aerial, passing the lead through the holes.
8   If the facia-mounted console is already fitted, remove it, and then partially detach the left-hand facia lining.
9   Drill a hole in the rubber plug exposed and pass the aerial lead through it.
10 Refit the air intake grille and side vent.
11 Route the aerial lead under the panel lining and refit the lining.
12 Partially withdraw the facia under-cover to gain access to the power leads already connected.
13 Route the leads to the radio location.
14 Connect the in-line fuse holder into the radio feed wire within the engine compartment adjacent to the fuse block.

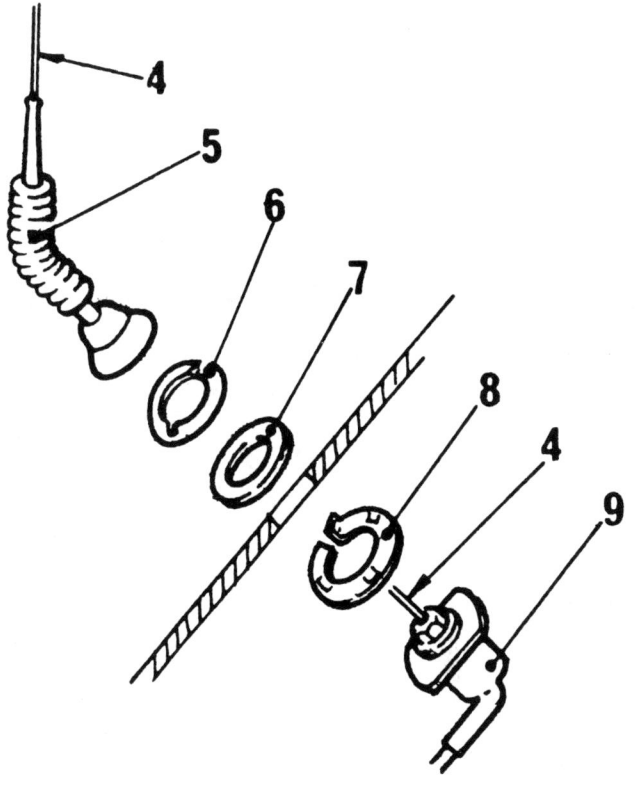

Fig. 9.11 Aerial fixing components (Sec 26)

4	Aerial lead	7	Grommet
5	Gaiter	8	Washer
6	Ring	9	Base

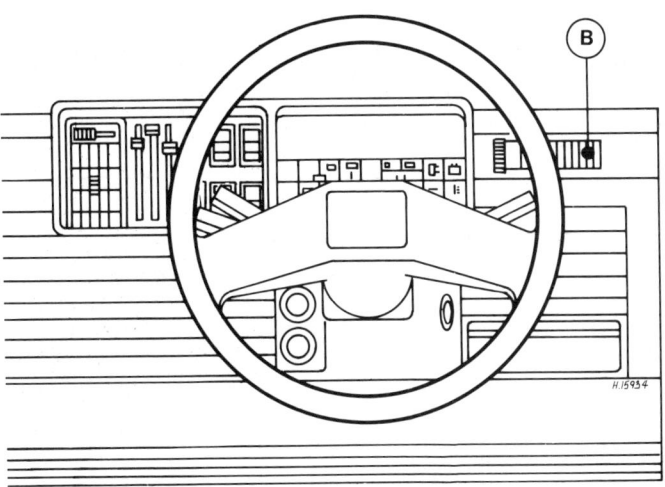

Fig. 9.9 Facia side vent (B) (Sec 26)

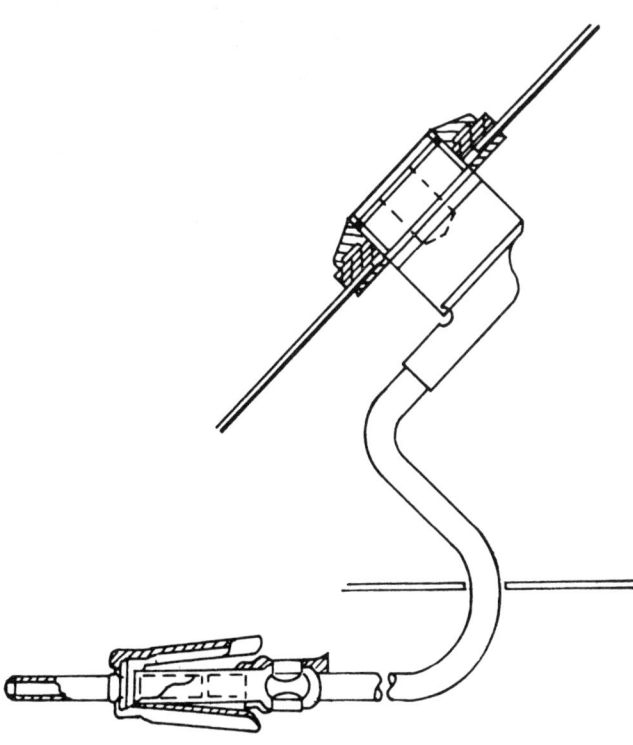

Fig. 9.10 Aerial mounting (Sec 26)

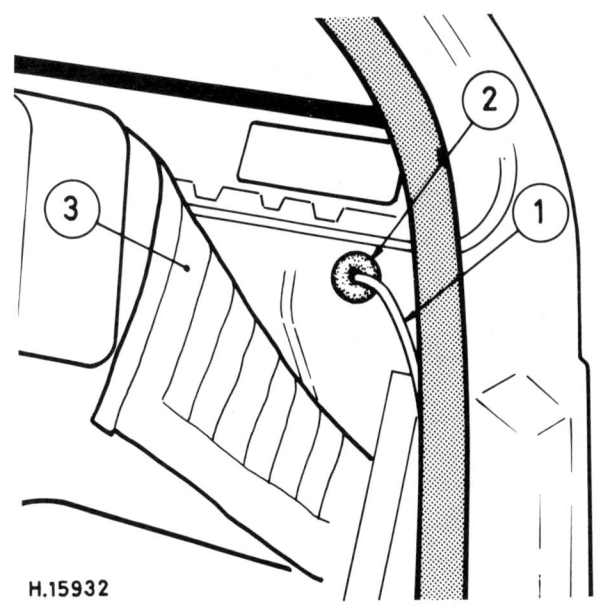

Fig. 9.12 Facia lead-through for aerial (Sec 26)

| 1 | Plug | 3 | Lining |
| 2 | Aerial lead | | |

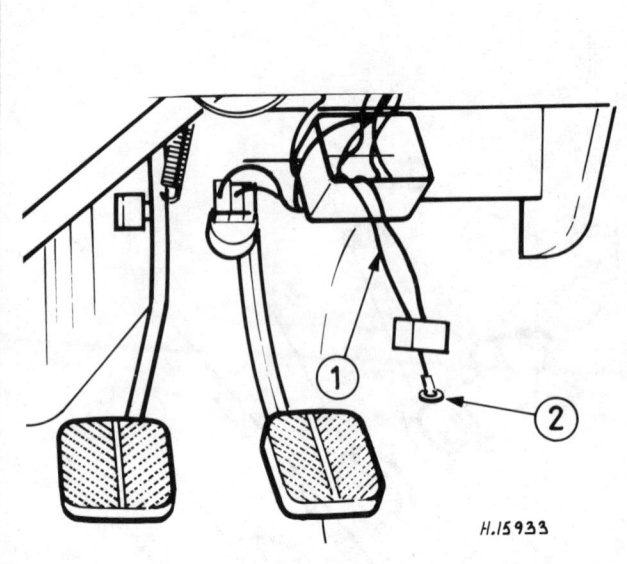

Fig. 9.13 Under facia power lead (1) and earth lead (2) (Sec 26)

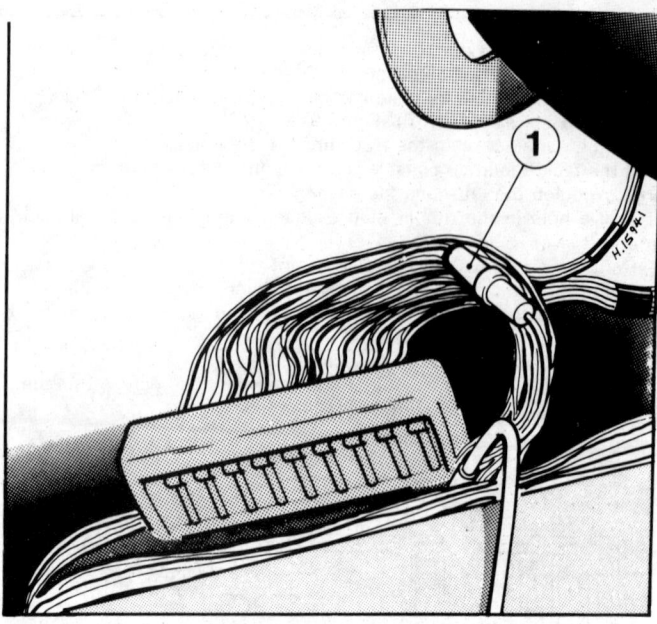

Fig. 9.14 Radio in-line fuse holder (1) (Sec 26)

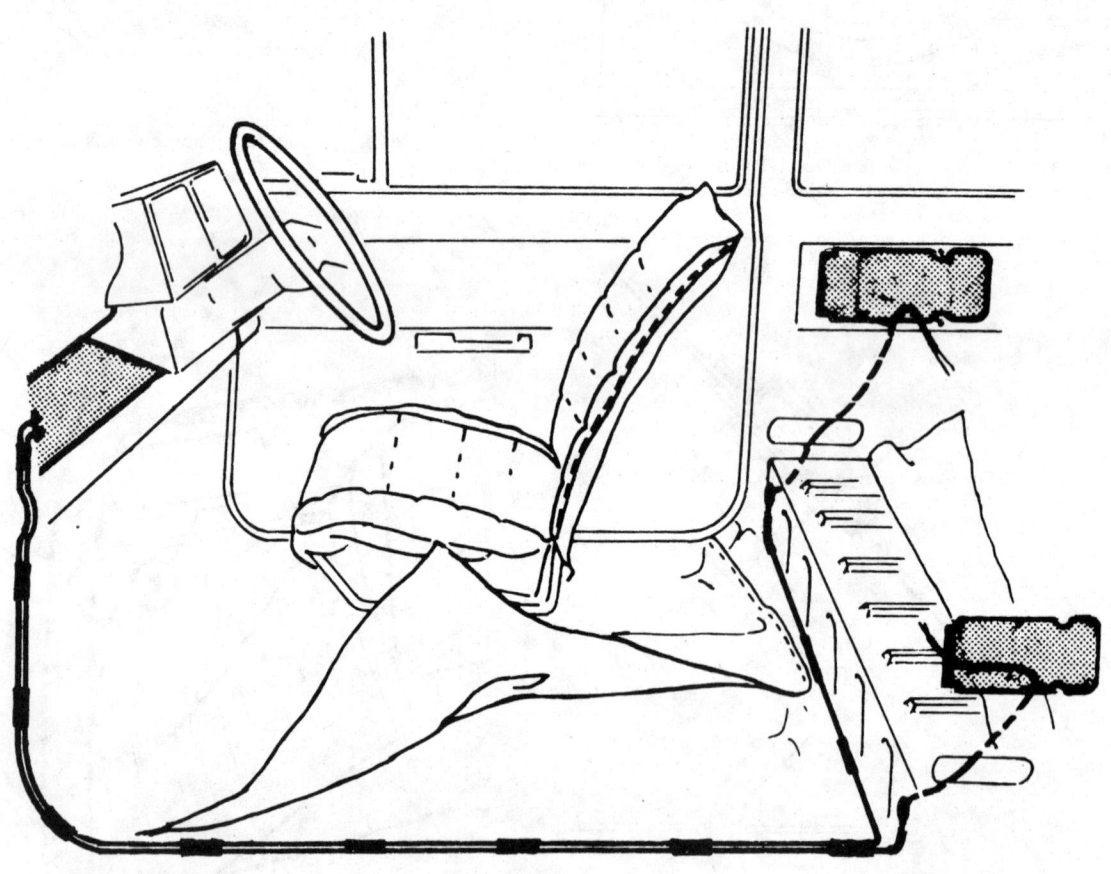

Fig. 9.15 Speaker wire routing (Sec 26)

Speakers

15 The speakers should be fitted behind the rear side trim panels. To do this, remove the left-hand door sill tread plate, the rear seat, luggage compartment mat and trim panels (refer to Chapter 12).

16 Run the speaker leads as shown in the diagram.

Receiver

17 Locate the receiver and connect the aerial, power and speaker leads to it. Make sure that there is a good earth bond between the receiver casing and the body of the car.

Interference suppression

18 The ignition coil (and alternator on early models) may require the fitting of suppressors. Refer to the next Section for details of the recommended methods.

19 Trim the aerial according to instructions with the radio.

27 Mobile radio equipment – interference-free installation (non-Fiat equipment)

Aerials – selection and fitting

The choice of aerials is now very wide. It should be realised that the quality has a profound effect on radio performance, and a poor, inefficient aerial can make suppression difficult.

A wing-mounted aerial is regarded as probably the most efficient for signal collection, but a roof aerial is usually better for suppression purposes because it is away from most interference fields. Stick-on wire aerials are available for attachment to the inside of the windscreen, but are not always free from the interference field of the engine and some accessories.

Motorised automatic aerials rise when the equipment is switched on and retract at switch-off. They require more fitting space and supply leads, and can be a source of trouble.

There is no merit in choosing a very long aerial as, for example, the type about three metres in length which hooks or clips on to the rear of the car, since part of this aerial will inevitably be located in an interference field. For VHF/FM radios the best length of aerial is about one metre. Active aerials have a transistor amplifier mounted at the base and this serves to boost the received signal. The aerial rod is sometimes rather shorter than normal passive types.

A large loss of signal can occur in the aerial feeder cable, especially over the Very High Frequency (VHF) bands. The design of feeder cable is invariably in the co-axial form, ie a centre conductor surrounded by a flexible copper braid forming the outer (earth) conductor. Between the inner and outer conductors is an insulator material which can be in solid or stranded form. Apart from insulation, its purpose is to maintain the correct spacing and concentricity. Loss of signal occurs in this insulator, the loss usually being greater in a poor quality cable. The quality of cable used is reflected in the price of the aerial with the attached feeder cable.

The capacitance of the feeder should be within the range 65 to 75 picofarads (pF) approximately (95 to 100 pF for Japanese and American equipment), otherwise the adjustment of the car radio aerial trimmer may not be possible. An extension cable is necessary for a long run between aerial and receiver. If this adds capacitance in excess of the above limits, a connector containing a series capacitor will be required, or an extension which is labelled as 'capacity-compensated'.

Fitting the aerial will normally involve making a $\frac{7}{8}$ in (22 mm) diameter hole in the bodywork, but read the instructions that come with the aerial kit. Once the hole position has been selected, use a centre punch to guide the drill. Use sticky masking tape around the area for this helps with marking out and drill location, and gives protection to the paintwork should the drill slip. Three methods of making the hole are in use:

(a) Use a hole saw in the electric drill. This is, in effect, a circular hacksaw blade wrapped round a former with a centre pilot drill.

(b) Use a tank cutter which also has cutting teeth, but is made to shear the metal by tightening with an Allen key.

(c) The hard way of drilling out the circle is using a small drill, say $\frac{1}{8}$ in (3 mm), so that the holes overlap. The centre metal drops out and the hole is finished with round and half-round files.

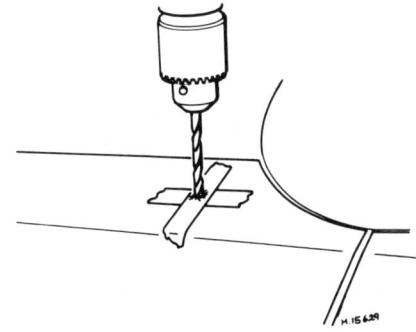

Fig. 9.16 Drilling the bodywork for aerial mounting (Sec 27)

Whichever method is used, the burr is removed from the body metal and paint removed from the underside. The aerial is fitted tightly ensuring that the earth fixing, usually a serrated washer, ring or clamp, is making a solid connection. *This earth connection is important in reducing interference.* Cover any bare metal with primer paint and topcoat, and follow by underseal if desired.

Aerial feeder cable routing should avoid the engine compartment and areas where stress might occur, eg under the carpet where feet will be located. Roof aerials require that the headlining be pulled back and that a path is available down the door pillar. It is wise to check with the vehicle dealer whether roof aerial fitting is recommended.

Loudspeakers

Speakers should be matched to the output stage of the equipment, particularly as regards the recommended impedance. Power transistors used for driving speakers are sensitive to the loading placed on them.

Before choosing a mounting position for speakers, check whether the vehicle manufacturer has provided a location for them. Generally door-mounted speakers give good stereophonic reproduction, but not all doors are able to accept them.

For door mounting, first remove the trim, which is often held on by 'poppers' or press studs, and then select a suitable gap in the inside door assembly. Check that the speaker would not obstruct glass or winder mechanism by winding the window up and down. A template

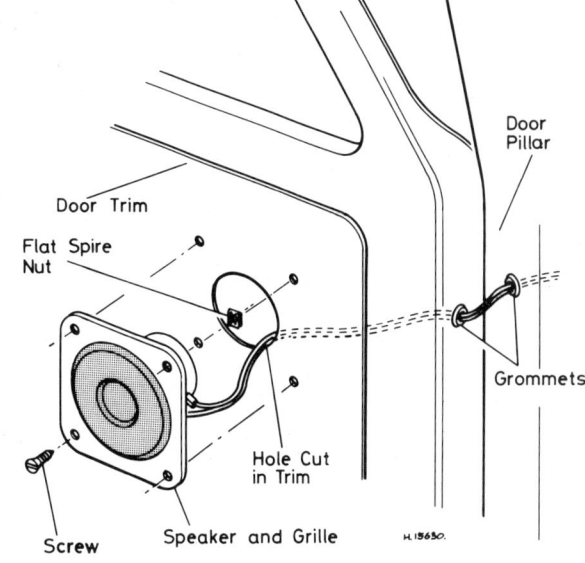

Fig. 9.17 Door-mounted speaker installation (Sec 27)

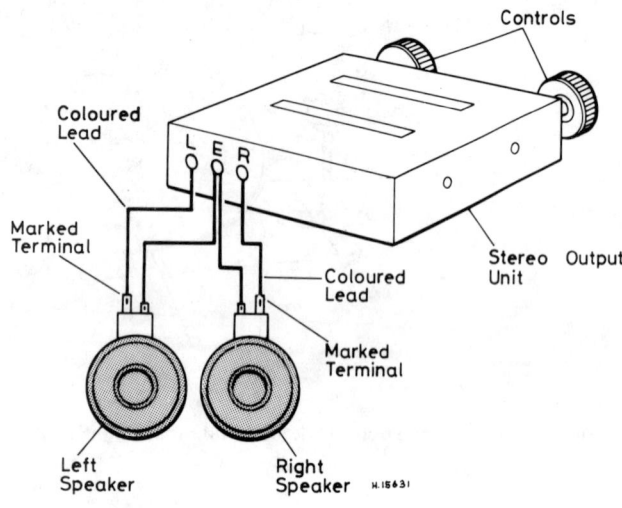

Fig. 9.18 Speaker connecting leads (Sec 27)

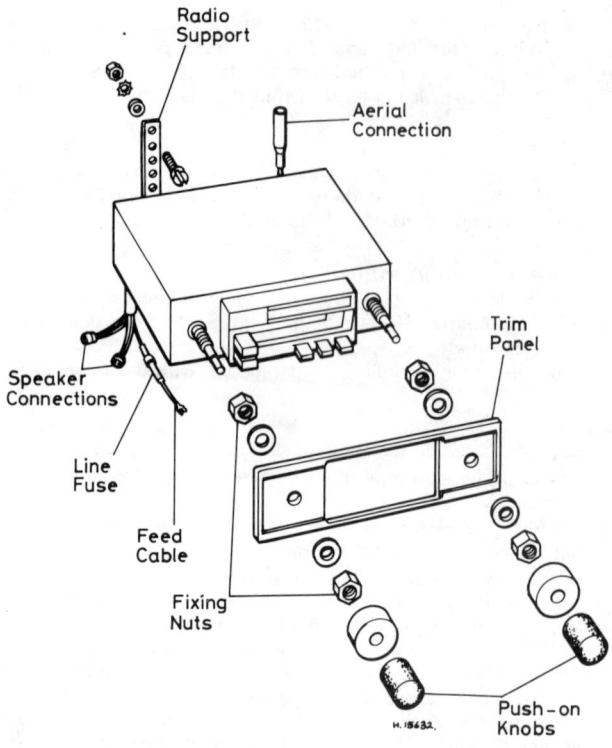

Fig. 9.19 Mounting components for radio/cassette (Sec 27)

is often provided for marking out the trim panel hole, and then the four fixing holes must be drilled through. Mark out with chalk and cut cleanly with a sharp knife or keyhole saw. Speaker leads are then threaded through the door and door pillar, if necessary drilling 10 mm diameter holes. Fit grommets in the holes and connect to the radio or tape unit correctly. Do not omit a waterproofing cover, usually supplied with door speakers. If the speaker has to be fixed into the metal of the door itself, use self-tapping screws, and if the fixing is to the door trim use self-tapping screws and flat spire nuts.

Unit installation

Many vehicles have a dash panel aperture to take a radio/audio unit, a recognised international standard being 189.5 mm x 60 mm. Alternatively a console may be a feature of the car interior design and this, mounted below the dashboard, gives more room. If neither facility is available a unit may be mounted on the underside of the parcel shelf; these are frequently non-metallic and an earth wire from the case to a good earth point is necessary. A three-sided cover in the form of a cradle is obtainable from car radio dealers and this gives a professional appearance to the installation; in this case choose a position where the controls can be reached by a driver with his seat belt on.

Installation of the radio/audio unit is basically the same in all cases, and consists of offering it into the aperture after removal of the knobs (not push buttons) and the trim plate. In some cases a special mounting plate is required to which the unit is attached. It is worthwhile supporting the rear end in cases where sag or strain may occur, and it is usually possible to use a length of perforated metal strip attached between the unit and a good support point nearby. In general it is recommended that tape equipment should be installed at or nearly horizontal.

Connections to the aerial socket are simply by the standard plug terminating the aerial downlead or its extension cable. Speakers for a stereo system must be matched and correctly connected, as outlined previously.

Note: *While all work is carried out on the power side, it is wise to disconnect the battery earth lead.* Before connection is made to the vehicle electrical system, check that the polarity of the unit is correct. Most vehicles use a negative earth system, but radio/audio units often have a reversible plug to convert the set to either + or − earth. *Incorrect connection may cause serious damage.*

The power lead is often permanently connected inside the unit and terminates with one half of an in-line fuse carrier. The other half is fitted with a suitable fuse (3 or 5 amperes) and a wire which should go to a power point in the electrical system. This may be the accessory terminal on the ignition switch, giving the advantage of power feed with ignition or with the ignition key at the 'accessory' position. Power

to the unit stops when the ignition key is removed. Alternatively, the lead may be taken to a live point at the fusebox with the consequence of having to remember to switch off at the unit before leaving the vehicle.

Before switching on for initial test, be sure that the speaker connections have been made, for running without load can damage the output transistors. Switch on next and tune through the bands to ensure that all sections are working, and check the tape unit if applicable. The aerial trimmer should be adjusted to give the strongest reception on a weak signal in the medium wave band, at say 200 metres.

Interference

In general, when electric current changes abruptly, unwanted electrical noise is produced. The motor vehicle is filled with electrical devices which change electric current rapidly, the most obvious being the contact breaker.

When the spark plugs operate, the sudden pulse of spark current causes the associated wiring to radiate. Since early radio transmitters used sparks as a basis of operation, it is not surprising that the car radio will pick up ignition spark noise unless steps are taken to reduce it to acceptable levels.

Interference reaches the car radio in two ways:

(a)   by conduction through the wiring.
(b)   by radiation to the receiving aerial.

Initial checks presuppose that the bonnet is down and fastened, the radio unit has a good earth connection (not through the aerial downlead outer), no fluorescent tubes are working near the car, the aerial trimmer has been adjusted, and the vehicle is in a position to receive radio signals, ie not in a metal-clad building.

Switch on the radio and tune it to the middle of the medium wave (MW) band off-station with the volume (gain) control set fairly high. Switch on the ignition (but do not start the engine) and wait to see if irregular clicks or hash noise occurs. Tapping the facia panel may also produce the effects. If so, this will be due to the voltage stabiliser, which is an on-off thermal switch to control instrument voltage. It is located usually on the back of the instrument panel, often attached to the speedometer. Correction is by attachment of a capacitor and, if still troublesome, chokes in the supply wires.

Switch on the engine and listen for interference on the MW band. Depending on the type of interference, the indications are as follows.

A harsh crackle that drops out abruptly at low engine speed or when the headlights are switched on is probably due to a voltage regulator.

A whine varying with engine speed is due to the alternator. Try temporarily taking off the fan belt — if the noise goes this is confirmation.

Regular ticking or crackle that varies in rate with the engine speed is due to the ignition system. With this trouble in particular and others in general, check to see if the noise is entering the receiver from the wiring or by radiation. To do this, pull out the aerial plug, (preferably shorting out the input socket or connecting a 62 pF capacitor across it). If the noise disappears it is coming in through the aerial and is *radiation noise*. If the noise persists it is reaching the receiver through the wiring and is said to be *line-borne*.

Interference from wipers, washers, heater blowers, turn-indicators, stop lamps, etc is usually taken to the receiver by wiring, and simple treatment using capacitors and possibly chokes will solve the problem. Switch on each one in turn (wet the screen first for running wipers!) and listen for possible interference with the aerial plug in place and again when removed.

Note that if most of the vehicle accessories are found to be creating interference all together, the probability is that poor aerial earthing is to blame.

Component terminal markings

Throughout the following sub-sections reference will be found to various terminal markings. These will vary depending on the manufacturer of the relevant component. If terminal markings differ from those mentioned, reference should be made to the following table, where the most commonly encountered variations are listed.

Alternator	Alternator terminal (thick lead)	Exciting winding terminal
DIN/Bosch	B+	DF
Delco Remy	+	EXC
Ducellier	+	EXC
Ford (US)	+	DF
Lucas	+	F
Marelli	+B	F

Ignition coil	Ignition switch terminal	Contact breaker terminal
DIN/Bosch	15	1
Delco Remy	+	−
Ducellier	BAT	RUP
Ford (US)	B/+	CB/−
Lucas	SW/+	−
Marelli	BAT/+B	D

Voltage regulator	Voltage input terminal	Exciting winding terminal
DIN/Bosch	B+/D+	DF
Delco Remy	BAT/+	EXC
Ducellier	BOB/BAT	EXC
Ford (US)	BAT	DF
Lucas	+/A	F
Marelli		F

Suppression methods – ignition

Suppressed HT cables are supplied as original equipment by manufacturers and will meet regulations as far as interference to neighbouring equipment is concerned. It is illegal to remove such suppression unless an alternative is provided, and this may take the form of resistive spark plug caps in conjunction with plain copper HT cable. For VHF purposes, these and 'in-line' resistors may not be effective, and resistive HT cable is preferred. Check that suppressed cables are actually fitted by observing cable identity lettering, or measuring with an ohmmeter – the value of each plug lead should be 5000 to 10 000 ohms.

A 1 microfarad capacitor connected from the LT supply side of the ignition coil to a good nearby earth point will complete basic ignition

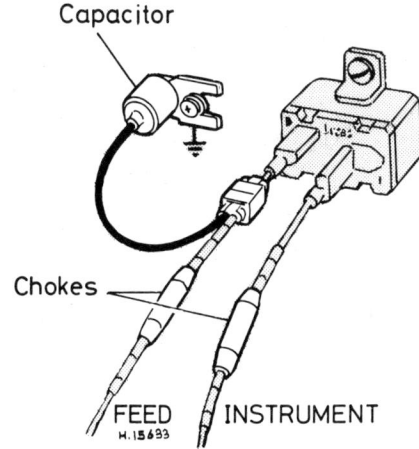

Fig. 9.20 Voltage stabiliser interference suppression (Sec 27)

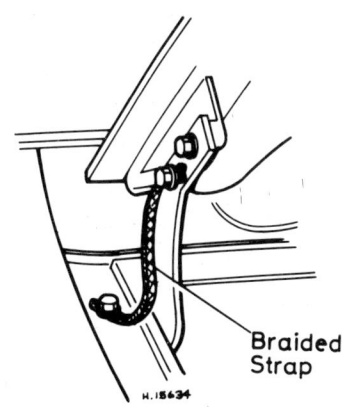

Fig. 9.21 Bonnet to body earth strap (Sec 27)

interference treatment. *NEVER fit a capacitor to the coil terminal to the contact breaker – the result would be burnt out points in a short time.*

If ignition noise persists despite the treatment above, the following sequence should be followed:

(a) Check the earthing of the ignition coil; remove paint from fixing clamp.

(b) If this does not work, lift the bonnet. Should there be no change in interference level, this may indicate that the bonnet is not electrically connected to the car body. Use a proprietary braided strap across a bonnet hinge ensuring a first class electrical connection. If, however, lifting the bonnet increases the interference, then fit resistive HT cables of a higher ohms-per-metre value.

(c) If all these measures fail, it is probable that re-radiation from metallic components is taking place. Using a braided strap between metallic points, go round the vehicle systematically – try the following: engine to body, exhaust system to body, front suspension to engine and to body, steering column to body (especially French and Italian cars), gear lever to engine and to body (again especially French and Italian cars), Bowden cable to body, metal parcel shelf to body. When an offending component is located it should be bonded with the strap permanently.

(d) As a next step, the fitting of distributor suppressors to each lead at the distributor end may help.

(e) Beyond this point is involved the possible screening of the distributor and fitting resistive spark plugs, but such advanced treatment is not usually required for vehicles with entertainment equipment.

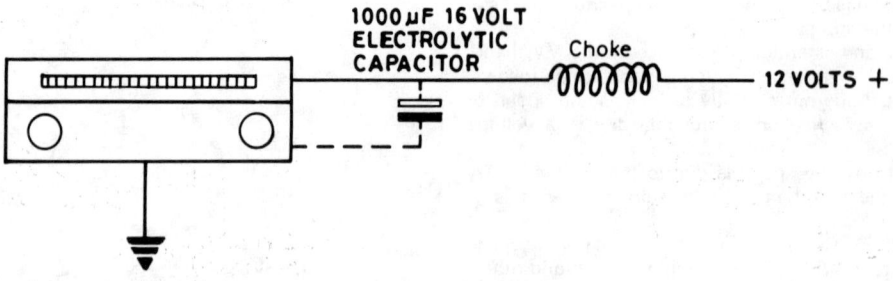

Fig. 9.22 In-line choke (Sec 27)

Suppression methods – generators

Alternators should be fitted with a 3 microfarad capacitor from the B+ main output terminal (thick cable) to earth. Additional suppression may be obtained by the use of a filter in the supply line to the radio receiver.

It is most important that:

(a) *Capacitors are never connected to the field terminals of an alternator.*
(b) *Alternators must not be run without connection to the battery.*

Suppression methods – voltage regulators

Alternator regulators come in three types:

(a) *Vibrating contact regulators separate from the alternator. Used extensively on continental vehicles.*
(b) *Electronic regulators separate from the alternator.*
(c) *Electronic regulators built-in to the alternator.*

In case (a) interference may be generated on the AM and FM (VHF) bands. For some cars a replacement suppressed regulator is available. Filter boxes may be used with non-suppressed regulators. But if not available, then for AM equipment a 2 microfarad or 3 microfarad capacitor may be mounted at the voltage terminal marked D+ or B+ of the regulator. FM bands may be treated by a feed-through capacitor of 2 or 3 microfarad.

Electronic voltage regulators are not always troublesome, but where necessary, a 1 microfarad capacitor from the regulator + terminal will help.

Integral electronic voltage regulators do not normally generate much interference, but when encountered this is in combination with alternator noise. A 1 microfarad or 2 microfarad capacitor from the warning lamp (IND) terminal to earth for Lucas ACR alternators and Femsa, Delco and Bosch equivalents should cure the problem.

Suppression methods – other equipment

Wiper motors – Connect the wiper body to earth with a bonding strap. For all motors use a 7 ampere choke assembly inserted in the leads to the motor.

Heater motors – Fit 7 ampere line chokes in both leads, assisted if necessary by a 1 microfarad capacitor to earth from both leads.

Horn – A capacitor and choke combination is effective if the horn is directly connected to the 12 volt supply. The use of a relay is an alternative remedy, as this will reduce the length of the interference-carrying leads.

Electrostatic noise – Characteristics are erratic crackling at the receiver, with disappearance of symptoms in wet weather. Often shocks may be given when touching bodywork. Part of the problem is the build-up of static electricity in non-driven wheels and the acquisition of charge on the body shell. It is possible to fit spring-loaded contacts at the wheels to give good conduction between the rotary wheel parts and the vehicle frame. Changing a tyre sometimes helps – because of tyres' varying resistances. In difficult cases a trailing flex which touches the ground will cure the problem. If this is not acceptable it is worth trying conductive paint on the tyre walls.

Fluorescent tubes – Vehicles used for camping/caravanning frequently have fluorescent tube lighting. These tubes require a relatively high voltage for operation and this is provided by an inverter (a form of oscillator) which steps up the vehicle supply voltage. This can give rise to serious interference to radio reception, and the tubes themselves can contribute to this interference by the pulsating nature of the lamp discharge. In such situations it is important to mount the aerial as far away from a fluorescent tube as possible. The interference problem may be alleviated by screening the tube with fine wire turns spaced an inch (25 mm) apart and earthed to the chassis. Suitable chokes should be fitted in both supply wires close to the inverter.

Radio/cassette case breakthrough

Magnetic radiation from dashboard wiring may be sufficiently intense to break through the metal case of the radio/cassette player. Often this is due to a particular cable routed too close and shows up as ignition interference on AM and cassette play and/or alternator whine on cassette play.

The first point to check is that the clips and/or screws are fixing all parts of the radio/cassette case together properly. Assuming good earthing of the case, see if it is possible to re-route the offending cable – the chances of this are not good, however, in most cars.

Next release the radio/cassette player and locate it in different positions with temporary leads. If a point of low interference is found, then if possible fix the equipment in that area. This also confirms that local radiation is causing the trouble. If re-location is not feasible, fit the radio/cassette player back in the original position.

Alternator interference on cassette play is now caused by radiation from the main charging cable which goes from the battery to the output terminal of the alternator, usually via the + terminal of the starter motor relay. In some vehicles this cable is routed under the

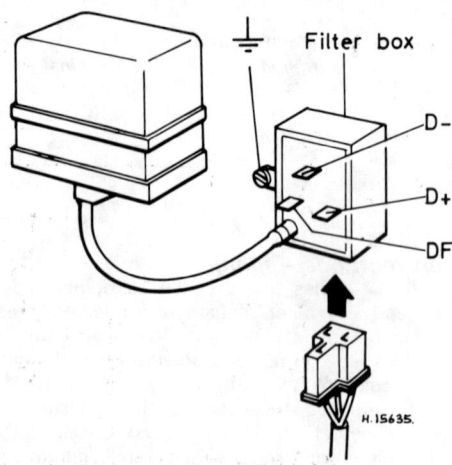

Fig. 9.23 Typical filter box for alternator voltage regulator (contact points type) (Sec 27)

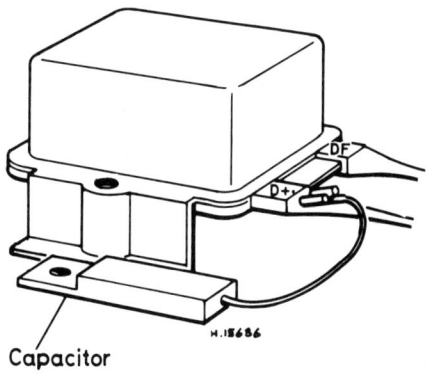

Fig. 9.24 Suppressor fitted to contact points type voltage regulator (Sec 27)

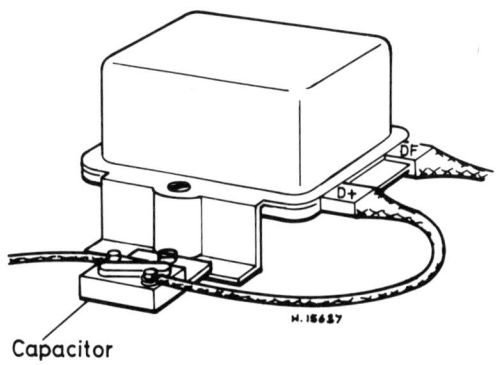

Fig. 9.25 Suppressor fitted to electronic type voltage regulator (Sec 27)

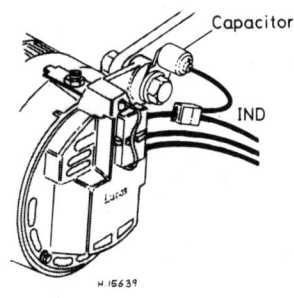

Fig. 9.26 Suppressor fitted to alternator with integral voltage regulator (Sec 27)

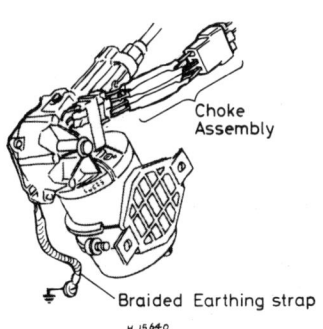

Fig. 9.27 Wiper motor suppressor (Sec 27)

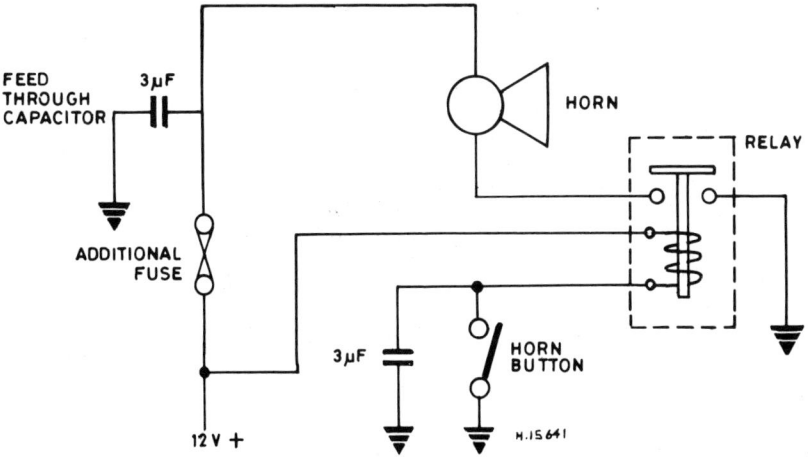

Fig. 9.28 Horn relay used to reduce interference (Sec 27)

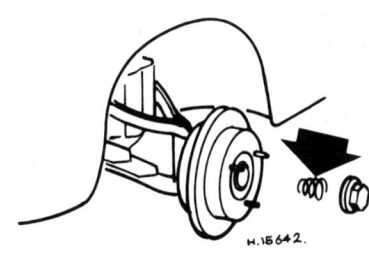

Fig. 9.29 Roadwheel spring contacts (Sec 27)

dashboard, so the solution is to provide a direct cable route. Detach the original cable from the alternator output terminal and make up a new cable of at least 6 mm² cross-sectional area to go from alternator to battery with the shortest possible route. *Remember – do not run the engine with the alternator disconnected from the battery.*

Ignition breakthrough on AM and/or cassette play can be a difficult problem. It is worth wrapping earthed foil round the offending cable run near the equipment, or making up a deflector plate well screwed down to a good earth. Another possibility is the use of a suitable relay to switch on the ignition coil. The relay should be mounted close to the ignition coil; with this arrangement the ignition coil primary current is not taken into the dashboard area and does not flow through the ignition switch. A suitable diode should be used since it is possible that at ignition switch-off the output from the warning lamp alternator terminal could hold the relay on.

Connectors for suppression components

Capacitors are usually supplied with tags on the end of the lead, while the capacitor body has a flange with a slot or hole to fit under a nut or screw with washer.

Connections to feed wires are best achieved by self-stripping connectors. These connectors employ a blade which, when squeezed down by pliers, cuts through cable insulation and makes connection to the copper conductors beneath.

Chokes sometimes come with bullet snap-in connectors fitted to the wires, and also with just bare copper wire. With connectors, suitable female cable connectors may be purchased from an auto-accessory shop together with any extra connectors required for the cable ends after being cut for the choke insertion. For chokes with bare wires, similar connectors may be employed together with insulation sleeving as required.

VHF/FM broadcasts

Reception of VHF/FM in an automobile is more prone to problems than the medium and long wavebands. Medium/long wave transmitters are capable of covering considerable distances, but VHF transmitters are restricted to line of sight, meaning ranges of 10 to 50 miles, depending upon the terrain, the effects of buildings and the transmitter power.

Because of the limited range it is necessary to retune on a long journey, and it may be better for those habitually travelling long distances or living in areas of poor provision of transmitters to use an AM radio working on medium/long wavebands.

When conditions are poor, interference can arise, and some of the suppression devices described previously fall off in performance at very high frequencies unless specifically designed for the VHF band. Available suppression devices include reactive HT cable, resistive distributor caps, screened plug caps, screened leads and resistive spark plugs.

For VHF/FM receiver installation the following points should be particularly noted:

(a) Earthing of the receiver chassis and the aerial mounting is important. Use a separate earthing wire at the radio, and scrape paint away at the aerial mounting.

(b) If possible, use a good quality roof aerial to obtain maximum height and distance from interference generating devices on the vehicle.

(c) Use of a high quality aerial download is important, since losses in cheap cable can be significant.

(d) The polarisation of FM transmissions may be horizontal, vertical, circular or slanted. Because of this the optimum mounting angle is at 45° to the vehicle roof.

Citizens' Band radio (CB)

In the UK, CB transmitter/receivers work within the 27 MHz and 934 MHz bands, using the FM mode. At present interest is concentrated on 27 MHz where the design and manufacture of equipment is less difficult. Maximum transmitted power is 4 watts, and 40 channels spaced 10 kHz apart within the range 27.60125 to 27.99125 MHz are available.

Aerials are the key to effective transmission and reception. Regulations limit the aerial length to 1.65 metres including the loading coil and any associated circuitry, so tuning the aerial is necessary to obtain optimum results. The choice of a CB aerial is dependent on whether it is to be permanently installed or removable, and the

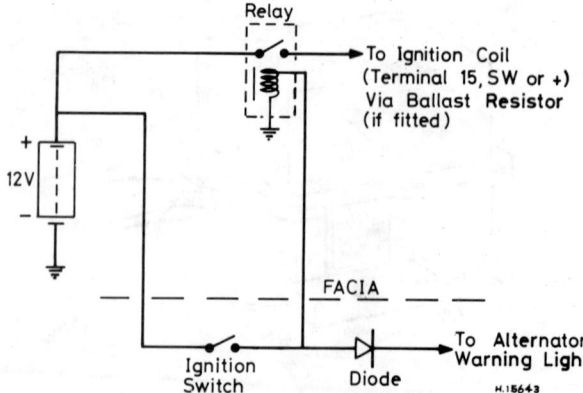

Fig. 9.30 Ignition coil relay to suppress casing breakthrough (Sec 27)

performance will hinge on correct tuning and the location point on the vehicle. Common practice is to clip the aerial to the roof gutter or to employ wing mounting where the aerial can be rapidly unscrewed. An alternative is to use the boot rim to render the aerial theftproof, but a popular solution is to use the 'magmount' – a type of mounting having a strong magnetic base clamping to the vehicle at any point, usually the roof.

Aerial location determines the signal distribution for both transmission and reception, but it is wise to choose a point away from the engine compartment to minimise interference from vehicle electrical equipment.

The aerial is subject to considerable wind and acceleration forces. Cheaper units will whip backwards and forwards and in so doing will alter the relationship with the metal surface of the vehicle with which it forms a ground plane aerial system. The radiation pattern will change correspondingly, giving rise to break-up of both incoming and outgoing signals.

Interference problems on the vehicle carrying CB equipment fall into two categories:

(a) Interference to nearby TV and radio receivers when transmitting.

(b) Interference to CB set reception due to electrical equipment on the vehicle.

Problems of break-through to TV and radio are not frequent, but can be difficult to solve. Mostly trouble is not detected or reported because the vehicle is moving and the symptoms rapidly disappear at the TV/radio receiver, but when the CB set is used as a base station any trouble with nearby receivers will soon result in a complaint.

It must not be assumed by the CB operator that his equipment is faultless, for much depends upon the design. Harmonics (that is, multiples) of 27 MHz may be transmitted unknowingly and these can fall into other user's bands. Where trouble of this nature occurs, low pass filters in the aerial or supply leads can help, and should be fitted in base station aerials as a matter of course. In stubborn cases it may be necessary to call for assistance from the licensing authority, or, if possible, to have the equipment checked by the manufacturers.

Interference received on the CB set from the vehicle equipment is, fortunately, not usually a severe problem. The precautions outlined previously for radio/cassette units apply, but there are some extra points worth noting.

It is common practice to use a slide-mount on CB equipment enabling the set to be easily removed for use as a base station, for example. Care must be taken that the slide mount fittings are properly earthed and that first class connection occurs between the set and slide-mount.

Vehicle manufacturers in the UK are required to provide suppression of electrical equipment to cover 40 to 250 MHz to protect TV and VHF radio bands. Such suppression appears to be adequately effective at 27 MHz, but suppression of individual items such as alternators, clocks, stabilisers, flashers, wiper motors, etc, may still be necessary. The suppression capacitors and chokes available from auto-electrical suppliers for entertainment receivers will usually give the required results with CB equipment.

Other vehicle radio transmitters

Besides CB radio already mentioned, a considerable increase in the use of transceivers (ie combined transmitter and receiver units) has taken place in the last decade. Previously this type of equipment was fitted mainly to military, fire, ambulance and police vehicles, but a large business radio and radio telephone usage has developed.

Generally the suppression techniques described previously will suffice, with only a few difficult cases arising. Suppression is carried out to satisfy the 'receive mode', but care must be taken to use heavy duty chokes in the equipment supply cables since the loading on 'transmit' is relatively high.

28 Fault diagnosis – electrical system

Note: *Electrical faults not dealt with below can usually be attributed to defects in current supply (blown fuse or defective relay, loose connections or broken wires) or earth return (loose or corroded mountings).*

Symptom	Reason/s
Starter motor fails to turn engine	Battery discharged Battery defective internally Battery terminal leads or earth strap loose or corroded Engine earth strap broken or insecure Loose or broken connection in starter motor circuit Starter motor switch or solenoid faulty Starter motor brushes worn, sticking, or brush wires loose Commutator dirty, worn or burnt Starter motor armature faulty Field coils earthed
Starter motor turns engine very slowly	Battery in discharged condition Starter motor brushes worn, sticking, or brush wires loose Loose wires in starter motor circuit Starter motor armature faulty
Starter motor operates without turning engine	Starter motor pinion sticking Pinion or flywheel gear teeth worn or broken
Starter motor noisy or excessively rough in engagement	Pinion or flywheel gear teeth worn or broken Starter motor retaining bolts loose
Battery will not hold charge	Electrolyte level too low Battery defective internally Electrolyte too weak (after spillage or leakage) Alternator drivebelt slipping Loose connections or broken wires in charging circuit Short circuit causing battery drain Alternator faulty
Ignition light fails to go out when engine running	Alternator drivebelt slipping or broken Fault in charging circuit Fault in alternator
Ignition light fails to come on with ignition on and engine stopped	Ignition light bulb blown Fault in bulb holder, printed circuit or wiring Alternator faulty
Fuel or temperature gauges give no reading	Wiring to gauges disconnected Fuel gauge tank unit faulty Temperature gauge transmitter faulty Wiring from transmitters to gauges broken or disconnected Gauges faulty Fuse blown
Fuel or temperature gauges give maximum readings all the time	Fuel gauge tank unit faulty Wiring from fuel gauge to tank unit earthed Wiring from temperature gauge to transmitter earthed Gauges faulty Temperature gauge transmitter faulty
Instrument readings increase with engine speed	Voltage stabilizer faulty
Lights do not come on	Light bulb filament burnt out Fuse blown Battery discharged Excessive corrosion on bulbs or bulb holders Wiring loose, disconnected or broken Light switch faulty

Symptom	Reason/s
Light(s) very dim	Bulb or bulbholder not making good earth connection
	Incorrect bulb fitted
	Lamp glasses dirty
	Reflector tarnished or dirty
	Corroded or poor electrical connections
Wiper motor fails to work	Fuse blown
	Wiring loose, disconnected, or broken
	Switch faulty
	Brushes worn
	Armature faulty
	Field coils faulty
Wiper motor works very slowly	Commutator dirty or burnt
	Armature faulty
	Brushes worn
	Armature bearings dry or misaligned
	Drive to wheelboxes bent or unlubricated
	Wheelboxes binding or damaged
Wiper motor works but blades remain static	Wheelboxes damaged or worn
	Wiper motor gearbox parts badly worn
	Wiper arms loose on spindles

Chapter 10 Steering

Contents

Fault diagnosis – steering 13
General description 1
Maintenance 2
Rack damper – adjustment 9
Steering angles and front wheel alignment 12
Steering column lock/switch – removal and refitting 7
Steering column – overhaul 8

Steering column – removal and refitting 6
Steering gear – overhaul 11
Steering gear – removal and refitting 10
Steering rack gaiter – renewal 4
Steering wheel – removal and refitting 5
Tie-rod end balljoint – renewal 3

Specifications

System type .... Rack and pinion with universally-jointed column

Turning circle .... 9.2 m (30.2 ft)

Number of turns of steering wheel (lock to lock) 3.4

Steering angles (at kerb weight)
Camber (at wheel rim) .... 1° to 2° positive
Castor .... 2° 30' to 3° 30' positive
Toe .... Parallel (0°) to 4° toe-out

Steering angles of roadwheels on turns
Inner wheel .... 32° 15' to 35° 15'
Outer wheel .... 30° 0' to 33° 0'

Rack lubricant capacity .... 140 cc

Torque wrench settings

	Nm	lbf ft
Steering wheel nut	49	36
Steering coupling pinch-bolt	27	20
Steering gear mounting bolts	25	18
Tie-rod balljoint taper pin nut	34	25
Tie-rod end locknut	49	36
Steering column pressed steel mounting bracket bolts	8	6
Roadwheel bolts	86	63
Pinion bearing plate bolt	30	22
Rack damper cover plate bolt	30	22

1 General description

The steering gear is of rack and pinion type with a universally-jointed shaft supported in a tubular column.

The front wheel toe setting and castor are adjustable as described in Section 12, the camber angle is set in production.

A two-spoked steering wheel is fitted.

2 Maintenance

1 The steering rack and tie-rod end balljoints are sealed for life and require no lubrication.

2 At the intervals specified in Routine Maintenance, check the rack gaiters for splits. Extend the gaiters with the fingers in case splits at the base of the pleats are overlooked.

3   With an assistant moving the steering wheel a few degrees quickly in each direction, check for wear (lost movement) at the tie-rod end balljoints. If wear is detected, renew any worn components as described later in this Chapter.

4   At the specified periods, check the front wheel alignment as described in Section 12.

3   Tie-rod end balljoint – renewal

1   Wear of the tie-rod end balljoints can only be overcome by renewal, no adjustment being possible. The balljoints are grease-sealed and require no attention during their life, except to check their dust excluding boots for splits at the specified inspection intervals.

2   Jack up the front of the car and remove the roadwheel from the side on which the balljoint is to be renewed.

3   Unscrew the self-locking nut from the tie-rod end ball stud, but do not remove it (photo).

4   Using a suitable tool, disconnect the balljoint.

5   Release the locknut on the tie-rod, unscrewing it only just enough to be able to unscrew the tie-rod end from the tie-rod.

6   With the tie-rod end removed, wire brush the threads on the tie-rod without disturbing the position of the locknut; apply grease to the threads and screws on the new tie-rod end until the locknut can be tightened by turning it through the same amount of rotation it was given when unscrewed.

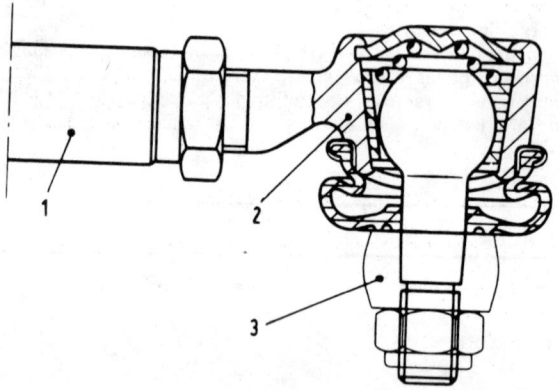

Fig. 10.1 Sectional view of typical balljoint (Sec 3)

1   Tie-rod   3   Steering arm
2   Balljoint socket

3.3 Tie-rod end balljoint

7   Reconnect the balljoint taper pin to the eye of the steering arm and tighten the retaining nut to the specified torque. *Never grease the taper pin or eye;* the pin will otherwise turn when the nut is tightened. If a taper pin is inclined to rotate when a nut is being tightened, apply pressure to the socket of the joint to force the taper pin into closer contact with the tapered hole in the eye. If a taper pin is pointing downward, a strong lever can be used to apply the extra pressure. Where the taper pin of a balljoint points upward, a jack placed under the joint socket will produce the desired result.

8   Although the careful fitting of the new tie-rod end will have approximately maintained the original front wheel alignment of the car, manufacturing differences alone of the new component make it essential to check the setting, as described in Section 12.

4   Steering rack gaiter – renewal

1   If lubricant is found to be leaking from the gaiters (at the ends of the housing), first check that the gaiter clips are secure.

2   If the lubricant is leaking from the gaiter through a split, the gaiter can be removed in the following way, without the necessity of withdrawing the gear from the car.

3   Remove the tie-rod end from the side concerned, as described in the preceding Section.

4   Release the gaiter clips; draw the gaiter from the rack housing and off the tie-rod.

5   If the gaiter has only just split, road dirt is unlikely to have entered and lubricant can be wiped away. If it is severely grit contaminated, the steering gear should be completely removed, the original lubricant flushed out and new lubricant pumped in.

6   If the gear does not have to be removed from the car, slide the new gaiter into positon and secure it with the inboard clip.

7   On these models, the steering gear lubricant is grease, therefore reducing the possibility of oil seal leakage. When recharging the gaiter with this type of lubricant, give full steering lock to the side being replenished so that the extended section of the rack will take the grease into the housing as it returns.

8   Fit the outboard clip.

9   Fit the tie-rod end as described in the preceding Section and then check the front wheel alignment (Section 12).

5   Steering wheel – removal and refitting

1   Disconnect the battery negative lead.

2   Set the steering in the straight ahead attitude.

3   Prise out the horn button from the centre of the steering wheel (photo).

4   Extract the two horn switch contact springs now exposed (photos).

5   Unscrew and remove the steering wheel securing nut, then pull the wheel from the column shaft. If it is tight on its splines, thump the rear of the rim, at opposite points, with the palms of the hands.

6   Refit by reversing the removal operations. Set the wheel in the straight ahead position with the spokes in the lower part of the wheel.

7   Tighten the fixing nut to the specified torque.

6   Steering column – removal and refitting

1   Disconnect the battery.

2   Remove the steering wheel as previously described.

3   Working under the column shroud, extract the screw and bolt. The screw holds the shroud and the bolt secures the steering column combination switches (photo).

4   Release the screw which holds the clamp retainer for the switches. This screw is accessible through the large hole in the shroud (photo).

5   Disconnect the combination switch wiring harness plugs at the side of the steering column and withdraw the switches off the end of the column.

6   Disconnect the choke control cable from the carburettor.

7   Extract the end screws from the full width parcels shelf and lower the shelf (photo).

8   Withdraw the steering column shroud until the washer control connections can be disconnected and the shroud removed completely.

5.3 Removing horn pad

5.4A Steering wheel nut and horn contact springs

5.4B Steering wheel thrustwasher

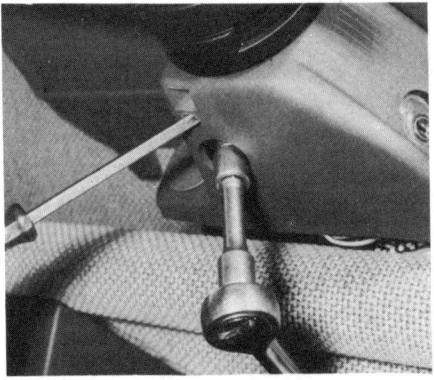

6.3 Shroud fixing screw and column, switch clamp bolt

6.4 Steering column switch and clamp

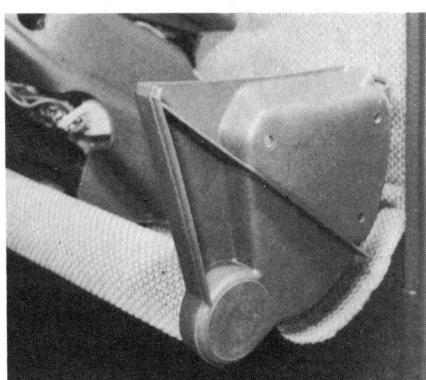

6.7 Front parcels shelf end brackets

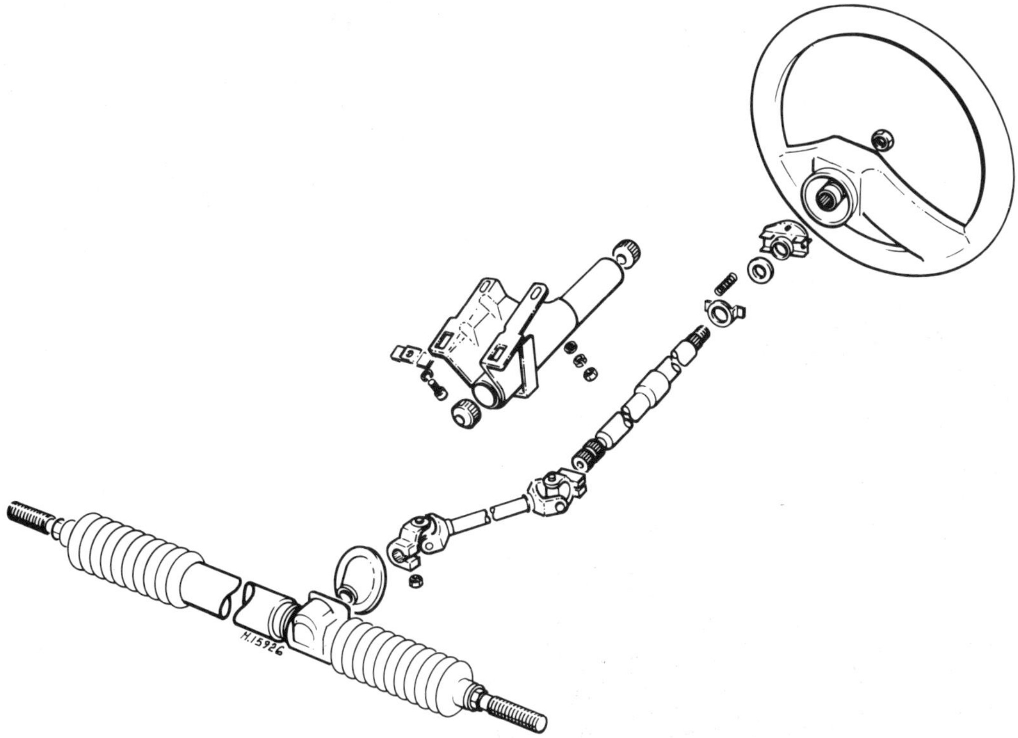

Fig. 10.2 Steering arrangement (Sec 6)

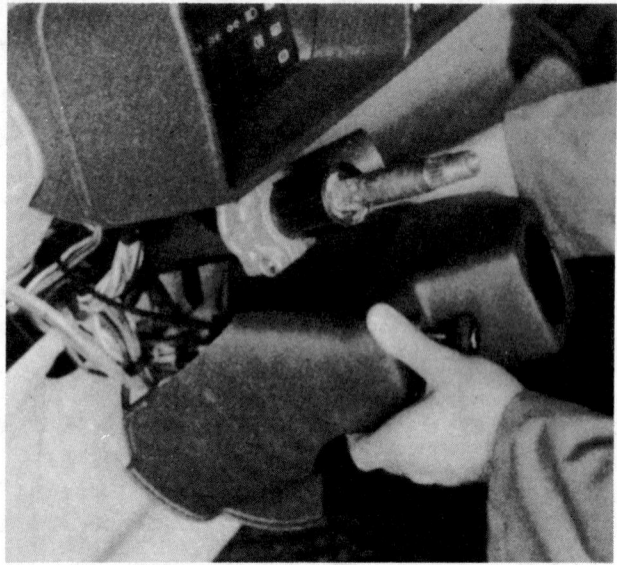

Fig. 10.3 Withdrawing steering column shroud (Sec 6)

7.3A Ignition switch/lock fixing screw

9   Unbolt the steering column pressed-steel bracket and lower the column to rest on the front seat.
10 Working between the foot pedals, extract the pinch-bolt and pull the coupling from the splines of the pinion shaft of the steering gear. If the coupling is tight, open its jaws slightly with a screwdriver.
11 Withdraw the column assembly from the car.
12 Refit the upper mounting bracket after the bottom end of the column has been reconnected; try to position the bracket so that the retaining bolts and washers are tightened into their original, scored marks on the bracket. This will ensure that the universally jointed section of the column shaft maintains its originally fitted attitude.
Note: *Do not tighten beyond the specified torque.*
13 Refitting and reconnection of all the other components is a reversal of removal and disconnection.

7   Steering column lock/switch – removal and refitting

1   Remove the steering wheel as described in Section 5.
2   Remove the combination switches and column shroud as described in the preceding Section.
3   The lock/switch may be removed from its housing by extracting the retaining screw, depressing the small spring-loaded plunger and turning the key to the START position. Ease the wiring harness through the housing as the lock cylinder/switch is withdrawn (photos).
4   If the lock housing must be removed, then the shear-head bolts must be drilled out. When the new ones are screwed in, tighten them until their heads break off.
5   The ignition switch may be detached from the rear of the lock after extracting the retaining screws.
6   Refitting is a reversal of removal.

8   Steering column – overhaul

1   Withdraw the steering column as described in Section 6.
2   If the reason for overhaul is to renew the column bearings, insert the ignition key and turn it to release the steering column lock.
3   The bearing retaining staking at the ends of the column tube will have to be relieved and the shaft then pushed backwards and forwards to eject the bearings.
5   Apply grease to the bearings; tap them into position (until they seat against the crimped stops in the column tube), then stake over the ends of the tube. Make sure that the staking does not coincide with the split in the bush.

7.3B Ignition switch/lock removed showing retaining plunger

6   Reassembly and refitting are reversals of the removal and dismantling sequences. Note that the splined couplings must be correctly located on their shafts before the pinch bolt can be passed through the groove in the shaft. Never hammer the bolt to drive it through – readjust the coupling position by sliding it slightly up or down the shaft.

9   Rack damper – adjustment

1   The yoke in the rack housing presses the rack into mesh with the pinion. This cuts out any backlash between the gears. Also owing to its pressure, it introduces some stiffness into the rack, which cuts out excessive reaction from the road to the steering wheel.
2   In due course, wear reduces the pressure exerted by the damping yoke. The pressure is controlled by the yoke cover plate and a spring.
3   The yoke setting should be reset if the rack has been dismantled for overhaul.
4   The need for resetting of the yoke if the car has run a long mileage, but the rack is not being dismantled, is not easy to detect. On bumpy roads the shock induced through the steering will give a feeling of play, and sometimes faint clonking can be heard. In extreme cases free-play

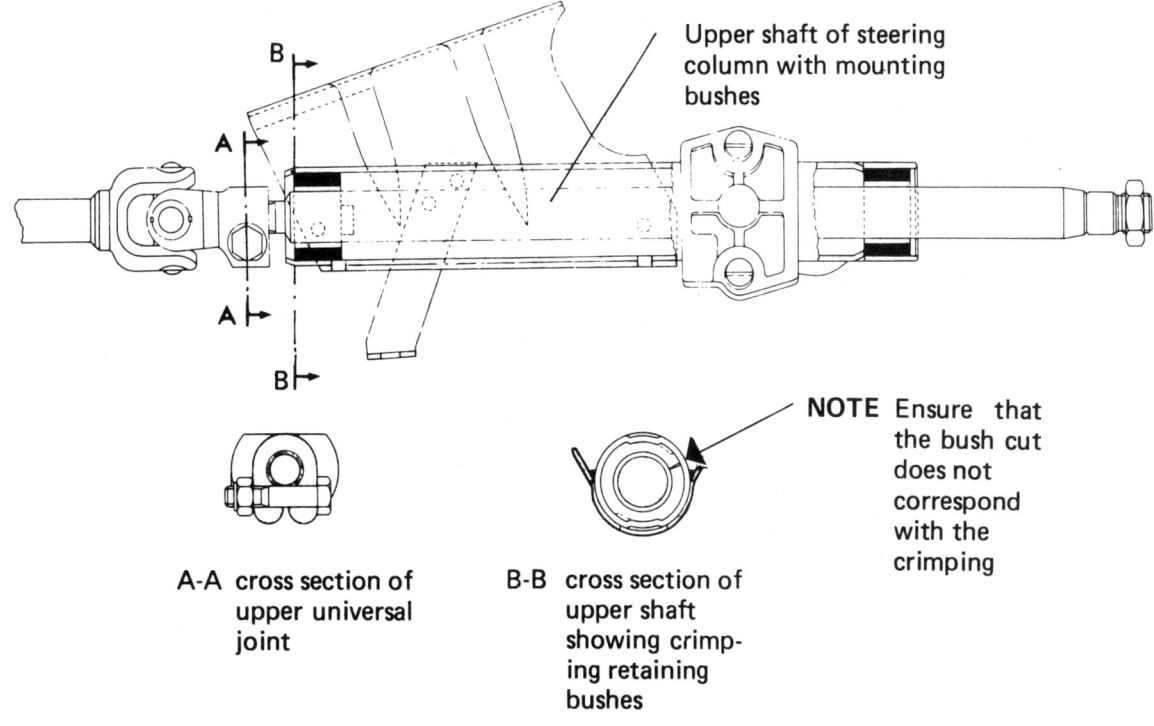

B-B cross section of
upper shaft showing crimping retaining
bushes

A-A cross section of
upper universal
joint

NOTE Ensure that
the bush cut
does not
correspond
with the
crimping

Fig. 10.4 Sectional view of steering column showing bushes (Sec 8)

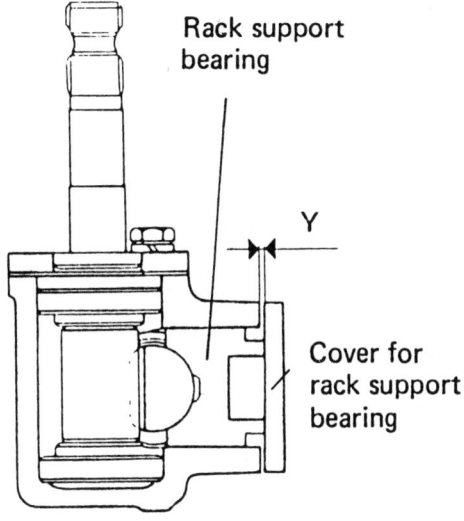

Fig. 10.5 Rack damper and cover plate gap (Y) (Sec 9)

Rack support
bearing

Cover for
rack support
bearing

Y

in the steering may be felt, though this is rare. If the steering is
compared with that of a new rack on another car, the lack of friction
damping is quite apparent in the ease of movement of the steering
wheel of the worn unit.
5   Turn the steering to the straight-ahead position.
6   Take the cover plate off the damping yoke, remove the spring and
shims, and refit it. Refit the bolts, but only tighten them enough to hold
the yoke firmly against the rack.
7   Turn the pinion through 180° either way to settle the rack.
8   Measure the gap between the cover plate and the rack housing.
(See Fig. 10.5).
9   Select shims to a thickness 0.002 to 0.005 in. (0.05 to 0.13 mm)
more than the measured gap. (Shims are available 0.1 and 0.15 mm
thick).
10 Remove the cover plate again, and refit the spring.
11 Smear each shim with soft setting gasket compound, and fit them
and the cover plate.

10 Steering gear – removal and refitting

1   Raise the front of the car and support it securely.
2   Remove the roadwheels.
3   Unscrew the nut which holds each tie-rod end balljoint to the eye
of the steering arm, then using a balljoint splitter tool, disconnect the
balljoints from the steering arms.
4   Working within the car, centralise the steering wheel so that the
roadwheels, if fitted, would be in the straight-ahead positon. Mark the
relationship of the column lower coupling to the splined pinion, then
unscrew and remove the coupling pinch bolt.
5   Working within the engine compartment, unbolt and remove the
rubber insulated clamps which hold the steering gear to the rear
bulkhead (photo).

10.5 Steering rack and mounting clamp

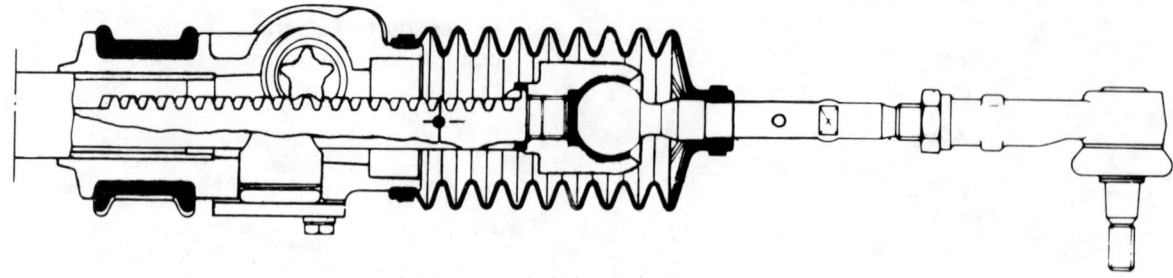

Fig. 10.6 Cut-away view of one side of the steering rack (Sec 11)

6   Support the steering gear and withdraw it first downward from the bulkhead (to draw the splined pinion from the column coupling), then remove it sideways from under one of the wheel arches.

7   Refitting is a reversal of the removal process; be sure to align the pinion shaft and column coupling marks, otherwise the position of the steering wheel in the straight-ahead attitude will be altered.

8   If a new or overhauled gear has been fitted, check the front wheel alignment (Section 12).

11 Steering gear – overhaul

1   If the car has covered a high mileage and the steering gear is badly worn, it is recommended that a factory-reconditioned or new unit is fitted rather than fit a large number of new components to the old one.

2   For those wishing to dismantle the original gear, proceed in the following way.

3   Remove the steering gear from the car as previously described and clean away external dirt.

4   Remove the tie-rod ends and gaiters.

5   Take off the clamps that held the rack to the car, and their rubber packing.

6   Take off its cover plate, and remove the rack damping yoke with spring, and shims, and oil sealing ring.

7   Remove the two bolts holding the pinion bearing plate to the housing. Take out the pinion, with oil seal, gasket, shim and top ball bearing.

8   Mount the rack housing in a vice, but be careful not to crush it.

9   Unstake the lock for the locknuts for the adjustable head for the balljoints at the ends of the rack. The locknut is the inner one. Undo the locknuts themselves.

10   Take off the ends of the rack housing the adjustable heads for the balljoints, bringing with them the balljoints, and their sockets and springs.

11   Slide the rack out of the housing.

12   Take out the lower bearing for the pinion.

13   Check all parts for signs of excessive wear or damage, or corrosion. New gaskets, a new seal for the pinion shaft, and new rubber boots should be fitted.

14   As the parts are refitted, smear them with specified grease.

15   Avoid scraping the rack housing bearings as the rack teeth pass through.

16   Fit the pinion bearing plate with a selected shim pack to give a dimension (X) Fig. 10.7 of between 0.025 and 0.13 mm (0.001 and 0.005 in). Shims are available in four sizes.

17   Check the torque necessary to start the pinion turning. In the absence of a suitable gauge, wind a cord around the pinion splines and attach the end to a spring balance. The turning torque should be between 19.5 and 28.5 kgf cm (16 to 25 lbf in) or a reading on the spring balance of between 6.8 and 9.0 kg (15.0 and 20.0 lb).

18   Reconnect the balljoints to the ends of the rack. Tighten the adjustable heads until the balljoints are slightly stiff to turn in their seats. Make sure that the trackrods will rotate through 360°, at an angle of 60°. Lock the heads and stake the locknuts.

19   Extend the rack fully in one direction, smear it with special grease (Fiat K854) and fit the gaiter. Repeat with the rack extended in the opposite direction. As the total lubricant capacity is 140 cc divide it equally on both sides of the rack.

20   Grease the threads and screw on the tie-rod end balljoints equally.

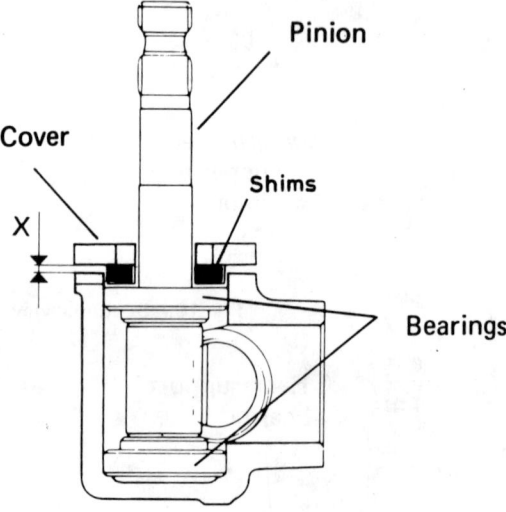

Fig. 10.7 Pinion bearing cover clearance (X) (Sec 11)

12 Steering angles and front wheel alignment

1   Accurate front wheel alignment is essential to provide good steering and roadholding characteristics and to ensure slow and even tyre wear. Before considering the steering angles, check that the tyres are correctly inflated, that the front wheels are not buckled, the hub bearings are not worn or incorrectly adjusted and that the steering linkage is in good order, without slackness or wear at the joints.

2   Wheel alignment consists of four factors:

Camber, is the angle at which the road wheels are set from the vertical when viewed from the front or rear of the vehicle. Positive camber is the angle (in degrees) that the wheels are tilted outwards at the top from the vertical.

Castor, is the angle between the steering axis and a vertical line when viewed from each side of the vehicle. Positive castor is indicated when the steering axis is inclined towards the rear of the vehicle at its upper end.

Steering axis inclination, is the angle when viewed from the front or rear of the vehicle between vertical and an imaginary line drawn between the top and bottom strut mountings.

Toe, is the amount by which the distance between the front inside edges of the roadwheel rims differs from that between the rear inside edges. If the distance between the front edges is less than that at the rear, the wheels are said to toe-in. If the distance between the front inside eges is greater that that at the rear, the wheels toe-out.

3   Due to the need for precision gauges to measure the small angles of the steering and suspension settings, it is preferable that adjustment of camber and castor is left to a service station having the necessary equipment.

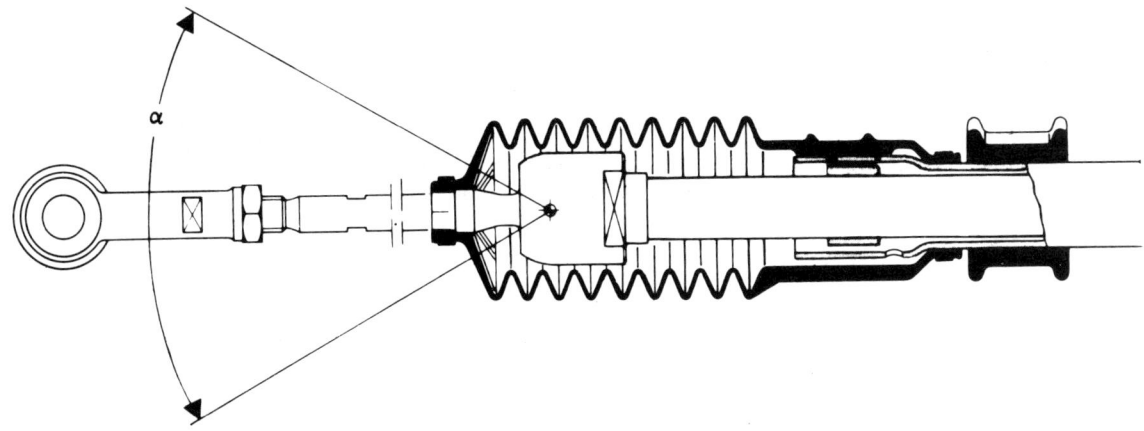

α = Angle of ball joint rotation 60° + $^{6°}_{0°}$

Fig. 10.8 Inner balljoint arc of travel (Sec 11)

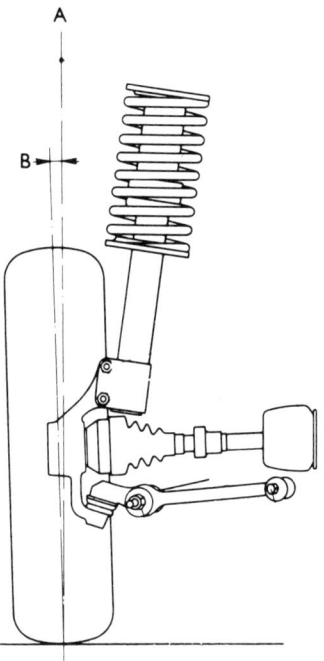

Fig. 10.9 Camber angle diagram (Sec 12)

A   Vertical   B   Camber angle (positive)

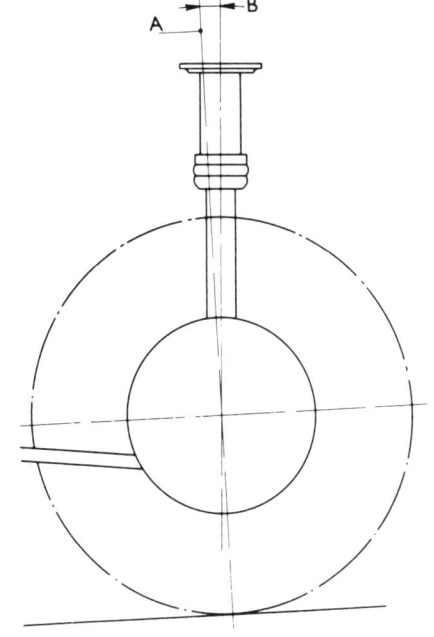

Fig. 10.10 Castor angle diagram (Sec 12)

A   Vertical   B   Castor angle (positive)

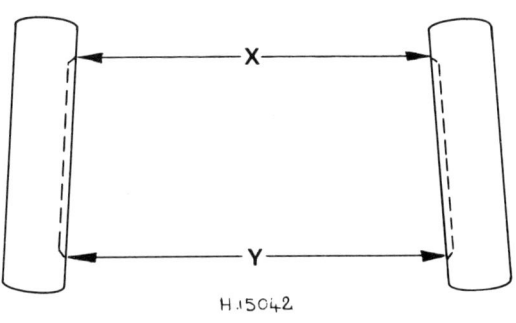

H.15042

Fig. 10.11 Front wheel alignment diagram (Sec 12)

X = Front dimension   Y – X = toe-out
Y = Rear dimension

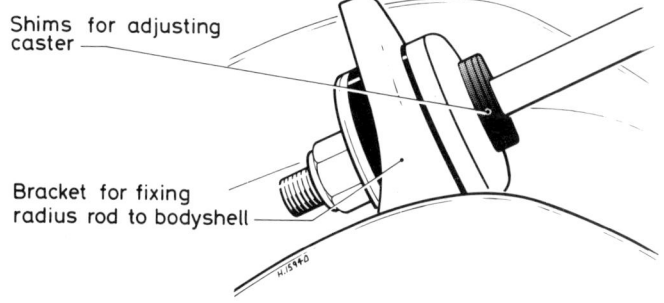

Shims for adjusting caster

Bracket for fixing radius rod to bodyshell

Fig. 10.12 Location of castor adjusting shims (Sec 12)

4   For information purposes however, adjustment of castor is carried out by altering the number of shims at the radius rod on the body bracket. Camber is set in production and any variation from setting given in the Specifications will normally be due to accident damage.
5   To check the front wheel alignment, first make sure that the lengths of both tie-rods are equal when the steering is in the straight-ahead position. Adjust if necessary by releasing the tie-rod end locknuts and turning the tie-rods until the lengths of the exposed threads are equal on each side.
6   Obtain a tracking gauge. These are available in various forms from accessory stores or one can be fabricated from a length of steel tubing suitably cranked to clear the sump and bellhousing and having a setscrew and locknut at one end.
7   With the gauge, measure the distance between the two wheel inner rims (at hub height) at the rear of the wheel. Push the vehicle forward to rotate the wheel through 180° (half a turn) and measure the distance between the wheel inner rims, again at hub height, at the front of the wheel. This last measurement should differ from the first by the appropriate toe-in or toe-out according to specification (see Specifications Section).
8   Where the toe-in or toe-out is found to be incorrect, release the tie-rod balljoint locknuts and turn the tie-rods equally. Only turn them a quarter of a turn at a time before re-checking the alignment. Do not grip the threaded part of the tie-rod/balljoint during adjustment and make sure that the gaiter outboard clip is released otherwise the gaiter will twist as the tie-rod is rotated. Turn each tie-rod in the same direction when viewed from the centre line of the car otherwise the rods will become unequal in length. This would cause the steering wheel spoke position to alter and cause problems on turns with tyre scrubbing. On completion, tighten the tie-rod locknuts without disturbing their setting, check that the balljoint is at the centre of its arc of travel and then retighten the bellows clip.

13 Fault diagnosis – steering

Symptom	Reason(s)
Stiff action	Lack of rack lubrication
	Seized tie-rod end balljoints
	Seized suspension lower balljoint
Free movement at steering wheel	Wear in tie-rod balljoints
	Wear in rack teeth
Knocking when traversing uneven surface	Incorrectly adjusted rack slipper

Chapter 11 Suspension

Contents

Fault diagnosis	11	Maintenance	2
Front hub carrier – removal and refitting	6	Radius rod – removal and refitting	5
Front suspension lower track control arm – removal and		Rear axle – removal and refitting	9
refitting	4	Rear leaf spring – removal and refitting	8
Front suspension strut – removal and refitting	3	Rear shock absorber – removal, testing and refitting	7
General description	1	Rear wheel alignment	10

Specifications

Type
Front suspension	Independent, MacPherson strut with track control and radius rods
Rear suspension	Axle tube with leaf springs and telescopic hydraulic shock absorbers

Torque wrench settings

	Nm	lbf ft
Front suspension		
Track control arm to body	40	29.5
Track control arm balljoint nut	79	58
Tie-rod end balljoint nut	34	25
Strut upper mounting nuts	25	18
Strut lower clamp bolts	35	26
Radius rod front nut	49	36
Radius rod to track control arm	70	52
Strut spindle nut	25	18
Rear suspension		
Shock absorber lower mounting bolt	50	37
Shock absorber upper mounting bolt	50	37
Spring U-bolt nuts	50	37
Spring shackle bolts	30	22
Spring front pivot bolt	30	22

1 General description

The front suspension is of independent type having MacPherson struts with coil springs.

The rear suspension consists of a tubular axle, leaf springs and hydraulic telescopic dampers.

2 Maintenance

1 This is largely a visual inspection to check that the front strut gaiters are not split, that the leaf spring or shock absorber rubber bushes are not worn and that there is no sign of fluid leakage from the strut or shock absorber.

2 Periodically, check the tightness of all suspension fixing nuts and bolts.

3 Front suspension strut – removal and refitting

1 Raise the front of the car and remove the roadwheel.

2 Disconnect the brake hydraulic hose from the suspension strut.

3 Unbolt the caliper and tie it up out of the way.

3.4A Disconnecting tie-rod end balljoint

3.4B Disconnecting suspension lower arm balljoint

3.4C Radius rod connection to lower arm

3.6 Front strut upper mounting

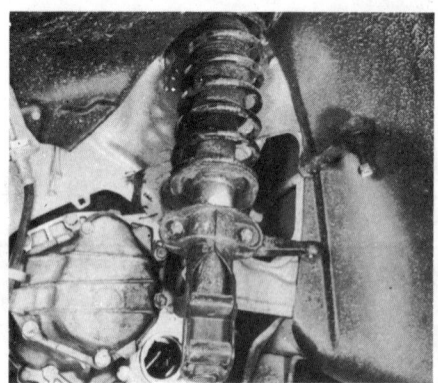

3.7 Front strut

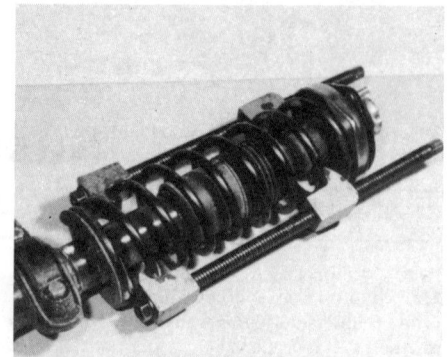

3.10 Strut spring compressors

4   Using a balljoint splitter tool, disconnect the tie-rod end and the suspension lower control arm balljoints. Release the radius rod from the control arm (photos).

5   Unscrew the bolts from the hub carrier clamp at the base of the strut. Slide the carrier down off the strut.

6   Working at the strut mounting turret inside the engine compartment unscrew the mounting nuts, *not the centre spindle nut (photo)*.

7   Withdraw the strut downwards and out from under the wing (photo).

8   If the strut is defective because of leakage or lack of damping action, then it can only be renewed, no repair to the hydraulic assembly is possible.

9   The coil spring should be removed in the following way to renew the strut tube or a defective gaiter.

10   Engage at least two spring compressors over as many spring coils as possible and compress the spring until the upper and lower coils come away from their seats. Spring compressors may be hired or purchased from many motor accessory stores (photo).

11   Unscrew the spindle top nut while holding the flats at the upper end of the spindle with an open-ended spanner.

12   Withdraw the strut upper mounting and the spring (held compressed).

13   Renew the gaiter or strut as necessary, fit the coil spring and top mounting and tighten the spindle nut.

14   Gently release the spring compressors and remove them.

15   Refit the strut by reversing the removal operations, tighten all nuts and bolts to the specified torque.

---

4   Front suspension lower track control arm – removal and refitting

1   In the interests of safety, support the car on the side from which the track control arm is being removed, but do not raise the roadwheel off the floor.

2   Using a suitable balljoint splitter tool, disconnect the control arm balljoint from the hub carrier.

3   Disconnect the radius rod from the track control arm.

4   Unscrew and remove the track control arm inboard pivot bolt and remove the arm.

5   If the control arm flexible bush is worn, renew the arm.

6   Refitting is a reversal of removal. **Note:** *If difficulty is experienced in loosening or tightening a balljoint taper pin nut due to the taper pin turning in its eye, apply pressure with a jack or long lever to the balljoint socket to force the taper pin further into its conical seat.*

---

5   Radius rod – removal and refitting

1   Unbolt the radius rod from the front suspension lower track control arm (photo).

2   Unscrew the nut from the front end of the radius rod and disconnect it from the body bracket (photo).

3   Note the number of castor adjusting shims (see Chapter 10, Section 12) used on the rear side of the body bracket. Refit these at reassembly.

4   If new components have been fitted have the castor angle checked.

---

6   Front hub carrier – removal and refitting

1   Raise the front of the car and support it securely.

2   Remove the roadwheel.

3   With an assistant depressing the brake pedal hard, unscrew the driveshaft nut. A long wrench bar will be required as it is very tight.

4   Unbolt the brake caliper and tie it up out of the way.

5   Using a balljoint splitter tool, disconnect the tie-rod end from the steering arm as described in Chapter 10.

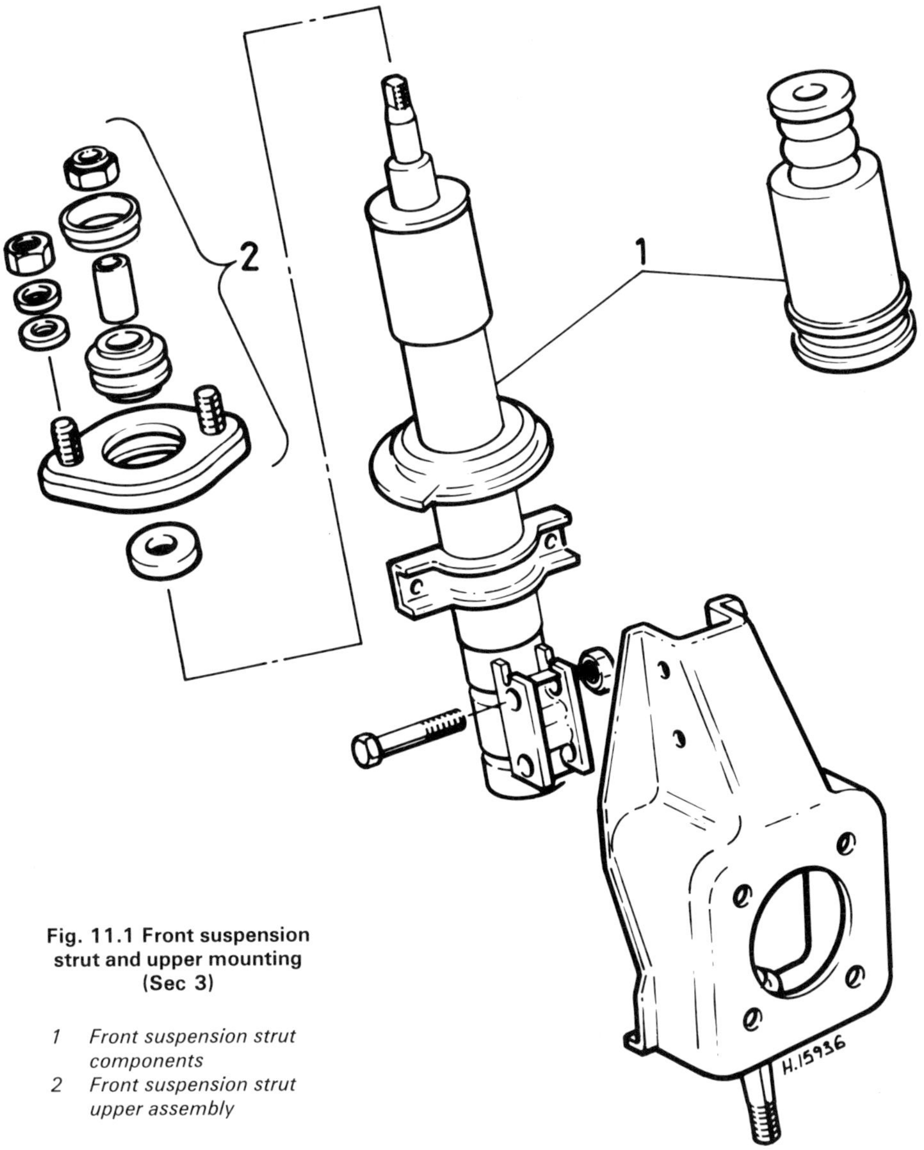

Fig. 11.1 Front suspension strut and upper mounting (Sec 3)

1   Front suspension strut components
2   Front suspension strut upper assembly

H.15936

5.1 One side of the front suspension

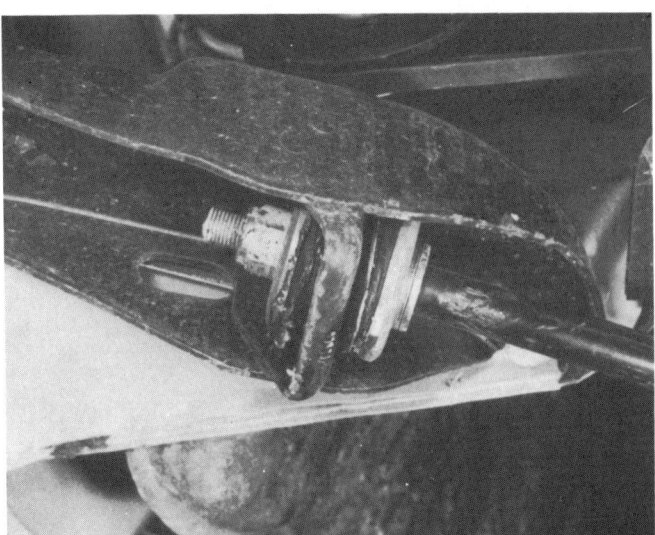

5.2 Radius rod front connection to body bracket

6   Unscrew the bolts which secure the hub carrier to the clamp at the base of the suspension strut.
7   Again using the splitter tool, disconnect the balljoint just below the hub carrier. Disconnect the radius rod.
8   Pull the hub carrier downwards off the strut and then outwards, at the same time pressing the driveshaft out of it in an inward direction. If the driveshaft will not release from the carrier, press it out using the centre screw from a three-legged puller.
9   Unscrew the brake disc fixing bolt and roadwheel alignment stud. Remove the disc.
10 Unbolt the hub/flange assembly.
11 If the bearings are worn, refer to Chapter 7, Section 5.
12 If the balljoint is worn then the complete hub carrier must be renewed.
13 Commence reassembly by offering the hub carrier onto the outboard end of the driveshaft, fit the washer and loosely screw on the nut.
14 Reconnect the hub carrier to the strut base clamp and to the suspension lower control arm balljoint.
15 Reconnect the tie-rod end balljoint to the steering arm.
16 Refit the brake disc and caliper.
17 Reconnect the radius rod.
18 Have an assistant apply the footbrake hard and tighten the driveshaft nut to the specified torque. Stake the nut into its shaft groove.
19 Fit the roadwheel and lower the car.

7   Rear shock absorber – removal, testing and refitting

1   Unscrew the bolts from the shock absorber top and bottom mountings and lift the shock absorber from the car (photos).
2   Grip the bottom mounting in the jaws of a vice so that the shock absorber is held vertically.

3   Fully extend and contract the unit five or six times. Any evidence of jerkiness, lack of resistance or seizure can only be remedied by renewal.
4   Fit new rubber top and bottom bushes if the original ones are worn or deformed.

8   Rear leaf spring – removal and refitting

1   Raise the rear of the car and support it securely, but have the roadwheel still in contact with the floor.
2   Unscrew the shackle bolts from the rear end of the spring and disconnect the spring eye (photo).
3   Unscrew the spring U-bolts and lower the spring.
4   Disconnect the pivot bolt from the front end of the spring (photo).
5   The spring flexible bushes may be renewed using a press or by drawing them out and in using a nut, bolt and distance pieces.
6   When refitting the spring, the axle may be jacked up if necessary to align the shackle bolt holes.
7   Fully tighten the shackle and pivot bolt nuts after the weight of the car has again been lowered onto the roadwheels.

9   Rear axle – removal and refitting

1   Raise the rear of the car and support securely.
2   Remove the roadwheels.
3   Disconnect the handbrake cables from the levers at the brake backplate and release them from the axle tube retainers.
4   Disconnect the brake hydraulic hose at its connection with the rigid pipe on the underside of the floor pan. Cap the open ends of hose and pipe to prevent loss of fluid.
5   Unbolt the spring U-bolts.

7.1A Rear shock absorber upper mounting

7.1B Rear shock absorber lower mounting

8.2 Leaf spring rear shackle

8.3 Leaf spring U-bolts

8.4 Leaf spring front pivot

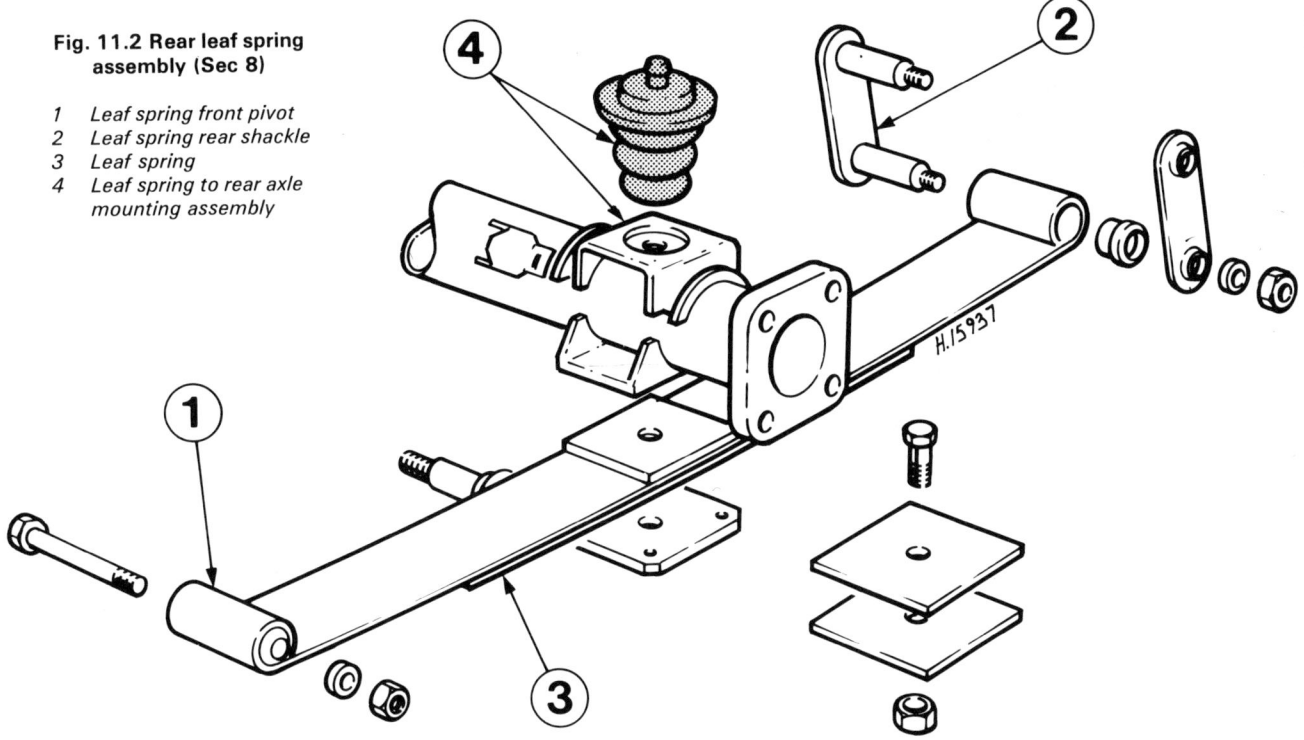

Fig. 11.2 Rear leaf spring assembly (Sec 8)

1 Leaf spring front pivot
2 Leaf spring rear shackle
3 Leaf spring
4 Leaf spring to rear axle mounting assembly

6 Remove the rubber buffer from one side box member.
7 Lift the axle slightly and withdraw it sideways through the space between the roadspring and sidemember.
8 Refitting is a reversal of removal.
9 Bleed the rear hydraulic circuit.

10 Rear wheel alignment

1 The toe-in and positive camber of the rear wheels are set during production of the car and cannot be adjusted.

11 Fault diagnosis – suspension

Symptom	Reason(s)
Front suspension	
Car wanders	Worn track control arm balljoints
Wheel wobble or vibration	Faulty strut or weak coil spring
Excessive pitching or rolling on corners or during braking	Faulty strut Weak coil spring
Rear suspension	
Poor roadholding and wander	Faulty shock absorber Weak leaf spring Worn spring flexible bushes

Chapter 12 Bodywork

Contents

Bonnet – removal and refitting 7
Bonnet lock – adjustment 8
Bonnet release cable – renewal 9
Bumpers – removal and refitting 5
Centre console – removal and refitting 25
Door – dismantling and reassembly 12
Door – removal and refitting 13
Door trim panel – removal and refitting 11
Front parcels shelf and facia panel – removal and refitting 20
Front seat – removal and refitting 18
Front wing – removal and refitting 6
General description 1
Maintenance – bodywork and underframe 2

Major body damage – repair 4
Minor body damage – repair 3
Radiator grille – removal and refitting 10
Rear seat – removal and refitting 19
Rear side trim panel – removal and refitting 14
Rear view mirrors 22
Roof rack 23
Seat belts 21
Side rear opening window – removal and refitting 17
Sun roof 24
Tailgate – removal and refitting 15
Windscreen and tailgate glass – removal and refitting 16

1 General description

1   The Panda comes in one body style, three-door Hatchback. Construction is of all steel welded type with front and rear crumple zones.
2   Impact resistant bumpers and a laminated windscreen are fitted.
3   The car is well equipped, but a sunroof and Denovo tyres are available as factory-fitted options.

2 Maintenance – bodywork and underframe

1   The general condition of a vehicle's bodywork is the one thing that significantly affects its value. Maintenance is easy but needs to be regular. Neglect, particulary after minor damage, can lead quickly to further deterioration and costly repair bills. It is important also to keep watch on those parts of the vehicle not immediately visible, for instance the underside, inside all the wheel arches and the lower part of the engine compartment.
2   The basic maintenance routine for the bodywork is washing – preferably with a lot of water, from a hose. This will remove all the loose solids which may have stuck to the vehicle. It is important to flush these off in such a way as to prevent grit from scratching the finish. The wheel arches and underframe need washing in the same way to remove any accumulated mud which will retain moisture and tend to encourage rust. Paradoxically enough, the best time to clean the underframe and wheel arches is in wet weather when the mud is thoroughly wet and soft. In very wet weather the underframe is usually cleaned of large accumulations automatically and this is a good time for inspection.

3   Periodically, except on vehicles with a wax-based underbody protective coat, it is a good idea to have the whole of the underframe of the vehicle steam cleaned, engine compartment included, so that a thorough inspection can be carried out to see what minor repairs and renovations are necessary. Steam cleaning is available at many garages and is necessary for removal of the accumulation of oily grime which sometimes is allowed to become thick in certain areas. If steam cleaning facilities are not available, there are one or two excellent grease solvents available which can be brush applied. The dirt can then be simply hosed off. Note that these methods should not be used on vehicles with wax-based underbody protective coating or the coating will be removed. Such vehicles should be inspected annually, preferably just prior to winter, when the underbody should be washed down and any damage to the wax coating repaired. Ideally, a completely fresh coat should be applied. It would also be worth considering the use of such wax-based protection for injection into door panels, sills, box sections etc, as an additional safeguard against rust damage.
4   After washing paintwork, wipe off with a chamois leather to give an unspotted clear finish. A coat of clear protective wax polish will give added protection against chemical pollutants in the air. If the paintwork sheen has dulled or oxidised, use a cleaner/polisher combination to restore the brilliance of the shine. This requires a little effort, but such dulling is usually caused because regular washing has been neglected. Care needs to be taken with metallic paintwork, as special non-abrasive cleaner/polisher is required to avoid damage to the finish. Always check that the door and sill drain holes and pipes are completely clear so that water can be drained out. Bright work should be treated in the same way as paintwork. Windscreens and windows can be kept clear of the smeary film which often appears by the use of a proprietary glass cleaner. Never use any form of wax or other body or chromium polish on glass (photos).

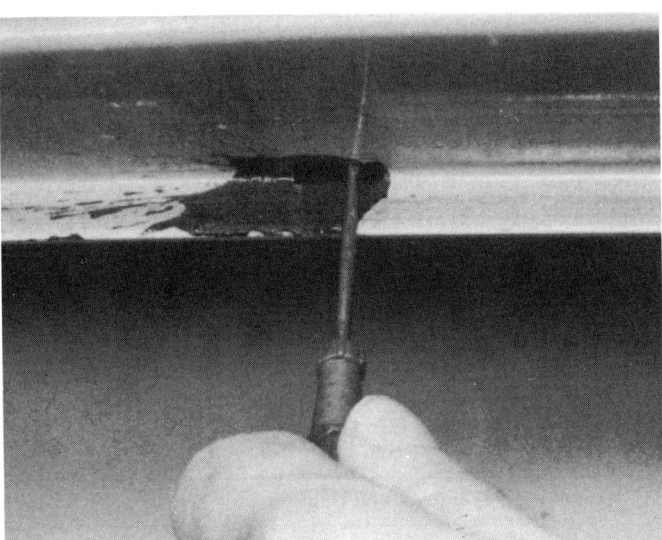

2.4A Door drain hole

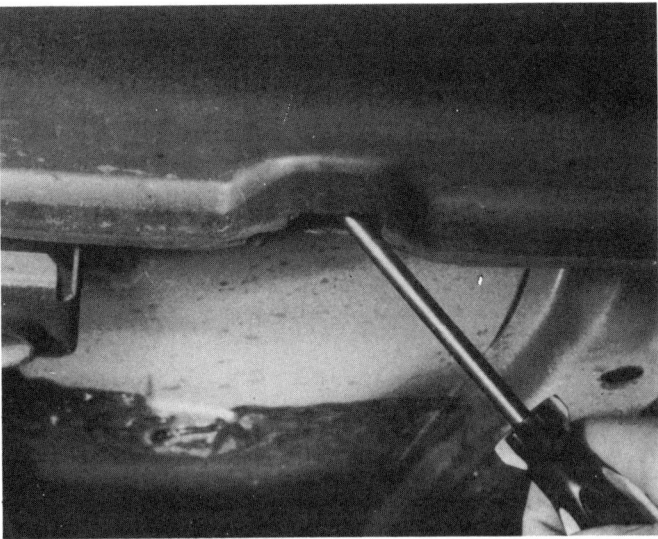

2.4B Sill drain hole

3 Minor body damage – repair

The photographic sequences on pages 166 and 167 illustrate the operations detailed in the following sub-sections.

Repair of minor scratches in bodywork

If the scratch is very superficial, and does not penetrate to the metal of the bodywork, repair is very simple. Lightly rub the area of the scratch with a paintwork renovator, or a very fine cutting paste, to remove loose paint from the scratch and to clear the surrounding bodywork of wax polish. Rinse the area with clean water.

Apply touch-up paint to the scratch using a fine paint brush; continue to apply fine layers of paint until the surface of the paint in the scratch is level with the surrounding paintwork. Allow the new paint at least two weeks to harden: then blend it into the surrounding paintwork by rubbing the scratch area with a paintwork renovator or a very fine cutting paste. Finally, apply wax polish.

Where the scratch has penetrated right through to the metal of the bodywork, causing the metal to rust, a different repair technique is required. Remove any loose rust from the bottom of the scratch with

a penknife, then apply rust inhibiting paint to prevent the formation of rust in the future. Using a rubber or nylon applicator fill the scratch with bodystopper paste. If required, this paste can be mixed with cellulose thinners to provide a very thin paste which is ideal for filling narrow scratches. Before the stopper-paste in the scratch hardens, wrap a piece of smooth cotton rag around the top of a finger. Dip the finger in cellulose thinners and then quickly sweep it across the surface of the stopper-paste in the scratch; this will ensure that the surface of the stopper-paste is slightly hollowed. The scratch can now be painted over as described earlier in this Section.

Repair of dents in bodywork

When deep denting of the vehicle's bodywork has taken place, the first task is to pull the dent out, until the affected bodywork almost attains its original shape. There is little point in trying to restore the original shape completely, as the metal in the damaged area will have stretched on impact and cannot be reshaped fully to its original contour. It is better to bring the level of the dent up to a point which is about $\frac{1}{8}$ in (3 mm) below the level of the surrounding bodywork. In cases where the dent is very shallow anyway, it is not worth trying to pull it out at all. If the underside of the dent is accessible, it can be hammered out gently from behind, using a mallet with a wooden or plastic head. Whilst doing this, hold a suitable block of wood firmly against the outside of the panel to absorb the impact from the hammer blows and thus prevent a large area of the bodywork from being 'belled-out'.

Should the dent be in a section of the bodywork which has a double skin or some other factor making it inaccessible from behind, a different technique is called for. Drill several small holes through the metal inside the area – particularly in the deeper section. Then screw long self-tapping screws into the holes just sufficiently for them to gain a good purchase in the metal. Now the dent can be pulled out by pulling on the protruding heads of the screws with a pair of pliers.

The next stage of the repair is the removal of the paint from the damaged area, and from an inch or so of the surrounding 'sound' bodywork. This is accomplished most easily by using a wire brush or abrasive pad on a power drill, although it can be done just as effectively by hand using sheets of abrasive paper. To complete the preparation for filling, score the surface of the bare metal with a screwdriver or the tang of a file, or alternatively, drill small holes in the affected area. This will provide a really good 'key' for the filler paste.

To complete the repair see the Section on filling and re-spraying.

Repair of rust holes or gashes in bodywork

Remove all paint from the affected area and from an inch or so of the surrounding 'sound' bodywork, using an abrasive pad or a wire brush on a power drill. If these are not available a few sheets of abrasive paper will do the job just as effectively. With the paint removed you will be able to gauge the severity of the corrosion and therefore decide whether to renew the whole panel (if this is possible) or to repair the affected area. New body panels are not as expensive as most people think and it is often quicker and more satisfactory to fit a new panel than to attempt to repair large areas of corrosion.

Remove all fittings from the affected area except those which will act as a guide to the original shape of the damaged bodywork (eg headlamp shells etc). Then, using tin snips or a hacksaw blade, remove all loose metal and any other metal badly affected by corrosion. Hammer the edges of the hole inwards in order to create a slight depression for the filler paste.

Wire brush the affected area to remove the powdery rust from the surface of the remaining metal. Paint the affected area with rust inhibiting paint; if the back of the rusted area is accessible treat this also.

Before filling can take place it will be necessary to block the hole in some way. This can be achieved by the use of aluminium or plastic mesh, or aluminium tape.

Aluminium or plastic mesh is probably the best material to use for a large hole. Cut a piece to the approximate size and shape of the hole to be filled, then position it in the hole so that its edges are below the level of the surrounding bodywork. It can be retained in position by several blobs of filler paste around its periphery.

Aluminium tape should be used for small or very narrow holes. Pull a piece off the roll and trim it to the approximate size and shape required, then pull off the backing paper (if used) and stick the tape over the hole; it can be overlapped if the thickness of one piece is insufficient. Burnish down the edges of the tape with the handle of a screwdriver or similar, to ensure that the tape is securely attached to the metal underneath.

Bodywork repairs – filling and re-spraying

Before using this Section, see the Sections on dent, deep scratch, rust holes and gash repairs.

Many types of bodyfiller are available, but generally speaking those proprietary kits which contain a tin of filler paste and a tube of resin hardener are best for this type of repair. A wide, flexible plastic or nylon applicator will be found invaluable for imparting a smooth and well contoured finish to the surface of the filler.

Mix up a little filler on a clean piece of card or board – measure the hardener carefully (follow the maker's instructions on the pack) otherwise the filler will set too rapidly or too slowly.

Using the applicator apply the filler paste to the prepared area; draw the applicator across the surface of the filler to achieve the correct contour and to level the filler surface. As soon as a contour that approximates to the correct one is achieved, stop working the paste – if you carry on too long the paste will become sticky and begin to 'pick up' on the applicator. Continue to add thin layers of filler paste at twenty-minute intervals until the level of the filler is just proud of the surrounding bodywork.

Once the filler has hardened, excess can be removed using a metal plane or file. From then on, progressively finer grades of abrasive paper should be used, starting with a 40 grade production paper and finishing with 400 grade wet-and-dry paper. Always wrap the abrasive paper around a flat rubber, cork, or wooden block – otherwise the surface of the filler will not be completely flat. During the smoothing of the filler surface the wet-and-dry paper should be periodically rinsed in water. This will ensure that a very smooth finish is imparted to the filler at the final stage.

At this stage the 'dent' should be surrounded by a ring of bare metal, which in turn should be encircled by the finely 'feathered' edge of the good paintwork. Rinse the repair area with clean water, until all of the dust produced by the rubbing-down operation has gone.

Spray the whole repair area with a light coat of primer – this will show up any imperfections in the surface of the filler. Repair these imperfections with fresh filler paste or bodystopper, and once more smooth the surface with abrasive paper. If bodystopper is used, it can be mixed with cellulose thinners to form a really thin paste which is ideal for filling small holes. Repeat this spray and repair procedure until you are satisfied that the surface of the filler, and the feathered edge of the paintwork are perfect. Clean the repair area with clean water and allow to dry fully.

The repair area is now ready for final spraying. Paint spraying must be carried out in a warm, dry, windless and dust free atmosphere. This condition can be created artificially if you have access to a large indoor working area, but if you are forced to work in the open, you will have to pick your day very carefully. If you are working indoors, dousing the floor in the work area with water will help to settle the dust which would otherwise be in the atmosphere. If the repair area is confined to one body panel, mask off the surrounding panels; this will help to minimise the effects of a slight mis-match in paint colours. Bodywork fittings (eg chrome strips, door handles etc) will also need to be masked off. Use genuine masking tape and several thicknesses of newspaper for the masking operations.

Before commencing to spray, agitate the aerosol can thoroughly, then spray a test area (an old tin, or similar) until the technique is mastered. Cover the repair area with a thick coat of primer; the thickness should be built up using several thin layers of paint rather than one thick one. Using 400 grade wet-and-dry paper, rub down the surface of the primer until it is really smooth. While doing this, the work area should be thoroughly doused with water, and the wet-and-dry paper periodically rinsed in water. Allow to dry before spraying on more paint.

Spray on the top coat, again building up the thickness by using several thin layers of paint. Start spraying in the centre of the repair area and then, using a circular motion, work outwards until the whole repair area and about 2 inches of the surrounding original paintwork is covered. Remove all masking material 10 to 15 minutes after spraying on the final coat of paint.

Allow the new paint at least two weeks to harden, then, using a paintwork renovator or a very fine cutting paste, blend the edges of the paint into the existing paintwork. Finally, apply wax polish.

4 Major body damage – repair

1 This sort of work should be left to your Fiat dealer or specialist body repair works.
2 It is essential to have the body aligned on special jigs to ensure that the specified steering and suspension settings are maintained during repair. This is of course beyond the scope of the home mechanic.

5 Bumpers – removal and refitting

1 The front and rear impact resistant type bumpers are secured with bolts and nuts. The bolt heads are fitted with domed covers in the interest of neatness.
2 Before removing the rear bumper, disconnect the leads from the rear number plate lamp.

6 Front wing – removal and refitting

1 The wing is spot welded in position and the seam welds will have to be cut in order to remove the wing, and the new one welded in position.
2 A detachable plastic undershield is fitted to each front wing.
3 New wings are supplied in primer and should be refinished to match the car after fitting and a protective under coating applied.

7 Bonnet – removal and refitting

1 Open the bonnet and support securely on its prop.
2 Mark the position of the hinge plates on the underside of the bonnet. Strips of masking tape are useful for this (photo).
3 Have an assistant support the other side of the bonnet. Then unscrew the hinge bolts and lift the bonnet away to a safe place.
4 Refit by reversing the removal operations. Align the hinges to the marks made on the masking tape during removal.
5 Adjust the bonnet lock if necessary to provide smooth, positive closure as described in the next Section.

7.2 Bonnet hinge

8 Bonnet lock – adjustment

1 The bonnet lock which is attached to the front rail may be moved up, down or sideways to align with the striker and to provide positive locking action when the bonnet is closed (photos).

8.1A Bonnet lock

8.1B Bonnet striker

8.2 Bonnet lid buffer

2   Adjustment should be carried out in conjunction with the rubber closure buffers, screwing these in or out to increase or decrease the pressure required to engage the striker with the lock (photo).

9   Bonnet release cable – renewal

1   Open the bonnet and disconnect the cable from the lock lever. If the reason for renewal is because the cable has broken, release the lock lever by inserting a hooked length of wire through the radiator grille slots or by reaching up through the engine compartment from under the front of the car.
2   Working inside the car under the facia panel, disconnect the end of the cable from the control handle (photo).

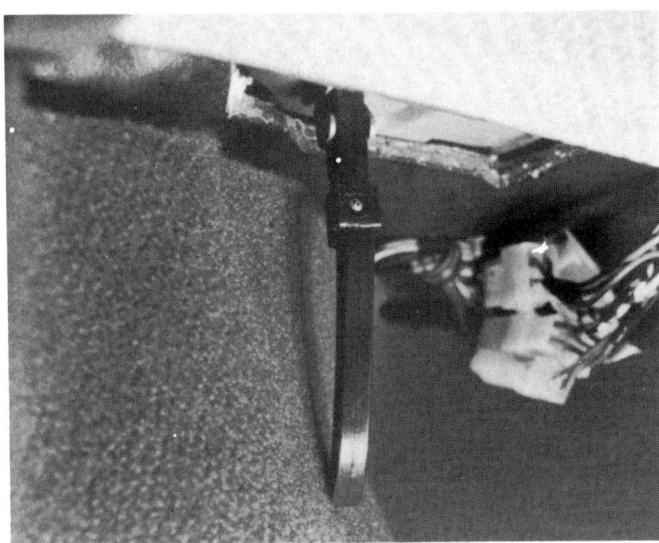

9.2 Bonnet release handle

3   Withdraw the cable through the bulkhead into the car interior.
4   Refitting is a reversal of removal. Eliminate all cable slack before securing the cable to the lock lever. The cable is then looped and crimped.

10   Radiator grille – removal and refitting

1   The grille is pop riveted in position and cannot be removed.
2   If it must be renewed because of damage, drill out the rivets and rivet the new one into position.

11   Door trim panel – removal and refitting

1   Open the door, extract the fixing screws and remove the door pocket (photo).
2   Extract the single screw and take off the window winder handle (photo).
3   Remove the door pull/remote lock handle and withdraw it from the trim panel until it can be unhooked from the link rod by turning it through 90° (photo).
4   Insert the fingers under the edge of the trim panel or use a broad bladed tool and jerk the panel from the door, this will release the retaining clips.
5   Refitting is a reversal of removal. Set the window winder handle vertical with the handle knob uppermost when the glass is closed.

11.1 Door pocket screw

12 Door – dismantling and reassembly

1   Remove the trim panel as described in the preceding Section.
2   Extract the lock fixing screws from the edge of the door and withdraw the lock.
3   The door exterior handle is secured inside the door cavity by a forked spring clip.
4   Release the glass carrier clamps from the cable and slip the cables off the pulleys.
5   Unbolt and remove the window regulator (photo).
6   To remove the main glass from the door, temporarily fit the winder handle and lower the glass fully.
7   Prise out the weatherstrip from the upper edge of the door panel.
8   Unscrew and remove the glass carrier bolts (photo).
9   Withdraw the glass carrier.
10   Withdraw the glass upwards out of the door and towards the outside of the car, rotating its leading edge also in an upward direction.
11   If the opening quarterlight is to be removed, this can be done independently of the main glass. Wind the main glass fully down and extract the screws which hold the top of the glass channel. Remove the pivot and the window catch (photo).

11.2 Window winder handle screw

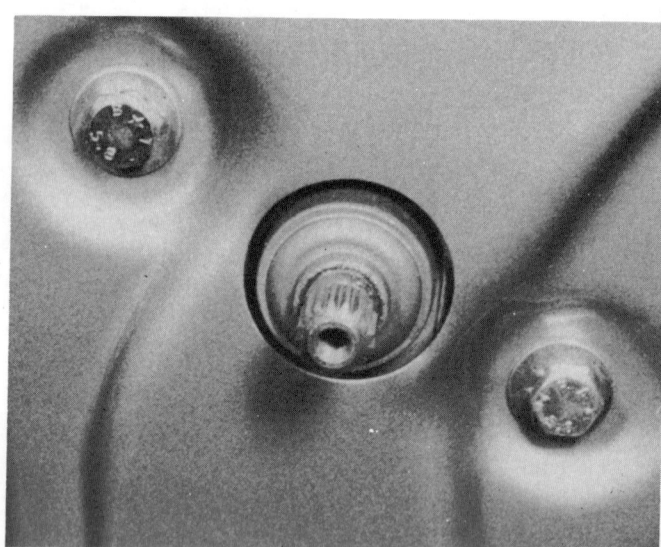

12.5 Window regulator fixing bolts

11.3 Door pull/remote control handle screw

12.8 Door glass lower fixing

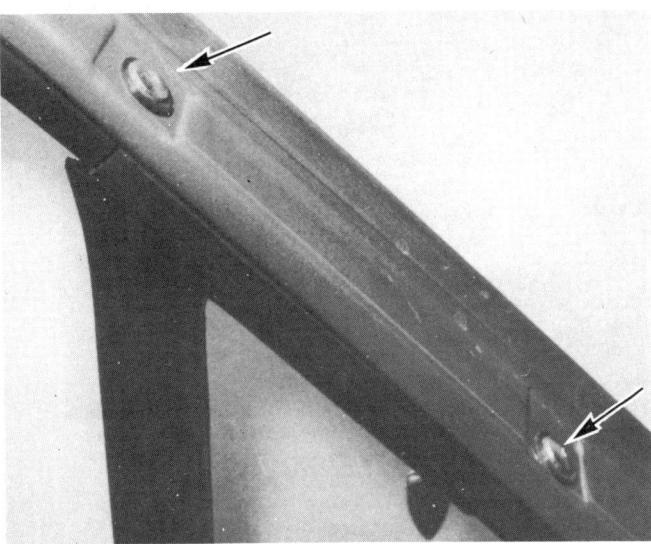

12.11 Door opening quarterlight screws

12 Remove the quarterlight with weatherstrip.
13 Reassembly is a reversal of dismantling.

13 Door – removal and refitting

1 Open the door fully and support its lower edge on a jack or blocks covered with cloth to prevent damage to the paintwork.

2 The hinge bolts are covered and are accessible if the top hinge cover is tapped towards the front of the car and the lower hinge cover plate is prised out. The door check is part of the hinge (photo).
3 Mark the position of the hinges on the body using masking tape and unscrew the bolts. Lift the door away.
4 Refitting is a reversal of removal. The position of the door may be adjusted if the hinge bolts are not fully tightened and the door moved up, down or sideways within the clearance provided in the bolt hole cut-outs.
5 If necessary, unscrew the striker and move it to achieve smooth positive closure (photo).

14 Rear side trim panel – removal and refitting

1 Open the door and pull away the weatherseal channel from the rear vertical edge of the door aperture.
2 Remove the seal cushion and back (Section 19) and the seat tube support sockets (photos).
3 Pull the side upper trim panel off by inserting the fingers under its edge and jerking its retaining clips out of their holes. Ease the seat belt and frame from the panel.
4 Extract the self-tapping screws and retaining pins and remove the lower trim panel.
5 Refitting is a reversal of removal.

15 Tailgate – removal and refitting

1 Open the tailgate fully.
2 Disconnect the leads from the tailgate glass heater element.
3 Remove the small trim panel from the inside of the tailgate.
4 Disconnect the electrical leads from the tailgate wiper motor.
5 Disconnect the washer tube from the washer jet.
6 With an assistant supporting the weight of the tailgate, or using a

13.2A Door upper hinge (cover removed)

13.2B Door lower hinge (blanking plate removed)

13.2C Door check

13.5 Door striker

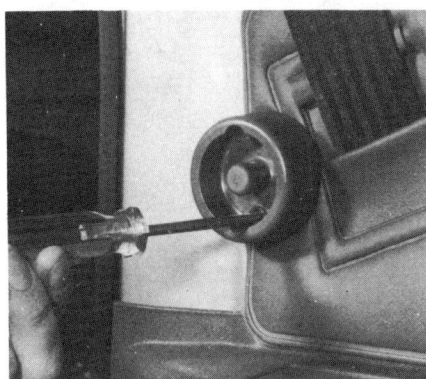

14.2A Seat tube support socket

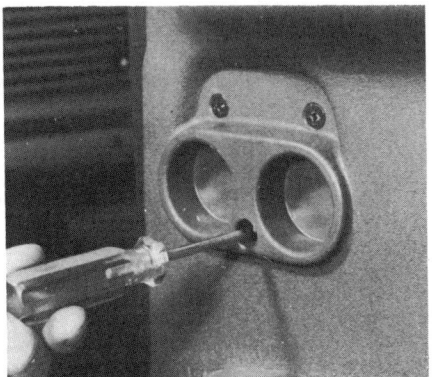

14.2B Seat tube support socket

This sequence of photographs deals with the repair of the dent and paintwork damage shown in this photo. The procedure will be similar for the repair of a hole. It should be noted that the procedures given here are simplified — more explicit instructions will be found in the text

In the case of a dent the first job — after removing surrounding trim — is to hammer out the dent where access is possible. This will minimise filling. Here, the large dent having been hammered out, the damaged area is being made slightly concave

Now all paint must be removed from the damaged area, by rubbing with coarse abrasive paper. Alternatively, a wire brush or abrasive pad can be used in a power drill. Where the repair area meets good paintwork, the edge of the paintwork should be 'feathered', using a finer grade of abrasive paper

In the case of a hole caused by rusting, all damaged sheet-metal should be cut away before proceeding to this stage. Here, the damaged area is being treated with rust remover and inhibitor before being filled

Mix the body filler according to its manufacturer's instructions. In the case of corrosion damage, it will be necessary to block off any large holes before filling — this can be done with aluminium or plastic mesh, or aluminium tape. Make sure the area is absolutely clean before ...

... applying the filler. Filler should be applied with a flexible applicator, as shown, for best results; the wooden spatula being used for confined areas. Apply thin layers of filler at 20-minute intervals, until the surface of the filler is slightly proud of the surrounding bodywork

Initial shaping can be done with a Surform plane or Dreadnought file. Then, using progressively finer grades of wet-and-dry paper, wrapped around a sanding block, and copious amounts of clean water, rub down the filler until really smooth and flat. Again, feather the edges of adjoining paintwork

The whole repair area can now be sprayed or brush-painted with primer. If spraying, ensure adjoining areas are protected from over-spray. Note that at least one inch of the surrounding sound paintwork should be coated with primer. Primer has a 'thick' consistency, so will find small imperfections

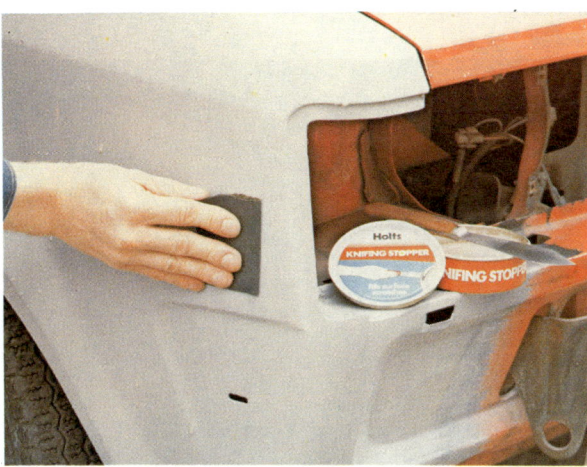

Again, using plenty of water, rub down the primer with a fine grade wet-and-dry paper (400 grade is probably best) until it is really smooth and well blended into the surrounding paintwork. Any remaining imperfections can now be filled by carefully applied knifing stopper paste

When the stopper has hardened, rub down the repair area again before applying the final coat of primer. Before rubbing down this last coat of primer, ensure the repair area is blemish-free — use more stopper if necessary. To ensure that the surface of the primer is really smooth use some finishing compound

The top coat can now be applied. When working out of doors, pick a dry, warm and wind-free day. Ensure surrounding areas are protected from over-spray. Agitate the aerosol thoroughly, then spray the centre of the repair area, working outwards with a circular motion. Apply the paint as several thin coats

After a period of about two weeks, which the paint needs to harden fully, the surface of the repaired area can be 'cut' with a mild cutting compound prior to wax polishing. When carrying out bodywork repairs, remember that the quality of the finished job is proportional to the time and effort expended

15.6A Tailgate strut upper fixing

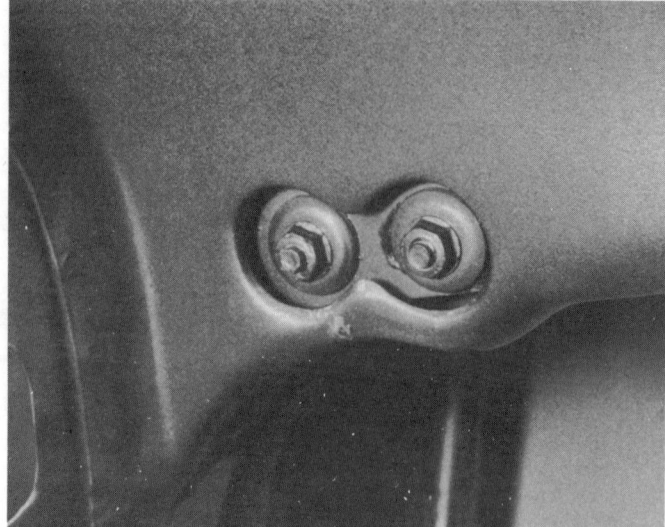

15.7 Tailgate hinge nuts

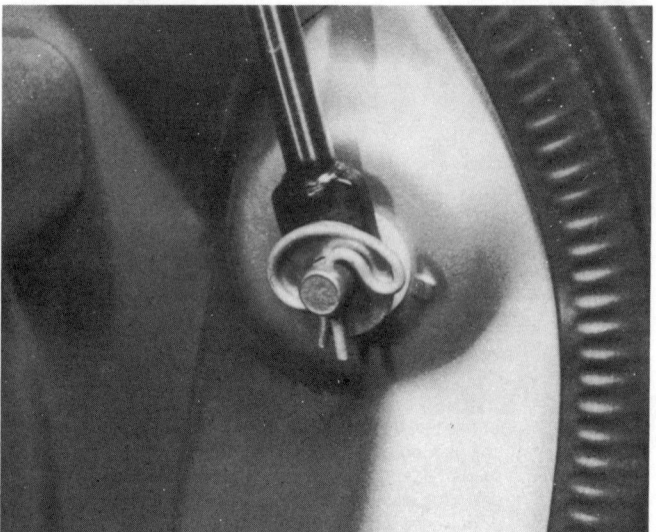

15.6B Tailgate strut lower fixing

15.10 Tailgate lock

wooden prop, disconnect the struts. Do this by pulling out the spring clips from the pivots (photo).

7   Working inside the car at the rear of the headlining, remove the narrow panel and unscrew the hinge mounting nuts (photo).

8   Lift the tailgate from the car.

9   Refitting is a reversal of removal, but do not fully tighten the hinge bolts until the tailgate has been gently closed and its gap all around the edge checked to be of equal width. If necessary, move the tailgate within the clearance provided at the bolt holes. Fully tighten on completion.

10 The lock striker may be moved after releasing its fixing bolts to give smooth, positive closure with the lock (photo).

16 Windscreen and tailgate glass – removal and refitting

The windscreen glass is of the laminated type and even if cracked, can be removed in one piece.

It is strongly recommended that you leave windscreen renewal to the experts. Laminated screens will not stand the amount of stress toughened glass will tolerate during fitting. For those who are prepared to do the work themselves, however, carry out the following sequence of operations.

1   Remove the wiper arms and blades.

2   Sitting in the front seats, apply pressure with the feet (suitably protected with soft shoes or slippers) to the top corners of the glass and push the glass and rubber surround off the body flange. Have an assistant ready to catch the glass.

3   Make sure that the rubber surround and the body flange are clean and free from old sealant. If the rubber has hardened or otherwise deteriorated, renew it.

4   Fit the rubber surround to the glass, smear petroleum jelly lightly into the body flange groove of the rubber surround, then insert a length of nylon or terylene cord into the groove so that the ends of the cord overlap at the centre of the bottom of the screen.

5   Engage the bottom edge of the rubber with the body flange and, with an assistant applying gentle pressure to the glass, withdraw the two ends of the cord simultaneously to engage the lip of the rubber with the body flange. Apply the pressure from outside the glass so that it follows the two places where the cord is being drawn out.

6   Renewal of the rear screen is similar to the procedure just described, but it is of toughened glass. When shattered, therefore, make sure that all the glass fragments are removed from the rubber surround before using it again.

7   Renewal of the side fixed glass is also carried out as just described. If the window is of opening type, refer to the next Section.

17.1 Side window latch

17.2 Side window hinge bolt

18.1 Front seat slide

17 Side rear opening window – removal and refitting

1 The window catch is secured with three screws (photo).
2 The hinges are fixed to the glass using a bolt inserted through a hole in the glass. Exert care when unscrewing or tightening the bolt.

18 Front seat – removal and refitting

1 The front seat slide rails are welded to the floor. Remove a seat by simply sliding it fully forward out of the rails.

19 Rear seat – removal and refitting

1 Open the tailgate and release the clips (A) by pulling lever (F) at the base of the seat back.
2 Working at the top of the seat back, grip the bar (B) and release its left-hand end by twisting it upward. Pull the bar from the mounting at its opposite end.
3 Release the bar (C) at the front of the seat cushion in the same way.

20 Front parcels shelf and facia panel – removal and refitting

1 If a radio has been fitted, remove it and its mounting tray (refer to Chapter 10).
2 From each end of the parcels shelf, extract the screws which hold the end brackets in position. Lower and remove the shelf.
3 Remove the instrument panel as described in Chapter 9.

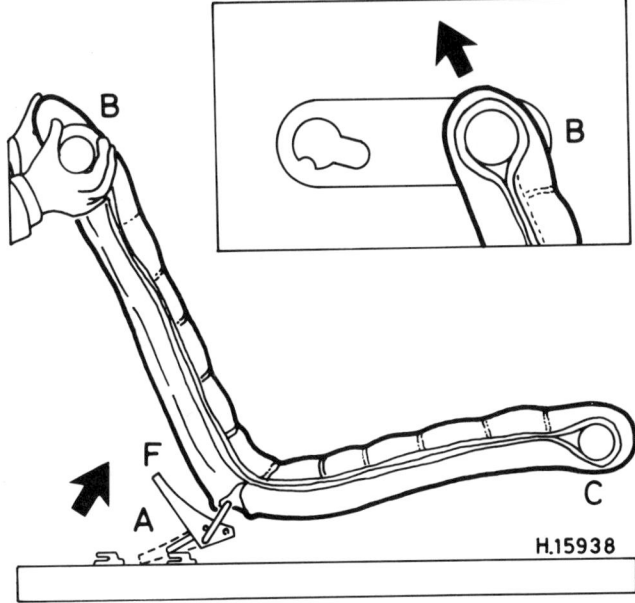

Fig. 12.1 Rear seat removal diagram (Sec 19)

A   Clip   C   Lower bar
B   Upper bar   F   Lever

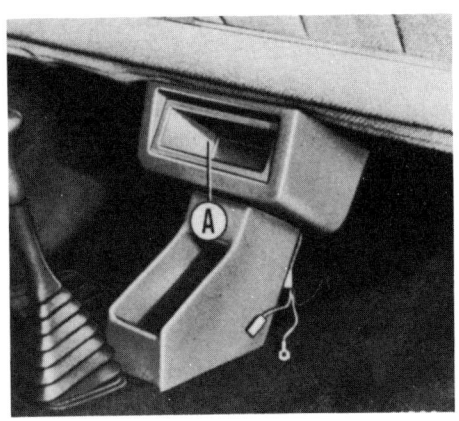

Fig. 12.2 Alternative types of radio mounting trays (Sec 20)

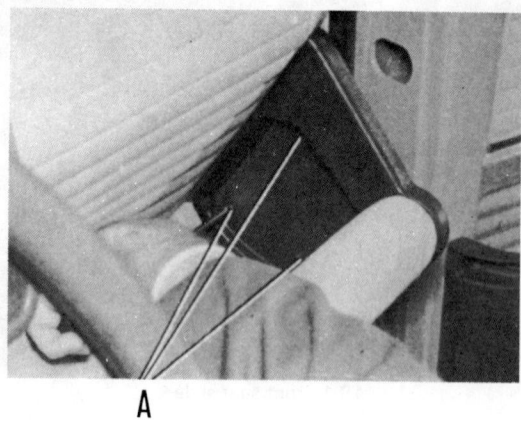

Fig. 12.3 Front parcels shelf end bracket and fixing screws (A)
(Sec 20)

20.4 Side air vent screw

4   Extract the fixing screws and remove the side air vents (photo).
5   Carefully release the facia panel flexible cover from the metal
panel by disconnecting the upper and lower anchor plate teeth.

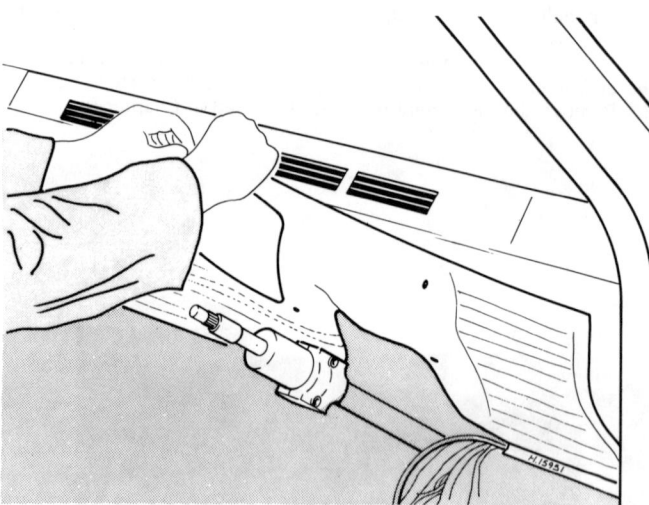

Fig. 12.4 Releasing facia panel flexible cover (Sec 20)

21 Seat belts

1   The seat belts should be checked regularly for wear, cuts or
fraying.
2   No repair is possible and any fault in the belt can only be remedied
by renewal.
3   The seat belt reel is secured by a single bolt and is located behind
the rear side trim panel (see Section 14 for removal) (photo).

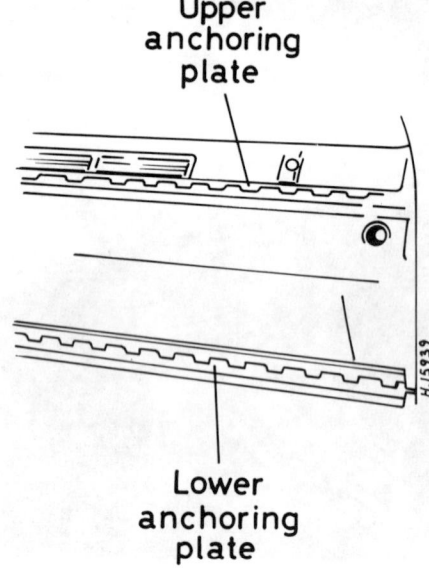

Upper
anchoring
plate

Lower
anchoring
plate

Fig. 12.5 Facia cover anchor plates (Sec 20)

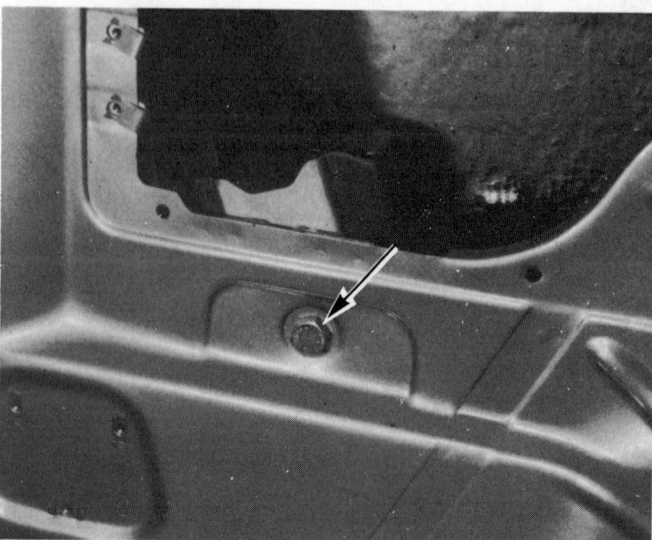

21.3 Seat belt reel fixing bolt

4   Never attempt to alter the belt anchorage points and if a belt is
removed, always maintain the originally fitted sequence of the
mounting components – spacer, plain and wave washer (photos).
5   If a seat belt requires cleaning, use only warm water and
detergent, never solvent or a chemical cleaner.

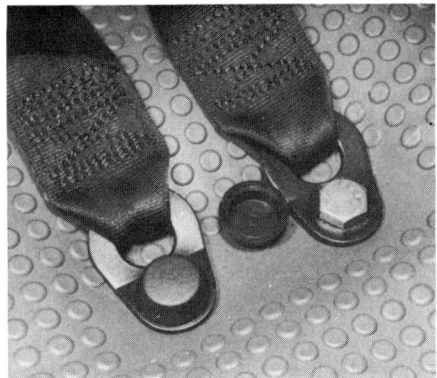

21.4A Seat belt anchorage

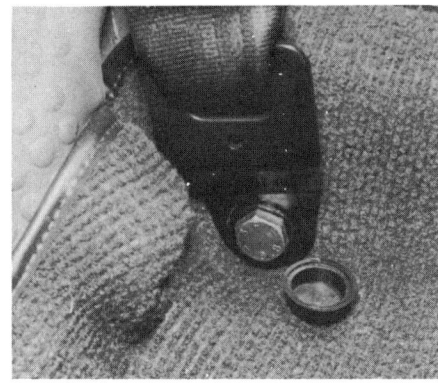

21.4B Seat belt anchorage

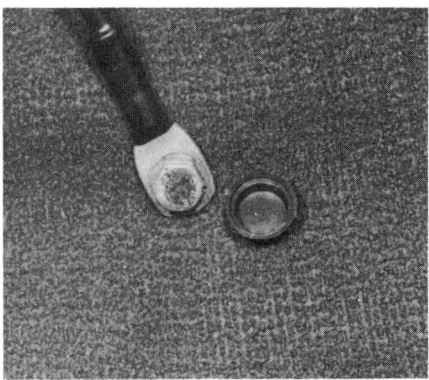

21.4C Seat belt stalk

22.2 Exterior mirror fixing screw

22.3A Exterior mirror remote control

22.3B Removing exterior mirror control knob

22 Rear view mirrors

Interior

1   The mirror, clock and courtesy lamp base which are mounted above the windscreen are all secured by a screw.

Exterior

2   The door-mounted mirrors are secured by external screws (photo).
3   On some versions the mirror is of remotely-controlled adjustable type. Pull off the rubber cover from the control handle and unscrew the ring nut (photos).

23 Roof rack

1   Provision for fitting a roof rack is made by two tapped holes on the roof towards the upper edge of the tailgate.
2   The front of the rack should be held using clamps located under the top edge of the front door body opening.

Fig. 12.6 Remotely-controlled type exterior mirror (Sec 22)

    C   Mirror   *D   Control knob*

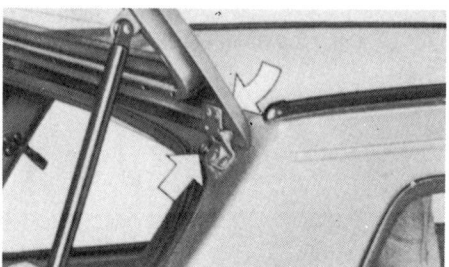

Fig. 12.7 Roof rack rear mounting hole (Sec 23)

Fig. 12.8 Roof rack front clamp mounting point (Sec 23)

Fig. 12.10 Sunroof partially open (Sec 24)

A   Lever   B   Hook

24 Sun roof

1   The optional Fiat sunroof is of roll-back dual panel type.
2   To open the sunroof, release the lever (A), fold the roof fabric forward without trapping it under the frame and then roll it back and fasten with strap (B) and the roof hook.
3   The lever (A) will be located between the strap and the fabric.
4   To close, reverse the opening operations making sure that the pin (C) of the lever (A) is located in the seat (D). Finally hook the strap (B) to the end of the lever (A).

25 Centre console – removal and refitting

1   Extract the screw which holds the upper part and remove that section.
2   The base can be removed from the door after extracting the screws (photo).
3   If a cigar lighter is fitted, make sure that the connecting leads are disconnected before withdrawing the console too far.
4   Refitting is a reversal of removal.

Fig. 12.11 Sunroof flexible strap (B) (Sec 24)

Fig. 12.9 Sunroof (Sec 24)

B   Strap

25.2 Centre console screw

Index

A

Accelerator pedal and linkage – 70
Air cleaner
    servicing, removal and refitting – 64
Alternator
    description, maintenance and precautions – 126
    overhaul – 126
    removal and refitting – 126
Antifreeze – 55

B

Battery
    maintenance – 125
    removal and refitting – 125
Bleeding the brakes – 120
Bodywork – 160 *et seq*
Bodywork
    bonnet – 162, 163
    bumpers – 162
    centre console – 172
    description – 160
    doors – 163, 164, 165
    front parcels shelf and facia panel – 169
    front wing – 162
    maintenance, bodywork and underframe – 160
    radiator grille – 163
    rear side trim panel – 165
    rear view mirrors – 171
    repair
        major damage – 162
        minor damage – 161
    roof rack – 171
    seat belts – 170
    seats – 169
    side rear opening window – 169
    sun roof – 172
    tailgate – 165, 168
    windscreen glass – 168
Bodywork repair sequence (colour) – 166, 167
Bonnet
    lock adjustment – 162
    release cable renewal – 163
    removal and refitting – 162
Braking system – 112 *et seq*
Braking system
    caliper – 116
    description – 112
    disc pads – 112
    fault diagnosis – 123
    front disc – 117
    handbrake – 121, 122
    hydraulic system bleeding – 120
    hydraulic rigid pipes and flexible hoses – 120
    maintenance – 112
    master cylinder – 118
    pedal – 122
    pressure regulating valve – 119
    rear drum – 117
    rear hydraulic wheel cylinder – 117
    rear shoe linings – 114
    specifications – 112
    torque wrench settings – 112
Bulbs, lamp
    renewal – 129
    specifications – 125
Bumpers removal and refitting – 162

C

Caliper
    removal, overhaul and refitting – 116
Cam followers
    examination and renovation – 43
Camshaft
    examination and renovation – 43
    reassembly – 48
Capacities, general – 6
Carburettor
    description and maintenance – 67
    idle speed and mixture adjustment – 68
    overhaul – 69
    removal and refitting – 69
    specifications – 63
Choke control cable
    adjustment and renewal – 71

Clock
setting – 134
Clutch – 82 *et seq*
Clutch
adjustment – 82
cable renewal – 82
description – 82
fault diagnosis – 85
inspection – 84
pedal removal and refitting – 84
refitting – 84
release mechanism – 84
removal – 84
specifications – 82
Coil, ignition – 80
Compression ratio – 24
Condenser
testing and renewal – 78
Connecting rods
examination and renovation – 42
Contact breaker points
servicing – 76
Conversion factors – 13
Coolant pump
overhaul – 58
removal and refitting – 58
Coolant temperature switch – 58
Cooling and heating systems – 54 *et seq*
Cooling system
coolant mixtures – 55
coolant pump – 58
coolant temperature switch – 58
description – 54
draining, flushing and refilling – 55
drivebelt – 57
electric cooling fan and switch – 57
fault diagnosis – 62
maintenance – 54
radiator – 56
specifications – 54
thermostat – 56
torque wrench settings – 54
Courtesy lamp, clock, mirror assembly
removal and refitting – 134
Crankcase ventilation system – 29
Crankshaft and bearings
examination and renovation – 42
reassembly – 46
Cylinder block and crankcase
examination and renovation – 42
Cylinder head
dismantling and decarbonising – 40
reassembly – 49
removal and refitting – 29

D

Decarbonising – 40
Differential – 96
Dimensions, general – 6
Disc brake pads
inspection and renewal – 112
Distributor
overhaul – 79
removal and refitting – 79
Doors
dismantling and reassembly – 164
removal and refitting – 165
trim panel removal and refitting – 163
Drivebelt
tensioning, removal and refitting – 57
Driveshafts
description – 106
fault diagnosis – 111

joints renewal – 108
maintenance – 107
removal and refitting – 107
torque wrench settings – 106
Driveshafts, hubs, wheels and tyres – 106 *et seq*
Dwell angle
checking – 78

E

Electrical system – 124 *et seq*
Electrical system
alternator – 126
battery – 125
bulbs – 129
clock – 134
courtesy lamp, clock, mirror assembly – 134
description – 125
fault diagnosis – 20, 145
fuses and relays – 128
headlamps – 131, 132
heated tailgate window – 136
instrument panel – 132
radio equipment, mobile – 139
radio (Fiat accessory) – 136
specifications – 124
speedometer cable – 134
starter motor – 126, 128
switches – 129
torque wrench settings – 125
washer system – 136
wipers – 134, 135
wiring diagrams – 177 to 183
Electric cooling fan and switch – 57
Engine – 24 *et seq*
Engine
ancillary components
refitting – 50
removal – 39
cam followers – 43
camshaft – 43, 48
connecting rods – 33, 44
crankcase ventilation system – 29
crankshaft and bearings – 42, 46
cylinder block and crankcase – 42
cylinder head – 29, 40, 49
decarbonising – 40
description – 26
dismantling – 39
examination and renovation – 42
fault diagnosis – 22, 52
flywheel – 43, 47
mountings – 36
oil and filter – 29
oil pump – 36, 45
oil seals and gaskets – 46
operations possible without removing engine – 29
piston rings – 42
pistons – 33, 42
reassembly – 46
reconnection to transmission – 50
refitting (with transmission) – 51
removal
downwards (with transmission) – 38
method – 37
upwards (with transmission) – 39
rockers and rocker shaft – 44
separation from transmission – 39
specifications – 24
start-up after overhaul – 51
sump pan – 32
timing chain and sprockets – 35, 43, 48
torque wrench settings – 26
valves – 37
Exhaust system – 71

Index

A

Accelerator pedal and linkage – 70
Air cleaner
    servicing, removal and refitting – 64
Alternator
    description, maintenance and precautions – 126
    overhaul – 126
    removal and refitting – 126
Antifreeze – 55

B

Battery
    maintenance – 125
    removal and refitting – 125
Bleeding the brakes – 120
Bodywork – 160 *et seq*
Bodywork
    bonnet – 162, 163
    bumpers – 162
    centre console – 172
    description – 160
    doors – 163, 164, 165
    front parcels shelf and facia panel – 169
    front wing – 162
    maintenance, bodywork and underframe – 160
    radiator grille – 163
    rear side trim panel – 165
    rear view mirrors – 171
    repair
        major damage – 162
        minor damage – 161
    roof rack – 171
    seat belts – 170
    seats – 169
    side rear opening window – 169
    sun roof – 172
    tailgate – 165, 168
    windscreen glass – 168
Bodywork repair sequence (colour) – 166, 167
Bonnet
    lock adjustment – 162
    release cable renewal – 163
    removal and refitting – 162
Braking system – 112 *et seq*
Braking system
    caliper – 116
    description – 112
    disc pads – 112
    fault diagnosis – 123
    front disc – 117
    handbrake – 121, 122
    hydraulic system bleeding – 120
    hydraulic rigid pipes and flexible hoses – 120
    maintenance – 112
    master cylinder – 118
    pedal – 122
    pressure regulating valve – 119
    rear drum – 117
    rear hydraulic wheel cylinder – 117
    rear shoe linings – 114
    specifications – 112
    torque wrench settings – 112
Bulbs, lamp
    renewal – 129
    specifications – 125
Bumpers removal and refitting – 162

C

Caliper
    removal, overhaul and refitting – 116
Cam followers
    examination and renovation – 43
Camshaft
    examination and renovation – 43
    reassembly – 48
Capacities, general – 6
Carburettor
    description and maintenance – 67
    idle speed and mixture adjustment – 68
    overhaul – 69
    removal and refitting – 69
    specifications – 63
Choke control cable
    adjustment and renewal – 71

F

Fault diagnosis – 20 *et seq*
Fault diagnosis
    braking system – 123
    clutch – 85
    cooling system – 62
    driveshafts – 111
    electrical system – 20, 145
    engine – 22, 52
    fuel system – 72
    ignition system – 81
    steering – 154
    suspension – 159
    transmission – 105
Firing order – 24
Flywheel
    examination and renovation – 43
    reassembly – 47
Front brake discs
    inspection and renovation or renewal – 117
Front suspension – 155, 156
Front wheel alignment – 152
Front wing
    removal and refitting – 162
Fuel pump
    cleaning – 65
    overhaul (non-sealed type) – 66
    removal and refitting – 66
    testing – 65
Fuel system – 63 *et seq*
Fuel system
    accelerator pedal and linkage – 70
    air cleaner – 64
    carburettor – 67, 68, 69
    choke control cable – 71
    description and maintenance – 64
    fault diagnosis – 72
    fuel pump – 65, 66
    fuel tank – 66
    fuel tank transmitter – 66
    specifications – 63
Fuel tank
    capacity – 6
    removal and refitting – 66
Fuel tank transmitter
    removal and refitting – 66
Fuses and relays – 128

G

Gearchange lever and linkage
    removal, refitting and adjustment – 87

H

Handbrake
    adjustment – 121
    cable renewal – 122
Headlamps
    beam alignment – 132
    removal and refitting – 131
Heater
    removal and refitting – 60
High tension leads – 80
Horn and switch – 129
Hub bearings
    maintenance – 107
    renewal
        front – 110
        rear – 110

Hydraulic system (brake)
    bleeding – 120
    rigid pipes and flexible hoses
        inspection and renewal – 120

I

Ignition system – 74 *et seq*
Ignition system
    coil – 80
    condenser – 78
    contact breaker – 76
    description – 74
    distributor – 79
    dwell angle – 78
    fault diagnosis – 80
    HT leads – 80
    spark plugs – 75, 80
    specifications – 74
    timing – 78
Instrument panel
    removal and refitting – 132

J

Jacking – 7

L

Lubricants and fluids recommended – 19
Lubrication chart – 19

M

Main bearings – 42, 46
Maintenance, routine
    bodywork
        and underside – 18, 160
        hinges and controls lubrication – 18
    brakes
        disc pad and shoe lining wear check – 18, 112, 114
        fluid level check/top-up – 18, 112
        handbrake adjustment – 18, 121
        hoses check – 18, 120
        hydraulic fluid renewal – 18, 120
    clutch
        cable adjustment – 18, 82
    cooling system
        coolant level check/top-up – 18, 54
        coolant renewal – 18, 55
        drivebelt tension and condition check – 18, 57
    driveshafts and hubs – 18, 107
    electrical system
        alternator – 126
        battery – 18, 125
        headlamps beam alignment check – 18, 132
        lights check – 18
        washers and wipers check – 18
    engine
        cylinder head bolts torque check (new cars) – 18, 31
        oil change – 18, 29
        oil filter renewal – 18, 29
        oil level check/top-up – 18
        valve clearances check/adjust – 18, 37
    exhaust system – 18, 71
    fuel system
        air cleaner element renewal – 18, 64
        carburettor idle speed and mixture check/adjust – 18, 68
        fuel pump cleaning – 65
    ignition system
        contact points check/renew – 18, 76

dwell angle and timing check/adjust – 18, 78
spark plugs check/re-gap/renewal – 18, 80
safety precautions – 14
schedules – 18
steering and suspension
front wheel alignment check – 18, 152
gaiters check – 18, 148, 155
joints check – 18, 152
transmission
oil change – 18, 86
oil level check/top-up – 18, 86
tyres pressures and tread wear check – 18, 106, 111
Manifolds – 71
Master cylinder (brake)
removal, overhaul and refitting – 118
Mirrors, rear view – 171
Mountings, engine
removal and refitting – 36

O

Oil filter
renewal – 29
Oil pump
examination and renovation – 45
removal and refitting – 36
Oil seals and gaskets – 46

P

Pedal
removal and refitting
brake – 122
clutch – 84
Piston/connecting rods
removal and refitting – 33
Pistons and piston rings
examination and renovation – 42
Pressure regulating valve – 119

R

Radiator
removal and refitting – 56
Radiator grille
removal and refitting – 163
Radio equipment, mobile
interference-free installation – 139
Radio (Fiat accessory)
fitting – 136
Rear axle – 158
Rear brakes
drum inspection and renovation or renewal – 117
hydraulic wheel cylinder removal, overhaul and refitting – 117
shoe linings inspection and renewal – 114
Rear suspension – 155, 158
Repair procedures, general – 10
Roadwheels see Wheels
Rockers and rocker shaft
examination and renovation – 44
Roof rack – 171

S

Safety – 14
Seat belts – 170
Seats
removal and refitting
front – 169
rear – 169

Spare parts
buying – 9
to carry in car – 21
Spark plugs
conditions (colour chart) – 75
general – 80
specifications – 74
Speedometer cable
renewal – 134
Starter motor
description and in-car testing – 126
overhaul – 128
removal and refitting – 126
Steering – 147 et seq
Steering
angles and front wheel alignment – 152
column – 148, 150
column lock/switch – 150
description – 147
fault diagnosis – 154
gear – 151, 152
maintenance – 147
rack – 148, 150
specifications – 147
tie-rod and balljoint renewal – 148
torque wrench settings – 147
wheel – 148
Steering column
lock/switch removal and refitting – 150
overhaul – 150
removal and refitting – 148
Steering gear
overhaul – 152
removal and refitting – 151
Steering rack
damper adjustment – 150
gaiter renewal – 148
Steering wheel
removal and refitting – 148
Sump pan
removal and refitting – 32
Sun roof – 172
Suspension – 155 et seq
Suspension
description – 155
fault diagnosis – 159
front
hub carrier removal and refitting – 156
lower track control arm removal and refitting – 156
strut removal and refitting – 155
maintenance – 155
radius rod removal and refitting – 156
rear
axle removal and refitting – 158
leaf spring removal and refitting – 158
shock absorber removal, testing and refitting – 158
rear wheel alignment – 159
specifications – 155
torque wrench settings – 155
Switches
removal and refitting
courtesy lamp – 129
horn – 129
rocker – 129
steering column – 150

T

Tailgate
removal and refitting – 165
Tailgate window, heated – 136
Thermostat
removal, testing and refitting – 56
Timing chain
examination and renovation – 43

Timing chain and sprockets
reassembly – 48
removal and refitting – 35
Timing, ignition – 74, 78
Tools   .
general – 11
to carry in car – 21
Towing – 7
Transmission – 86 *et seq*
Transmission
components inspection – 95
description – 86
differential overhaul – 96
fault diagnosis – 105
gearchange lever and linkage – 87
maintenance – 86
reassembly – 99
removal and refitting – 89
removal of main assemblies – 90
shaft geartrains overhaul – 95
specifications – 86
torque wrench settings – 86
Tyres
general – 111
pressures – 106
specifications – 106

V

Valves
clearances adjustment – 37
Vehicle identification numbers – 9

W

Washer system – 136
Weights, general – 6
Wheels
changing – 7
general – 111
specifications – 106
Window, side rear opening
removal and refitting – 169
Windscreen glass
removal and refitting – 168
Wipers
blade and arm removal and refitting – 134
motor and linkage removal and refitting – 135
Wiring diagrams – 177 to 183
Working facilities – 12

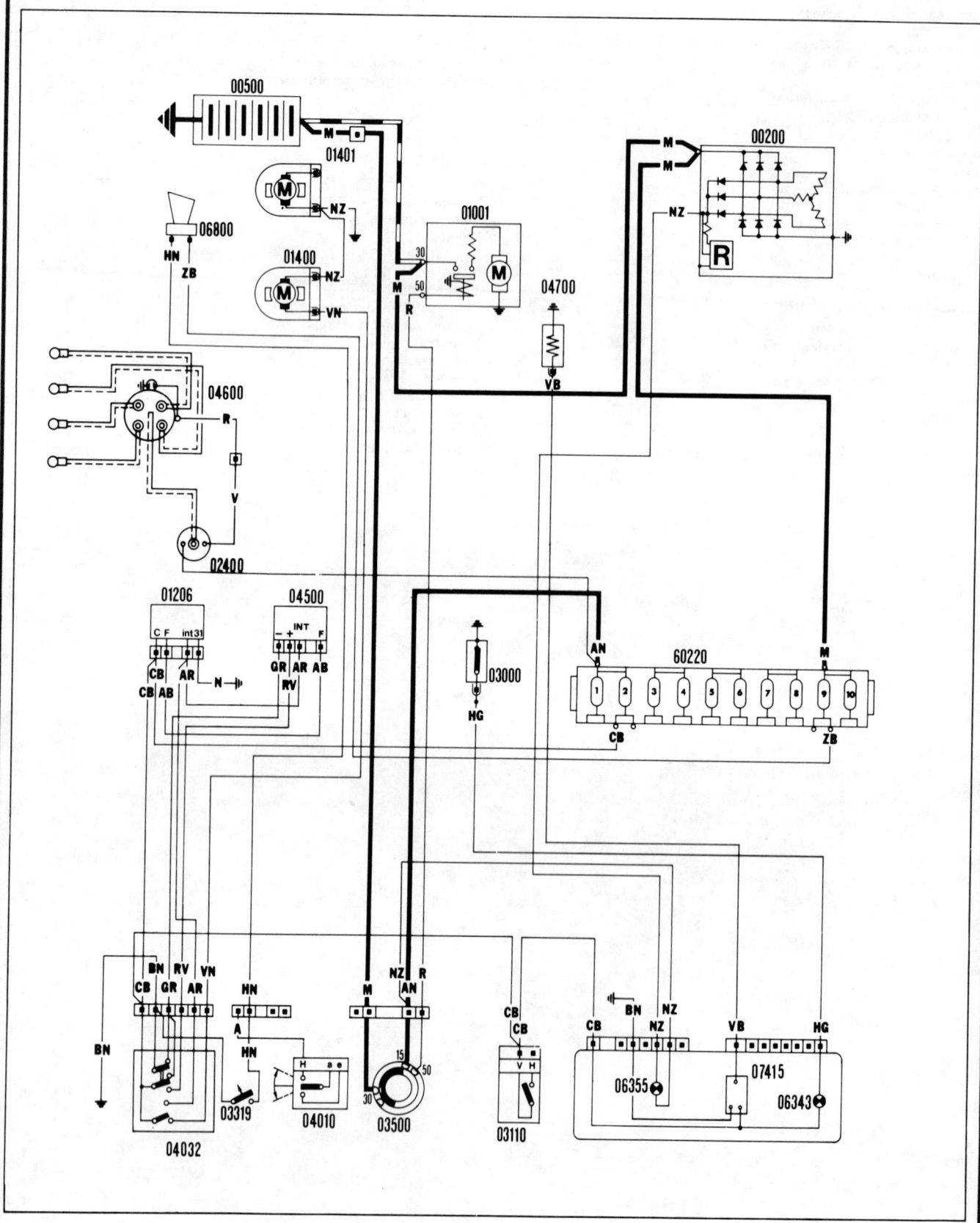

Wiring diagram for starting, ignition, recharging, coolant temperature, horn, oil pressure and windscreen wash/wipe

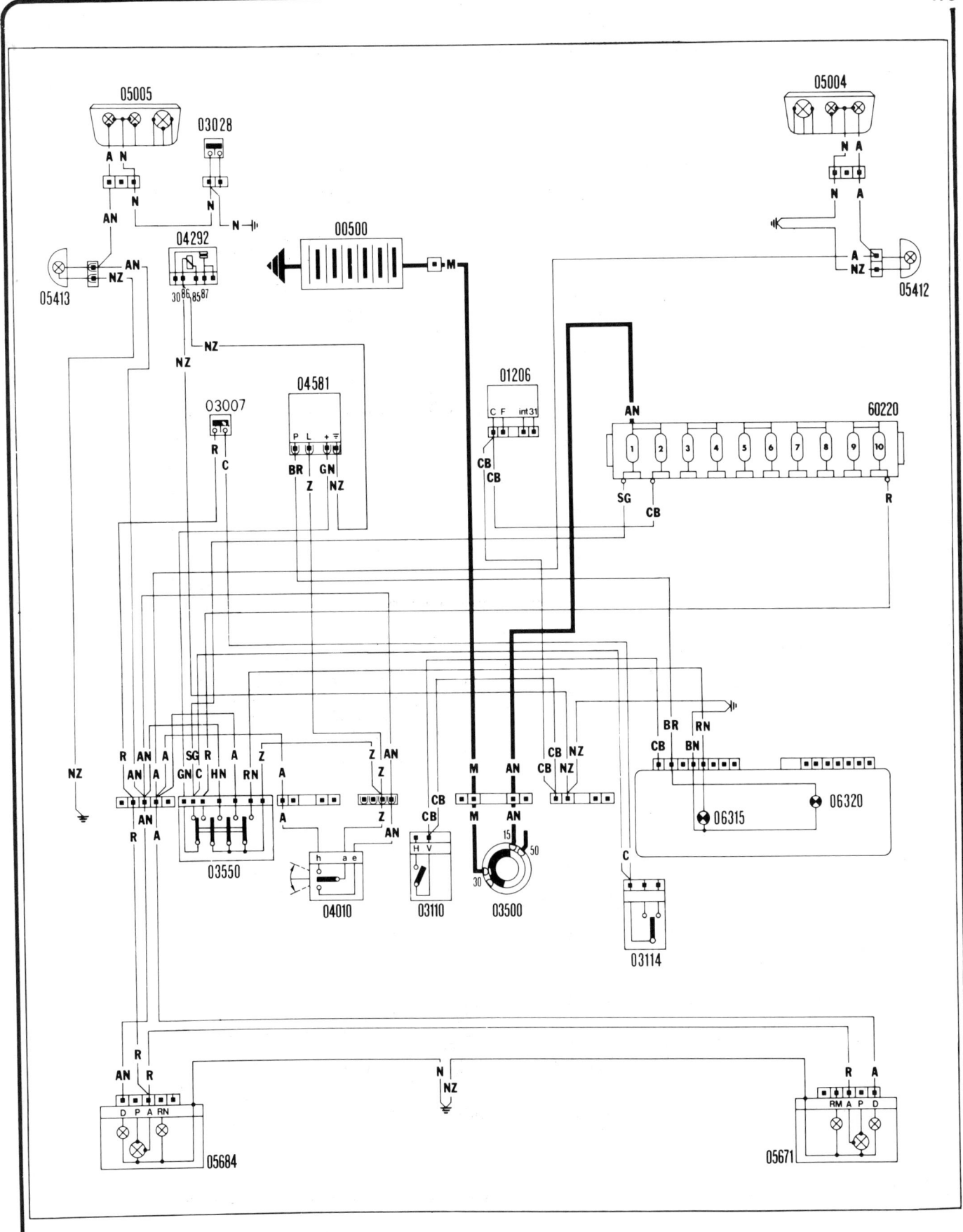

Wiring diagram for direction indicators, hazard warning lights and brake lights

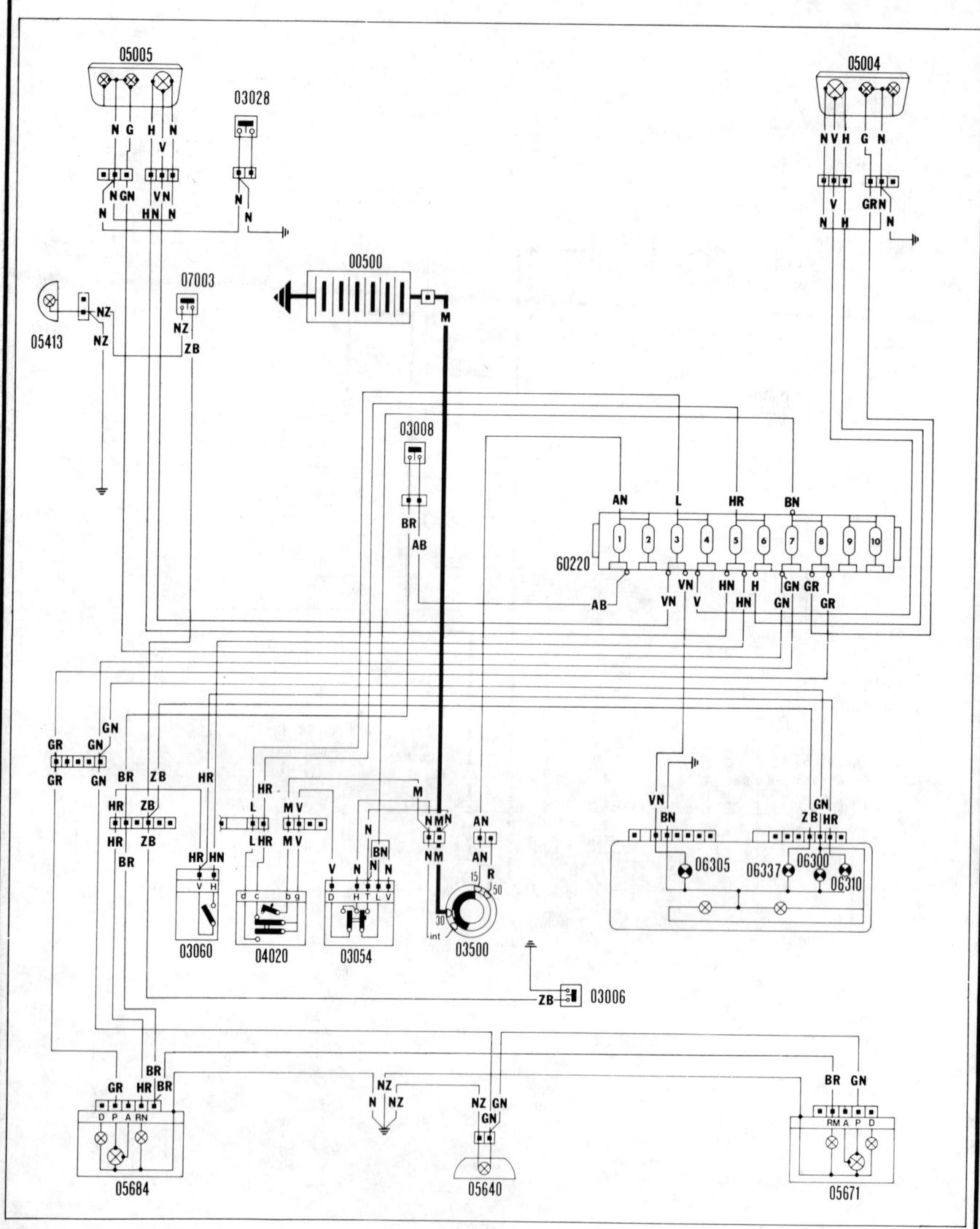

Wiring diagram for sidelights, headlights, number plate light, rear foglight, reversing light and warning lights for brake fluid and handbrake

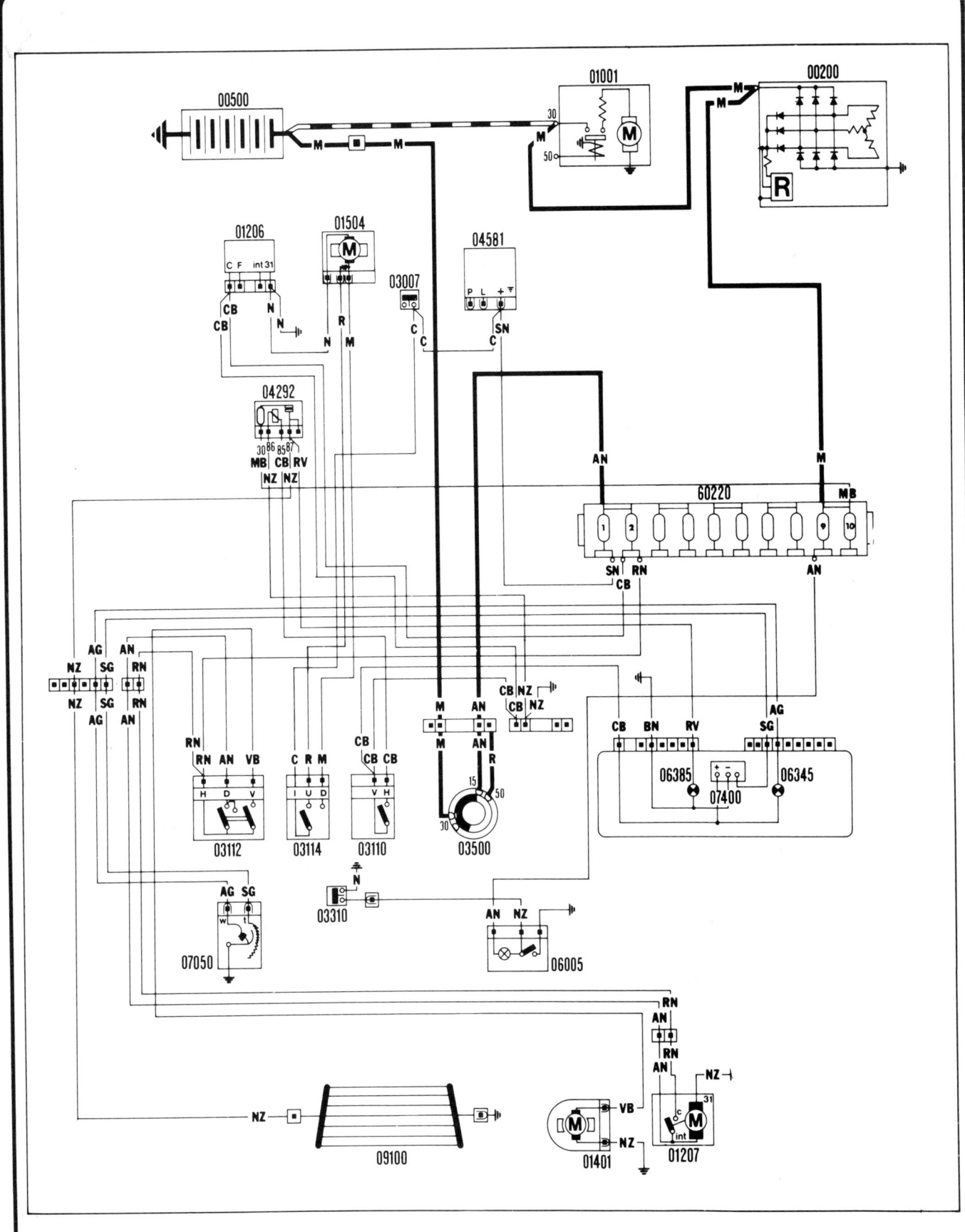

Wiring diagram for heated rear window, rear wash/wipe, fuel gauge, fuel reserve and courtesy lights

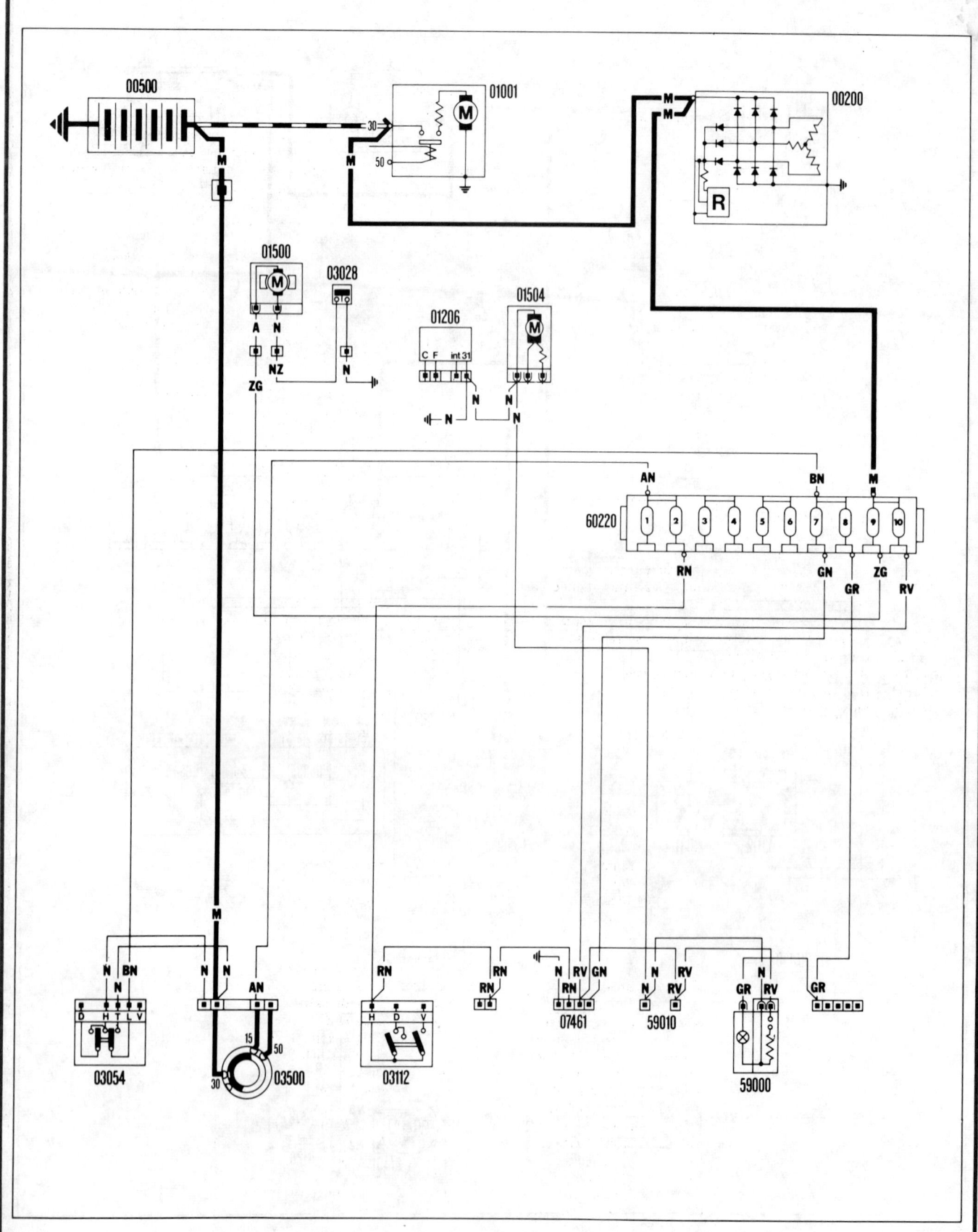

Wiring diagram for radiator fan, cigarette lighter, radio and digital clock

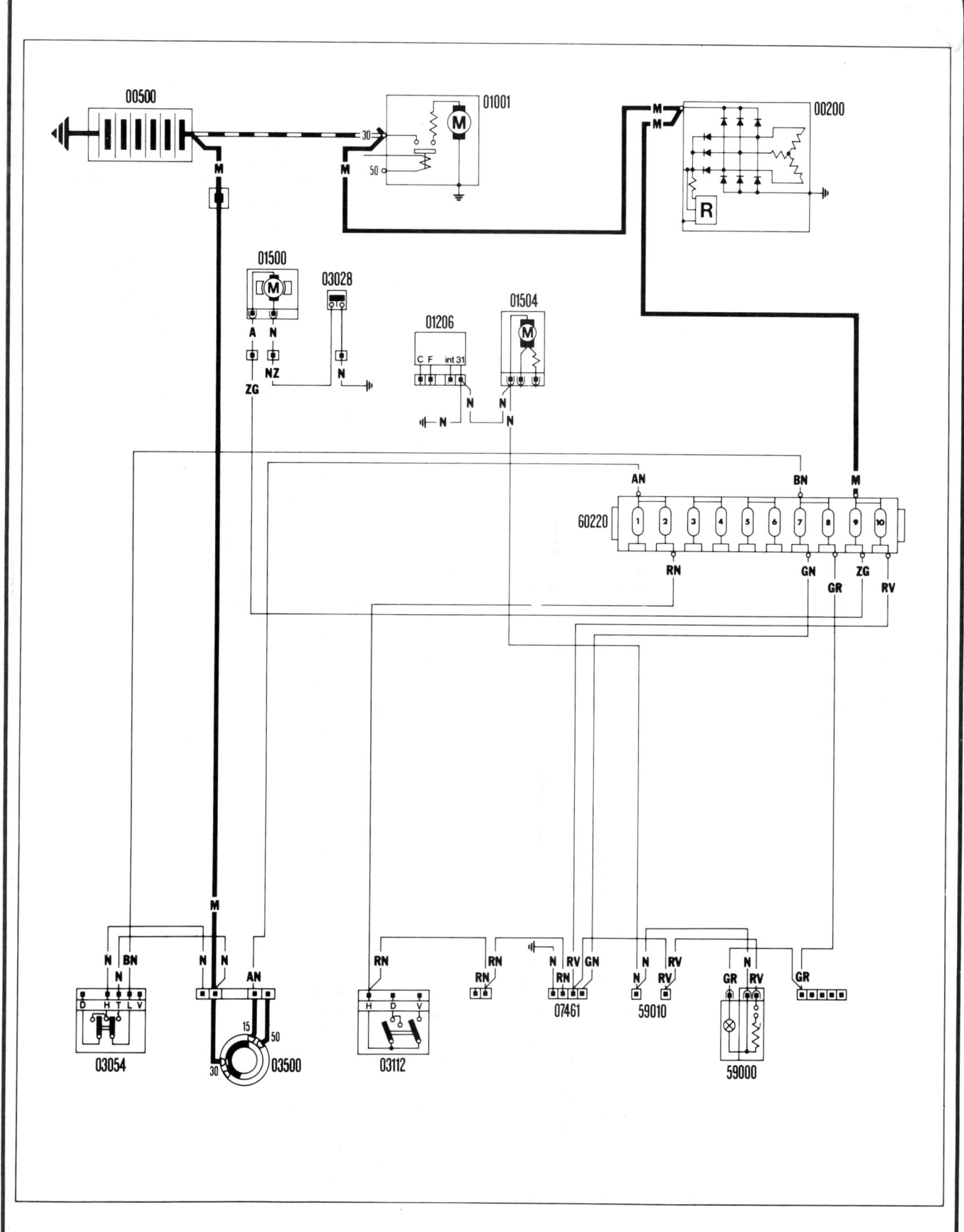

Wiring diagram for radiator fan, cigarette lighter, radio and digital clock

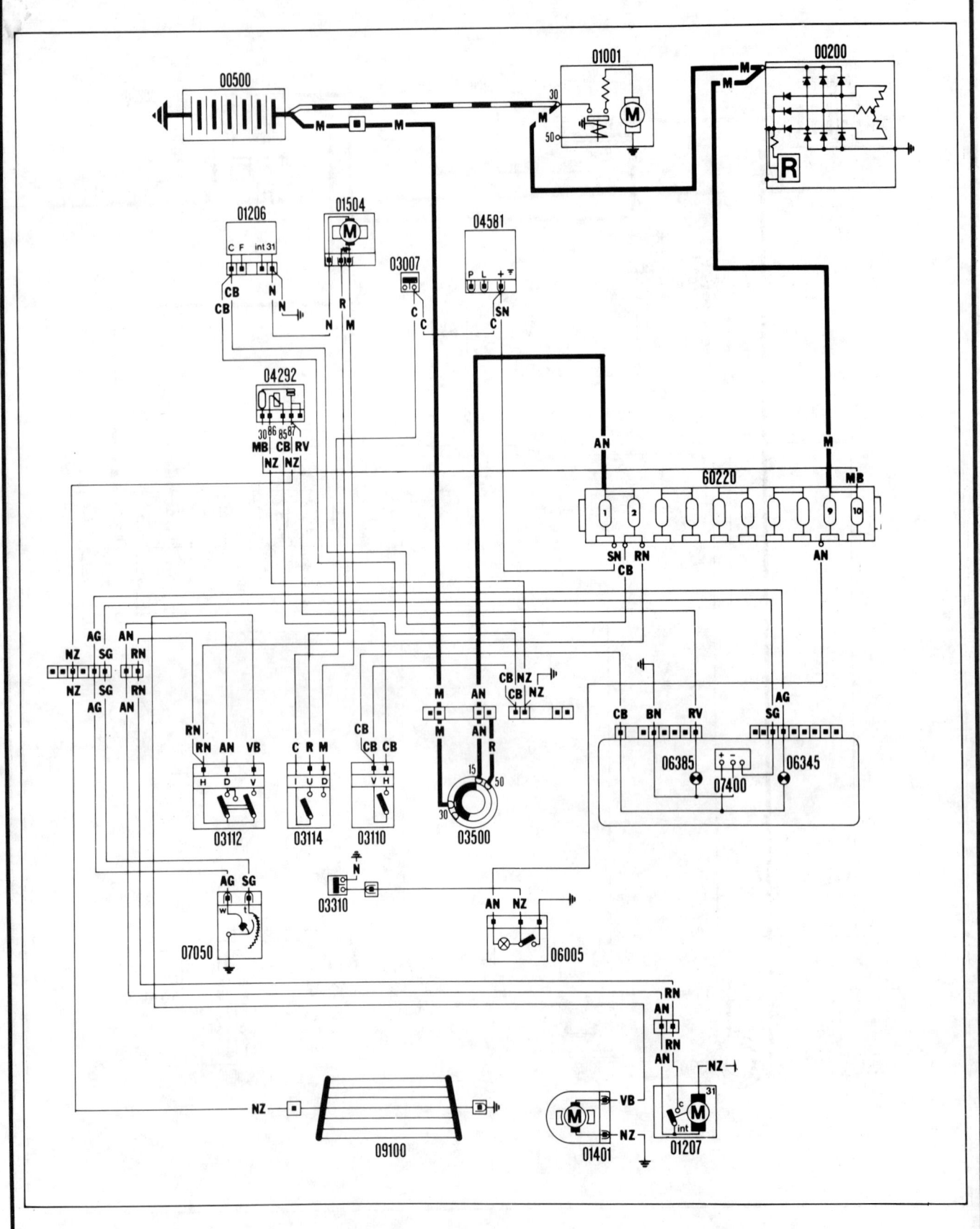

Wiring diagram for heated rear window, rear wash/wipe, fuel gauge, fuel reserve and courtesy lights

Key to wiring diagrams

00200	Alternator with built-in voltage regulator
00500	Battery
01001	Starter motor
01206	Windscreen wiper motor
01207	Rear window wiper motor
01400	Windscreen washer pump
01401	Rear window washer pump
01500	Radiator cooling fan
01504	Heater fan
02400	Ignition coil
02475	Contact breaker with advance device
03000	Engine oil pressure switch
03006	Handbrake warning light switch
03007	Brake lights switch
03008	Reversing light switch
03028	Radiator thermal switch
03029	Coolant warning light switch
03054	Outside lights switch
03060	Rear foglight switch
03110	Heated rear window switch
03112	Rear window washer switch
03114	Heater fan switch
03310	Push button on left door for courtesy light
03319	Horn push button
03500	Ignition switch
03550	Hazard warning lights switch
04010	Steering column switch unit, direction indicators
04020	Steering column switch unit, headlamps, dipped and main beam
04031	Steering column switch unit, windscreen wiper
04032	Steering column switch unit, windscreen wash/wipe
04292	Heated rear window relay
04500	Windscreen wiper intermittent device
04581	Direction indicator flasher unit
04600	Ignition distributor
04700	Water temperature sender unit
05004	Right front light cluster with headlamp, main beam and dipped, sidelight and direction indicator
05005	Left front light cluster with headlamp, main beam and dipped, sidelight and direction indicator
05412	Right front side direction indicator
05413	Left front side direction indicator
05640	Number plate light
05671	Right rear light cluster with sidelight, direction indicator brake light and reversing light
05684	Left rear light cluster with sidelight, direction indicator brake light and rear foglight
06005	Courtesy light on rear view mirror with switch
06300	Sidelights warning light
06305	Main beam headlamps warning light
06310	Rear foglight warning light
06315	Hazard warning lights warning light
06320	Direction indicators warning light
06336	Handbrake warning light
06337	Brake fault and handbrake warning light
06343	Engine oil pressure warning light
06345	Fuel reserve warning light
06350	Coolant warning light
06355	Battery recharging warning light
06385	Heater rear window warning light
06800	Horn
07003	Brake fluid level sensor
07050	Fuel gauge
07415	Coolant temperature gauge
07461	Digital clock (if fitted)
09100	Heated rear window
59000	Cigar lighter
59010	Radio power lead (if fitted)
60220	10 place fusebox

Colour code

A	Light blue	CB	Orange-White
B	White	CN	Orange-Black
C	Orange	GL	Yellow-Blue
G	Yellow	GN	Yellow-Black
H	Grey	GR	Yellow-Red
L	Blue	GV	Yellow-Green
M	Brown	HG	Grey-Yellow
N	Black	HN	Grey-Black
R	Red	HR	Grey-Red
S	Pink	LB	Blue-White
V	Green	LG	Blue-Yellow
Z	Violet	LN	Blue-Black
AB	Light blue-White	LR	Blue-Red
AG	Light blue-Yellow	LV	Blue-Green
AN	Light blue-Black	MB	Brown-White
AR	Light blue-Red	NZ	Black-Violet
AV	Light blue-Green	RB	Red-White
BG	White-Yellow	RG	Red-Yellow
BL	White-Blue	RN	Red-Black
BN	White-Black	RV	Red-Green
BR	White-Red	SN	Pink-Black
BV	White-Green	VB	Green-White
BZ	White-Violet	VN	Green-Black
CA	Orange-Light blue	VR	Green-Red